'IMPROVED BY CULTIVATION'

An Anthology of

English-Canadian

Prose to 1914

Edited and with Introduction

& Notes by

R. G. Moyles

broadview press • *1994*

Canadian Cataloguing in Publication Data
Improved by cultivation

Includes bibliographical references.
ISBN 1-55111-049-0
1. Canadian prose literature (English).* I. Moyles, R.G. (Robert Gordon), 1939-   .

PS8325.I56 1994.   C810.8   C94-931610-5
PR9197.25.I56 1994

Broadview Press
Post Office Box 1243, Peterborough, Ontario, Canada, K9J 7H5

in the United States of America
3576 California Road, Orchard Park, NY 14127

in the United Kingdom
c/o Drake Marketing, Saint Fagan's Road, Fairwater, Cardiff, CF53AE

Broadview Press gratefully acknowledges the support of the Canada Council, the Ontario
Arts Council, the Ontario Publishing Centre,
and the Ministry of National Heritage.

Cover: Frederick Challener (1869–1959), *A Song at Twilight*, 1893, oil on canvas.
National Gallery of Canada (gift of the Royal Canadian Academy of Arts, 1894).

This book was set in Monotype Bembo and designed by George Kirkpatrick.

PRINTED IN CANADA
5 4 3 2 1 94 95 96

'IMPROVED BY CULTIVATION'

Contents

Introduction

> "They are naturally a fine people,
> and possess capabilities
> and talents, which, when improved by
> cultivation, will render them second to
> no people in the world."
>   —Susanna Moodie

This anthology derives its *raison d'être* from a proposition often voiced by literary historians, to the effect that the discovery of a Canadian identity is best undertaken through an examination of what we have written and what has been written about us. Indeed, as Robert Kroetsch opines, "In a sense, we haven't got an identity until somebody tells our story. The [story] makes us real."[1] Not only is that true in the present tense, but in the past as well. For "creating our identity" by "telling our story" has been, though often unintentional, sporadic, and ill-defined, a preoccupation of Canadians since the first explorers set foot on our "foreign" soil. And it is to the many stories from the previous century that we must turn when we wish to discover who we are and where we have come from. We cannot fully understand the present unless we understand our past.

Not many years ago it would have seemed rash to suggest that we do indeed have a story-telling past. For it was long maintained by critics that, prior to the twentieth century, Canada did not have many stories worth reading and certainly not enough to shape an imaginative identity. This, at least, was the opinion of those who dictated literary tastes and controlled the literary canon. Canadian critics believed (or agreed with those who insisted) that a nineteenth-century Canadian "literature" was practically non-existent. The case was stated, succinctly and with a tone of finality, as far back as 1891 when Archibald Lampman made this assertion: "A good deal is being said about Canadian literature, and most of it takes the form of question and answer as to whether a Canadian literature exists. *Of course it does not.*"[2]

Lampman's statement was long accepted (indeed, well into the present century) as being irrefutable because by "literature" he (as did so many others) meant "a body of work of sufficient excellence as measured by the severest standards, and sufficiently marked with local colour."[3] That is, there were in Canada no writers "of outstanding individuality" — no Thackerays, or Austens, or even Kiplings; no one to vivify or define the Canadianness of Canada. Thus, apart from a very few writers, like Haliburton and Roberts and Leacock, who managed to avoid the labels of "popular romantics" or "lame versifiers," there seemed to be few other writers worth mentioning or reading.

In the last few decades, however, such elitist and imperialistic assessments have been supplanted by an emphasis on the socio-historical importance of literature. Literary historians, unencumbered by the restrictions of a purely evaluative approach, have shown that there is a vast body of early prose literature — much of it relegated to oblivion (or, worse, to school anthologies) — that is not only intrinsically enjoyable but which, read wisely, reveals much about an emerging Canadian identity. Ignored or forgotten were the narratives of such travellers as George Munro Grant, Paul Kane, Samuel Hearne, and Leonidas Hubbard; the social memoirs of Lady Agnes Macdonald, Georgina Binnie Clark, Annie Frechette, and Agnes Deans Cameron; the romantic fiction of J. Macdonald Oxley, Gilbert Parker, William Bleasdell Cameron, Allan Sullivan, and Norman Duncan; these and much, much more. As George Woodcock states, in his last essay in *The Century that Made Us*, by the end of the nineteenth century Canada, in spite of many claims to the contrary, did indeed exist "as an imaginative concept" in the minds of our early writers and artists.[4]

This anthology attempts to support that contention — to vivify the richness and variety of our pre-twentieth century prose literature beyond that manifest in recently reprinted novels. It does so through an organization which suggests that there are five classes of prose to which early Canadian writers have made significant or outstanding contributions: personal memoirs, humorous/satirical sketches, animal stories, travel/exploration narratives, and short fiction. The first three have been acknowledged as such by many literary historians. Woodcock, for example, suggests that "The most felicitous and also the most characteristic prose writing by British North Americans until the end of the nineteenth century fell into three categories: the autobiographical memoir consisting of a series of episodes and reflections, like Susanna Moodie's *Roughing it in the Bush*; the satirical sketch; and the animal tale."[5] The last two stem from my own research which indicates that Woodcock and others have not been generous enough: the literature of travel and exploration pertaining to Canada can claim to be among the best and most informative which exists in that genre; and, among the romantic short-story writers of the late nineteenth and early twentieth centuries, whose work floods the many popular magazines of the day, some of the most read and acclaimed were Canadians. Though the inclusion of each will be justified in separate introductions, it might be said briefly in their defence that writing by early travellers and explorers — among them Hearne, Mackenzie, Kane, and Munro Grant — contains much that is essential to an understanding of our "imaginative landscape"; and in the neglected fiction of Gilbert Parker, Marjorie Pickthall, Lily Dougall, Sara Jeannette Duncan, and Duncan Campbell Scott we glimpse the real beginnings of a genuine Canadian literature.

I have, then, divided the anthology into five distinct generic categories: Literature of Travel and Exploration, Memoirs and Personal Sketches, Satirical and Humorous Sketches, Animal Stories, and Short Stories. And within each I have tried to offer not only well-known representative pieces but much that has unjustifiably been ignored or neglected. Thus, while the well-known personal memoirs of Moodie and Traill help define the category in which they appear, there are many other writers who validate Woodcock's contention that the "memoir" is a peculiarly Canadian kind of prose: Lady Agnes Macdonald, Annie Fréchette, and Frances Beavan are every bit as incisive, entertaining and enlightening as Traill or Moodie. Similarly, while one must always acknowledge the influential work of Haliburton and Leacock, the comic genius of Robert Barr and E.W. Thomson are also well worth celebrating. And so, too, though perhaps not always in terms of artistic success, are the works of such little-known writers as John Donkin, Frances Beaven, Lily Dougall, Gilbert Parker, Norman Duncan, and others.

No doubt some of the pieces offered here will cause some readers moments of embarrassment or even distress. They were, after all, written at a time (or various times) when social, religious, political, and personal attitudes were far different from those of today. And the Canada that was mirrored in and shaped by this literature was done so through a set of metaphors that is (or is fast becoming) foreign to our imaginations. In the first instance, much of the literature is perforce (by virtue of colonization) quite British in its generic foundation, its metaphorical origins, and its attitudes. It is, moreover, not merely British but imperialistic, deriving its dominant rhetoric from a military caste system which had appropriated the language of Arthurian chivalry, embellished with muscular Christianity, as a means of expanding its empire. That is not only true of those writers who were British, but of those born in Canada as well: to be Canadian was to be British and imperialistic.

It will be obvious, therefore, that there are certain stereotypical images and attitudes which recur throughout much of the literature presented here. There is an unquestioning acceptance (once or twice satirized) of the superiority of all things British — from a system of law and justice to social etiquette; there is a great deal of male chauvinism to contend with; there is much condescension when discussing both natives and French Canadians; and there is an annoying derivativeness in terms of literary subject and style. But that is what makes the whole so interesting and informative: we need to understand — and be able to discuss with objectivity — the kinds of attitudes (distasteful though they now might be) that determined Canada's culture in the nineteenth century.

If we look closely enough, of course, we will see that, though some of the writers promoted the stereotypes, others openly rebelled; still others agonized over whether or not to adhere to the accepted standards. In other words, there are no simple assessments; the literature is as complex as early Canadian life itself. To dismiss it simply because it is derivative or chauvinistic is to dismiss an important element of the Canadian social fabric. And, as Carole Gerson states in *A Purer Taste*, an excellent introduction to nineteenth-century Canadian fiction, "When examined within its own context, early Canadian fiction illustrates the social role of fiction and the relation between cultural attitudes and literary performance in a community struggling towards self-definition."[6]

This anthology includes representative prose to 1914, a date which, for most historians, marks the symbolic end of the nineteenth century. When Canada became Britain's ally in its great fight for freedom (1914-18), she began her final push towards nationalism and independence; landlord colonialism was being displaced by an equal partnership. A sentimental attachment to Britain would continue, but Canadians would see themselves as a North American nation, friendly with but distinct from Great Britain. Their literature, too, would become more nationalistic and/or Canadian in its outlook. New and perhaps better writers, seeking a new identity, would emerge and, apart from a few treasures, the old writers (some of them still alive in 1914) would be forgotten and relegated to the literary basement. This anthology is yet another attempt, among many in recent years, to rediscover that literature and the Canada it portrayed.

Notes

[1] "A Conversation with Margaret Laurence," in *creation* (Toronto: New Press, 1970), 63.

[2] "Two Canadian Poets," in Douglas M. Daymond & Leslie Monkman, eds., *Towards a Canadian Literature: Volume I: 1752-1940* (Ottawa: Tecumseh Press, 1984), 134.

[3] Ibid.

[4] *The Century That Made Us: Canada 1814-19141* (Toronto: Oxford, 1989), 266.

[5] Ibid., 249.

[6] *A Purer Taste: The Writing and Reading of Fiction in English Nineteenth-Century Canada* (Toronto: U of T Press, 1989), 154.

Part One: Travel & Exploration Narratives

Travel and Exploration Narratives

Commentary

One must begin with an important *caveat*. Most of our travel and exploration narratives were issued as books — they were, like the actual events themselves, meant to be extended excursions; to take readers on long tours with either a discovery at the end (the object of exploration) or a series of novel experiences to be savoured (the delights of travel). To be a true "armchair traveller" one must travel the whole journey with one's writer — i.e., read the book from beginning to end. Therefore, when any anthologist offers excerpts (or "choice selections") from any such book he or she may be accused of distorting the structure of the work and altering its purpose.

For some literary historians there is no defence against such an accusation. For others, however, the accusation itself is unwarranted. The chief value in exploration literature, they argue, is not in any "overarching scheme" (or design) but in its anecdotalism. As Stephen Greenblatt suggests, this type of discourse is more interesting "at the level of anecdote" than it is as "sustained narrative." Its strength, Greenblatt argues, lies in "the shock of the unfamiliar, the provocation of an intense curiosity, the local excitement of intense wonders." And it is as recurring anecdote rather than extended narrative that exploration literature works best — both as metaphor and vicarious experience.[1] An anthology, therefore, rather than distorting the whole, merely isolates, or perhaps highlights, the dominant metaphors prominent in the discourse.

Leaving that contentious argument to provoke discussion, my chief reasons for offering the following selections are quite practical: first, to introduce readers to the genre; and, second, to entice them to read the whole works from which they come, and others similar to them. For the field is a vast and rich one: Canadian travel and exploration literature (descriptions of travel and exploration within and on the fringes of what is now Canada) comprises thousands of books and articles from the earliest accounts in Hakluyt's *Principal*

Navigations (1598) to Agnes Deans Cameron's *The New North* (1910). They range from descriptions of ventures dedicated to a single purpose, such as George Vancouver's *Voyage of Discovery to the North Pacific* Ocean (1801), to those undertaken for pure fun, such as Horton Rhys's *A Theatrical Trip for a Wager* (1861); from quasi-scientific reports, such as Henry Youle Hind's *Narrative of the Canadian Red River Exploring Expedition* (1860) to idiosyncratic musings, such as J. Ewing Ritchie's *To Canada With the Emigrants* (1886); from descriptions of holiday trips by Governors General to hunting expeditions by aristocratic sportsmen.

And the pleasures which they offer are more than one can enunciate. One can experience the vicarious thrill of discovery as one breaks through the massive forest with Mackenzie and is confronted by the magnificence of the Pacific Ocean; or toil with David Thompson through the mountains to find the Columbia River basin; or view for the first time the awesome Grand Falls of Labrador (higher than Niagara) with John McLean. By reading travel narratives one can visit Indian encampments, Newfoundland outports in their infancy, Niagara or Montmorency Falls before commercial effrontery, take a trip on the new CPR, ride the streets of Muddy York, or see the sights of early Calgary. Just as a rage for "continental tourism" gripped the Englishman of the eighteenth century, so in the nineteenth century most who could afford it had to experience the "wildness" of British North America. And most were compelled to commit their impressions to print.

The selections which follow, then, though but a small token of the whole, are intended to provide a sense of that variety and pleasure. There are the explicit exploration narratives of Hearne, Mackenzie, and Hubbard, all of which, though preoccupied with "getting somehwere," have enough anecdotal pauses to make each "vicarious trip" (i.e., each reading) entirely worthwhile. At the other extreme are the avowed travel narratives of such people as J. Ewing Ritchie in which no destination is necessary; it is enough to wander, savour the moment and enjoy the novelty of experience. And, somewhere in between are the many engaging narratives of the traveller-explorer — those who undertook trips for pleasure and profit — such as Alexander Henry, the elder, trader, explorer, raconteur, who witnessed so much of the expansion of Canada into the Great Lakes region; and Paul Kane, artist and explorer, who vivified Western native life before it virtually vanished. Taken together, and read with good judgement and discrimination, they provide fascinating glimpses of early Canada — its topographical diversity, its challenges to adventurers, its native society, and its emerging history.

Notes

[1] See *Marvelous Possessions: The Wonder of the New World* (Chicago: University of Chicago Press, 1991), 2.

Extra Reading

Victor G. Hopwood, "Explorers by Land" and "Explorers by Sea," in Carl F. Klinck, ed., *Literary History of Canada* 2nd. ed., Vol I. (Toronto: U of T Press, 1976), 19-54.

R.G. Moyles, "Literature of Exploration, Travel and Description," in *English Canadian Literature to 1900*. (Detroit: Gale Research, 1976), 209-69.

Elizabeth Waterston and R.G. Moyles, "Travel Books: 1860-1920," in Carl F. Klinck, ed., Literary History of Canada, 2nd ed., Vol. I. (Toronto: U of T Press, 1976), 361-79.

Richard Whitbourne

The New World as Paradise was a constant image in early travel and exploration literature. A good representative of this kind is Richard Whitbourne's A Discourse and Discovery of Newfoundland *(1620), a popular book (several times reprinted) whose intentional idyllic qualities are acknowledged in a later reprint entitled* Westward Ho to Avalon *(1870). Whitbourne, called by D.W. Prowse "the John Smith of our colonial history," had been visiting Newfoundland since 1580, was there when Sir Humphrey Gilbert took possession of it in 1583, and in 1618 was governor of Vaughan's Newfoundland colony. He was therefore well qualified to write about the island, to "discover" its natural resources, though his salesmanship may have caused him to distort some realities. In the following excerpt, the spelling has been modernized.*

A Discourse and Discovery of Newfoundland

Most dread Sovereign, it is to be seen by the cosmographers' maps, and well approved, that the Newfoundland is an island, bordering upon the continent of America, from which it is divided by sea: so far distant as England is from the nearest part of France, and lieth between 46 and 53 degrees north latitude. It is as spacious as Ireland, and lies near the course that ships usually hold in their return from the West Indies, and near half the way between Ireland and Virginia.

I shall not much need to commend the wholesome temperature of that country, seeing the greatest part thereof lieth about four degrees nearer the south than any part of England doth. And it hath been well approved by some of our nation, who have lived there many years, that in the winter season it is as pleasant and healthful as England is. And although the example of one summer be no certain rule for other years, yet thus much also can I truly affirm, that in the year 1615 of the many thousands of English, French, Portugals, and others, that were then upon that coast (amongst whom I sailed to and fro more than one hundred and fifty leagues), I neither saw nor heard in all that travel, of any man or boy of either of these nations that died there during the whole voyage; neither was there so much as any one of them sick....

The soil of this country is so fruitful as that in any divers places; there the summer naturally produces out of the fruitful womb of the earth, without the labour of man's hand, great plenty of green peas and vetches, fair, round, full and wholesome as our vetches are in England; of which I have there fed on many times. The hawmes [pods] of them are good fodder for cattle and other beasts in the winter, with the help of hay, of which there may be made great store with little labour, in divers places of the country. Then have you there fair strawberries, red and white, and fair repasse berries [raspberries], and gooseberries, as there be in England, as also multitudes of bilberries, which are called by some, whorts, and many other delicate berries (which I cannot name) in great abundance. There are also many other fruits, as small pears, cherries, filberds [hazelnuts], etc. And of these berries and fruits the store is there so great that the mariners of my ship and barque's company have gathered at once more than half a hogshead would hold of which divers times, eating their fill, I never heard of any man whose health was thereby any way impaired.

There are also herbs, for salads and broth, as parsley, alexander, sorrel, etc. And also flowers, as the red and white damask rose, with other kinds; which are most beautiful and delightful, both to the sight and smell. And questionless the country is stored with many physical herbs and roots, albeit their virtues are not known, because not sought after; yet within these few years, many of our nation finding themselves ill, have bruised some of the herbs and strained the juice into beer, wine or *aqua-vitae*, and by God's assistance, after a few drinkings, it hath restored them to their former health. The like virtue it hath to cure a wound, or any swelling, either by washing the grieved places with some of the herbs boiled, or by applying them so thereunto (plaster-wise) which I have seen by often experience.

This being the natural fruitfulness of the earth, producing such variety of things fit for food without the labour of man, I might in reason hence infer that if the same were manured and husbanded in some places, as our grounds are, it would be apt to bear corn no less fertile than the English soil. But I need not confine myself to probabilities therein: seeing our men that have wintered there divers years did for a trial and experiment thereof sow some small quantity of corn which I saw growing very fair; and they found the increase to be great, and the grain very good; and it is well known to me and divers that trade there yearly, how that cabbage, turnips, lettuce, parsley, and such like, prove so well there as elsewhere.

On divers parts of the country there is great store of deer, and some hares, many foxes, squirrels, beavers, wolves, and bears, with other sorts of beasts, serving as well for necessity as for profit and delight. Neither let me seem ridiculous to annex a matter of novelty, rather than weight, to this discourse.

In the year 1615 it was well known to 48 persons of my company, and other divers men, that three several times the wolves and beasts of the country came down near them to the sea-side, where they were laboring about their fish, howling and making a noise, so that each time my mastif-dog went unto them (as the like in that country hath not been seen). The one began to fawn and play with the other, and so went together into the woods, and continued with them every of these times nine or ten days and did return unto us without any hurt. Hereof I am no way superstitious, yet it is something strange to me that the wild beasts being followed by a stern mastif-dog should grow to familiarity with him, seeing their natures are repugnant. Surely much rather the people, by our discreet and gentle usage, may be brought to society, being already naturally inclined thereunto.

But to return to our purpose, and to speak something of the great plenty of fowl in that country, as well land-fowl as water-fowl; the variety of both kinds is infinite. The land-fowl; (besides great number of small birds flying up and down, some without name, that live by scraping their food from the earth in the hardest winter that is) there are also hawks, great and small, partridges, thrush, and thrussels abundance very fat. As also filladies, nightingales and such like small birds that sing most pleasantly. There are also birds that live by prey, as ravens, gripes, crows, etc. For water-fowl there is certainly so good, and as much variety, as in any part of the world; as geese, ducks, pigeons, gulls, penguins, and many other sorts. These penguins are as big as geese, and fly not, for they have but a little short wing, and they multiply so infinitely upon a certain flat island that men drive them from thence upon a board into their boats, by hundreds at a time; as if God made the innocency of so poor a creature to become such an admirable instrument for the sustenation of man. There are also godwits, curlews, and a certain kind of fowl that are called oxen and kine, with such like; which fowl do not only steed [supply] those that trade thither greatly for food, but also they are a great furthering to divers ships voyages, because the abundance of them is such that the fishermen do bait their hooks with the quarters of seafowl on them: and therewith some ships do yearly take a great part of their fishing voyages with such bait before they can get others....

Now also I will not omit to relate something of a strange creature which I saw there in the year 1610, in a morning early, as I was standing by the riverside in the harbour of St. John's, which very swiftly came swimming towards me, looking cheerfully on my face, as it had been a woman. By the face, eyes, nose, mouth, chin, ears, neck, and forehead, it seemed to be so beautiful and in those parts so well proportioned, having round about the head many blue streaks, resembling hair, but certainly it was no hair, for I beheld it long and another of my company also yet living, that saw the same coming so swiftly towards me, whereat I stepped back. For it was come within the length of a longpike, supposing it would have sprung aland to me, because I had often seen huge whales to spring a great height above the water, and divers other great fishes the like. And so might this strange creature have done to me if I had stood still where I was (as I verily believe it had such a purpose). But when it saw that I went from it, it did thereupon dive a little under water and swam towards the place where a little before I had landed, and it did often look back towards me, whereby I beheld the shoulders and back down to the middle to be so square, white and smooth as the back of a man; and from the middle to the hinder part it was pointing in proportion something like a broad hooked arrow. How it was in the forepart from the neck and shoulders, I could not discern; but it came shortly after to a boat in the same harbour (wherein one William Hawkrige, then my servant, was); and the same creature did put both its hands upon the side of the boat and did strive much to come in to him, and divers so others then in the same boat; whereat they were afraid and one of them struck it a full blow on the head, whereby it fell off from them; and afterwards it came to two other boats in the said harbour where they lay by the shore. The men in them, for fear, fled to land and beheld it. This (I suppose) was a mermaid or merman. Now, because divers have writ much of mermaids, I have presumed to relate what is most certain of such a strange creature that was thus there seen. Whether it were a mermaid or no, I leave others to judge.

Alexander Henry

Alexander Henry's Travels and Adventures in Canada and the Indian Territories Between the Years 1760 *and* 1776 *(New York: Riley, 1809) is one of the most vivid and exciting pieces of exploration and descriptive literature in the Canadian canon. Henry, born in New Jersey in 1739, came to Canada as an enterprising merchant, supplying goods to General Amherst's army as it "mopped up" after Wolfe's conquest of Quebec. He stayed in Canada, obtained a licence to trade with the Indians, and became a successful merchant-prince. He was, as well, the first white man to explore the Great Lakes Territory. His book describes his trading adventures from 1760 to 1776, vividly depicting such events as the massacre at Fort Michilimackinac in 1763, his year as a prisoner of the Indians, and his later travels to the Great Lakes and the prairies. The following excerpt from his* Travels *describes the first of those events.*

The Massacre at Fort Michilimackinac

When I reached Michilimackinac, I found several other traders who had arrived before me from different parts of the country, and who, in general, declared the dispositions of the Indians to be hostile to the English, and even apprehended some attack. M. Laurent Ducharme distinctly informed Major Etherington, that a plan was absolutely conceived, for destroying him, his garrison and all the English in the upper country; but, the commandant, believing this and other reports to be without foundation, proceeding only from idle or ill-disposed persons, and of a tendency to do mischief, expressed much displeasure against M. Ducharme, and threatened to send the next person who should bring a story of the same kind a prisoner to Detroit.

The garrison at this time consisted of ninety privates, two subalterns and the commandant; and the English merchants at the fort were four in number. Thus strong, few entertained anxiety concerning the Indians, who had no weapons but small arms.

Meanwhile, the Indians from every quarter were daily assembling in unusual numbers, but with every acceptance of friendship, frequenting the fort and disposing of their peltries in such a manner as to dissipate almost every one's fears. For myself, on one occasion, I took the liberty of observing to Major Etherington that in my judgment, no confidence ought to be placed in them, and that I was informed no less than four hundred lay about the fort.

In return the major only rallied me on my timidity; and it is to be confessed that if this officer neglected admonition on his part, so did I on mine. Shortly after my first arrival at Michilimackinac, in the preceding year, a Chipeway, named Wa'wa'tam', began to come often to my house, betraying, in his demeanour, strong marks of personal regard. After this had continued for some time, he came on a certain day bringing with him his whole family, and at the same time a large present consisting of skins, sugar and dried meat. Having laid these in a heap, he commenced his speech, in which he informed me that some years before he had observed a fast, devoting himself, according to the custom of his nation, to solitude and to the mortification of his body, in the hope to obtain from the Great Spirit protection through all his days; that on this occasion, he had dreamed of adopting an Englishman as his son, brother, and friend; that from the moment in which he first beheld me, he had recognized me as the person whom the Great Spirit had been pleased to point out to him for a brother; that he hoped I would not refuse his present; and that he should forever regard me as one of his family.

I could do no otherwise than accept the present, and declare my willingness to have so good a man as this appeared to be for my friend and brother. I offered a present in return for that which I had received, which Wa'wa'tam' accepted, and then, thanking me for the favour which he said that I had rendered him, he left me, and soon after set out for his winter's hunt.

Twelve months had now elapsed, since the occurrence of this incident, and I had almost forgotten the person of my *brother*, when, on the second day of June, Wa'wa'tam' came again to my house in a temper of mind visibly melancholy and thoughtful. He told me that he had just returned from his *wintering-ground*, and I asked after his health; but, without answering my question, he went on to say that he was very sorry to find me returned from the Sault; that he had intended to go to that place himself immediately after his arrival at Michilimackinac; and that he wished me to go there, along with him and his family, the next morning. To all this, he joined an inquiry, whether or not the commandant had heard bad news, adding that during the winter he himself had been frequently disturbed with the *noise of evil birds*; and further suggesting that there were numerous Indians near the fort, many of whom had never shown themselves within it. — Wa'wa'tam' was about forty-five years of age, of an excellent character among his nation, and a chief.

Referring much of what I had heard to the peculiarities of the Indian character, I did not pay all the attention which they will be found to have deserved, to the entreaties and remarks of my visitor. I answered that I could not think of going to the Sault, so soon as the next morning, but would follow him there, after the arrival of my clerks. Finding himself unable to prevail with me, he withdrew for that day; but, early the next morning, he came again, bringing with him his wife, and a present of dried meat. At this interview, after stating that he had several packs of beaver, for which he intended to deal with me, he expressed, a second time, his apprehensions, from the numerous Indians who were round the fort, and earnestly pressed me to consent to an immediate departure for the Sault. As a reason for this particular request, he assured me that all the Indians proposed to come in a body, that day, to the fort, to demand liquor of the commandant, and that he wished me to be gone, before they should grow intoxicated.

I had made, at the period to which I am now referring, so much progress in the language in which Wa'wa'tam' addressed me, as to be able to hold an ordinary conversation in it; but, the Indian manner of speech is so extravagantly figurative, that it is for a very perfect master to follow and comprehend it entirely. Had I been further advanced in this respect, I think that I should have gathered so much information, from this my friendly monitor, as would have put me into possession of the design of the enemy, and enabled me to save as well others as myself; as it was, it unfortunately happened that I turned a deaf ear to every thing, leaving Wa'wa'tam' and his wife, after long and patient but ineffectual efforts, to depart alone, with dejected countenances, and not before they had each let fall some tears.

In the course of the same day, I observed that the Indians came in great numbers into the fort, purchasing tomahawks (small axes, of one pound weight), and frequently desiring to see silver armbands, and other valuable ornaments, of which I had a large quantity for sale. These ornaments, however, they in no instance purchased; but after turning them over, left them, saying that they would call again the next day. Their motive, as it afterward appeared, was no other than the very artful one of discovering, by requesting to see them, the particular places of their deposit, so that they might lay their hands on them in the moment of pillage with the greater certainty and despatch.

At night I turned in my mind the visits of Wa'wa'tam'; but, though they were calculated to excite uneasiness, nothing induced me to believe that serious mischief was at hand. The next day, being the fourth of June, was the king's birthday.

The morning was sultry. A Chipeway came to tell me that his nation was going to play at *bag'gat'iway* with the Sacs or Saakies, another Indian nation, for a high wager. He invited me to witness the sport, adding that the commandant was to be there, and would bet on the side of the Chipeways. In consequence of this information, I went to the commandant, and expostulated with him a little, representing that the Indians might possibly have some sinister end in view; but, the commandant only smiled at my suspicions.

Bag'gat'iway, called by the Canadians *le jeu de la crosse*, is played with a bat and ball. The bat is about four feet in length, curved, and terminating in a sort of racket. Two posts are planted in the ground, at a considerable distance from each other, as a mile or more. Each party has its post, and the game consists in throwing the ball up to the post of the adversary. The ball, at the beginning, is placed in the middle of the course, and each party endeavours as well to throw the ball out of the direction of its own post, as into that of the adversary's.

I did not go myself to see the match which was now to be played without the fort, because, there being a canoe prepared to depart on the following day for Montreal, I employed myself in writing letters to my friends; and even when a fellow-trader, Mr. Tracy, happened to call upon me, saying that another canoe had just arrived from Detroit, and proposing that I should go with him to the beach, to inquire the news, it so happened that I still remained to finish my letters; promising to follow Mr. Tracy in the course of a few minutes. Mr. Tracy had not gone more than twenty paces from my door, when I heard an Indian war-cry, and a noise of general confusion.

Going instantly to my window, I saw a crowd of Indians, within the fort, furiously cutting down and scalping every Englishman they found. In particular, I witnessed the fate of Lieutenant Jemette.

I had, in the room in which I was, a fowling-piece, loaded with swan-shot. This I immediately seized, and held it for a few minutes, waiting to hear the drum beat to arms. In this dreadful interval, I saw several of my countrymen fall, and more than one struggling between the knees of an Indian, who, holding him in this manner, scalped him, while yet living.

At length, disappointed in the hope of seeing resistance made to the enemy, and sensible, of course, that no effort of my own unassisted arm could avail against four hundred Indians, I thought only of seeking shelter. Amid the slaughter which was raging, I observed many of the Canadian inhabitants of the fort, calmly looking on, neither opposing the Indians, nor suffering injury; and, from this circumstance, I conceived a hope of finding security in their houses.

Between the yard-door of my own house, and that of M. Langlade, my next neighbour, there was only a low fence, over which I easily climbed. At my entrance, I found the whole family at the windows, gazing at the scene of blood before them. I addressed myself immediately to M. Langlade, begging that he would put me into some place of safety, until the heat of the affair should be over; an act of charity by which he might perhaps preserve me from the general massacre; but, while I uttered my petition, M. Langlade, who had looked for a moment at me, turned again to the window, shrugging his shoulders, and intimating that he could do nothing for me: — *"Que voudriez-vous que j'en ferais?"*

This was a moment for despair; but, the next, a Pani woman, a slave of M. Langlade's, beckoned to me to follow her. She brought me to a door, which she opened, desiring me to enter, and telling me that it led to the garret, where I must go and conceal myself. I joyfully obeyed her directions; and she, having followed me up to the garret door, locked it after me, and with great presence of mind took away the key.

This shelter obtained, if shelter I could hope to find it, I was naturally anxious to know what might still be passing without. Through an aperture, which afforded me a view of the area of the fort, I beheld, in shapes the foulest and most terrible, the ferocious triumphs of barbarian conquerors. The dead were scalped and mangled; the dying were writhing and shrieking, under the unsatiated knife and tomahawk; and, from the bodies of some ripped open, their butchers were drinking the blood, scooped up in the hollow of joined hands, and quaffed amid shouts of rage and victory. I was shaken, not only with horror, but with fear. The suffering which I witnessed, I seemed on the point of experiencing. No long time elapsed, before every one being destroyed, who could be found, there was a general cry of "All is finished!" At the same instant, I heard some of the Indians enter the house in which I was.

The garret was separated from the room below, only by a layer of single boards, at once the flooring of the one and the ceiling of the other. I could therefore hear everything that passed; and the Indians, no sooner in, than they inquired whether or not any English man were in the house? M. Langlade replied that "He could not say — he did not know of any"; — answers in which he did not exceed the truth; for the Pani woman had not only hidden me by stealth, but kept my secret, and her own, M. Langlade was therefore, as I presume, as far from a wish to destroy me as he was careless about saving me, when he added to these answers that "They might examine for themselves, and would soon be satisfied as to the object of their question." Saying this, he brought them to the garret-door.

The state of my mind will be imagined. Arrived at the door, some delay was occasioned by the absence of the key, and a few moments were thus allowed me, in which to look around for a hiding place. In one corner of the garret was a heap of those vessels of birch-bark, used in maple-sugar making, as I have recently described.

The door was unlocked, and opening, and the Indians ascending the stairs before I had completely crept into a small opening, which presented itself, at one end of the heap. An instant after, four Indians entered the room, all armed with tomahawks, and all besmeared with blood upon every part of their bodies.

The die appeared to be cast. I could scarcely breathe; but I thought that the throbbing of my heart occasioned a noise loud enough to betray me. The Indians walked in every direction about the garret, and one of them approached me so closely that at a particular moment, had he put out his hand, he must have touched me. Still, I remained undiscovered; a circumstance to which the dark colour of my clothes, and the corner in which I was must have contributed. In a word, after taking several turns in the room, during want of light, in a room which had no window, and in which they told M. Langlade how many they had killed, and how many scalps they had taken, they returned downstairs, and I, with sensations not to be expressed, heard the door, which was the barrier between me and my fate, locked for the second time.

There was a feather-bed on the floor; and on this, exhausted as I was by the agitation of mind, I threw myself down and fell asleep. In this state I remained till the dusk of the evening, when I was awakened by a second opening of the door. The person that now entered was M. Langlade's wife, who was much surprised at finding me, but advised me not to be uneasy, observing that the Indians had killed most of the English, but that she hoped I might myself escape. A shower of rain having begun to fall, she had come to stop a hole in the roof. On her going away, I begged her to send me a little water to drink; which she did.

As night was now advancing, I continued to lie on the bed, ruminating on my condition, but unable to discover a resource from which I could hope for life. A flight to Detroit had no probable chance of success. The distance from Michilimackinac was four hundred miles; I was without provisions; and the whole length of the road lay through Indian countries, countries of an enemy in arms, where the first man whom I should meet would kill me. To stay where I was threatened nearly the same issue. As before, fatigue of mind and not tranquility suspended my cares and procured me further sleep.

The game of bag'gat'iway, as from the description above will have been perceived, is necessarily attended with much violence and noise. In the ardour of the contest the ball, as has been suggested, if it cannot be thrown to the goal desired, is struck in any direction of the adversary. At such a moment, therefore, nothing could be less liable to excite premature alarm than that the ball should be tossed over the pickets of the fort, nor that, having fallen there, it should be followed on the instant by all engaged in the game, as well the one party as the other, all eager, all struggling, all shouting, all in the unrestrained pursuit of a rude athletic exercise. Nothing could be less fitted to excite premature alarm — nothing, therefore, could be more happily devised, under the circumstances, than a stratagem like this; and this was, in fact, the stratagem which the Indians had employed, by which they had obtained possession of the fort and by which they had been enabled to slaughter and subdue its garrison and such of its other inhabitants as they pleased. To be still more certain of success, they had prevailed upon as many as they could by a pretext least liable to suspicion to come voluntarily without the pickets; and particularly the commandant and garrison themselves.

The respite which sleep afforded me during the night was put an end to by the return of morning. I was again on the rack of apprehension. At sunrise I heard the family stirring; and, presently after, Indian voices informing M. Langlade that they had not found my hapless self among the dead and that they supposed me to be somewhere concealed. M. Langlade appeared, from what followed, to be by this time acquainted with the place of my retreat, of which, no doubt, he had been informed by his wife. The poor woman, as soon as the Indians mentioned me, declared to her husband in the French tongue that he should no longer keep me in the house but deliver me up to my pursuers; giving as a reason for this measure that should the Indians discover his instrumentality in my concealment, they might revenge it on her children and that it was better that I should die than they. M. Langlade resisted at first this sentence of his wife's; but soon suffered her to prevail, informing the Indians that he had been told I was in his house, that I had come there without his knowledge, and that he would put me into their hands. This was no sooner expressed than he began to ascend the stairs, the Indians following upon his heels.

I now resigned myself to the fate with which I was menaced; and regarding every attempt at concealment as vain, I arose from the bed and presented myself full in view to the Indians who were entering the room. They were all in a state of intoxication and entirely naked except about the middle. One of them, named Wenniway, whom I had previously known, and who was upward of six feet in height, had his entire face and body covered with charcoal and grease, only that a white spot of two inches in diameter encircled either eye. This man, walking up to me, seized me with one hand by the collar of the coat while in the other he held a large carving-knife, as if to plunge into my breast; his eyes, meanwhile, were fixed steadfastly on mine. At length, after some seconds of the most anxious suspense, he dropped his arm, saying, "I won't kill you!" To this he added that he had been frequently engaged in wars against the English and had brought away many scalps; that, on a certain occasion, he had lost a brother whose name was Musinigon and that I should be called after him.

A reprieve, upon any terms, placed me among the living and gave me back the sustaining voice of hope; but Wenniway ordered me down stairs and there informing me that I was to be taken to his cabin where, and indeed every where else, the Indians were all mad with liquor, death again was threatened and not as possible only but as certain. I mentioned my fears on this subject to M. Langlade, begging him to represent the danger to my master. M. Langlade, in this instance, did not withhold his compassion and Wenniway immediately consented that I should remain where I was until he found another opportunity to take me away.

Thus far secure, I reascended my garret-stairs, in order to place myself the furthest possible out of the reach of insult from drunken Indians; but I had not remained there for more than an hour when I was called to the room below, in which was an Indian who said I must go with him out of the fort, Wenniway having sent him to fetch me. This man, as well as Wenniway himself, I had seen before. In the preceding year I had allowed him to take goods on credit, for which he was still in my debt; and some short time previous to the surprise of the fort he had said, upon my upbraiding him with want of honesty, that "He would pay me before long!" This speech now came fresh into my memory and led me to suspect that the fellow had formed a design against my life. I communicated the suspicion to M. Langlade; but he gave for an answer that "I was not now my own master and must do as I was ordered."

The Indian, on his part, directed that before I left the house I should undress myself, declaring that my coat and shirt would become him better than they did me. His pleasure, in this respect, being complied with, no other alternative was left me than either to go out naked, or to put on the clothes of the Indian, which he freely gave me in exchange. His motive for thus stripping me of my own apparel was no other, as I afterward learned, than this, that it might not be stained with blood when he should kill me.

I was now told to proceed; and my driver followed me close, until I had passed the gate of the fort, when I turned toward the spot where I knew the Indians to be encamped. This, however, did not suit the purpose of my enemy who seized me by the arm and drew me violently in the opposite direction to the distance of fifty yards above the fort. Here, finding that I was approaching the bushes and sand-hills, I determined to proceed no further but told the Indian that I believed he meant to murder me and that, if so, he might as well strike where I was as at any greater distance. He replied, with coolness, that my suspicions were just and that he meant to pay me in this manner for my goods. At the same time he produced a knife and held me in a position to receive the intended blow. Both this, and that which followed, were but the affair of a moment. By some effort, too sudden and too little dependent on thought to be explained or remembered, I was able to arrest his arm and give him a sudden push by which I turned him from me and released myself from his grasp. This was no sooner done than I ran toward the fort with all the swiftness in my power, the Indian following me and I expecting every moment to feel his knife. I succeeded in my flight; and, on entering the fort, I saw Wenniway standing in the midst of the area and to him I hastened for protection. Wenniway desired the Indian to desist; but the latter pursued me round him, making several strokes at me with his knife, and foaming at the mouth with rage at the repeated failure of his purpose. At length, Wenniway drew near to M. Langlade's house; and, the door being open, I ran into it. The Indian followed me; but, on my entering the house, he voluntarily abandoned the pursuit.

Preserved so often, and so unexpectedly, as it had now my lot to be, I returned to my garret with a strong inclination to believe that through the will of an overruling power no Indian enemy could do me hurt; but new trials, as I believed, were at hand when, at ten o'clock in the evening, I was roused from sleep and once more desired to descend the stairs. Not less, however, to my satisfaction than surprise I was summoned only to meet Major Etherington, Mr. Bostwick and Lieutenant Lesslie, who were in the room below.

These gentlemen had been taken prisoners while looking at the game, without the fort, and immediately stripped of all their clothes. They were now sent into the fort, under the charge of Canadians, because the Indians having resolved on getting drunk the chiefs were apprehensive that they would be murdered if they continued in the camp. — Lieutenant Jemette and seventy soldiers had been killed; and but twenty Englishmen, including soldiers, were still alive. These were all within the fort, together with nearly three hundred Canadians.

These being our numbers, myself and others proposed to Major Etherington to make an effort for regaining possession of the fort and maintaining it against the Indians. The Jesuit missionary was consulted on the project; but he discouraged us by his representations, not only of the merciless treatment we must expect from the Indians, should they regain their superiority, but of the little dependence which was to be placed upon our Canadian auxiliaries. Thus, the fort and prisoners remained in the hands of the Indians, though, through the whole night, the prisoners and whites were in actual possession, and they were without the gates.

[*Henry remained a prisoner of the Indians for a year, travelling with them throughout that part of the country, and in the chapters which follow this one he goes on to describe his further adventures in the "Indian territories."*]

Samuel Hearne

Samuel Hearne (born in 1745) joined the Hudson's Bay Company in 1766 and, for two years, served as a seaman on their trading vessels in the Hudson Bay. In 1769 he was appointed (ordered?) to undertake an exploring expedition to see if there was truth to the natives' assertion that vast quantities of copper were to be found near the Arctic Ocean, and to see if there was an easy passage, by sea or river, across the barren lands. His first two expeditions failed miserably; the Indians robbed and deserted him, and he suffered terribly from the harsh arctic conditions. In December of 1770, however, he again set out (with the more reliable Matonabbee as guide) and, for one and a half years, he explored the region of the Coppermine River. His discoveries were fairly inconsequential — there was no copper to warrant excitement and the river proved to be shallow and unnavigable — but the record of his experiences, published three years after his death, secured for him a lasting fame. The following excerpt is taken from Chapter VI of that book, A Journey from Prince of Wales's Fort, in Hudson's Bay, to the Northern Ocean *(London: Strahan & Cadell, 1795).*

Transactions at the Coppermine River

July 14, 1771. We had scarcely arrived at the Coppermine River when four Copper Indians joined us, and brought with them two canoes. They had seen all the Indians who were sent from us at various times, except Matonabbee's brother, and three others that were first dispatched from Congecathawhacgaga.

On my arrival here I was not a little surprised to find the river differ so much from the description which the Indians had given of it at the Factory; for, instead of being so large as to be navigable for shipping, as it had been represented by them, it was at that part scarcely navigable for an Indian canoe, being no more than one hundred and eighty yards wide, every where full of shoals, and no less than three falls were in sight at first view.

Near the water's edge there is some wood; but not one tree grows on or near the top of the hills between which the river runs. There appears to have been formerly a much greater quantity than there is at present; but the trees seem to have been set on fire some years ago, and, in consequence, there is at present ten sticks lying on the ground, for one green one which is growing beside them. The whole timber appears to have been, even in its greatest prosperity, of so crooked and dwarfish a growth as to render it of little use for any purpose but firewood.

Soon after our arrival at the riverside, three Indians were sent off as spies, in order to see if any Esquimaux were inhabiting the river-side between us and the sea. After walking about three- quarters of a mile by the side of the river, we put up, when most of the Indians went a-hunting, and killed several musk-oxen and some deer. They were employed all the remainder of the day and night in splitting and drying the meat by the fire. As we were not then in want of provisions, and as deer and other animals were so plentiful, that each day's journey might have provided for itself, I was at a loss to account for this unusual economy of my companions; but was soon informed, that those preparations were made with a view to have victuals enough ready-cooked to serve us to the river's mouth, without being obliged to kill any in our way, as the report of guns, and the smoke of the fires, would be liable to alarm the natives, if any should be near at hand, and give them an opportunity of escaping.

Early in the morning of the fifteenth, we set out, when I immediately began my survey, which I continued about ten miles down the river, till heavy rain coming on we were obliged to put up; and the place where we lay that night was the end, or edge of the woods, the whole space between it and the sea being entirely barren hills and wide open marshes. In the course of this day's survey, I found the river as full of shoals as the part which I had seen before; and in many places it was so greatly diminished in its width, that in our way we passed by two more capital falls.

Early in the morning of the sixteenth, the weather being fine and pleasant, I again proceeded with my survey, and continued it for ten miles down the river; but still found it the same as before, being everywhere full of falls and shoals. At this time (it being about noon) the three men who had been sent as spies met us on their return, and informed my companions that five tents of Esquimaux were on the west side of the river. The situation, they said, was very convenient for surprising them; and, according to their account, I judged it to be about twelve miles from the place we met the spies. When the Indians received this intelligence, no farther attendance or attention was paid to my survey, but their whole thoughts were immediately engaged in planning the best method of attack, and how they might steal on the poor Esquimaux the ensuing night, and kill them all while asleep. To accomplish this bloody design more effectually, the Indians thought it necessary to cross the river as soon as possible; and, by the account of the spies, it appeared that no part was more convenient for the purpose than that where we had met them, it being there very smooth, and at a considerable distance from any fall. Accordingly, after the Indians had put all their guns, spears, targets, &c. in good order, we crossed the river, which took up some time.

When we arrived on the west side of the river, each painted the front of his target or shield; some with the figure of the Sun, others with that of the Moon, several with different kinds of birds and beasts of prey, and many with the images of imaginary beings, which, according to their silly notions, are the inhabitants of the different elements, Earth, Sea, Air, &c.

On enquiring the reason for their doing so, I learned that each man painted his shield with the image of that being on which he relied most for success in the intended engagement. Some were contented with a single representation; while others, doubtful, as I suppose, of the quality and power of any single being, had their shields covered to the very margin with a group of hieroglyphics, quite unintelligible to every one except the painter. Indeed, from the hurry in which this business was necessarily done, the want of every colour but red and black, and the deficiency of skill in the artist, most of those paintings had more the appearance of a number of accidental blotches, than "of any thing that is on earth, or in the water under the earth"; and though some few of them conveyed a tolerable idea of the thing intended, yet even these were many degrees worse than our country-sign paintings in England.

When this piece of superstition was completed, we began to advance towards the Esquimaux tents; but were very careful to avoid crossing any hills, or talking loud, for fear of being seen or overheard by the inhabitants; by which means the distance was not only much greater than it otherwise would have been, but, for the sake of keeping in the lowest grounds, we were obliged to walk through entire swamps of stiff marly clay, sometimes up to the knees. Our course, however, on this occasion, though very serpentine, was not altogether so remote from the river as entirely to exclude me from a view of it the whole way: on the contrary, several times (according to the situation of the ground) we advanced so near it, as to give me an opportunity of convincing myself that it was as unnavigable as it was in those parts which I had surveyed before, and which entirely corresponded with the accounts given of it by the spies.

It is perhaps worth remarking, that my crew, though an undisciplined rabble, and by no means accustomed to war or command, seemingly acted on this horrible occasion with the utmost uniformity of sentiment. There was not among them the least altercation or separate opinion; all were united in the general cause, and as ready to follow where Matonabbee led, as he appeared to be ready to lead, according to the advice of an old Copper Indian, who had joined us on our first arrival at the river where this bloody business was first proposed.

Never was reciprocity of interest more generally regarded among a number of people, than it was on the present occasion by my crew, for not one was a moment in want of any thing that another could spare; and if ever the spirit of disinterested friendship expanded the heart of a Northern Indian, it was here exhibited in the most extensive meaning of the word. Property of every kind that could be of general use now ceased to be private, and every one who had any thing which came under that description, seemed proud of an opportunity of giving it, or lending it to those who had none, or were most in want of it.

The number of my crew was so much greater than that which five tents could contain, and the warlike manner in which they were equipped so greatly superior to what could be expected of the poor Esquimaux, that no less than a total massacre of every one of them was likely to be the case, unless Providence should work a miracle for their deliverance.

The land was so situated that we walked under cover of rocks and hills till we were within two hundred yards of the tents. There we lay in ambush for some time, watching the motions of the Esquimaux; and here the Indians would have advised me to stay till the fight was over, but to this I could by no means consent; for I considered that when the Esquimaux came to be surprised, they would try every way to escape, and if they found me alone, not knowing me from an enemy, they would probably proceed to violence against me when no person was near to assist. For this I determined to accompany them, telling them at the same time, that I would not have any hand in the murder they were about to commit, unless I found it necessary for my own safety. The Indians were not displeased at this proposal; one of them immediately fixed me a spear, and another lent me a broad bayonet for my protection, but at that time I could not be provided with a target; nor did I want to be encumbered with such an unnecessary piece of lumber.

While we lay in ambush, the Indians performed the last ceremonies which were thought necessary before the engagement. These chiefly consisted in painting their faces; some all black, some all red, and others with a mixture of the two; and to prevent their hair from blowing into their eyes, it was either tied before and behind, and on both sides, or else cut short all round. The next thing they considered was to make themselves as light as possible for running; which they did, by pulling off their stockings, and either cutting off the sleeves of their jackets, or rolling them up close to their armpits; and though the muskettos at that time were so numerous as to surpass of credibility, yet some of the Indians actually pulled off their jackets and entered the lists quite naked, except their breech-cloths and shoes. Fearing I might have occasion to run with the rest, I thought it also advisable to pull off my stockings and cap, and to tie my hair as close up as possible.

By the time the Indians had thus made themselves completely frightful, it was near one o'clock in the morning of the seven-teenth; when finding all the Esquimaux quiet in their tents, they rushed forth from their ambuscade, and fell on the poor unsuspecting creatures, unperceived till close at the very eves of their tents, when they soon began the bloody massacre, while I stood neuter in the rear.

In a few seconds the horrible scene commenced; it was shocking beyond description; the poor unhappy victims were surprised in the midst of their sleep, and had neither time nor power to make any resistance; men, women, and children, in all upward of twenty, ran out of their tents stark naked, and endeavoured to make their escape; but the Indians having possession of all the landside, to no place could they fly for shelter. One alternative only remained, that of jumping into the river; but, as none of them attempted it, they all fell a sacrifice to Indian barbarity!

The shrieks and groans of the poor expiring wretches were truly dreadful; and my horror was much increased at seeing a young girl, seemingly about eighteen years of age, killed so near me, that when the first spear was stuck into her side she fell down at my feet, and twisted round my legs, so that it was with difficulty that I could disengage myself from her dying grasps. As two Indian men pursued this unfortunate victim, I solicited very hard for her life; but the murderers made no reply till they had stuck both their spears through her body, and transfixed her to the ground. They then looked me sternly in the face, and began to ridicule me, by asking if I wanted an Esquimaux wife; and paid not the smallest regard to the shrieks and agony of the poor wretch, who was twining round their spears like an eel! Indeed, after receiving much abusive language from them on the occasion, I was at length obliged to desire that they would be more expeditious in dispatching their victim out of her misery, otherwise I should be obliged, out of pity, to assist in the friendly office of putting an end to the existence of a fellow-creature who was so cruelly wounded. On this request being made, one of the Indians hastily drew his spear from the place where it was lodged, and pierced it through her breast near the heart. The love of life, however, even in this most miserable state, was so predominant, that though this might justly be called the most merciful act that could be done for the poor creature, it seemed to be unwelcome, for though much exhausted by pain and loss of blood, she made several efforts to ward off the friendly blow. My situation and the terror of my mind at beholding this butchery, cannot easily be conceived, much less described; though I summed up all the fortitude I was master of on the occasion, it was with difficulty that I could refrain from tears; and I am confident that my features must have feelingly expressed how sincerely I was affected at this barbarous scene I then witnessed; even at this hour I cannot reflect on the transaction of that horrid day without shedding tears.

Alexander Mackenzie

*A partner in the North West fur-trading company, Alexander Macken-
zie's consuming passion was to find a route across the continent to the
Pacific Ocean. In 1789 he tested a theory that the river which flowed out of
Great Slave Lake (now the Mackenzie) led to the Pacific Ocean but discovered that it flowed to the Arctic instead. A second expedition in 1793,
however, was successful and Mackenzie became the first white man to
journey overland to the Pacific, reaching it in July of that year. The record
of that expedition is fascinating in its vivification of hardship and determination, and in its depiction of first contacts with the coast Indians. The
following passage is from* Voyages from Montreal... Through the
Continent of North America to the Frozen and Pacific Oceans
(London: Cadell, 1801).

On the Shore of the Pacific Ocean

We continued our route with a considerable degree of expedition,
and as we proceeded the mountains appeared to withdraw from us.
The country between them soon opened to our view, which apparently added to their awful elevation. We continued to descend till
we came to the brink of a precipice, from whence our guides discovered the river to us, and a village on its banks. This precipice, or
rather succession of precipices, is covered with large timber, which
consists of the pine, the spruce, the hemlock, the birch, and other
trees. Our conductors informed us, that it abounded in animals,
which, from their description, must be wild goats. In about two
hours we arrived at the bottom, where there is a conflux of two rivers, that issue from the mountains. We crossed the one which was to
the left. They are both very rapid, and continue so till they unite
their currents, forming a stream of about twelve yards in breadth.
Here the timber was also very large; but I could not learn from our
conductors why the most considerable hemlock trees were stripped
of their bark to the tops of them. I concluded, indeed, at that time
that the inhabitants tanned their leather with it. Here were also the
largest and loftiest elder and cedar trees that I had ever seen. We were

now sensible of an entire change in the climate, and the berries were quite ripe.

The sun was about to set, when our conductors left us to follow them as well as we could. We were prevented, however, from going far astray, for we were hemmed in on both sides and behind by such a barrier as nature never before presented to my view. Our guides had the precaution to mark the road for us, by breaking the branches of trees as they passed. This small river must, at certain seasons, rise to an uncommon height and strength of current most probably on the melting of the snow; as we saw a large quantity of drift wood lying twelve feet above the immediate level of the river. This circumstance impeded our progress, and the protruding rocks frequently forced us to pass through the water. It was now dark, without the least appearance of houses, though it would be impossible to have seen them, if there had been any, at the distance of twenty yards, from the thickness of the woods. My men were anxious to stop for the night; indeed the fatigue they had suffered justified the proposal, and I left them to their choice; but as the anxiety of my mind impelled me forwards, they continued to follow me; till I found myself at the edge of the woods; and, notwithstanding the remonstrances that were made, I proceeded, feeling rather than seeing my way, till I arrived at a house, and soon discovered several fires, in small huts, with people busily employed in cooking their fish. I walked into one of them without the least ceremony, threw down my burden, and, after shaking hands with some of the people, sat down upon it. They received me without the least appearance of surprize, but soon made signs for me to go up to the large house, which was erected, on upright posts, at some distance from the ground. A broad piece of timber with steps cut in it, led to the scaffolding even with the floor, and by this curious kind of ladder I entered the house at one end; and having passed three fires, at equal distances in the middle of the building, I was received by several people, sitting upon a very wide board, at the upper end of it. I shook hands with them, and seated myself beside a man, the dignity of whose countenance induced me to give him that preference. I soon discovered one of my guides seated a little above me, with a neat mat spread before him, which I supposed to be the place of honour, and appropriated to strangers. In a short time my people arrived, and placed themselves near me, when the man by whom I sat, immediately rose, and fetched, from behind a plank of about four feet wide, a quantity of roasted salmon.

He then directed a mat to be placed before me and Mr. Mackay, who was now sitting by me. When this ceremony was performed, he brought a salmon for each of us, and half an one to each of my men. The same plank served also as a screen for the beds, whither the women and children were already retired; but whether that circumstance took place on our arrival, or was the natural consequence of the late hour of the night, I did not discover. The signs of our protector seemed to denote, that we might sleep in the house, but as we did not understand him with a sufficient degree of certainty, I thought it prudent, from the fear of giving offence, to order the men to make a fire without, that we might sleep by it. When he observed our design, he placed boards for us that we might not take our repose on the bare ground, and ordered a fire to be prepared for us. We had not been long seated round it, when we received a large dish of salmon roes, pounded fine and beat up with water so as to have the appearance of a cream. Nor was it without some kind of seasoning that gave it a bitter taste. Another dish soon followed, the principal article of which was also salmon-roes, with a large proportion of gooseberries, and an herb that appeared to be sorrel. Its acidity rendered it more agreeable to my taste than the former preparation. Having been regaled with these delicacies, for such they were considered by that hospitable spirit which provided them, we laid ourselves down to repose with no other canopy than the sky; but I never enjoyed a more sound and refreshing repose, though I had a board for my bed, and a billet for my pillow.

At five this morning I awoke, and found that the natives had lighted a fire for us, and were sitting by it. My hospitable friend immediately brought me some berries and roasted salmon, and his companions soon followed his example. The former, which consisted among many others, of gooseberries, whirtleberries and raspberries, were the finest I ever saw or tasted, of their respective kinds. They also brought the dried roes of fish to eat with the berries.

Salmon is so abundant in this river, that these people have a constant and plentiful supply of that excellent fish. To take them with more facility, they had, with great labour, formed an embankment or weir across the river for the purpose of placing their fishing machines, which they disposed both above and below it. I expressed my wish to visit this extraordinary work, but these people are so superstitious, that they would not allow me a nearer examination than I could obtain by viewing it from the bank. The river is about fifty yards in breadth, and by observing a man fish with a dipping net, I judged it to be about ten feet deep at the foot of the fall. The weir is a work of great labour, and contrived with considerable ingenuity. It was near four feet above the level of the water, at the time I saw it, and nearly the height of the bank on which I stood to examine it. The stream is stopped nearly two thirds by it. It is constructed by fixing small trees in the bed of the river in a slanting position (which could be practicable only when the water is much lower than I saw it) with the thick part down-wards; over these is laid a bed of gravel, on which is placed a range of lesser trees, and so on alternately till the work is brought to its proper height. Beneath it the machines are placed, into which the salmon fall when they attempt to leap over. On either side there is a large frame of timber-work six feet above the level of the upper water, in which passages are left for the salmon leading directly into the machines, which are taken up at pleasure. At the foot of the fall dipping nets are also successfully employed.

The water of this river is of the colour of asses milk, which I attributed in part to the limestone that in many places forms the bed of the river, but principally to the rivulets which fall from mountains of the same material.

These people indulge an extreme superstition respecting their fish, as it is apparently their only animal food. Flesh they never taste, and one of their dogs having picked and swallowed part of a bone which we had left, was beaten by his master till he disgorged it. One of my people also having thrown a bone of the deer into the river, a native, who had observed the circumstance, immediately dived and brought it up, and, having consigned it to the fire, instantly proceeded to wash his polluted hands.

As we were still at some distance from the sea, I made application to my friend to procure us a canoe or two, with people to conduct us thither. After he had made various excuses, I at length comprehended that his only objection was to the embarking venison in a canoe on their river, as the fish would instantly smell it and abandon them, so that he, his friends, and relations, must starve. I soon eased his apprehensions on that point, and desired to know what I must do with the venison that remained, when he told me to give it to one of the strangers whom he pointed out to me, as being of a tribe that eat flesh. I now requested him to furnish me with some fresh salmon in its raw state; but, instead of complying with my wish, he brought me a couple of them roasted, observing at the same time, that the current was very strong, and would bring us to the next village, where our wants would be abundantly supplied. In short, he requested that we would make haste to depart. This was rather unexpected after so much kindness and hospitality, but our ignorance of the language prevented us from being able to discover the cause.

At eight this morning, fifteen men armed, the friends and relations of these people, arrived by land, in consequence of notice sent them in the night, immediately after the appearance of our guides. They are more corpulent and of a better appearance than the inhabitants of the interior. Their language totally different from any I had heard; the Atnah and Chin tribe, as far as I can judge from the very little I saw of that people, bear the nearest resemblance to them. They appear to be of a quiet and peaceable character, and never make any hostile incursions into the lands of their neighbours.

Their dress consists of a single robe tied over the shoulders, falling down behind, to the heels, and before, a little below the knees, with a deep fringe round the bottom. It is generally made of the bark of the cedar tree, which they prepare as fine as hemp; though some of these garments are interwoven with strips of the sea-otter skin, which give them the appearance of a fur on one side. Others have stripes of red and yellow threads fancifully introduced toward the borders, which have a very agreeable effect. The men have no other covering than that which I have described, and they unceremoniously lay it aside when they find it convenient. In addition to this robe, the women wear a close fringe hanging down before them about two feet in length, and half as wide. When they sit down they draw this between their thighs. They wear their hair so short, that it requires little care or combing. The men have theirs in plaits, and being smeared with oil and red earth, instead of a comb they have a small stick hanging by a string from one of the locks, which they employ to alleviate any itching or irritation in the head. The colour of the eye is grey with a tinge of red. They have all high cheek-bones, but the women are more remarkable for that feature than the men. Their houses, arms, and utensils I shall describe hereafter.

I presented my friend with several articles, and also distributed some among others of the natives who had been attentive to us. One of my guides had been very serviceable in procuring canoes for us to proceed on our expedition; he appeared also to be very desirous of giving these people a favourable impression of us; and I was very much concerned that he should leave me as he did, without giving me the least notice of his departure, or receiving the presents which I had prepared for him, and he so well deserved. At noon I had an observation which gave 52.28.11. North longitude.

Anna Brownell Jameson

Anna Jameson, a celebrated writer in England — her Diary of an En-
nuyée *(1826) being very popular — came to Canada in December of
1836 to attempt a reconciliation with her husband, Robert Jameson, who
was then Vice-Chancellor of Upper Canada. The attempt failing,
Jameson returned to England seven months later, but in the meantime
travelled a great deal and absorbed much of what was interesting and distinctive about the new land.* Winter Studies and Summer Rambles
*(1838), her account of those travels, has become a Canadian travel classic
— it is intimate (but not overbearing), detailed and frank, amusing and
incisive. The following selection from that book describes, as did hundreds
of writers, Niagara Falls; but Jameson's is unique in its unexpectedness
and in its avoidance of stereotypes.*

Niagara Falls in Winter

Well! I have seen these Cataracts of Niagara, which have thundered
in my mind's ear ever since I can remember — which have been my
"childhood's thought, my youth's desire," since first my imagination was awakened to wonder and to wish. I have beheld them, and
shall I whisper it to you? — but, O tell it not among the Philistines!
— I wish I had not! I wish they were still a thing unbeheld — a thing
to be imagined, hoped, and anticipated — something to live for: —
the reality has displaced from my mind an illusion far more magnificent than itself — I have no words for my utter disappointment:
yet I have not the presumption to suppose that all I have heard and
read of Niagara is false or exaggerated — that every expression of
astonishment, enthusiasm, rapture, is affectation or hyperbole. No! it
must be my own fault. Terni, and some of the Swiss cataracts leaping
from their mountains, have affected me a thousand times more than
all the immensity of Niagara. O I could beat myself! and now there is
no help! — the first moment, the first impression is over — is lost;
though I should live a thousand years, long as Niagara itself shall roll,
I can never see it again for the first time. Something is gone that cannot be restored. What has come over my soul and senses? — I am no
longer Anna — I am metamorphosed — I am translated — I am an

ass's head, a clod, a wooden spoon, a fat weed growing on Lethe's bank, a stock, a stone, a petrifaction, — for have I not seen Niagara, the wonder of wonders; and felt — no words can tell what disappointment!

But, to take things in order: we set off for the falls yesterday morning, with the intention of spending the day there, sleeping, and returning the next day to Niagara. The distance is fourteen miles, by a road winding along the banks of the Niagara river, and over the Queenston heights; — and beautiful must this land be in summer, since even now it is beautiful. The flower garden, the trim shrubbery, the lawn, the meadow with its hedgerows, when frozen up and wrapt in snow, always give me the idea of some-thing not only desolate but dead: Nature is the ghost of herself, and trails a spectral pall; I always feel a kind of pity — a touch of melancholy — when at this season I have wandered among withered shrubs and buried flower-beds; but here, in the wilderness, where Nature is wholly independent of art, she does not die, nor yet mourn; she lies down to rest on the bosom of Winter, and the aged one folds her in his robe of ermine and jewels, and rocks her with his hurricanes, and hushes her to sleep. How still it was! how calm, how vast the glittering white waste and the dark purple forests! The sun shone out, and the sky was without a cloud; yet we saw few people, and for many miles the hissing of our sleigh, as we flew along upon our dazzling path, and the tinkling of the sleigh-bells, were the only sounds we heard. When we were within four or five miles of the falls, I stopped the sleigh from time to time to listen for the roar of the cataracts, but the state of the atmosphere was not favourable for the transmission of sound, and the silence was unbroken.

Such was the deep, monotonous tranquillity which prevailed on every side — so exquisitely pure and vestal-like the robe in which all Nature lay slumbering around us, I could scarce believe that this whole frontier district is not only remarkable for the prevalence of vice — but of dark and desperate crime.

Mr. A., who is a magistrate, pointed out to me a lonely house by the way-side, where, on a dark stormy night in the preceding winter, he had surprised and arrested a gang of forgers and coiners; it was a fearful description. For some time my impatience had been thus beguiled — impatience and suspense much like those of a child at a theatre before the curtain rises. My imagination had been so impressed by the vast height of the Falls, that I was constantly looking in an upward direction, when, as we came to the brow of a hill, my companion suddenly checked the horses, and exclaimed, "The Falls!"

I was not, for an instant, aware of their presence; we were yet at a distance, looking down upon them; and I saw at one glance a flat extensive plain; the sun having withdrawn its beams for the moment, there was neither light, nor shade, nor colour. In the midst were seen the two great cataracts, but merely as a feature in the wide landscape. The sound was by no means overpowering, and the clouds of spray, which Fanny Butler called so beautifully the "everlasting incense of the waters," now condensed ere they rose by the excessive cold, fell round the base of the cataracts in fleecy folds, just concealing that furious embrace of the waters above and the waters below. All the associations which in imagination I had gathered round the scene, its appalling terrors, its soul-subduing beauty, power and height, and velocity and immensity, were all diminished in effect, or wholly lost.

I was quite silent — my very soul sank within me. On seeing my disappointment (written, I suppose, most legibly in my countenance) my companion began to comfort me, by telling me of all those who had been disappointed on the first view of Niagara, and had confessed it. I did confess but I was not to be comforted. We held on our way to the Clifton hotel, at the foot of the hill; most desolate it looked with its summer verandahs and open balconies cumbered up with snow, and hung round with icicles — its forlorn, empty rooms, broken windows, and dusty dinner tables. The poor people who kept the house in winter had gathered themselves for warmth and comfort into a little kitchen, and when we made our appearance, stared at us with a blank amazement, which showed what a rare thing was the sight of a visitor at this season.

While the horses were cared for, I went up into the highest balcony to command a better view of the cataracts; a little Yankee boy, with a shrewd, sharp face, and twinkling black eyes, acting as my gentleman usher. As I stood gazing on the scene which seemed to enlarge upon my vision, the little fellow stuck his hands into his pockets, and looking up in my face, said,

"You be from the old country, I reckon?"

"Yes."

"Out over there, beyond the sea?"

"Yes."

"And did you come all that way across the sea for these here falls?"
"Yes."

"My!!" Then after a long pause, and eyeing me with a most comical expression of impudence and fun, he added, "Now, do you know what them 'ere birds are, out yonder?" pointing to a number of gulls which were hovering and sporting amid the spray, rising and sinking and wheeling around, appearing to delight in playing on the verge of this "hell of waters" and almost dipping their wings into the foam. My eyes were, in truth, fixed on these fair, fearless creatures, and they had suggested already twenty fanciful similitudes, when I was roused by his question.

"Those birds" said I. "Why, what are they?"

"Why, them's EAGLES!"

"Eagles?" it was impossible to help laughing.

"Yes," said the urchin sturdily; "and I guess you have none of them in the old country?"

"Not many eagles, my boy; but plenty of gulls!" and I gave him a pretty considerable pinch by the ear.

"Ay!" said he, laughing; "well now you be dreadful smart — smarter than many folks that come here!"

We now prepared to walk to the Crescent fall, and I bound some crampons to my feet, like those they use among the Alps, without which I could not for a moment have kept my footing on the frozen surface of the snow. As we approached the Table Rock, the whole scene assumed a wild and wonderful magnificence; down came the dark-green waters, hurrying with them over the edge of the precipice enormous blocks of ice brought down from Lake Erie. On each side of the Falls, from the ledges and overhanging cliffs, were suspended huge icicles, some twenty, some thirty feet in length, thicker than the body of a man, and in colour of a paly green, like the glaciers of the Alps; and all the crags below, which projected from the boiling eddying waters, were encrusted, and in a manner built round with ice, which had formed into immense crystals, like basaltic columns, such as I have seen in the pictures of Staffa and the Giant's Causeway; and every tree, and leaf, and branch, fringing the rocks and ravines, was wrought in ice. On them, and on the wooden buildings erected near the Table Rock, the spray from the cataract had accumulated and formed into the most beautiful crystals and tracery work; they looked like houses of glass, welted and moulded into regular and ornamental shapes, and hung round with a rich fringe of icy points. Wherever we stood we were on unsafe ground, for the snow, when heaped up as now to the height of three or four feet, frequently slipped in masses from the bare rock, and on its surface the spray, for ever falling, was converted into a sheet of ice, smooth, compact, and glassy, on which I could not have stood a moment without my *crampons*. It was very fearful, and yet I could not tear myself away, but remained on the Table Rock, even on the very edge of it, till a kind of dreamy fascination came over me; the continuous thunder, and might and movement of the lapsing waters, held all my vital spirits bound up as by a spell. Then, as at last I turned away, the descending sun broke out, and an Iris appeared below the American Fall, one extremity resting on a snow mound; and motionless there it hung in the midst of restless terrors, its beautiful but rather pale hues contrasting with the death-like colourless objects around; it reminded me of the faint ethereal smile of a dying martyr. We wandered about for nearly four hours, and then returned to the hotel: there my good-natured escort from Toronto, Mr. Campbell, was waiting to conduct us to his house, which is finely situated on an eminence not far from the great cataract. We did not know, till we arrived there, that the young and lovely wife of our host had been confined only the day before. This event had been concealed from us, lest we should have some scruples about accepting hospitality under such circumstances; and, in truth, I *did* feel at first a little uncomfortable, and rather *de trop*; but the genuine kindness of our reception soon overcame all scruples: we were made welcome, and soon felt ourselves so; and, for my own part, I have always sympathies ready for such occasions, and shared very honestly in the grateful joy of these kind people. After dinner I went up into the room of the invalid — a little nest of warmth and comfort; and though the roar of the neighbouring cataract shook the house as with a universal tremor, it did not quite overpower the soft voice of the weak but happy mother, nor even the feeble wail of the new-born baby, as I took it in my arms with a whispered blessing, and it fell asleep in my lap. Poor little thing! — it was an awful sort of lullaby, that ceaseless thunder of the mighty waters ever at hand, yet no one but myself seemed to heed, or even to hear it; such is the force of custom, and the power of adaptation even in our most delicate organs. To sleep at the hotel was impossible, and to intrude ourselves on the Campbells equally so. It was near midnight when we mounted our sleigh to return to the town of Niagara, and, as I remember, I did not utter a word during the whole fourteen miles. The air was still, though keen, the snow lay around, the whole earth seemed to slumber in a ghastly, calm repose; but the heavens were wide awake. There the Aurora Borealis was holding her revels, and dancing and flashing, and varying through all shapes and all hues pale amber, rose tint, blood red — and the stars shone out with a fitful, restless brilliance; and every now and then a meteor would shoot athwart the skies, or fall to earth, and all around me was wild, and strange, and exciting — more like a fever dream than a reality.

Today I am suffering, as might be expected, with pain and stiffness, unable to walk across the room; but the pain will pass: and on the whole I am glad I have made this excursion. The Falls did not make on my mind the impression I had anticipated, perhaps for that reason, even because I had *anticipated* it. Under different circumstances it might have been otherwise; but "it was sung to me in my cradle," as the Germans say, that I should live to be disappointed — even in the Falls of Niagara.

Paul Kane

Paul Kane, who was born in Ireland in 1810 and moved with his family to York, Upper Canada, around 1822, is best known as an artist-explorer; that is, as an artist who, like George Catlin and Frederic Remington, set out to explore the North American wilderness before it disappeared and to describe it in pictures. Kane did this between 1845 and 1848, travelling throughout Western Canada, making some 700 sketches of native lifestyle, new settlements and natural scenery. Many of the canvases he painted from those sketches are now in the Royal Ontario Museum and are well known to Canadians, having been reproduced many times. Kane also published an account of his travels, Wanderings of an Artist Among the Indians of North America *(London: Longman, 1859), and that too has become a Canadian classic. The following selection is from that book.*

Christmas at Fort Edmonton

On the evening of the 5th we arrived at Fort Edmonton, where I was most kindly received by Mr. Harriett, and provided with a comfortable room to myself — a luxury I had not known for many months. This was to be my headquarters for the winter; and certainly no place in the interior is at all equal to it, either in comfort or interest. All the Company's servants, with their wives and children, numbering about 130, live within the palings of the fort in comfortable log-houses, supplied with abundance of firewood.

Along the banks of the river in the vicinity of the fort, about twenty feet below the upper surface, beds of hard coal are seen protruding, which is, however, not much used, except in the blacksmith's forge, for which purpose it seems to be admirably adapted. The want of proper grates or furnaces in those distant regions, where iron is at present so scarce, prevents its general use as fuel.

Provisions are in the greatest plenty, consisting of fresh buffalo meat, venison, salted geese, magnificent whitefish, and rabbits in abundance, with plenty of good potatoes, turnips and flour. The potatoes are very fine, and the turnips do well here. Of wheat, they can of course have only one crop; but with very indifferent farming they manage to get from twenty to twenty-five bushels per acre. The crop, however, is sometimes destroyed by early frost. The corn is ground in a windmill, which had been erected since my last visit, and seemed to make very good flour. Indian corn has been tried but it did not succeed, owing to the very short summer.

Outside, the buffaloes range in thousands close to the fort; deer are to be obtained at an easy distance; rabbits run about in all directions, and wolves and lynxes prowl after them all through the neighbouring woods. As for seeing aborigines, no place can be more advantageous. Seven of the most important and war-like tribes on the continent are in constant communication with the fort, which is situated in the country of the Crees and Assiniboines, and is visited at least twice in the year by the Blackfeet, Sar-cees, Gros-Vents, Paygans, and Blood Indians, who come to sell the dried buffalo meat and fat for making pemmican which is prepared in large quantities for the supply of the other posts.

The buffaloes were extremely numerous this winter, and several had been shot within a few hundred yards of the fort. The men had already commenced gathering their supply of fresh meat for the summer in the ice-pit. This is made by digging a square hole, each containing 700 or 800 buffalo carcases. As soon as the ice in the river is of sufficient thickness, it is cut into square blocks of uniform size with saws; with these blocks the floor of the pit is regularly paved, and the blocks cemented together by pouring water in between them, and allowing it to freeze solid. In like manner, the walls are solidly built up to the surface of the ground. The head and feet of the buffalo, when killed, are cut off, and the carcase, without being skinned, is divided into quarters, and piled in layers in the pit as brought in, until it is filled up, when the whole is covered with a thick coating of straw, which is again protected from the sun and rain by a shed. In this manner the meat keeps perfectly good through the whole summer and eats much better than fresh killed meat, being more tender and better flavoured.

Shortly after my arrival, Mr. Harriett, myself, and two or three gentlemen of the establishment, prepared for a buffalo hunt. We had our choice of splendid horses, as about a dozen are selected and kept in stables for the gentlemen's use from the wild band of 700 or 800, which roam about the fort, and forage for themselves through the winter, by scraping the snow away from the long grass with their hoofs. These horses have only one man to take care of them, who is called the horsekeeper; he follows them about and encamps near them with his family, turning the band should he perceive them going too far away. This would appear to be a most arduous task; but instinct soon teaches the animals that their only safety from their great enemies, the wolves, is by remaining near the habitations of man; and by keeping in one body they are enabled to fight the bands of wolves, which they often drive off after severe contests. Thus they do not stray far away, and they never leave the band. These horses are kept and bred there for the purpose of sending off the pemmican and stores to other forts during the summer; in winter they are almost useless, on account of the depth of snow. In the morning we breakfasted most heartily on white fish and buffalo tongues, accompanied by tea, milk, sugar, and *galettes*, which the voyageurs consider a great luxury. These are cakes made of simple flour and water, and baked by clearing away a place near the fire; the cake is then laid on the hot ground, and covered with hot ashes, where it is allowed to remain until sufficiently baked. They are very light and pleasant, and are much esteemed. We then mounted our chosen horses, and got upon the track the men had made on the river by hauling wood. This we followed for about six miles, when we espied a band of buffaloes on the bank; but a dog, who had sneaked after us, running after them, gave the alarm too soon, and they started off at full speed, much to our disappointment. We caught the dog, and tied his legs together, and left him lying in the road to await our return.

After going about three miles further, we came to a place where the snow was trodden down in every direction, and on ascending the bank, we found ourselves in the close vicinity of an enormous band of buffaloes, probably numbering nearly 10,000. An Indian hunter started off for the purpose of turning some of them towards us; but the snow was so deep, that the buffaloes were either unable or unwilling to run far, and at last came to a dead stand. We therefore secured our horses, and advanced towards them on foot to within forty or fifty yards, when we commenced firing, which we continued to do until we were tired of a sport so little exciting; for, strange to say, they never tried either to escape or to attack us.

Seeing a very large bull in the herd, I thought I would kill him, for the purpose of getting the skin of his enormous head, and preserving it. He fell; but as he was surrounded by three others that I could not frighten away, I was obliged to shoot them all before I could venture near him, although they were all bulls, and they are not generally saved for meat. The sport proving rather tedious, from the unusual quietness of the buffaloes, we determined to return home, and send the men for the carcases, and remounted our horses. But, before we came to the river, we found an old bull standing right in our way, and Mr. Harriett, for the purpose of driving him off, fired at him and slightly wounded him, when he turned and made a furious charge. Mr. Harriett barely escaped by jumping his horse on one side. So close, indeed, was the charge, that the horse was slightly struck on the rump. The animal still pursued Mr. Harriett at full speed, and we all set after him, firing ball after ball into him, as we ranged up close to him, without any apparent effect than that of making him more furious, and turning his rage on ourselves. This enabled Mr. Harriett to reload, and plant a couple more balls in him, which evidently sickened him. We were now all close to him, and we all fired deliberately at him. At last, after receiving sixteen bullets in his body, he slowly fell, dying harder than I had ever seen an animal die before.

On our return, we told the men to get the dogsledges ready to go in the morning to bring in the cows we had killed, numbering twenty-seven, with the head of the bull I wanted; whereupon the squaws and halfbreed women, who have always this job to do, started off to catch the requisite number of dogs. About the fort there are always two or three hundred who forage for themselves like the horses, and lie outside. These dogs are quite as valuable there as horses, as it is with them that everything is drawn over the snow. Two of them will easily draw in a large cow; yet no care is taken of them, except that of beating them sufficiently before using them, to make them quiet for the time they are in harness.

It would be almost impossible to catch these animals, who are almost as wild as wolves, were it not for the precaution which is taken in the autumn of catching the dogs singly by stratagem, and tying light logs to them, which they can drag about. By this means the squaws soon catch as many as they want, and bring them into the fort, where they are fed — sometimes — before being harnessed. This operation is certainly (if it were not for the cruelty exhibited) one of the most amusing scenes I had witnessed. Early next morning I was aroused by a yelling and screaming that made me rush from my room, thinking that we were all being murdered; and there I saw the women harnessing the dogs. Such a scene! The women were like so many furies with big sticks, thrashing away at the poor animals, who rolled and yelled in agony and terror, until each team was yoked up and started off.

During the day the men returned, bringing the quartered cows ready to be put in the ice-pit, and my big head, which, before skinning, I had put in the scales, and found that it weighed exactly 202 lbs. The skin of the head I brought home with me.

The fort at this time of the year presented a most pleasing picture of cheerful activity; every one was busy; the men, some in hunting and bringing in the meat when the weather permitted, some in sawing boards in the saw-pit, and building the boats, about thirty feet long and six feet beam, which go as far as York Factory, and are found more convenient for carrying goods on the Saskatchewan and Red River than canoes. They are mostly built at Edmonton, because there are more boats required to take the peltries to York Factory than is required to bring goods back; and more than one-half of the boats built here never return. This system requires them to keep constantly building.

The women find ample employment in making mocassins and clothes for the men, putting up pemmican in ninety-pound bags, and doing all the household drudgery, in which the men never assist them. The evenings are spent round their large fires in eternal gossiping and smoking. The sole musician of the establishment, a fiddler, is now in great requisition amongst the French part of the inmates, who give full vent to their national vivacity, whilst the more sedate Indian looks on with solemn enjoyment.

No liquor is allowed to the men or Indians; but the want of it did not in the least seem to impair their cheerfulness. True, the gentlemen of the fort had liquor brought out at their own expense; but the rules respecting its use were so strict and so well known, that none but those to whom it belonged either expected, or asked, to share it.

On Christmas day the flag was hoisted, and all appeared in their best and gaudiest style, to do honour to the holiday. Towards noon every chimney gave evidence of being in full blast, whilst savoury steams of cooking pervaded the atmosphere in all directions. About two o'clock we sat down to dinner. Our party consisted of Mr. Harriett, the chief, and three clerks, Mr. Thebo, the Roman Catholic missionary from Manitou Lake, about thirty miles off, Mr. Rundell, the Wesleyan missionary, who resided within the pickets, and myself, the wanderer, who, though returning from the shores of the Pacific, was still the latest importation from civilized life. The dining-hall in which we assembled was the largest room in the fort, probably about fifty by twenty-five feet, well warmed by large fires, which are scarcely ever allowed to go out. The walls and ceilings are boarded, as plastering is not used, there being no limestone within reach but these boards are painted in a style of the most startling barbaric gaudiness, and the ceiling filled with centre-pieces of fantastic gilt scrolls, making altogether a saloon which no white man would enter for the first time without a start, and which the Indians always looked upon with awe and wonder.

The room was intended as a reception room for the wild chiefs who visited the fort; and the artist who designed the decorations was no doubt directed to "astonish the natives." If such were his instructions, he deserves the highest praise for having faithfully complied with them, although, were he to attempt a repetition of the same style in one of the rooms of the Vatican, it might subject him to some severe criticisms from the fastidious. No tablecloth shed its snowy whiteness over the board; no silver candelabra or gaudy china interfered with its simple magnificence. The bright tin plates and dishes reflected jolly faces, and burnished gold can give no truer zest to a feast.

Perhaps it might be interesting to some dyspeptic idler, who painfully strolls through a city park, to coax an appetite to a sufficient intensity to enable him to pick an ortolan, if I were to describe to him the fare set before us, to appease appetites nourished by constant outdoor exercise in an atmosphere ranging at 40 ° to 50° below zero. At the head, before Mr. Harriett, was a large dish of boiled buffalo hump; at the foot smoked & boiled buffalo calf. Start not, gentle reader, the calf is very small, and is taken from the cow by the Caesarean operation long before it attains its full growth. This, boiled whole, is one of the most esteemed dishes amongst the epicures of the interior. My pleasing duty was to help a dish of mouffle, or dried moose nose; the gentleman on my left distributed, with graceful impartiality, the white fish, delicately browned in buffalo marrow. The worthy priest helped the buffalo tongue, whilst Mr. Rundell cut up the beavers' tails. Nor was the other gentleman left unemployed, as all his spare time was occupied in dissecting a roast wild goose. The centre of the table was graced with piles of potatoes, turnips, and bread conveniently placed, so that each could help himself without interrupting the labours of his companions. Such was our jolly Christmas dinner at Edmonton; and long will it remain in my memory, although no pies, or puddings, or blanc manges, shed their fragrance over the scene.

In the evening the hall was prepared for the dance to which Mr. Harriett had invited all the inmates of the fort, and was early filled by the gaily dressed guests. Indians, whose chief ornament consisted in the paint on their faces, voyageurs with bright sashes and neatly ornamented mocassins, half-breeds glittering in every ornament they could lay their hands on; whether civilized or savage, all were laughing, and jabbering in as many different languages as there were styles of dress. English, however, was little used, as none could speak it but those who sat at the dinner-table. The dancing was most picturesque, and almost all joined in it. Occasionally I, among the rest, led out a young Cree squaw, who sported enough beads round her neck to have made a pedlar's fortune, and having led her into the centre of the room, I danced round her with all the agility I was capable of exhibiting, to some highland-reel tune which the fiddler played with great vigour, whilst my partner with grave face kept jumping up and down, both feet off the ground at once, as only an Indian can dance. I believe, however, that we elicited a great deal of applause from Indian squaws and children, who sat squatting round the room on the floor. Another lady with whom I sported the light fantastic toe, whose poetic name was Cun-ne-wa-bum, or "One that looks at the Stars," was a half-breed Cree girl; and I was so much struck by her beauty, that I prevailed upon her to promise to sit for her likeness, which she afterwards did with great patience, holding her fan, which was made of the tip end of swan's wing with an ornamental handle of porcupine's quills, in a most coquettish manner.

After enjoying ourselves with such boisterous vigour for several hours, we all gladly retired to rest about twelve o'clock, the guests separating in great good humour, not only with themselves but with their entertainers.

J. Ewing Ritchie

Mr. Ritchie, a well-known London journalist and social reformer, was one of many British journalists who came to Canada to write about it for prospective immigrants. (He would later write books on Australia and South Africa.) He was, however, a much better writer than most and had a keener sense of what was distinctive about the West. His book To Canada With the Emigrants: A Record of Actual Experiences *(London: Fisher Unwin, 1885) is one of the most engaging of its kind, offering amusing and revealing descriptive accounts of many aspects of western Canadian society.*

Amongst the Cow-Boys

I am writing from Calgary, a little but growing collection of huts and wooden houses planted on a lovely plain with hills all around, a river at my feet, on the banks of which some poplars flourish, and I can almost fancy I am in Derbyshire itself. It is a gay place, this rising town, at the foot, as it were, of the Rockies, and just now is unusually gay, as the Queen's birthday is being celebrated with athletic sports and a ball; and, besides, a new clergyman has made his appearance, the Rev. Parks Smith, from a Bermondsey parish, who is to preach in the new Assembly Hall, which is to be set apart as a church on Sundays. I am going to hear him, and already I feel somewhat of a Pharisee — I have on a clean collar, which I religiously preserved for the occasion, and have had my boots blackened. The sight is so novel that I have spent half an hour on the prairie contemplating the effect of that operation. Already I feel six inches higher.

I can't say that I think quite so much of Calgary as do the people who live in it. In splendour, in wealth, in dignity, and importance, they evidently anticipate it will be a second Babylon. Well, a good deal has to be done first. The situation is pleasant, I admit. You incline to think well of Calgary after the dreary ride across the prairie, and you have quite a choice of hotels, and of shops, all well stocked; but then these shops are little better than huts, and the hotels certainly don't throw the shops into the shade.

For instance, I am in the leading hotel. It is too far from the railway, but that is because the C.P.R. have moved their station a little further on, where the new town of Calgary is springing up. We have an open room, where I am writing — a dark dining-room on one side, and then, on the other, a little row of closets, which they dignify by the name of bedrooms. I am the proud possessor of one. It holds a bed, whereon, I own, I slept soundly; a row of pegs, on which to hang one's clothes; and a little shelf, on which is placed a tiny wash-hand basin; while above that is a glass, in which it is impossible to get a good view of yourself — a matter of very small consequence, as the glass certainly reflects very poorly the looker's personal charms, whatever they may be. I ought to have said there is a window; and as my bedroom is on the ground floor (upper rooms are rare in these wooden houses in the North-West), I am much exercised in my mind as to whether that window may not be opened in the course of the night, and the roll of dollars I have hidden under my pillow carried off. Then, just as I am getting into bed, I discover somebody else's boots. That is awkward — very. It is with a sigh of relief I discover that they are not feminine. Suppose the owner of those boots comes into my bedroom and claims to be the rightful owner? Suppose he resorts to physical force? Suppose, in such a case, I got the worst of it?

Fortunately, before I can answer these questions satisfactorily to myself, I am asleep, and yet they are not so irrelevant as you fancy.

Last night, for instance, as I was sitting in the cool air, smoking one of the peculiarly bad cigars in which the brave men of Canada greatly rejoice, and for which they pay as heavily as if they were of the finest brands, a half-drunken man came up, abusing me in every possible way, threatening to smash every bone in my body, and altogether behaving himself in a way the reverse of polite. Perhaps you say, Why did you not knock him down? In novels heroes always do, and come clear off; but I am not writing fiction, and in real life I have always found discretion to be the better part of valour. The fact is, the fellow was a strapping Hercules, and I could see in a moment, if the appeal were to force, what the issue might be. Yet I had not done anything intentionally to offend him. He had come galloping up to the hotel, as they all do here — the horses are not trained to trot — and his horse had bucked him off. I believe I did say something to a friend of a mildly critical nature, but I question whether the rider heard it. The fact was, he was angry at having been thrown, and seeing that I was a stranger, he evidently thought he could pour the vials of his wrath on me. I must admit that in a little while he came up and apologized, and there was an end of the matter. But the worst part of it was that his friend remarked to me that this drunken insulting ruffian was one of the best fellows in the place. If so, Calgary has to be thankful for very small mercies indeed.

You ask, How could the fellow be drunk, seeing that there is a prohibitory liquor-law in existence? I have every reason to believe that Calgary is a very drunken place, nevertheless. I have already referred to one case of drunkenness. I may add that, in the afternoon of the same day, I had seen another in the shape of an old gentleman who was going to head a revolt which would cut off the North-West from the Dominion, and which would make her a Crown colony. He was very drunk as he stood on the bar opposite me declaiming all this bunkum. I remarked his state to the landlord, who seemed to feel how unfair it was that men could get drunk on the sly, and that a decent landlord, like himself, should be deprived of the privilege of selling them decent liquor. I own it is very hard on the publicans. At Moose Jaw one of them told me he would give five hundred pounds for a liquor license. "They call this a free country," said an indignant English settler to me, "and yet I can't get a drop of good liquor. Pretty freedom, ain't it?" Unfortunately, the Government, while it prohibits the sale of liquor, does not exterminate the desire for it — perhaps only increases it — as we always cry for what we can't get. Unfortunately, also, it is true that, as long as this demand exists, the supply will be found somehow.

In Montana there are a lot of blackguards and daredevils who will run the thing in some-how. Liquor is also brought in by the railway as coal-oil, oatmeal, flour, varnish, and then it is doctored up and sold at £1 the bottle to the thirsty souls. Now, what is the consequence? Why, that, as a local journal remarks, liquor is sold; the dealers are pests and outlaws; they sell their poison for ten times the price of what people who don't belong to the Blue Ribbon Army call good liquor, and then vanish with their ill-gotten money out of the country, excepting such as they may leave behind them in the shape of fines, when found out. I do think the hotelkeeper has much reason to complain of prohibition. It presses hardly on him, and does not put drunkenness down. I mentioned these facts to a Baptist minister from England, whom I met in Toronto. He would not believe them; I gave him cuttings from newspapers to support my view. His reply was that they were hoaxes. I have now been in Calgary a day, and already I find that these hoaxes, as my friend calls them, are veritable facts.

I believe that many of my travelling companions were a little fresh last night, from their soberness and dejection of manner this morning. They were away down town, and had not returned when I retired to rest; and this morning several of the householders complain of having had their doors knocked at at most unseasonable hours.

At meals I meet queer company. We have a Chinese cook. I have a faint idea that he has murderous designs on us all, his smile is so childlike and bland; yet I prefer his placid pleasant round face to those of his female helps, sour and ill-looking, who earn wages such as an English servant-girl never dreams of. His messes seem to be appreciated, and little is left after mealtime. It is enough for me to see the men eat. Every particle of food is conveyed into the mouth by means of the knife, which is also freely used if sugar or salt be required. Our dining-room is simply a shed, and a very dark one, having a canvas on one side and unpainted deal on the other. Few houses at Calgary are painted, though a painted house looks so much prettier than a deal one that I wonder painting is not more resorted to, especially when you remember how paint preserves the wood. Many of the houses here are brought all the way from Ontario, and, perhaps, this accounts for their smallness. They chiefly consist of two rooms, one a shop, the other a sitting and night-room; and the larger number have been erected within the last few months. What we call in England a gentleman's house, I should say does not exist in the whole district. A gentleman would find existence intolerable here, though the air is fine, and the extent of the prairie is unbounded. There are two newspapers in the town, and the professions are all well represented.

As to my companions, the less I say of them the better. They are young and vigorous, and use language not generally tolerated in polite society. Their talk is chiefly of horses and bets. They ride recklessly up and down the dusty path which forms the main street, and would not break their hearts if they knocked a fellow down; or they drive light waggons on four wheels, creating the most overwhelming clouds of dust as they rush by. As to their saddles, they are as unlike English ones as can well be imagined, rising at each end, so as to give the rider a very safe seat, while their stirrups are as long almost as the foot itself; but the saddles have this advantage, that they never give the horses sore backs. As to the horses, they are all branded, and turned loose on to the prairie when not required. Most of the men are prospectors — people who go round the country in search of mines; or cow-boys — that is, men employed in the cattle ranches in the district. The cow-boy is a fearful sight. His hands and face are as brown as leather, he wears a straw hat — or one of felt — with a very wide brim. His coat or jacket is, perhaps, decorated with Indian work. Around his waist he wears a belt, which he makes useful in many ways. Then he has brown leather leggings, ornamented down the sides with leather fringes, and on his heels he puts a tremendous pair of spurs. The men on the mountains have much the same style of dress, and are fine specimens of muscular, rather than intellectual or moral, development. On the whole, I am not unduly enamoured of these pioneers of civilization; but, then, I was born in the old country, and learned Dr. Watts's hymns, and was taught to

> Thank the goodness and the grace
> That on my birth has smiled,
> And made me in these Christian days
> A happy English child.

I see a good deal more of Calgary than I wish to. I feel that I have been made a fool of by the station-master. I am, as you may be aware, at the foot of the Rocky Mounrains. They are some 60 miles off, yet; already I have seen their far-off peaks, glistening with snow, rising into the summer sky. As I have got so far, I must see them. There are trees up there, and the sight of a tree would be good for sore eyes; there are cooling shades out there, and here, though it is but early morning, it is too hot to stir. The scenery out there is the finest to be seen in all the Canadian continent, and I would carry away with me, to think of in after years, something of their beauty. I travelled all this way for that purpose, and hoped to have been off before, and now find I must wait, owing to a blunder on the part of the station-master. He promised he would let me know if he sent a freight train to the Rocky Mountains. Well, he sent off a train at one o'clock this morning, and never let me know anything about it, and the consequence is I must stay two more days in this dreary spot, without conveniences such as I could find in the meanest cottage in England, and at a cost which would enable me to live in luxury and fare sumptuously at home. One lesson I have learned, which I repeat for the benefit of my readers. Never depend upon other people; hear all they say, and then act for yourself. Had I done so, I should have been now in the Rocky Mountains. I trusted in others, and I am, in consequence, the victim of misplaced confidence.

I gather a few items of interest to intending emigrants. Crops raised in the vicinity of Calgary during 1883 gave the following yields per acre — Wheat, 33 bushels; barley, 40 bushels; oats, 60 bushels. The Government farm a few miles off, which I have visited, does well. The country round offers especial advantages to sheep and dairy farmers, cheese manufacturers, and hog raisers. My own impression is, and I have mentioned it to several persons who all think it excellent, that any man would easily make his fortune who set up a poultry farm. Eggs and fowls are almost entirely unknown, and if the producer did not find a market here, he could easily send his produce by the railway to where it was wanted. Eggs and fowls help one as well as anything to keep body and soul together.

I am glad I went to church yesterday. My presence there gave quite a tone to the place (said the head man to me this morning), and so far I may presume I did good service. The congregation consisted chiefly of men, and the collection amounted to nearly 16 dollars — pretty good, considering (said the above mentioned gentleman) there are two or three schism shops in the place. In the evening I went to the Wesleyan Methodist schism shop, as he called it, and heard a sermon, which touched me more than any sermon I have heard in a long time. As I came out the effect was startling. The sun was sinking in crimson glory just behind the green hills by which Calgary is surrounded. Far off a dim splendour of pink testified to the existence of a prairie fire, while before me stood a gigantic Indian, with his big black head rising out of a pyramid of gorgeous robes, really dazzling to behold. There is an Indian Mission near here, but the Indians are not the only heathens out here.

I have just had a ride in a buck-cart, which is the kind of vehicle the colonists use. It is of boards on four wheels, on which is placed a seat for a couple of persons, while the luggage is piled up behind. Some of them have springs, as fortunately was the case with the one on which I rode, or I should have had a very uncomfortable ride indeed. Perhaps I ought not to be so angry with the station-master as I was when I interviewed him this morning. I have just seen a man who got on to the freight train, but he tells me it was so uncomfortable that he preferred to wait, and got off after he had taken his passage.

Money seems scarce. I have just been to the post-office to send a letter to England. The postmaster could give me no change, and I had to take post-cards instead. I suppose all the money goes to the smugglers. In this small town 500 dollars are sent weekly to Winnipeg for liquor; so much for prohibition in Calgary.

As there is no bank here, people find it hard to get money. A young man waiting here to make up a mining party for the Rockies, tells me he had to telegraph to Toronto for 500 dollars, which were sent in the shape of a post-office order. The post-master charged him five dollars for cashing the order. I have just heard of a loan of 300 dollars effected; the borrower has agreed to pay, in the shape of interest, the moderate sum of four dollars a month.

Calgary, according to some, can have no enduring prosperity; if so, the land-grabbers who have scattered themselves all over it will be deeply disappointed.

Edmonton, where they get gold out of the river sand, and where they have already a kind of dredging machine employed for that purpose, it is said, will shortly have a railway to itself, and the men from the mountains, who are the mainstay of Calgary, will go that way.

I fancy I hear some one exclaim: On those wide plains over which sweeps the ice-laden air of the Rockies, what pleasant walks you must have! My dear sir, you are quite mistaken. Perhaps, as you set out, there comes a herd of wild horses — and then I remember how poor George Moore was knocked down by one, and avoid the boundless prairie accordingly.

Then there are the dogs, "their name is Legion," and they are big, and as wild as they are big, and I am not partial to hydrophobia. No; it is better to sit at the door of my tent and watch the flight of the horses, the fights of the dogs, and the stream of dust a mile long which denotes that some Jehu is at hand, who will pull up at the door, deeply drink water, smoke a cigar, use a little strong language, and then mount again and ride off into boundless space. Here and there a pedestrian may be seen making his way to his solitary hut or shop, where at no time do you see any sign of life; and how the people here make a living (with the exception of the hotel-keepers, who are always busy) puzzles me. I meet good fellows, I own. They are friendly in their way. As humour is a thing unknown in Canada and the North-West, they generally grin when I make a remark, which I do at very protracted intervals, fearing to be worn out before the long day is done. Nevertheless, I begin to doubt whether I am not relapsing into the wild life of those around me. Fortunately, I have not yet acquired the habit of speaking through my nose, nor do I make that fearful sound — a hawking in the throat — which is a signal that your neighbour is preparing to expectorate, and which renders travelling, even in a first-class car, almost insupportable; but my hands are tanned. I sit with my waistcoat open, and occasionally in my shirt-sleeves. I care little to make any effort to be polite; I am clean forgetting all my manners, and feel that in a little while I shall be as rough as a cow-boy, or as the wild wolf of the prairie. It is clear I must not tarry at Calgary too long.

Dillon Wallace

Towards the end of the nineteenth century and in the early decades of the twentieth, explorers turned their attention to the last great unexplored wilderness of the world — that of Labrador. And in doing so they captured the imagination of the world. Perhaps the most captivating — and most controversial — of these was the Leonidas Hubbard/Dillon Wallace/Mina Hubbard expeditions. In 1903 Hubbard, a New York writer, and his friend Dillon Wallace, undertook to traverse the interior of Labrador but, being ill-prepared, they lost their way, and Hubbard died of starvation. The following selection from Wallace's The Lure of the Labrador Wild *(1905) describes their return trip, after they had given up hope of achieving their goal, and shortly before Hubbard died.*

A footnote: somewhat suspicious of Wallace's account, Mina Hubbard decided, in 1905, to follow her husband's footsteps and become the first person to cross Labrador. She did so. Almost at the same moment Wallace also decided to do the same thing. Theirs was a race for fame, one that also, in the books that followed, captivated a whole nation of avid readers.

Hubbard's Last Camp in Labrador

We began our march back to the Susan Valley with a definite plan. Some twenty-five miles below, on the Susan River, we had abandoned about four pounds of wet flour; twelve or fifteen miles below the flour there was a pound of powdered milk, and four or five miles still further down the trail a pail with perhaps four pounds of lard. Hubbard considered the distances and mapped out each day's march as he hoped to accomplish it. We had in our possession, besides the caribou bones and hide, one and one-sixth pounds of pea meal. Could we reach the flour? If so, that perhaps would take us on to the milk powder, and that to the lard; and then we should be within easy distance of Grand Lake and Blake's winter hunting cache.

Hubbard was hopeful; George and I were fearful. Hubbard's belief that we should be able to reach the flour was largely based on his expectation that we should get fish in the outlet to Lake Elson. His idea was that the water of the lake would be much warmer than that of the river. He had, poor chap, the fatal faculty, common to persons of the optimistic temperament, of making himself believe what he wanted to believe. Neither George nor I remarked on the possibilities or probabilities of our getting fish in Lake Elson's outlet, and just before we said good-bye to the canoe Hubbard turned to me and said:

"Wallace, don't you think we'll get them there? Aren't you hopeful we shall?"

"Yes, I hope," I answered. "But I fear. The fish, you know, b'y, haven't been rising at all for several days, and perhaps it's better not to let our hopes run too high; for then, if they fail us, the disappointment won't be so hard to bear."

"Yes, that's so," he replied; "but it makes me feel good to look forward to good fishing there. We *will* get fish there. We *will!* Just say we will, b'y; for that makes me feel happy."

"We *will* — we'll say we will," I repeated to comfort him.

Under ordinary conditions we should have found our packs, in their depleted state, very easy to carry; but, as it was, they weighed us down grievously as we trudged laboriously up the hill from the river and over the ridge to the marsh on the farther side of which lay Lake Elson. On the top of the ridge and on the slope where it descended to the marsh we found a few mossberries, which we ate while we rested. Crossing the marsh, we stepped from bog to bog when we could, but a large part of the time were knee-deep in the icy water and mud. Our feet at this time were wrapped in pieces of camp blanket, tied to what remained of the moccasin uppers with pieces of our old trolling line. George and I were all but spent when we reached our old camping ground on the outlet to Lake Elson, and what it cost Hubbard to get across that marsh I can only imagine.

As soon as we arrived Hubbard tried the fish. It did not take him long to become convinced that there was no hope of inducing any to rise. It was a severe blow to him, but he rallied his courage and soon apparently was as full of confidence as ever that we should be able to reach the flour. While Hubbard was trying the fish, George looked the old camp over carefully for refuse, and found two goose heads, some goose bones, and the lard pail we had emptied there.

"I'll heat the pail," he said, "and maybe there'll be a little grease sticking to it that we can stir in our broth." Then, after looking at us for a moment, he put his hand into the pail and added: "I've got a little surprise here. I thought I'd keep it until the bones were boiled, but I guess you might as well have it now."

From out of the pail he brought three little pieces of bacon — just a mouthful for each. I cannot remember what we said, but as I write I can almost feel again the thrill of joy that came to me upon beholding those little pieces of bacon. They seemed like a bit of food from home, and they were to us as the rarest dainty.

George reboiled the bones with a piece of the hide and the remainder of the deer's stomach, and with this and the goose bones and head we finished our supper. We were fairly comfortable when we went to rest. The hunger pangs were passing now. I have said that at this time I was in an abnormal state of mind. I suppose that was true of us all. The love of life had ceased to be strong upon us. For myself I know that I was conscious only of a feeling that I must do all I could to preserve my life and to help the others. Probably it was the beginning of the feeling of indifference, or reconciliation with the inevitable, that mercifully comes at the approach of death.

In the morning (Thursday, October 15) we again went over our belongings, and decided to abandon numerous articles we had hitherto hoped to carry through with us — my rifle and cartridges, some pistol ammunition, the sextant, the tarpaulin, fifteen rolls of photograph films, my fishing rod, maps, and notebook, and various other odds and ends, including the cleaning rod Hubbard's father had made for him.

"I wonder where father and mother are now," said Hubbard, as he took a last look at the cleaning rod. For a few moments he clung to it lovingly; then he handed it to me with the words, "Put it with your rifle and fishing rod, b'y." And as I removed the cartridge from the magazine, and held the rifle up for a last look before wrapping it in the tarpaulin, he said: "It almost makes me cry to see you leave the fishing rod. If it is at all possible, we must see that the things are recovered. If they are, I want you to promise me that when you die you'll will the rod to me. It has got us more grub than anything else in the outfit, and it's carried us over some bad times. I'd like to have it, and I'd keep it and cherish it always."

I promised him that he certainly should have it. Well, the rod *was* recovered. And now when I look at the old weather-beaten piece of wood as it reposes comfortably in my den at home, I recall this incident, and my imagination carries me back to those last fishing days when Hubbard used it; and I can see again his gaunt form arrayed in rags as he anxiously whipped the waters on our terrible struggle homeward. It is the only thing I have with which he was closely associated during those awful days, and it is my most precious possession.

As we were chewing on a piece of hide and drinking the water from the reboiled bones at breakfast, Hubbard told us he had had a realistic dream of rejoining his wife. The boy was again piteously homesick, and when we shouldered with difficulty our lightened packs and began the weary struggle on, my heart was heavy with a great dread. Dark clouds hung low in the sky, but the day was mild. Once or twice while skirting Lake Elson we halted to pick the few scattering mossberries that were to be found, once we halted to make tea to stimulate us, and at our old camp on Mountaineer Lake we again boiled the bones and used the water to wash down another piece of the caribou hide.

In the afternoon George took the lead, I followed, and Hubbard brought up the rear. Suddenly George stopped, dropped his pack, and drew Hubbard's pistol, which he carried because he was heading the procession. Hubbard and I also halted and dropped our packs. Into the brush George disappeared, and we heard, at short intervals, the pistol crack three times. Then George reappeared with three spruce grouse. How our hearts bounded! How we took George's hand and pressed it, while his face lighted up with the old familiar grin! We fingered the birds to make sure they were good and fat. We turned them over and over and gloated over them. George plucked them at once that we might see their plump bodies. It is true we were not so very hungry, but those birds meant that we could travel just so much the farther.

We pushed on that we might make our night camp at the place where we had held the goose banquet on the third of August — that glorious night when we were so eager to proceed, when the northern lights illuminated the heavens and the lichens gleamed on the barren hill. Hubbard, I noticed, was lagging, and I told George quietly to set a slower pace. Then, to give Hubbard encouragement, I fell to the rear. The boy was staggering fearfully, and I watched him with increasing consternation. "We must get him out of here! We must! We *must!*" I kept saying to myself. The camping place was only two hundred yards away when he sank on the trail. I was at his side in a moment. He looked up at me with a pitiful smile, and spoke so low I could scarcely hear him.

"B'y, I've got to rest here — a little — just a little while... you understand.... My legs — have given out."

"That's right, b'y, take a little rest," I said. "You'll be alright soon. But rest a little. I'll rest a bit with you; and then we'll leave your pack here, and you walk to camp light, and I'll come back for your pack."

In a few minutes he got bravely up. We left his pack and together walked slowly on to join George at the old goose camp on Goose Creek. Then I returned for the pack that had been left behind.

George boiled one of the grouse for supper. Hubbard told us he was not discouraged. His weakness, he said, was only momentary, and he was sure he would be quite himself in the morning, ready to continue the march homeward. After supper, as he was lying before the fire, he asked me, if I was not too tired, to read him the latter part of the sixth chapter of Matthew. I took the Book and read as he requested, closing with the words:

"Wherefore, if God so clothe the grass of the field, which today is, and tomorrow is cast into the oven, shall he not much more clothe you, O ye of little faith? Therefore take no thought, saying, What shall we eat? or, What shall we drink? or, Wherewithal shall we be clothed? (For all these things do the Gentiles seek:) for your heavenly Father knoweth that ye have need of all these things. But seek ye first the Kingdom of God and His righteousness; and all these things shall be added unto you. Take therefore no thought for the morrow; for the morrow shall take thought for the things of itself. Sufficient unto the day is the evil thereof."

"How beautiful, how encouraging that is!" said Hubbard, as I put away the Book. He crawled into the tent to go to sleep. Then: "I'm so happy, b'y, so very, very happy tonight ... for we're going home ... we're going home." And he slept.

Before I lay down I wrote in my diary:

"Hubbard is in very bad shape — completely worn out physically and mentally — but withal a great hero, never complaining and always trying to cheer us up."

George said he was sick when he went to rest, and that added to my concern.

Friday morning (October 16) came clear, mild, and beautiful. I was up at break of day to start the fire, and soon was followed by George and a little later by Hubbard. We all said we were feeling better. George shot a foolhardy whiskey jack that ventured too near the camp, and it went into the pot with a grouse for breakfast. The meal eaten, we all felt very much stronger, but decided that more outfit must be abandoned. I gave George my extra undershirt and a blue flannel shirt, both of which he donned. Every scrap we thought at the time we could do without, including many photograph films and George's blanket, was cached.

After Hubbard read aloud John 15, we resumed the struggle. Naturally George and I relieved Hubbard of everything he would permit us to. The fact was, we could not have taken much more and moved. When Hubbard broke down on the trail, it was strictly necessary for me to make two trips with the packs; although his weighed something less than ten pounds, I could not have carried it in addition to my own if my life had depended upon it.

Just below the place where Hubbard caught so many fish that day in August that we killed the geese, we stopped for a moment to rest. Hardly had we halted when George grabbed Hubbard's rifle, exclaiming "Deer!" About four hundred yards below us, a magnificent caribou, his head held high, dashed across the stream and into the bush. He was on our lee and had winded us. No shot was fired. One fleeting glance, and he was gone. Our feelings can be imagined. His capture would have secured our safety.

We struggled on. At midday we ate our last grouse. At this stopping place George abandoned his waterproof camp bag and his personal effects that he might be able to carry Hubbard's rifle. This relieved Hubbard of seven pounds, but he again failed before we reached our night camp. It was like the previous evening. With jaws set he tottered grimly on until his legs refused to carry him farther, and he sank to the ground. Again I helped him into camp, and returned for his pack.

We pitched the tent facing a big rock so that the heat from the fire, blazing between, might be reflected into the tent, the front of which was thrown wide open. Of course George and I did all the camp work. Fortunately there was not much to do; our camps being pitched on the sites of previous ones, we had stakes ready to hand for the tent, and in this part of the country we were able to find branches and logs that we could burn without cutting. We still had one axe with us, but neither George nor I had the strength to swing it.

The night was cold and damp. For supper we had another piece of the caribou hide, and water from the much-boiled bones with what I believe was the last of the pea meal — about two spoonfuls that Hubbard shook into the pot from the package, which he then threw away. As we reclined in the open front of the tent before the fire, I again read from the Bible, and again a feeling of religious exaltation came to Hubbard. "I'm so happy, and oh! so sleepy," he murmured, and was quiet. He did not make his usual entry in his diary. In my own diary for this date I find:

"Hubbard's condition is pitiable, but he bears himself like the hero that he is — trying always to cheer and encourage us. He is visibly failing. His voice is very weak and low. I fear he will break down at every step. O God, what can we do! How can we save him!"

On Saturday (October 17) threatening clouds overcast the sky, and a raw wind was blowing. It penetrated our rags and set us a-shiver. At dawn we had more water from the bones and more of the hide. Cold and utterly miserable, we forced our way along. Our progress was becoming slower and slower. But every step was taking us nearer home, we said, and with that thought we encouraged ourselves. At noon we came upon our first camp above the Susan River. There George picked up one of our old flour bags. A few lumps of moldy flour were clinging to it, and he scraped them carefully into the pot to give a little substance to the bone water. We also found a box with a bit of baking powder still in it. The powder was streaked with rust from the tin, but we ate it all.

Then Hubbard made a find — a box nearly half full of pasty mustard. After we had each eaten a mouthful, George put the remainder in the pot. He was about to throw the box away when Hubbard asked that it be returned to him. Hubbard took the box and sat holding it in his hand.

"That box came from Congers," he said, as if in a reverie. "It came from my home in Congers. Mina has had this very box in her hands. It came from the little grocery store where I've been so often. Mina handed it to me before I left home. She said the mustard might be useful for plasters. We've eaten it instead. I wonder where my girl is now. I wonder when I'll see her again. Yes, she had that very box in her hands — in *her* hands! She's been such a good wife to me."

Slowly he bent his head, and the tears trickled down his cheeks.

George and I turned away.

It was near night when we reached the point near the junction of the Susan River and Goose Creek where we were to cross the river to what had been our last camping ground in the awful valley, and which was to prove our last camp in Labrador. Hubbard staggered along during the afternoon with the greatest difficulty, and finally again sank to the ground, completely exhausted. George took his pack across the river. While he crouched there on the trail, Hubbard's face bore an expression of absolute despair. At length I helped him to his feet, and in silence we forded the shallow stream.

Our camp was made a short distance below the junction of the streams, among the fir trees a little way from the river bank. Here and there through the forest were numerous large rocks. Before one of these we pitched the tent, with the front of it open to receive the heat from the fire as it was reflected from the rock. More bone water and hide served us for supper, with the addition of a yeast cake from a package George had carried throughout the trip and never used. Huddling in front of the tent, we counselled.

"Well, boys," said Hubbard, "I'm busted. I can't go any farther — that's plain. I can't go any farther. We've got to do something."

In the silence the crackling of the logs became pronounced.

"George," Hubbard continued, "maybe you had better try to reach Blake's camp, and send in help if you're strong enough to get there. If you find a cache, and don't find Blake, try to get back with some of the grub. There's that old bag with a little flour in it — you might find that. And then the milk powder and the lard farther down. Maybe Wallace could go with you as far as the flour and bring back a little of it here. What do you say, b'y?"

"I say it's well," I answered. "We've got to do something, at once."

"It's the only thing to do," said George. "I'm willin', and I'll do the best I can to find Blake and get help."

"Then," said Hubbard, "you'd better start in the morning, boys. If you don't find the bag, you'd better go on with George, Wallace; for then there would no use of your trying to get back here. Yes, boys, you'd better start in the morning. I'll be quite comfortable here alone until help comes."

"I'll come back, flour or no flour," I said, dreading the thought of his staying there alone in the wilderness.

We planned it all before Hubbard went to sleep. George and I, when we started in the morning, were ready to carry as little as possible. I thought I should be able to reach the flour bag and be back within three days. We were to prepare for Hubbard a supply of wood, and leave him everything on hand that might be called food — the bones and the remainder of the hide, a sack with some lumps of flour sticking to it, and the rest of the yeast cakes. George and I were to depend solely on the chance of finding game.

"I'm much relieved now," said Hubbard, when it had all been settled. "I feel happy and contented. I feel that our troubles are about ended. I am very, very happy and contented."

He lay down in his blanket. After a little he said:

"B'y, I'm rather chilly; won't you make the fire a little bigger."

I threw on more wood, and when I sat down I told him I should keep the fire going all night; for the air was damp and chill.

"Oh, thank you, b'y," he murmured, "thank you. You're so good." After another silence, the words came faintly. "B'y, won't you read to me those two chapters we've had before? — the fourteenth of John and the thirteenth of First Corinthians ... I'd like to hear them again, b'y ... I'm very ... sleepy ... but I want to hear you read before ... I go... to sleep."

Leaning over so that the light of the fire might shine on the Book, I turned to the fourteenth of John and began: "'Let not your heart be troubled.'" I paused to glance at Hubbard. He was asleep. Like a weary child, he had fallen asleep with the first words. The dancing flames lit up his poor, haggard, brown face; but upon it now there was no look of suffering; it was radiant with peace.

George lay on his side, also asleep. Thus I began a night of weary vigil and foreboding. My heart was heavy with a presentiment of something dreadful. In the forest beyond the fire the darkness was intense. There was a restless stir among the fir tops; then a weary, weary sighing. The wind had arisen. I dozed. But what was that! I sat suddenly erect.

On the canvas above me sounded a patter, patter, patter. Rain!

Gradually the real and seeming became blended. Beyond the fire-glow, on the edge of the black pall of night, horrid shapes began to gather. They leered at me, and mocked me, and oh! they were telling me something dreadful was going to happen. A sudden jerk, and I sat up and stared wildly about me. Nothing but the sighing tree-tops, and the patter, patter, patter of the rain. The fire had died down. I struggled to my feet, and threw on more wood.

Again the horrid shapes leered at me from out the gloom. Then I heard myself exclaiming, "No, no, no!" The nameless dread was strong upon me. I listened for Hubbard's breathing. *Had it ceased?* I crawled over and peered long and anxiously at his face — his face which was so spectral and wan in the uncertain firelight. Twice I did this. A confused sense of things evil and malicious, a confused sense of sighing wind and pattering rain, a confused sense of starts and jerks and struggles with wood, and the night wore on.

The black slowly faded into drab. The trees, dripping with moisture, gradually took shape. The day of our parting had come.

Agnes Deans Cameron

Born in Victoria, British Columbia, in 1863, Agnes Deans Cameron became a school teacher (one of the few professions then open to women) and was successful — for a while. In 1906 she came up against the silly bureaucracy of the school board, and was forced to resign. She then moved to Chicago, where her considerable writing talent resulted in a job as journalist and editor. This led to many interesting (and daring) assignments which resulted in many articles. In 1908, with her niece Jessie Cameron Brown, Agnes undertook a trip through the Arctic. This was recounted in her only published book, The New North: A Woman's Journey Through Canada to the Arctic *(New York: Appleton, 1909) which became a minor classic. Cameron died prematurely of appendicitis in 1912.*

Down the Athabasca River

If you have to do with Indian or half-breed boatmen in the North you plan to begin your journey in the evening, even though you hope to run only a few miles before nightfall. This ensures a good start next morning, whereas it would be humanly impossible to tear men away from the flesh-pots (beer pots) of Athabasca Landing early in any day. It took these chaps all the afternoon to say good-bye, for each one in the village had to be shaken hands with, every dog apostrophized by name.

The Athabasca Transport of which we form joyous part makes a formidable flotilla: seven specially-built scows or "sturgeon-heads." Each runs forty to fifty feet with a twelve-foot beam and carries ten tons. The oars are twenty feet long. It takes a strong man to handle the forty-foot steering-sweep which is mounted with an iron pivot on the stem.

Our particular shallop is no different from the others, except that there is a slightly raised platform in the stern-sheets, evidently a dedication to the new Northern Manager of the H. B. Co. We share the pleasant company of a fourth passenger, Mrs. Harding, on her way home to Fort Resolution on Great Slave Lake. The second sturgeon-head carries seven members of the Royal Northwest Mounted Police, jolly laughing chaps, for are not they, too, like us, off duty?

Inspector Pelletier and three men are to go with our Fur Transport as far as Resolution and then diverge to the east, essaying a cross-continent cut from there to salt water on Hudson Bay. For this purpose they ship two splendidly made Peterborough canoes. The other three members of the force are young chaps assigned to Smith's Landing on the Slave River, sent there to protect the wood bison of that region, the world's last wild buffalo. The third craft we observe with due respect as "the cook boat." The remaining four scows carry cargo only, — the trade term being "pieces," each piece from eighty to a hundred pounds, a convenient weight for carrying on the portages.

June 6th at a quarter of seven saw the whole populace of Athabasca Landing on the river bank — dogs, babies, the officials of the Hudson's Bay, parson, priest, police, and even the barkeep, — and with the yelping of dogs and "Farewell, Nistow!" we are off. We are embarked on a 2500-mile journey, the longest water route on the continent, down which floats each year the food, clothing, and frugal supplies of a country as big as Europe.

The river is running five miles an hour and there is no need of the oars. The steersman is our admiration, as with that clumsy stern-sweep he dodges rocks, runs rifles, and makes bends. The scow is made of green wood, and its resilience stands it in good stead as, like a snake, it writhes through tight channels or over ugly bits of water. Everybody is in good humour; we are dreamers dreaming greatly. Why should we not be happy? Mrs. Harding is homeward-bound, Mr. Brabant on a new rung of the fur ladder of preferment, Inspector Pelletier and his associates starting on a quest of their own seeking. Sitting low among the "pieces" of the police boat, with only his head visible in the sunset glow, Dr. Sussex builds air-castles of that eleemosynary hospital of his on the Arctic Circle. The cook is whistling from the cook-boat. Five years ago he graduated from a business college, but the preparation of bannock and sow-belly appeals to the blood more insistently than trial balances and the petty cash book. As for ourselves, the Kid's smile is almost audible as she runs a loving hand over the oilskin cover of the camera. A favourite expression of mine in the latitudes below when the world smiled was, "Oh, I'm glad I'm alive and white." On this exclamation I start now, but stop at the word "white." North of Athabasca Landing white gives place to a tint more tawny.

A hundred yards out, the Policemen are boyish enough to launch those shiny Peterboroughs just to try them, and in and out among the big sturgeon-head, debonair dolphins, they dart. Then comes the rain, and one by one the clumsy boats turn toward shore. There are some things that even the enquiring mind cannot run to ground, things that just happen out of the blue. For fifteen successive springs I have tried to discover the first boy who brought marbles to school when marble-season came in, and I have never yet been able to put my finger on that elusive history-maker. So on this voyage, the fleet is started and stopped, landings are made, camping-places decided upon, and no ear can detect the sound of command.

The scows tie up, and without undressing we sleep on board, pulling a tarpaulin over us and letting the rain rain. At 5:30 next morning we hear the familiar "Nistow! Nistow!" of the awakened camp. This word literally means "brother-in-law," but it is the vocative used by the Cree in speaking to anybody he feels kindly toward. The cook makes a double entry with bacon and bannock, and there is exulting joy in our soul. Who would napkins bear, or finger-bowls? We had put them far behind, with the fardels.

It is the season of lengthening days and fading nights. At seven o'clock we are in the river again, and for three glorious hours we float, first one scow in front, then the other, social amenities in Cree being shouted from boat to boat. Then, in one voice from three boats, "Mooswa!" and far beyond white man's vision the boatmen sight a moose. There is a little red tape about the ethics of taking off those precious Peterboroughs which were to make history on the map, and in the delay the moose wandered into pleasant pastures. The boatmen were very much disgruntled, as the moose is treasure-trove, the chief fresh meat that his world offers the Indian. From here to the Arctic are no domestic animals, the taste of beef or mutton or pork or chicken is unknown, bread gives place to bannock (with its consequent indigestion "bannockburn"), and coffee is a beverage discredited. Tobacco to smoke, strong, black, sweetened tea to drink from a copper kettle, — this is luxury's lap....

It is Sunday, and we have music from a li'l fiddle made by a squaw at Lac Ste. Anne. Lac la Biche River we pass, and Calling River, and at five in the evening are at Swift Current, Peachy Pruden's place, and then Red Mud. Sunday night is clear and beautiful, and we float all night. Making a pillow of a squat packing-case consigned to the missionary at Hay River, and idly wondering what it might contain,

I draw up a canvas sheet. But it is too wonderful a night to sleep. Lying flat upon our backs and looking upward, we gaze at the low heaven full of stars, big, lustrous, hanging down so low that we can almost reach up and pluck them. Two feet away, holding in both hands the stern sweep, is the form of the Cree steersman, his thoughtful face a cameo against the shadow of the cut-banks. At his feet another half-breed is wrapped in his blanket, and from here to the bow the boat is strewn with these human cocoons. The reclining friend breaks the silence with a word or two of Cree in an undertone to the steersman, a screech-owl cries, from high overhead drops down that sound which never fails to stir vagrant blood — the "unseen flight of strong hosts prophesying as they go." It is the wild geese feeling the old spring fret even as we feel it. In imagination I pierce the distance and see the red panting throat of that longnecked voyageur as he turns to shout back raucous encouragement to his long, sky-clinging V.

Floating as we float, it is no longer a marvel to us that this North holds so many scientific men and finished scholars — colonial Esaus serving as cooks, dog-drivers, packers, trackers, oil-borers. The not knowing what is round the next corner, the old heart-hunger for new places and untrod ways, — who would exchange all this for the easy ways of fatted civilization!

At five in the morning there is a drawing-in of the fleet to Pelican Portage. Before two hours have passed the grasshopper has become a burden, and it is 102° in the shade, and no shade to be had. We are now a hundred miles from Athabasca Landing. On the left bank we come across a magnificent gas-well with a gush of flame twenty or thirty feet in height.

It seems that eleven years ago, seeking for petroleum, the Dominion Government had a shaft sunk here; their boring apparatus was heavy, the plunger with its attachment weighing nearly a ton. At eight hundred feet the operator broke into an ocean of gas, and the pressure blew him with plunger and appliances into the air as a ball comes from a cannon-bore. The flow of gas was so heavy that it clogged his drills with maltha and sand, and from then to now the gas has been escaping. Today the sound of the escape ricochets up and down the palisaded channel so that we cannot hear each other speak. There is gas enough here, if we could pipe it and bring it under control, to supply with free illumination every city of prairie Canada. It has destroyed all vegetation for a radius of twenty yards; but, oddly

enough, outside this range of demarcation the growth is more luxu-
riant and comes earlier and stays later than that of the surrounding
country. One red-headed Klondiker, ignorant of gas and its ways,
ten years ago struck a match to this escaping stream, was blown into
the bushes beyond, and came out minus hair, eye-brows and red
beard — the quickest and closest shave he ever had. The shells of
birds' eggs, tea-leaves from many a cheering copper-kettle, tufts of
rabbit-hair, and cracked shin-bones of the moose, with here a greasy
nine of diamonds, show this Stromboli of the Athabasca to be the
gathering-place of up and down-river wanderers. You can boil a
kettle or broil a moose-steak on this gas-jet in six minutes, and there
is no thought of accusing metre to mar your joy. The Doctor has
found a patient in a cabin on the high bank, and rejoices. The Indian
has consumption. The only things the Doctor could get at were rhu-
barb pills and cod-liver oil, but these, with faith, go a long way. They
may have eased the mind of poor Lo, around whose dying bunk we
hear the relatives scrapping over his residuary estate of rusty rifle,
much-mended fishing-net, and three gaunt dogs.

We pass House River, and the devout cross themselves and murmur a prayer. The point is marked by a group of graves covered with
canvas. Here years ago a family of four, travelling alone, contracted
diphtheria, and died before help could reach them. There is another
legend of which the boatmen unwillingly speak, the story of the
Wetigo, or Indian turned cannibal, who murdered a priest on this
lonely point, and ate the body of his victim. The taste for human
flesh, Philip Atkinson assures us, grows with the using, and this lunatic of long ago went back to the camps, secured an Indian girl as
bride, carried her to this point, took her life, and ate of her flesh. It is
a gruesome story.

Now begin the rapids, ninety miles of which we are to run. This
rough water on the Athabasca is one of the only two impediments to
navigation on the long course between Athabasca Landing and the
Polar Ocean. These first rapids, frankly, are a disappointment. The
water is high, higher than it has been for ten years, so the boiling over
the boulders is not very noticeable. The Pelican Rapid and the Stony
we shoot without turning a hair; the Joli Fou is a bit more insistent,
but, as the cook says, "nothing to write home about."

We drift in a drowsy dream of delight, and in the evening arrive at
the head of Grand Rapids. If we had looked slightingly on the rough
water passed, what we now see would satisfy the greediest. We tie up

and get a good view of what lies ahead, and get also our first real introduction to the mosquito. In mid-stream he had not bothered us much, but after supper it rained a little, the day had been warm, and with cymbals, banners, and brassbands, he comes in cohorts to greet us. The scows have their noses poked into the bank, the men have built smudge fires in front, but we decide that the best way to escape the mosquito is to go to bed. We lie down in the stern-sheets with our clothes on, make night-caps of our Stetson hats, pull the veils down over our necks, and try to sleep, but it is no avail. Each one of these mosquitoes is a Presbyterian mosquito and it has been ordained that this night he is to taste of white blood. It rains incessantly, and that hot hole in which we lie is one brown cloud of mosquitoes. The men on the bank have finally given it up as a bad job, and they set round the fires smoking and slapping different parts of their persons, swearing volubly in English. For the Cree language is devoid of invective. In the morning we are a sorry crowd, conversation is monosyllabic and very much to the point. It is the first serious trial to individual good-humour. When each one of your four million pores is an irritation-channel of mosquito-virus it would be a relief to growl at somebody about something. But the sun and smiles come out at the same time, and, having bled together, we cement bonds of friendship. What did Henry the Fifth say on the eve of Agincourt, "For he to-day who sheds his blood with me shall be my brother"?

Who would worry about mosquitoes with that splendid spectacular of the Grand Rapids at our feet? The great flood (Kitchee Abowstik) is divided into two channels by an island probably half a mile in length, with its long axis parallel to the flow of the river, and this island solves the question of progress. The main channel to the left is impassable; it is certain death that way. Between the island and the right shore is a passage which on its island side, with nice manipulation, is practicable for empty boats. Then the problem before us is to run the rough water at the near end of the island, tie up there, unload, transfer the pieces by hand-car over the island to its other end, let the empty scows down carefully through the channel by ropes, and reload at the other end.

Between the bank where we are and the island ahead is a stretch of roaring water dangerous enough looking. We have learned ere this, however, to sit tight and watch for events. The careless Indians have straightened into keen-eyed, responsible voyageurs, each muscle taut, every sense alert. Our boat goes first, one half-breed with huge pole braces himself as bowsman, the most able man takes the stern sweep, the others stand at the oars. Fifteen minutes of good head-work brings us to the island and we step out with relief. The other boats follow and anchor, and we have opportunity at close range to inspect these worst rapids of the Athabascan chain. The current on the west side of the dividing island looks innocent, and we understand how the greenhorn would choose this passage-way, to his destruction.

The transportation of pieces occupied four days, every moment of which we enjoyed. Grand Rapids Island is prodigal in wild flowers, — vetches, woodbine, purple and pink columbines, wild roses, several varieties of false Solomon's seal, our persisting friend dwarf cornel, and, treasure-trove, our first anemone, — that beautiful buttercup springing from its silvered sheath —

"And where a tear has dropt a wind-flower blows."

I measured a grass-stem and found it two feet three inches high, rising amid last year's prostrate growth.

At Grand Rapids Island we overtook two scows which had preceded us from The Landing and whose crews had waited here to assist in the transport. It gave us opportunity to observe these sixty representative half-breeds from Lac la Biche. Tall, strong, happy-go-lucky, with no sordid strain in their make-up, they are fellows that one cannot help feeling sympathy for. A natural link between the East and the West, the South of Canada and the North, they have bridged over the animosity and awkwardness with which the Red race elsewhere has approached the White.

In a glade our camp is made, inside our tents we arrange the mosquito-bar (a tent within a tent looking something like a good-sized dog-kennel), and here we lie in our blankets. The hum of the foiled mosquito is unction to our souls. It is, a relief, too, to remove the day's clothing, the first time in ninety-six hours....

When we pass the parallel of 55° N. we come into a very wealth of new words, a vocabulary that has found its way into no dictionary but which is accepted of all men. The steep bank opposite us is a "cut bank," an island or sandbar in a river is a "batture." A narrow channel is called a "she-ny," evidently a corruption of the French chenal. When it leads nowhere and you have to back down to get out, you have encountered a "blind she-ny." The land we have come from is known as "Outside" or "Le Grand Pays." Anywhere other than where we sit is "that side," evidently originating from the viewpoint of a man to whom all the world lay either on this side or that side of the river that stretched before him. When you obtain credit from a Hudson's Bay store, you "get debt." A Factor's unwillingness to advance you goods on credit would be expressed thus, "The Company will give me no debt this winter." From here northward the terms "dollars" and "cents" are unheard. An article is valued at "three skins" or "eight skins" or "five skins," harking back to the time when a beaver-skin was the unit of money. The rate of exchange today is from four skins to two skins for a dollar. Trapping animals is "making fur." "I made no fur last winter and The Company would give me no debt," is a painful picture of hard times. Whenever an Indian has a scanty larder, he is "starving," and you may be "starving" many moons without dying or thinking of dying. "Babiche" in the North is the tie that binds, and "sinew" is the thread, babiche being merely cured rawhide from moose or caribou, the sinew the longitudinal strands taken from either side of the spinal column of the same animals.

There is but one thing on this planet longer than the equator, and that is the arm of British justice, and the Mounted Police, these chaps sprawling at our feet, are the men who enforce it. The history of other lands shows a determined fight for the frontier, inch by inch advancement where an older civilization pushes back the native, — there are wars and feuds and bloody raids. Not so here. When the homesteader comes down the river we are threading and, in a flood, colonization follows him, he will find British law established and his home ready. The most compelling factor making for dignity and decency in this border-country is the little band of red-coated riders, scarcely a thousand in number. Spurring singly across the plains that we have traversed since leaving Winnipeg, they turn up on lone riverway or lakeside in the North just when most wanted.

Varied indeed is this man's duty, — "nursemaid to the Doukhobor" was a thrust literally true. His, too, was the task on the plains of seeing that the Mormon doesn't marry overmuch. He brands stray cattle, interrogates each new arrival in a prairie-waggon, dips every doubtful head of stock, prevents forest-fires, keeps weather records, escorts a lunatic to an asylum eight hundred miles away, herds wood bison on the Slave, makes a cross-continent dash from Great Slave Lake to Hudson Bay, preserves the balance of power between American whaler and Eskimo on the Arctic edge! At one time the roll-call of one troup of Mounted Police included in its rank and file three men who had held commissions in the British service, an ex-midshipman, a son of a Colonial Governor, a grandson of a Major General, a medical student from Dublin, two troopers of the Life Guards, an Oxford M. A., and half a dozen ubiquitous Scots. Recently an ex-despatch-bearer from De Wet joined the force at Regina, and although the cold shoulder was turned on him for a day or two, he soon made good. One of the young fellows stretched before us, now going to Fort Smith to round up wood bison, was born in Tasmania, ran away from school at fourteen, sheared sheep and hunted the wallaby, stoked a steamer from Australia to England and from England to Africa, and in the early days of bicycles was a professional racer.

Constable Walker, lying lazily on his back blowing blue spirals into the air, has in the long winter night made more than once, with dogs, that perilous journey from the Yukon to the Mackenzie mouth (one thousand miles over an unknown trail), carrying to the shut-in whalers their winter mail. On one of these overland journeys he cut off the tips of his four toes. His guide fainted, but Walker took babiche and, without a needle, sewed up the wound. On this trip he was fifty-seven days on the trail, during five days of which the thermometer hovered between sixty-two and sixty-eight degrees below.

Memoirs & Descriptive Sketches

Memoirs and Descriptive Sketches

Commentary

Memoirs and descriptive sketches — encompassing a wide variety of reflective writing in a variety of styles — are similar by virtue of the fact that each attempts to recount, describe or memorialize an aspect (or aspects) of lifestyle which the writer has experienced. The chief difference between the two is this: the writer of the memoir writes from within the experience while the author of a descriptive sketch is an observer of the experience. Memoirists, like Susanna Moodie or Agnes Macdonald, are not only active participants but most likely the subjects of the pieces; in other words, the memoir is autobiography. Readers of memoirs, therefore, will probably be as intrigued by the writer (the evidence of personality) as by the lifestyle being described. Writers of descriptive sketches, such as Harriet Jephson and Annie Fréchette, usually stand outside the events they describe: they are most likely visitors, more or less objectively observing a custom, event or experience, who try to vivify it for their readers.

Distinctions aside, memoirs and/or descriptive sketches (by either Canadians or non-Canadian visitors) constitute the bulk of Canada's published literature in the nineteenth and early twentieth centuries. In addition to hundreds of full-length works, similar to Catharine Parr Traill's *The Backwoods of Canada* (1836) and Susanna Moodie's *Roughing it in the Bush* (1852), there are thousands of shorter sketches scattered throughout several hundred Canadian, American, and British periodicals. American and British readers, in particular, were avid armchair visitors to Canada, relishing the lifestyles of Newfoundland fishermen, French Canadian *habitants*, prairie settlers, Ottawa River lumbermen, native Indians, and mounted policemen, among others, using as their vehicles of vicarious transportation such well-known magazines as *Harper's, Macmillan's, Scribner's, Pearson's, Outing,* and *Everybody's.*

And there were, as the preceding sentence indicates, several well-defined subjects which made such writing popular and which make it still worth reading. The hardships and challenges of early settlement in Upper Canada were predominant among them. In this section such sketches are represented by the autobiographical accounts of two sisters, Catharine Parr Traill and Susanna Moodie — whose settlement experiences, though different in sensibility, have become the best known of any — and by such little-known ones as that of Georgina Binnie-Clark. Contrasting with those is Francis Beaven's glimpse of daily routine in the household of an early settler in New Brunswick. More idyllic, less personal than either Moodie's or Traill's, it describes a community which, even in the 1840s, was well established in its social rituals.

While settlement literature very often depicts the challenges of everyday life, there was an abundance of literature which attempted to depict an elite social life (chiefly in Ottawa) — a lifestyle which fascinated readers throughout the nineteenth century (partly because it so often parodied English social life). Annie Howells Fréchette's sketch is typical of many such sketches, hers being a picture of life at Rideau Hall when the Marquis of Lorne and Princess Louise were resident there between 1878 and 1883. A little later, Lady Agnes Macdonald describes an official trip across Canada on which she rather daringly defies social propriety to ride on the cowcatcher of the locomotive. It is worth noting that the former, by an established writer, is by an outsider (though one who had privileged access); the latter, by an hitherto little-known writer (though equally accomplished), is from the pen of an "insider," the wife of one of our greatest prime ministers.

Two further preoccupations of early writers and readers are typified in sketches by John Donkin and Harriet Jephson. The former, a Northwest Mounted Policeman, offers a firsthand account of Louis Riel's final hours and his death by hanging. It is one of many such "historical moments" — among them glimpses of Wolfe's death, battles in the War of 1812, skirmishes during the 1837 rebellions, many moments during the Riel Rebellion, and so forth — which nineteenth-century readers found irresistible. The latter piece, by Jephson, is one of hundreds of similar descriptions of "quaint Quebec" which were favoured by magazine editors and which, in their stereotypical depiction of *habitant* lifestyle, say as much about their readers as they do about their subject.

This leaves but one memoir to account for — a rare one among the others. While many non-native writers comment freely on native life, only occasionally does one find a description of that lifestyle by a native. George Copway's description of Ojibway pastimes is just such a piece. Popular in its day, now little known, it provides an inside (though perhaps controversial) view of native customs. Chronologically, and properly, it takes precedence over all the other pieces in this section.

Again, there are cautions. Descriptive literature as a whole probably contains more stereotypes than any other kind. Since much of it was written primarily for a foreign audience, and often by newcomers or visitors, it tends to over-generalize and is often condescending (especially when describing natives and French Canadians). It also focuses narrowly on those aspects of Canadian life which non-Canadian readers found most intriguing (mainly because they were novel, quaint or unusual). Nevertheless, read wisely (with some understanding of the imperialist attitudes of the age), the best of it reveals a great deal about Canadian society. The selections offered here attest to that fact, taking us into different villages and social situations and illustrating how multi-faceted Canadian society was becoming as it expanded out of Ontario and into the far west.

Extra Reading

Carl Ballstadt, *Catharine Parr Traill and Her Works*. Toronto: ECW Press, 1983.

Georgina Binnie-Clark, *Wheat and Woman*. Susan Jackel, ed. Toronto: U. of T. Press, 1979.

Carole Gerson and Kathy Mezei, eds. *The Prose of Life: Sketches from Victorian Canada*. Toronto: ECW Press, 1981.

Audrey Morris, *Gentle Pioneers: Five Nineteenth-Century Canadians*. London: Hodder & Stoughton, 1968.

Michael Peterman, *Susanna Moodie and Her Works*. Toronto: ECW Press, [198?].

Louise Reynolds, *Agnes: The Biography of Lady Macdonald*. Toronto: Samuel Stevens Ltd., 1979. Rpt. 1990.

Carol Shields, *Susanna Moodie: Voice and Vision*. Ottawa: Borealis Press, 1977.

Clara Thomas, "The Strickland Sisters," in *The Clear Spirit* (Toronto: U of T Press, 1966) 42-73.

George Copway
(Kah-Ge-Ga-Gah-Bowh)

Though there are many descriptive accounts of native lifestyle by white ex-plorers and missionaries, only a very few are to be found written by natives themselves. One of these, the first such account, is George Copway's The Traditional History and Characteristic Sketches of the Ojibway Nation *published in 1850. In this highly successful book, Copway, a Christianized Ojibway and chief of his nation, describes the traditions — the religion, government, pastimes, legends and language — of his people. Though the book is marred by overt Christian proselytizing, it is still a valuable and well-written document. Copway was born in 1818 and died, in relative obscurity, in 1869. His books, long forgotten, are again becom-ing known to modern readers. The following extract is Chapter 4 of Copy-way's* Traditional History.

The Ojibway Nation:
Plays and Exercises

I believe all the Indian nations of this continent have amusements among them. Those of the prairie nations are different from those of the Ojibways, suitable to their wide, open fields. The plays I am about to describe are the principal games practised by the people of my nation. There are others; and chance games are considerably in vogue among them.

One of the most popular games is that of ball-playing, which of-tentimes engages an entire village. Parties are formed of from ten to several hundred. Before they commence, those who are to take a part in the play must provide each his share of staking, or things which are set apart; and one leader for each party. Each leader then appoints one of each company to be stake-holder.

Each man and each woman (women sometimes engage in the sport) is armed with a stick, one end of which bends somewhat like a small hoop, about four inches in circumference, to which is attached a net work of raw-hide, two inches deep, just large enough to admit the ball which is to be used on the occasion. Two poles are driven in the ground at a distance of four hundred paces from each other, which serves as goals for the two parties. It is the endeavour of each to take the ball to his hole. The party which carries the ball and strikes its pole wins the game.

The warriors, very scantily attired, young and brave fantastically painted — and women, decorated with feathers, assemble around their commanders, who are generally men swift on the race. They are to take the ball either by running with it or throwing it in the air. As the ball falls in the crowd the excitement begins. The clubs swing and roll from side to side, the players run and shout, fall upon and tread upon each other, and in the struggle some get rather rough treatment.

When the ball is thrown some distance on each side, the party standing near instantly pick it up, and run at full speed with three or four after him. The others send their shouts of encouragement to their own party. "Ha! ha! yah!" "A-ne-gook!" and these shouts are heard even from the distant lodges, for children and all are deeply interested in the exciting scene. The spoils are not all on which their interest is fixed, but is directed to the falling and rolling of the crowds over and under each other. The loud and merry shouts of the spectators, who crowd the doors of the wigwams, go forth in one continued peal, and testify to their happy state of feeling.

The players are clothed in fur. They receive blows whose marks are plainly visible after the scuffle. The hands and feet are unincumbered, and they exercise them to the extent of their power; and with such dexterity do they strike the ball, that it is sent out of sight. Another strikes it on its descent, and for ten minutes at a time the play is so adroitly managed that the ball does not touch the ground.

No one is heard to complain, though he be bruised severely, or his nose come in close communion with a club. If the last-mentioned catastrophe befall him, he is up in a trice, and sends his laugh forth as loud as the rest, though it be floated at first on a tide of blood.

It is very seldom, if ever, that one is seen to be angry because he has been hurt. If he should get so, they would call him a "coward," which proves a sufficient check to many evils which might result from many seemingly intended injuries.

While I was in La Point, Lake Superior, in the summer of 1836, when the interior band of Chippeways, with those of Sandy Lake,

Lac Counterville, Lac De Frambou, encamped in the island, the interior bands proposed to play against the Lake Indians. As it would be thought a cowardly act to refuse, the Lake Indians were ready at an early hour the next day, when about two hundred and fifty of the best and swiftest feet assembled on a level green, opposite the mansion-house of the Rev. Mr. Hall.

On our side was a thicket of thorns; on the other the lake shore, with a sandy beach of half a mile. Every kind of business was suspended, not only by the Indians, but by the whites of all classes.

There were but two rivals in this group of players. One of these was a small man from Cedar Lake, on the Chippeway river, whose name was "*Nai-nah-aun-gaib*" (Adjusted Feathers), who admitted no rival in bravery, daring or adventure, making the contest more interesting.

The name of the other competitor was "*Mah-koonce*" (Young Bear), of the shore bands.

The first, as I said before, was a small man. His body was a model for sculpture; well proportioned. His hands and feet tapered with all the grace and delicacy of a lady's. His long black hair flowed carelessly upon his shoulders. On the top of his raven locks waved in profusion seventeen signals (with their pointed fingers) of the feathers of that rare bird, the western eagle, being the number of the enemy he had taken with his own hand. A Roman nose with a classic lip, which wore at all times a pleasing smile. Such was *Nai-nah-aun-gaib*. That day he had not the appearance of having used paint of any kind. Before and after the play I counted five bullet-marks around his breast. Three had passed through; two were yet in his body. Besides these, there were innumerable marks of small shot upon his shoulders, and the graze of a bullet on his temple.

His rival on this occasion was a tall muscular man. His person was formed with perfect symmetry. He walked with ease and grace. On his arms were bracelets composed of the claws of grizzly bears. He bad been in the field of battle but five times; yet on his head were three signals of trophies.

The parties passed to the field; a beautiful green, as even as a floor. Here they exhibited all the agility and graceful motions. The one was as stately as the proud elk of the plains; while the other possessed all the gracefulness of the antelope of the western mountains.

Shout after shout arose from each party, and from the crowds of spectators. "Yah-hah-yah-hah" were all the words that could be distinguished. After a short contest, the antelope struck the post, and at that moment the applause was absolutely deafening. Thus ended the first day of the play, which was continued for some length of time.

After this day's game was over, the two champions met and indulged in a sort of personal encounter with the ball. This they continued a short time, then parted company, in good humour, and mingled with the crowd.

The Mocassin-play is simple, and can be played by two or three. Three mocassins are used for the purpose of hiding the bullets which are employed in the game. So deeply interesting does this play sometimes become, that an Indian will stake first his gun; next his steel-traps; then his implements of war; then his clothing; and lastly, his tobacco and pipe, leaving him, as we say, "*Nah-bah-wan-yah-ze-yaid*;" a piece of cloth with a string around his waist.

The "Tossing-play" is a game seldom seen among the whites. It is played in the wigwam. There is used in it an oblong knot, made of cedar boughs, of length say about seven inches. On the top is fastened a string, about fifteen inches long, by which the knot is swung. On the other end of this string is another stick, two and a half inches long, and sharply pointed. This is held in the hand, and if the player can hit the large stick every time it falls on the sharp one he wins.

"Bone-play," is another in-door amusement, so called, because the articles used are made of the hoof-joint bones of the deer. The ends are hollowed out, and from three to ten are strung together. In playing it they use the same kind of sharp stick, the end of which is thrown into the bones.

Doubtless the most interesting of all games is the "Maiden's Ball Play," in the Ojibway language, *Pak-pah-se-Kah-way.*

The majority of those who take part in this play are young damsels, though married women are not excluded. The ball is made of two deer skin bags, each about five inches long and one in diameter. These are so fastened together as to be at a distance of seven inches each from the other. It is thrown with a stick five feet long.

This play is practiced in summer under the shade of wide-spreading trees, beneath which each strives to find their homes, *tahwin*, and to run home with it. These having been appointed in the morning, the young women of the village decorate themselves for the day by painting their cheeks with vermilion, (how civilized, eh!) and disrobe themselves of as much unnecessary clothing as possible, braiding their hair with coloured feathers, which hang profusely down to the feet.

At the set time the whole village assemble, and the young men, whose loved ones are seen in the crowd, twist and turn to send sly glances to them, and receive their bright smiles in return.

The same confusion exists as in the game of ball played by the men. Crowds rush to a given point as the ball is sent flying through the air. None stop to narrate the accidents that befall them, though they tumble about to their no little discomfiture; they rise making a loud noise, something between a laugh and a cry, some limping behind the others, as the women shout. "*Ain goo*" is heard sounding like the notes of a dove, of which it is no bad imitation. Worked garters, mocassins, leggins and vermilion are generally the articles at stake. Sometimes the chief of the village sends a parcel before they commence, the contents of which are to be distributed among the maidens when the play is over. I remember that some winters before the teachers from the pale faces came to the lodge of my father, my mother was very sick. Many thought she would not recover her health. At this critical juncture, she told my father that it was her wish to see the "Maiden's Ball Play," and gave as a reason for her request that were she to see the girls at play, it would so enliven her spirits with the reminiscences of early days as to tend to her recovery.

Our family then resided at the upper end of Belmount Lake, above Crow River. The next day, at early dawn, the crier of my father was sent round to inform the village damsels that the Ball-game was to be played at the request of the chief's wife.

Two large spruce-trees were transplanted from the woods, to holes in the ice; and in the afternoon the people from the villages were on the shore of the Lake. Among them was my mother, wrapt up in furs and blankets to protect her from the cold. There was just enough snow upon the ground to make the footing very uncertain. I scarcely recollect any thing equal to the sport of that day. The crowds would fall and roll about, some laughing most heartily at themselves and at the distorted countenances of their companions, whose pain could not be concealed. When it was over, they all stood in a circle, and received the rewards allotted to each, consisting of beads, ribbons, scarlet cloths, &c. In a few moments more I heard them in their wigwams jesting and laughing at their day's sport.

Jumping is an exercise in which my countrymen have always engaged with considerable interest. Trials are made of jumping over a raised stick, or in the sand. This sport, as well as the use of the bow and arrow, young women are prohibited from engaging in.

Foot Racing is much practiced, mostly however by the young people. Thus in early life they acquire an elasticity of limb as well as health of body, which are of priceless value to them in subsequent years.

The first mortification my pride ever received was on a certain occasion when I engaged in one of these races in the presence of a crowd of warriors. The prize was a piece of scarlet cloth. As I reached forth my hand to grasp the prize, a rope that lay hid in the grass upset me so completely, that I turned half a dozen somersets and finally tumbled into a pool of water. When I got out I had the extreme pleasure of seeing my rival take the cloth, and of hearing him brag that he had actually beaten the chief's son. I wiped my drenched head as best I could, and my eyes of the dirt which adhered to them with all the tenacity of a leech, amid the shouts of laughter which was all the consolation I received in my misfortune. Since then I have walked seventy-five miles a day in the spring of the year, so that I can boast of this, if not of my first pedestrian feat.

I need not say in concluding this chapter, what every one probably knows, that the plays and exercises of the Indians have contributed much towards the formation and preservation of that noble, erect, and manly figure for which they are so remarkable.

Growing up in the daily practice of these has been and is now a sure preventive of disease. Not until recently has the rude and brutish system of wrestling been in vogue among them.

The law of the nation, like that of ancient Greece, has been enacted with a view to the health of its subjects. It obliged the people to engage in these exercises that they might inherit strong constitutions, and be prepared for the cold storms, and the piercing blasts that sweep around the lake shores.

The mildness added to the coldness of the climate conduce to the expansion of the ingenuity of my people. The old saying, "Necessity is the mother of invention," finds a verification in them. Did they possess the advantages of education possessed by the whites, many a bright star would shine forth in their ranks to bless and improve mankind. What they want is education. They have mind, but it requires culture.

A short time since, while on a steamboat on the waters of the upper Mississippi, a gentleman speaking of the Chippeways, said that they were a manly, noble race, that their motto seemed to be, "Suffering before treachery — death before dishonour." It was gratifying to my national pride to hear such an assertion made by an enlightened American.

Catharine Parr Traill

Older sister to Susanna Moodie (part of whose memoir follows), Catharine [Strickland] Traill emigrated to Canada with the Moodies and her husband, Thomas Traill, in 1832 and settled near Rice Lake, Ontario. Her book describing her early introduction to Canadian life, The Backwoods of Canada, *was published four years later, was an instant success, and was popular enough to be reprinted several times before her sister's book,* Roughing it in the Bush *(1852), became popular. Though fascinating in its factual detail, it lacks the immediacy and personality of Susanna's later memoir.*

Clearing the Land

November the 2d, 1833.

Many thanks, dearest mother, for the contents of the box which arrived in August. I was charmed with the pretty caps and worked frocks sent for my baby; the little fellow looks delightful in his new robes, and I can almost fancy is conscious of the accession to his wardrobe, so proud he seems of his dress. He grows fat and lively, and, as you may easily suppose, is at once the pride and delight of his foolish mother's heart.

His father, who loves him as much as I do myself, often laughs at my fondness, and asks me if I do not think him the ninth wonder of the world. He has fitted up a sort of rude carriage on the hand-sleigh for the little fellow — nothing better than a tea-chest, lined with a black bear-skin, and in this humble equipage he enjoys many a pleasant ride over the frozen ground.

Nothing could have happened more opportunely for us than the acquisition of my uncle's legacy, as it has enabled us to make some useful additions to our farm, for which we must have waited a few years. We have laid out a part of the property in purchasing a fine lot of land adjoining our home lot. The quality of our new purchase is excellent, and, from its situation, greatly enhances the value of the whole property.

We had a glorious burning this summer after the ground was all logged up; that is, all the large timbers chopped into lengths, and drawn together in heaps with oxen. To effect this the more readily we called a logging-bee. We had a number of settlers attend, with yokes of oxen and men to assist us. After that was over, my husband, with the men-servants, set the heaps on fire; and a magnificent sight it was to see such a conflagration all round us. I was a little nervous at first on account of the nearness of some of the log-heaps to the house, but care is always taken to fire them with the wind blowing in a direction away from the building. Accidents have sometimes happened, but they are of rarer occurrence than might be expected when we consider the subtlety and destructiveness of the element employed on the occasion.

If the weather be very dry, and a brisk wind blowing, the work of destruction proceeds with astonishing rapidity; sometimes the fire will communicate with the forest and run over many hundreds of acres. This is not considered favourable for clearing, as it destroys the underbrush and light timbers, which are almost indispensable for ensuring a good burning. It is, however, a magnificent sight to see the blazing trees and watch the awful progress of the conflagration, as it hurries onward, consuming all before it, or leaving such scorching mementos as have blasted the forest growth for years.

When the ground is very dry the fire will run all over the fallow, consuming the dried leaves, sticks, and roots. Of a night the effect is more evident; sometimes the wind blows particles of the burning fuel into the hollow pines and tall decaying stumps; these readily ignite, and after a time present an appearance that is exceedingly fine and fanciful. Fiery columns, the bases of which are hidden by the dense smoke wreaths, are to be seen in every direction, sending up showers of sparks that are whirled about like rockets and fire-wheels in the wind. Some of these tall stumps, when the fire has reached the summit, look like gas lamps newly lit. The fire will sometimes continue unextinguished for days.

After the burning is over the brands are collected and drawn together again to be reburnt; and, strange as it may appear to you, there is no work that is more interesting and exciting than that of tending the log-heaps, rousing up the dying flames and closing them in, and supplying the fires with fresh fuel.

There are always two burnings: first, the brush heaps, which have lain during the winter till the drying winds and hot suns of April and

May have rendered them sear, are set fire to; this is previous to forming the log-heaps.

If the season be dry, and a brisk wind abroad, much of the lighter timber is consumed, and the larger trees reduced during this first burning. After this is over, the rest is chopped and logged up for the second burning: and lastly, the remnants are collected and consumed till the ground be perfectly free from all encumbrances, excepting the standing stumps, which rarely burn out, and remain eye-sores for several years. The ashes are then scattered abroad, and the field fenced in with split timbers; the great work of clearing is over.

Our crops this year are oats, corn, and pumpkins, and potatoes, with some turnips. We shall have wheat, rye, oats, potatoes, and corn next harvest, which will enable us to increase our stock. At present we have only a yoke of oxen (Buck and Bright, the names of three-fourths of all the working oxen in Canada), two cows, two calves, three small pigs, ten hens, and three ducks, and a pretty brown pony: but she is such a skilful clearer of seven-railed fences that we shall be obliged to part with her. *Breachy* cattle of any kind are great disturbers of public tranquillity and private friendship; for which reason any settler who values the good-will of his neighbours would rather part with the best working yoke of oxen in the township than keep them if they prove *breachy*.

A small farmer at home would think very poorly of our Canadian possessions, especially when I add that our whole stock of farming implements consists of two reaping-hooks, several axes, a spade and a couple of hoes. Add to these a queer sort of harrow that is made in the shape of a triangle for the better passing between the stumps: this is a rude machine compared with the nicely painted instruments of the sort I have been accustomed to see used in Britain. It is roughly hewn, and put together without regard to neatness; strength for use is all that is looked to here. The plough is seldom put into the land before the third or fourth year, nor is it required; the general plan of cropping the first fallow with wheat or oats, and sowing grass-seeds with the grain to make pastures, renders the plough unnecessary till such time as the grass-lands require to be broken up. This method is pursued by most settlers while they are clearing bush-land; always chopping and burning enough to keep a regular succession of wheat and spring crops, while the former clearings are allowed to remain in grass.

The low price that is now given for grain of every kind, wheat having fetched only from two shillings and nine-pence to three shillings the bushel, makes the growing of it a matter of less importance than rearing and fatting of stock. Wages bear no proportion to the price of produce; a labourer receives ten and even eleven dollars and board a month, while wheat is selling at only three shillings, three shillings and sixpence or four shillings, and sometimes even still less. The returns are little compared with the outlay on the land; nor does the land produce that great abundance that men are apt to look for on newly cleared ground. The returns of produce, however, must vary with the situation and fertility of the soil, which is generally less productive in the immediate vicinity of the lakes and rivers than a little farther back from them, the land being either swampy or ridgy, covered with pines and beset with blocks of limestone and granite, the sub-soil poor and sandy.

This is the case on the small lakes and on the banks of the Otonabee; the back lots are generally much finer in quality, producing hard wood, such as basswood, maple, hickory, butternut, oak, beech, and ironwood; which trees always indicate a more productive soil than the pine tribe.

In spite of the indifference of the soil the advantage of a water frontage is considered a matter of great importance in the purchasing of land; and lots with water privileges usually fetch a much higher price than those farther removed from it. These lands are in general in the possession of the higher class of settlers, who can afford to pay something extra for a pretty situation and the prospect of future improvements when the country shall be under a higher state of cultivation and more thickly settled.

We cannot help regarding with infinite satisfaction the few acres that are cleared round the house and covered with crops. A space of this kind in the midst of the dense forest imparts a cheerfulness to the mind, of which those that live in an open country, or even a partially wooded one, can form no idea. The bright sunbeams and the blue and cloudless sky breaking in upon you, rejoices the eye and cheers the heart as much as the cool shade of a palm-grove would the weary traveller on the sandy wastes of Africa.

If we feel this so sensibly who enjoy the opening of a lake of full three-quarters of a mile in breadth directly in front of our windows, what must those do whose clearing is first opened in the depths of the forest, hemmed in on every side by a thick wall of trees, through the interminable shades of which the eye vainly endeavours to penetrate in search of other objects and other scenes; but so dense is the growth of timber that all beyond the immediate clearing is wrapped in profound obscurity. A settler on first locating on his lot knows no more of its boundaries and its natural features than he does of the North-West Passage.

Under such disadvantages it is ten chances to one if he chooses the best situation on the land for the site of his house. This is a very sufficient reason for not putting up an expensive building till the land is sufficiently cleared to allow its advantages and disadvantages to become evident. Many eligible spots often present themselves to the eye of the settler in clearing his land, that cause him to regret having built before he could obtain a better choice of ground. But circumstances will seldom admit of delay in building in the bush; a dwelling must be raised speedily, and that generally on the first cleared acre. The emigrant, however, looks forward to some no very distant period when he shall be able to gratify both his taste and love of comfort in the erection of a handsomer and better habitation than his log-house or his shanty, which he regards only in the light of a temporary accommodation.

On first coming to this country nothing surprised me more than the total absence of trees about the dwelling-houses and cleared lands; the axe of the chopper relentlessly levels all before him. Man appears to contend with the trees of the forest as though they were his most obnoxious enemies; for he spares neither the young sapling in its greenness nor the ancient trunk in its lofty pride; he wages war against the forest with fire and steel.

There are several sufficient reasons to be given for this seeming want of taste. The forest-trees grow so thickly together that they have no room for expanding and putting forth lateral branches; on the contrary, they run up to an amazing height of stem, resembling seedlings on a hot-bed that have not duly been thinned out. Trees of this growth when unsupported by others are tall, weak, and entirely divested of those graces and charms of outline and foliage that would make them desirable as ornaments to our grounds; but this is not the most cogent reason for not leaving them, supposing some more sightly than others were to be found.

Instead of striking deep roots in the earth, the forest-trees, with the exception of the pines, have very superficial hold in the earth; the roots running along the surface have no power to resist the wind when it bends the tops, which thus acts as a powerful lever in tearing them from their places.

The taller the tree the more liable it is to being uprooted by storms; and if those that are hemmed in, as in thickly-planted forests, fall, you may suppose the certain fate of any isolated tree, deprived of its former protectors, when left to brave the battle with the storm. It is sure to fall, and may chance to injure any cattle that are within its reach. This is the great reason why trees are not left in the clearing. Indeed, it is a less easy matter to spare them when chopping than I at first imagined, but the fall of one tree frequently brings down two, three, or even more smaller ones that stand near it. A good chopper will endeavour to promote this as much as possible by partly chopping through smaller ones in the direction they purpose the larger one to fall.

I was so desirous of preserving a few pretty sapling beech-trees that pleased me that I desired the choppers to spare them; but the only one that was saved from destruction in the chopping had to pass through a fiery ordeal, which quickly scorched and withered up its gay green leaves: it now stands a melancholy monument of the impossibility of preserving trees thus left. The only thing to be done if you desire trees is to plant them while young in favourable situations, when they take deep root and spread forth branches the same as the trees in our parks and hedgerows.

Another plan which we mean to adopt on our land is to leave several acres of forest in a convenient situation, and chop and draw out the old timbers for firewood, leaving the younger growth for ornament. This method of preserving a grove of trees is not liable to the objections formerly stated, and combines the useful with the ornamental.

There is a strange excitement created in the mind whilst watching the felling of one of the gigantic pines or oaks of the forest. Proudly and immoveably it seems at first to resist the storm of blows that assail its mossy trunk, from the united axes of three or even four choppers. As the work of destruction continues, a slight motion is perceived — an almost imperceptible quivering of the boughs. Slowly and slowly it inclines, while the loud rending of the trunk at length warns you that its last hold on earth is gone. The axe of the chopper has performed its duty; the motion of the falling tree becomes accelerated every instant, till it comes down in thunder on the plain, with a crash that makes the earth tremble, and the neighbouring trees reel and bow before it. Though decidedly less windy than our British isles, Canada is subject at times to sudden storms, nearly approaching to what might be termed whirlwinds and hurricanes. A description of one of these tempests I gave you in an early letter. During the present summer I witnessed another hurricane, somewhat more violent and destructive in its effect.

The sky became suddenly overcast with clouds of a highly electric nature. The storm came from the north-west, and its fury appeared to be confined within the breadth of a few hundred yards. I was watching with some degree of interest the rapid movements in the lurid, black, and copper-coloured clouds that were careering above the lake, when I was surprised by the report of trees falling on the opposite shore, and yet more so by seeing the air filled with scattered remnants of the pines within less than a hundred yards of the house, while the wind was scarcely felt on the level ground on which I was standing.

In a few seconds the hurricane had swept over the water, and with irresistible power laid low not less than thirty or forty trees, bending others to the ground like reeds. It was an awful sight to see the tall forest rocking and bowing before the fury of the storm, and with the great trunks falling one after the other, as if they had been a pack of cards thrown down by a breath. Fortunately for us the current of the wind merely passed over our open clearing, doing us no further damage than uprooting three big pinetrees on the ridge above the lake. But in the direction of our neighbour it did great mischief, destroying many rods of fencing, and crushing his crops with the prostrate trunks and scattered boughs, occasioning great loss and much labour to repair the mischief.

The upturned roots of trees thrown down by the wind are great nuisances and disfigurements in clearings, and cause much more trouble to remove than those that have been felled by the axe. Some of the stumps of these wind-fallen trees will right again if chopped from the trunk soon after they have been blown down, the weight of the roots and upturned soil being sufficient to bring them back into their former places; we have pursued this plan very frequently.

We have experienced one of the most changeable seasons this summer that was possible. The spring was warm and pleasant, but from the latter part of May till the middle of harvest we had heavy rains, cloudy skies, with moist hot days, and frequent tempests of thunder and lightning, most awfully grand, but seemingly less destructive than such storms are at home. Possibly the tall forest-trees divert the danger from the low dwellings, which are sufficiently sheltered from the effect of lightning. The autumn has also proved wet and cold. I must say at present I do not think very favourably of the climate; however, it is not right to judge by so short an acquaintance with it, as everyone says this summer has been unlike any of its predecessors.

The insects have been a sad annoyance to us, and I hailed the approach of the autumn as a respite from their attacks; for these pests are numerous and various, and no respecters of persons, as I have learned from experience.

I am longing for home-letters; let me hear from you soon.

Susanna Moodie

Settling near her sister, Catharine Parr Traill, in Cobourg, Upper Canada, Susanna, already a published poet before she arrived in Canada in 1832, stored up her impressions of the new country until 1852 when she wrote them in the relative comfort of her new home in Belleville. Roughing it in the Bush, *which has a less-popular sequel,* Life in the Clearings *(1853), is perhaps her best literary work and has become a classic of its kind. Part of its success lies in the author's willingness to reveal her personal feelings, her perceptive (though often biased) reading of character, and her ability to vivify unusual events and human eccentricity. The following excerpt is from Chapter 11 of* Roughing it in the Bush.

Canadian Customs: The Charivari

Our fate is sealed! 'Tis now in vain to sigh
For home, or friends, or country left behind.
Come, dry those tears, and lift the downcast eye
To the high heaven of hope, and be resign'd;
Wisdom and time will justify the deed,
The eye will cease to weep, the heart to bleed.
Love's thrilling sympathies, affections pure,
All that endear'd and hallow'd your lost home,
Shall on a broad foundation, firm and sure,
Establish peace; the wilderness become
Dear as the distant land you fondly prize,
Or dearer visions that in memory rise.

The moan of the wind tells of the coming rain that it bears upon its wings; the deep stillness of the woods, and the lengthened shadows they cast upon the stream, silently but surely foreshadow the bursting of the thunder-cloud; and who that has lived for any time upon the coast, can mistake the language of the waves — that deep prophetic surging that ushers in the terrible gale? So it is with the human heart — it has its mysterious warnings, its fits of sunshine and shade, of storm and calm, now elevated with anticipations of joy, now depressed by dark presentiments of ill.

All who have ever trodden this earth, possessed of the powers of thought and reflection, of tracing effects back to their causes, have listened to these voices of the soul, and secretly acknowledged their power; but few, very few, have had courage boldly to declare their belief in them: the wisest and the best have given credence to them, and the experience of every day proves their truth; yea, the proverbs of past ages abound with allusions to the same subject, and though the worldly may sneer, and the good man reprobate the belief in a theory which he considers dangerous, yet the former, when he appears led by an irresistible impulse to enter into some fortunate, but until then unthought of, speculation; and the latter, when he devoutly exclaims that God has met him in prayer, unconsciously acknowledges the same spiritual agency. For my own part, I have no doubts upon the subject, and have found many times, and at different periods of my life, that the voice in the soul speaks truly; that if we gave stricter heed to its mysterious warnings, we should be saved much after- sorrow.

Well do I remember how sternly and solemnly this inward monitor warned me of approaching ill, the last night I spent at home; how it strove to draw me back as from a fearful abyss, beseeching me not to leave England and emigrate to Canada, and how gladly would I have obeyed the injunction had it still been in my power. I had bowed to a superior mandate, the command of duty; for my husband's sake, for the sake of the infant, whose little bosom heaved against my swelling heart, I had consented to bid adieu for ever to my native shores, and it seemed both useless and sinful to draw back.

Yet, by what stern necessity were we driven forth to seek a new home amid the western wilds? We were not compelled to emigrate. Bound to England by a thousand holy and endearing ties, surrounded by a circle of chosen friends, and happy in each other's love, we possessed all the world can bestow of good — but *wealth*. The half-pay of a sub-altern officer, managed with the most rigid economy, is too small to supply the wants of a family, not enough to maintain his original standing in society. True, it may find his children bread, it may clothe them indifferently, but it leaves nothing for the indispensable requirements of education, or the painful contingencies of sickness and misfortune. In such a case, it is both wise and right to emigrate. Nature points it out as the only safe remedy for the evils arising out of an over-dense population, and her advice is always founded upon justice and truth.

Up to the period of which I now speak, we had not experienced much inconvenience from our very limited means. Our wants were few, and we enjoyed many of the comforts and even some of the luxuries of life; and all had gone smoothly and lovingly with us until the birth of our first child. It was then that prudence whispered to the father, "You are happy and contented now, but this cannot always last; the birth of that child, whom you have hailed with as much rapture as though she were born to inherit a noble estate, is to you the beginning of care. Your family may increase, and your wants will increase in proportion; out of what fund can you satisfy their demands? Some provision must be made for the future, and made quickly, while youth and health enable you to combat successfully with the ills of life. When you married for inclination, you knew that emigration must be the result of such an act of imprudence in over-populated England. Up and be doing, while you still possess the means of transporting yourself to a land where the industrious can never lack bread, and where there is a chance that wealth and independence may reward virtuous toil."

Alas! that truth should ever whisper such unpleasant realities to the lover of ease — to the poet, the author, the musician, the man of books, of refined taste and gentlemanly habits. Yet he took the hint, and began to bestir himself with the spirit and energy so characteristic of the glorious North, from whence he sprung.

"The sacrifice," he said, "must be made, and the sooner the better. My dear wife, I feel confident that you will respond to the call of duty; and hand-in-hand and heart-in-heart we will go forth to meet difficulties, and, by the help of God, to subdue them."

Dear husband! I take shame to myself that my purpose was less firm, that my heart lingered so far behind yours in preparing for this great epoch in our lives; that, like Lot's wife, I still turned and looked back, and clung with all my strength to the land I was leaving. It was not the hardships of an emigrant's life I dreaded. I could bear mere physical privations philosophically enough; it was the loss of the society in which I had moved, the want of congenial minds, of persons engaged in congenial pursuits, that made me so reluctant to respond to my husband's call.

I was the youngest in a family remarkable for their literary attainments; and, while yet a child, I had seen riches melt away from our once prosperous home, as the Canadian snows dissolve before the first warm days of spring, leaving the verdureless earth naked and bare.

There was, however, a spirit in my family that rose superior to the crushing influences of adversity. Poverty, which so often degrades the weak mind, became their best teacher, the stern but fruitful parent of high resolve and ennobling thought. The very misfortunes that overwhelmed, became the source from whence they derived both energy and strength, as the inundation of some mighty river fertilized the shores over which it spreads ruin and desolation. Without losing aught of their former position in society, they dared to be poor; to place mind above matter, and make the talents with which the great Father had liberally endowed them, work out their appointed end. The world sneered, and summer friends forsook them; they turned their backs upon the world, and upon the ephemeral tribes that live but in its smiles.

From out the solitude in which they dwelt, their names went forth through the crowded cities of that cold, sneering world, and were mentioned with respect by the wise and good; and what they lost in wealth, they more than regained in well-earned reputation.

Brought up in this school of self-denial, it would have been strange indeed if all its wise and holy precepts had brought forth no corresponding fruit. I endeavoured to reconcile myself to the changes that awaited me, to accommodate my mind and pursuits to the new position in which I found myself placed.

Many a hard battle had we to fight with old prejudices, and many proud swellings of the heart to subdue, before we could feel the least interest in the land of our adoption, or look upon it as our home.

All was new, strange, and distasteful to us; we shrank from the rude, coarse familiarity of the uneducated people among whom we were thrown; and they in turn viewed us as innovators, who wished to curtail their independence by expecting from them the civilities and gentle courtesies of a more refined community. They considered us proud and shy, when we were only anxious not to give offence. The semi-barbarous Yankee squatters, who had "left their country for their country's good," and by whom we were surrounded in our first settlement, detested us, and with them we could have no feeling in common. We could neither lie nor cheat in our dealings with them; and they despised us for our ignorance in trading and our want of smartness.

The utter want of that common courtesy with which a well-brought-up European addresses the poorest of his brethren, is severely felt at first by settlers in Canada. At the period of which I am now speaking, the titles of "sir," or "madam," were very rarely applied by inferiors. They entered your house without knocking; and while boasting of their freedom, violated one of its dearest laws, which considers even the cottage of the poorest labourer his castle, and his privacy sacred.

"Is your man to hum?" — "Is the woman within?" were the general inquiries made to me by such guests, while my bare-legged, ragged Irish servants were always spoken to as "sir" and "*men,*" as if to make the distinction more pointed.

Why they treated our claims to their respect with marked insult and rudeness, I never could satisfactorily determine, in any way that could reflect honour on the species, or even plead an excuse for its brutality, until I found that this insolence was more generally practised by the low, uneducated emigrants from Britain, who better understood your claims to their civility, than by the natives themselves. Then I discovered the secret.

The unnatural restraint which society imposes upon these people at home forces them to treat their more fortunate brethren with a servile deference which is repugnant to their feelings, and is thrust upon them by the dependent circumstances in which they are placed. This homage to rank and education is not sincere. Hatred and envy lie rankling at their heart, although hidden by outward obsequiousness. Necessity compels their obedience; they fawn, they cringe, and flatter the wealth on which they depend for bread. But let them once emigrate, the clog which fettered them is suddenly removed; they are free; and the dearest privilege of this freedom is to wreak upon their superiors the long-locked-up hatred of their hearts. They think they can debase you to their level by disallowing all your claims to distinction; while they hope to exalt themselves and their fellows into ladies and gentlemen by sinking you back to the only title you received from Nature — plain "man" and "woman." Oh, how much more honourable than their vulgar pretensions!

I never knew the real dignity of these simple epithets until they were insultingly thrust upon us by the working-classes of Canada.

But from this folly the native-born Canadian is exempt; it is only practised by the low-born Yankee, or the Yankeefied British peasantry and mechanics. It originates in the enormous reaction springing out of a sudden emancipation from a state of utter dependence into one of unrestrained liberty. As such, I not only excuse, but forgive it, for the principle is founded in nature; and, however disgusting and distasteful to those accustomed to different treatment from their inferiors, it is better than a hollow profession of duty and attachment urged upon us by a false and unnatural position. Still, it is very irksome until you think more deeply upon it; and then it serves to amuse rather than irritate.

And here I would observe, before quitting this subject that of all follies, that of taking out servants from the old country is one of the greatest, and is sure to end in the loss of the money expended in their passage, and to become the cause of deep disappointment and mortification to yourself.

They no sooner set foot upon the Canadian shores than they become possessed with this ultra-republican spirit. All respect for their employers, all subordination is at an end; the very air of Canada severs the tie of mutual obligation which bound you together. They fancy themselves not only equal to you in rank, but that ignorance and vulgarity give them superior claims to notice. They demand the highest wages, and grumble at doing half the work, in return, which they cheerfully performed at home. They demand to sit at your table, and to sit in your company, and if you refuse to listen to their dishonest and extravagant claims, they tell you that "they are free; that no contract signed in the old country is binding in 'Meriky'; that you may look out for another person to fill their place as soon as you like; and that you may get the money expended in their passage and outfit in the best manner you can."

I was unfortunately persuaded to take out a woman with me as a nurse for my child during the voyage, as I was in very poor health; and her conduct, and the trouble and expense she occasioned, were a perfect illustration of what I have described.

When we consider the different position in which servants are placed in the old and new world, this conduct, ungrateful as it then appeared to me, ought not to create the least surprise. In Britain, for instance, they are too often dependent upon the caprice of their employers for bread. Their wages are low; their moral condition still lower. They are brought up in the most servile fear of the higher classes, and they feel most keenly their hopeless degradation, for no effort on their part can better their position. They know that if once they get a bad character they must starve or steal; and to this conviction we are indebted for a great deal of their seeming fidelity and long and laborious service in our families, which we owe less to any moral perception on their part of the superior kindness or excellence of their employers, than to the mere feeling of assurance that as long as they do their work well, and are cheerful and obedient, they will be punctually paid their wages, and well housed and fed.

Happy is it for them and their masters when even this selfish bond of union exists between them!

But in Canada the state of things in this respect is wholly reversed. The serving class, comparatively speaking, is small, and admits of little competition. Servants that understand the work of the country are not easily procured, and such always can command the highest wages. The possession of a good servant is such an addition to comfort, that they are persons of no small consequence, for the dread of starving no longer frightens them into servile obedience. They can live without you, and they well know that you cannot do without them. If you attempt to practise upon them that common vice of English mistresses, to scold them for any slight omission or offence, you rouse into active operation all their new-found spirit of freedom and opposition. They turn upon you with a torrent of abuse; they demand their wages, and declare their intention of quitting you instantly. The more inconvenient the time for you, the more bitter become their insulting remarks. They tell you, with a high hand, that "they are as good as you; that they can get twenty better places by the morrow, and that they don't care a snap for your anger." And away they bounce, leaving you to finish a large wash, or a heavy job of ironing, in the best way you can.

When we look upon such conduct as the reaction arising out of their former state, we cannot so much blame them, and are obliged to own that it is the natural result of a sudden emancipation from former restraint. With all their insolent airs of independence, I must confess that I prefer the Canadian to the European servant. If they turn out good and faithful, it springs more from real respect and affection, and you possess in your domestic a valuable assistant and friend; but this will never be the case with a servant brought with you from the old country, for the reasons before assigned. The happy independence enjoyed in this highly-favoured land is nowhere better illustrated than in the fact that no domestic can be treated with cruelty or insolence by an unbenevolent or arrogant master.

Forty years has made as great a difference in the state of society in Canada as it has in its commercial and political importance. When we came to the Canadas, society was composed of elements which did not always amalgamate in the best possible manner.

The Canadian women, while they retain the bloom and freshness of youth, are exceedingly pretty; but these charms soon fade, owing, perhaps, to the fierce extremes of their climate, or the withering effect of the dry metallic air of stoves, and their going too early into company and being exposed, while yet children, to the noxious influence of late hours, and the sudden change from heated rooms to the cold, biting, bitter winter blast.

Though small in stature, they are generally well and symmetrically formed, and possess a graceful easy carriage. The early age at which they marry and are introduced into society, takes from them all awkwardness and restraint.

They have excellent practical abilities, which, with a little mental culture, would render them intellectual and charming companions. At present, too many of these truly lovely girls remind one of choice flowers half-buried in weeds.

Music and dancing are their chief accomplishments. Though possessing an excellent general taste for music, it is seldom in their power to bestow upon its study the time which is required to make a really good musician. They are admirable proficients in the other art, which they acquire readily, with the least instruction, often without any instruction at all, beyond that which is given almost intuitively by a good ear for time, and a quick perception of the harmony of motion.

The waltz is their favourite dance, in which old and young join with the greatest avidity; it is not unusual to see parents and their grown-up children dancing in the same set in a public ballroom.

On entering one of the public ballrooms, a stranger would be delighted with such a display of pretty faces and neat figures. I have hardly ever seen a really plain Canadian girl in her teens; and a downright ugly one is almost unknown.

The high cheek-bones, wide mouth, and turned-up nose of the Saxon race, so common among the lower classes in Britain, are here succeeded in the next generation, by the small oval face, straight nose, and beautifully-cut mouth of the American; while the glowing tint of the Albion rose pales before the withering influence of late hours and stove-heat.

They are naturally a fine people, and possess capabilities and talents, which, when improved by cultivation, will render them second to no people in the world; and that period is not too far distant.

To the benevolent philanthropist, whose heart has bled over the misery and pauperism of the lower classes in Great Britain, the almost entire absence of mendicity from Canada would be highly gratifying. Canada has few, if any, native beggars; her objects of charity are generally imported from the mother country, and these are never suffered to want food or clothing. The Canadians are a truly charitable people; no person in distress is driven with harsh and cruel language from their doors; they not only generously relieve the wants of suffering strangers cast upon their bounty, but they nurse them in sickness, and use every means in their power to procure them employment. The number of orphan children yearly adopted by wealthy Canadians, and treated in every respect as their own, is almost incredible.

It is a glorious country for the labouring classes, for while blessed with health, they are always certain of employment, and certain also to derive from it ample means of support for their families. An industrious, hard-working man in a few years is able to purchase from his savings a homestead of his own; and in process of time becomes one of the most important and prosperous class of settlers in Canada, her free and independent yeomen, who forms the bones and sinews of the rising country, and from among whom she already begins to draw her senators, while their educated sons become the aristocrats of the rising generation.

It has often been remarked to me by people long resident in the colony, that those who come to the country destitute of means, but able and willing to work, invariably improve their condition and become independent; while the gentleman who brings out with him a small capital is too often tricked and cheated out of his property, and drawn into rash and dangerous speculation which terminate in his ruin. His children, neglected and uneducated, but brought up with ideas far beyond their means, and suffered to waste their time in idleness, seldom take to work, and not unfrequently sink down to the lowest class.

It was towards the close of the summer of 1833, which had been unusually cold and wet for Canada, while Moodie was absent at D——, inspecting a portion of his government grant of land, that I was startled one night, just before retiring to rest, by the sudden firing of guns in our near vicinity, accompanied by shouts and yells, the braying of horns, the beating of drums, and the barking of all the dogs in the neighbourhood. I never heard a more stunning uproar of discordant and hideous sounds.

What could it all mean? The maid-servant, as much alarmed as myself, opened the door and listened.

"The goodness defend us!" she exclaimed, quickly closing it, and drawing a bolt seldom used. "We shall be murdered. The Yankees must have taked Canada, and are marching hither."

"Nonsense! that cannot be. Besides, they would never leave the main road to attack a poor place like this. Yet the noise is very near. Hark! they are firing again. Bring me the hammer and some nails, and let us secure the windows."

The next moment I laughed at my folly in attempting to secure a log hut, when the application of a match to its rotten walls would consume it in a few minutes. Still, as the noise increased, I was really frightened. My servant, who was Irish (for my Scotch girl, Bell, had taken to herself a husband, and I had been obliged to hire another in her place, who had been only a few days in the country), began to cry and wring her hands, and lament her hard fate in coming to Canada.

Just at this critical moment, when we were both self-convicted of an arrant cowardice, which would have shamed a Canadian girl of six years old, Mrs. O—— tapped at the door, and although generally a most unwelcome visitor, from her gossiping, mischievous propensities, I gladly let her in.

"Do tell me," I cried, "the meaning of this strange uproar?"

"Oh, 'tis nothing," she replied, laughing. "You and Mary looks as white as a sheet; but you need not be alarmed. A set of wild fellows have met to charivari Old Satan, who has married his fourth wife to-night, a young girl of sixteen. I should not wonder if some mischief happens among them, for they are a bad set, made up of all the idle loafers about Port H—— and C——."

"What is a charivari?" said I. "Do, pray, enlighten me."

"Have you been nine months in Canada, and ask that question? Why, I thought you knew everything! Well, I will tell you what it is. That charivari is a custom that the Canadians got from the French, in the Lower Province, and a queer custom it is. When an old man marries a young wife, or an old woman a young husband or two old people, who ought to be thinking of their graves, enter for the second or third time into the holy estate of wedlock, as the priest calls it, all the idle young fellows in the neighbourhood meet together to charivari them. For this purpose they disguise themselves, blackening their faces, putting their clothes on hind part before, and wearing horrible masks, with grotesque caps on their heads, adorned with cocks' feathers and bells. They then form in a regular body, and proceed to the bridegroom's house, to the sound of tin kettles, horns, and drums, cracked fiddles, and all the discordant instruments they can collect together. Thus equipped, they surround the house where the wedding is held, just at the hour when the happy couple are supposed to be about to retire to rest — beating upon the door with clubs and staves, and demanding of the bridegroom admittance to drink the bride's health, or in lieu thereof to receive a certain sum of money to treat the band at the nearest tavern.

"If the bridegroom refuses to appear and grant their request, they commence the horrible din you hear, firing guns charged with peas against the doors and windows, rattling old pots and kettles, and abusing him for his stinginess in no measured terms. Sometimes they break open the doors, and seize upon the bridegroom; and he may esteem himself a very fortunate man, under such circumstances, if he escapes being ridden upon a rail, tarred and feathered, and otherwise maltreated. I have known many fatal accidents arise out of an imprudent refusal to satisfy the demands of the assailants. People have even lost their lives in the fray; and I think the Government should interfere, and put down these riotous meetings. Surely it is very hard that an old man cannot marry a young gal, if she is willing to take him, without asking the leave of such a rabble as that. What right have they to interfere with his private affairs?"

"What, indeed?" said I, feeling a truly British indignation at such a lawless infringment upon the natural rights of man.

"I remember," continued Mrs. O——, who had got fairly started upon a favourite subject, "a scene of this kind, that was acted two years ago, at ——, when old Mr. P—— took his third wife. He was a very rich storekeeper, and had made during the war a great deal of money. He felt lonely in his old age, and married a young, handsome widow, to enliven his house. The lads in the village were determined to make him pay for his frolic. This got wind, and Mr. P—— was advised to spend the honeymoon in Toronto; but he only laughed, and said that 'he was not going to be frightened from his comfortable home by the threats of a few wild boys.' In the morning, he was married at the church, and spent the day at home, where he entertained a large party of his own and the bride's friends. During the evening all the idle chaps in the town collected round the house, headed by a mad young bookseller, who had offered himself for their captain, and, in the usual forms, demanded a sight of the bride, and liquour to drink her health. They were very good-naturedly received by Mr. P——, who sent a friend down to inquire on what terms they would consent to let him off, and disperse.

"The captain of the band demanded sixty dollars, as he, Mr. P——, could well afford to pay it.

"'That's too much, my fine fellows!' cried Mr. P—— from the open window. 'Say twenty-five, and I will send you down a cheque upon the Bank of Montreal for the money.'

"'Thirty! thirty! thirty! old boy!' roared a hundred voices. 'Your wife's worth that. Down with the cash, and we will give you three cheers, and three times three for the bride, and leave you to sleep in peace. If you hang back, we will raise such a 'larum about your ears that you shan't know that your wife's your own for a month to come!'

"'I'll give you twenty-five,' remonstrated the bridegroom, not the least alarmed at their threats, and laughing all the time in his sleeve.

"'Thirty; not one copper less!' Here they gave him such a salute of diabolical sounds that he ran from the window with his hands to his ears, and his friend came down to the verandah, and gave them the sum they required. They did not expect that the old man would have been so liberal, and they gave him the 'Hip, hip, hip, hurrah!' in fine style, and marched off to finish the night and spend the money at the tavern."

"And do such people allow themselves to be bullied out of their property by such ruffians?"

"Ah, my dear! 'tis the custom of the country, and 'tis not so easy to put it down."

Frances Beaven

A resident of New Brunwick for seven years, Mrs Beaven, in her engaging book, Sketches and Tales Illustrative of Life in the Backwoods of New Brunswick *(London, 1845), provides one of the most detailed (if sometimes idyllic) descriptions of life in the "lower provinces." In an idiosyncratic style, which has her taking the rounds of her village and commenting on everything she encounters, she describes the people, their houses, food, and "frolics," all punctuated by some very lively anecdotes.*

A Native New Brunswicker's House

Here is a house at which I have a call to make, and which will illustrate the *"menage"* of a New Brunswicker.... Melancthon Grey, whose most christian and protestant application was abbreviated into "Lank," was a true-blooded blue nose. His father had a noble farm of rich intervale on the banks of the river Saint John, and was well to do in the world. Lank was his eldest son, yet no heritage was his, save his axe and the arm which swung it. The law of primogeniture exists not in this country, and the youngest son is frequently heir to that land on which the older ones have borne the "heat and burthern of the day," and rendered valuable by their toil, until each chooses his own portion in the world, by taking unto himself a wife and a lot of forest land, thus another hard-won *homestead* is raised, and sons enough to choose among for heirs. Melancthon Grey had wedded his cousin, a custom common among the "blue noses," and which most likely had its origin in the patriarchal days of the earlier settler, when the inhabitants were few. Sybel was a sweet pretty girl, deficient, as the Americans all are, in those high-toned feelings which characterise the depth of woman's love in the countries of Europe, yet made, as they generally do, an affectionate wife, and a fond and doating mother. Those two names, Sybel and Melancthon, had a strange sound in the same household, awaking, as they always did in my dreamy fancy, a train of such differing memories. Sybel recalling the days of early Rome, the haughty Tarquin and his mysterious prophetess, while Melancthon brought back the "Reformation," and the best and most pious of its fathers. In the particular of names, the

Americans have a decided "penchant" for those of euphonious and peculiar sound — they are selected from sacred and profane history, ancient and modern. To them, however, there is little of meaning attached by those who give them save the sound. I have known one family reckon among its members a Solon and Solomon, a Hector and Wellington, a Bathsheba and Lucretia; and the two famous Johns, Bunyan and Wesley, have many a namesake. These, in their full length, are generally saved for holiday terms, and abbreviations are made for every-day use. In these they are ingenious in finding the shortest, and *Theodore*, that sweetest of all names, I have heard curtailed to "Od," which seems certainly an odd enough cognomen. Sybel's bridal portion consisted of a cow and some sheep — her father's waggon which brought her home contained some household articles her mother's care had afforded — Melancthon had provided a barrel of pork and one of flour, some tea and molasses, that staple commodity in transatlantic housekeeping. Amongst Sybel's chattels were a bake-pan and tea-kettle, and thus they commenced the world. Melancthon had not yet had time to make a gate at his dwelling, and our only mode of entrance must be either by climbing the "fence" or unshipping the "*bars*," which form one panel, and which are placed so as to be readily removed for the passage of a carriage, but from us this will require both time and strength, so at the risk of tearing our dress we will e'en take the fence. This is a feat which a novice does most clumsily, but those who are accustomed to it do most gracefully.

As we approach the dwelling the housewife's handy-work is displayed in a pole hung with many a skein of snow white yarn, glistening in the sunlight. Four years have passed since Sybel was a bride — her cheek has lost the bloom of girlhood, and has already assumed the hollow form of New Brunswick matrons; her dress is homespun, of her own manufacture, carded and spun by her own hands, coloured with dye stuffs gathered in the woods, woven in a pretty plaid, and neatly made by herself. This is also the clothing of her husband and children; a bright gingham hand-kerchief is folded inside her dress, and her rich dark hair is smoothly braided. In this particular the natives display a good taste — young women do not enshroud themselves in a cap the day after their marriage, as if glad to be done with the trouble of dressing their hair; and unless from sickness a cap is never worn by any one the least youthful. The custom commences with the children, for infants never have their heads covered during the day. At the first little bald heads seem unsightly to a stranger, but when the eye gets accustomed, they look much better in their own natural beauty then when decked out in lace and muslin. The plan of keeping the head cool seems to answer well, for New Brunswick may rival any country in the world for a display of lovely infants. Sybel has the delicacy of appearance which the constant in-door occupation of the women gives them, differing much from the coarse, but healthier look of those countries where the females assist in field labours. The "blue nose" considers it *"agin all nature"* for women to work out, and none are ever seen so employed, unless it be the families of emigrants before they are naturalised. A flush of delight crimsons Sybel's pale face as she welcomes me in, for simple and retired as her life is, she yet cherishes in her heart all the fondness for company and visiting inherent to her sex, and loves to enjoy them whenever opportunity permits. No excuse would be listened to, — I must stay dinner — my bonnet is untied, and placed upon the bed — Sybel has churned in the early cool of the morning, and she has now been working over the golden produce of her labours with a wooden ladle in a tray. With this ladle the butter is taken from the churn; the milk beaten out and formed by it into rolls — nothing else is employed, for moulds or prints are not used as in England. She has just finished, and placed it in her dairy, a little bark-lined recess adjoining the house — and now, on hospitable thoughts intent, she has caught up her pail and is gone for water — in this we are most luxurious in New Brunswick, never keeping any quantity in the house, but using it bright and sparkling as it gushes from the spring. While she is gone, we will take a pencilling of her dwelling. A beautiful specimen of still-life, in the shape of a baby six months old, reposes in its cradle — its eye-lids' long and silky fringes are lightly folded in sleep on its smooth round cheek. Another older one is swinging in the rocking chair, playing with some log chips and bark, the only toys of the log house — this single apartment serves the family for parlour, for kitchen, and hall — the chamber above being merely used as a store room, or receptacle for lumber — 'tis the state bed-room as well, and on the large airy-looking couch is displayed a splendid coverlet of home-spun wool, manufactured in a peculiar style, the possessing of which is the first ambition of a back-wood matron, and for which she will manoeuvre as much as a city lady would for some *bijou of a chiffi*onier, or centre table — Sybel has gained hers by saving each year a portion of the wool, until she had enough to accomplish this sure mark of industry, and of getting along in the world; for if they are not getting along or improving in circumstances their farms will not raise sheep enough to yield the wool, and if they are not industrious the yarn will not be spun for this much-prized coverlet, which, despite the local importance attached to it, is a useful, handsome and valuable article in itself. On a large chest beside the bed are laid piles of snow white blankets, and around the walls are hung the various woollen garments which form the wardrobe of the family. Bright-hued Indian baskets stand on top of each other — a pair of beaded moccasins and a reticule of porcupine quills are hung up for ornament. The pine table and willow-seated chairs are all made in the "bush," and even into this far back settlement has penetrated the prowess of the renowned "Sam Slick, of Slickville." One of his wooden-made yankee clocks is here — its case displaying "a most elegant picture" of Cupid, infrilled trowsers and morocco boots, the American prototype of the little god being allowed to appear so scantily clad as he is generally represented.

A long rifle is hung over the mantle-piece, and from the beams are suspended heads of Indian corn for seed; by them, tied in bunches, or in paper bags, is a complete "hortus siccus" of herbs and roots for medicinal as well as culinary purposes. Bone set and lobelia, sage and savory, sarsaparilla, and that mysterious bark which the natives say acts with a different effect, according as it is peeled up or down the tree — cat-nip and calamus root for the baby, with dried marigold leaves, balm of gilead buds, and a hundred others, for compounding the various receipts they possess, as remedies for every complaint in the world. Many of these they have learnt from the Indians, whose "ancient medicine men" are well versed in the healing powers with which the herbs of the forest and the field are gifted. On a small shelf is laid the library, which consists but of the bible, a new almanac, and Humberts Union Harmony, the province manual of sacred music, of which they are most particularly fond; but the air of the country is not favourable to song, and their melody always seemed to me "harmony not understood." Meanwhile, for the last half-hour, Sybel has been busily engaged in cooking, at which the natives are most expeditious and expert. I know not how they would be in other countries, but I know that at home they are first-rate — no other can come up to them in using the materials and implements they are possessed of. By the accustomed sun mark on the floor, which Sybel prefers to the clock, she sees 'tis now the hungry hour of noon, and blows the horn for Lank to come to dinner. This horn is a conk shell, bored at one end, and its sound is heard at a great distance. At the hours of meal-time it may be heard from house to house, and, ringing through the echoing woods from distant settlements, telling us, amid their loneliness, of happy meetings at the household board; but it comes too, at times, when its sounds are heralds of trouble and dismay. I have heard it burst upon the ear at the silent hour of midnight, and, starting from sleep, seen the sky all crimsoned with the flames of some far off dwelling, whose inmates thus called for assistance; but long ere that assistance could be given, the fire would have done its worst of destruction, perhaps of death. I have also heard it, when twilight gathered darkly o'er the earth, floating sad and mournfully since sunset, from some dwelling in the forest's depths, whose locality, but for the sounds, would not have been known. Some member of the family has been lost in the woods and the horn is blown to guide him homewards through the trackless wilderness. How sweet must those sounds be to the benighted wanderer, bearing, as they do, the voice of the heart, and telling of love and affectionate solicitude! But Melancthon has driven his ox-team to the barn and now, with the baby on his lap, which, like all the blue-noses, he loves to nurse, sits down to the table, where we join him. The dinner, as is often the case in the backwoods in summer, is "a regular pick-up one," that is, composed of any thing and every thing. People care little for meat in the hot weather; and in fact, a new settler generally uses his allowance of beef and pork during the long winter, so that the provision for the summer depends principally on fish, with which the country is amply supplied, and the produce of the dairy. The present meal consists of fine trout from the adjoining stream, potatoes white as snow-balls, and pulverising on the dish, some fried ham, and young french beans, which grow there in the greatest luxuriance, climbing to the top of their lofty poles till they can grow no higher. I have often thought them scions of that illustrious bean-stalk owned by Jack in the fairy tale. We have also a bowl of salad, and home-made vinegar prepared from maple sap, a large hot cake, made with Indian meal, and milk and dried blue-berries, an excellent substitute for currants. Biscuits, of snow white Tenessee flour, raised with cream and sal-a-ratus. This last article, which is used in place of yeast, or eggs, in compounding light cakes, can also be made at home from ley [lye] of the wood ashes, but it is mostly bought in town. The quantity of this used is suprising, country "store-keepers" purchasing barrels to supply their customers. A raspberry pie, and a splendid dish of strawberries and cream, with tea (the inseparable beverage of every meal in New Brunswick), forms our repast; and such would it be in ninety-nine houses out of a hundred of the class I am describing. Many of the luxuries, and all the necessaries of life, can be raised at home, by those who are industrious and spirited enough to take advantage of their resources. Melancthon this year expects to *bread himself*, as well as grow enough of hay to winter his stock.

Since he commenced farming he purchased what was not raised on the land by the sale of what was cut off it — that is, by selling ash timber and cordwood he procured what he required. This, however, can only be done where there is water conveyance to market. The indefatigable Melancthon had four miles to "haul " his marketable wood; but, when the roads were bad, he was chopping and clearing at the same time, and when the snow was well beaten down, with his little French horse and light sled he soon drew it to the place from whence the boats are loaded in the spring. Dinner being now finished, and after some conversation, which must of course be of a very local description, although it is brightened with many a quiet touch of wit, of which the natives possess a great original fund, and Melancthon, having finished in the forenoon harrowing in his buckwheat, had now gone with his axe to hew at a house-frame which he has in preparation, and Sybel and I having settled our affair of warp and woof, it is now time for me to proceed.

Annie Howells Fréchette

Born in Hamilton, Ontario, in 1844, Annie Howells moved with her newspaper-publisher father to the United States when she was five and back to Canada in her twenties when her father became the American consul at Quebec. Already an established writer (like her brother William Dean), she now turned to Canadian (particularly Quebec) subjects for her articles and stories. In 1876 she married Achille Fréchette, an Ottawa civil servant, and became quite a prominent participant in Ottawa literary activities. This descriptive sketch of the busy social and vice-regal life of Governor-General Lorne and The Princess Louise in the 1870s was written for an American audience and published in Harper's Magazine *63 (1881): 213-23.*

Life at Rideau Hall

Since the advent of the Princess Louise as its mistress, more than usual curiosity has been manifested regarding the life at Rideau Hall, the "White House" of Canada. Before that time, if it was thought of at all, it was only as the Government House; but since a Princess dwells there, a new interest attached itself to the place, and it is not strange if every little American "sovereign in her own right" should exercise her national perogative, and ask all the questions she likes about "court life" at Ottawa. Much of this curiosity has already been satisfied, for from the day the Marquis of Lorne and his royal wife landed upon Canadian soil, very little of the slightest interest concerning them has passed unnoted by the press.

So popular were their predecessors, Lord and Lady Dufferin, that the places which they left were difficult to fill. Indeed, I am sure there are people in Canada to-day who believe that they took their places with them, instead of leaving them to be filled. The Marquis and Marchioness of Lorne took the wisest and easiest way — they retained their individuality and *created* new places for themselves.

So unaffected is the life at Rideau Hall that it shows almost a republican simplicity when compared with the ceremony and parade kept up in many of the great country houses in England. No court etiquette is observed, and only the rules of good manners are adhered to. It is the very evident desire of the Governor-General and Princess to make all those who enter their home feel welcome and at their ease. The public sees very little beyond the usual formalities surrounding the two chief personages of the Dominion. Their home is jealously guarded from the world.

I often think, when I see the flag which always floats over Rideau Hall when the Princess is there, what a change has come into her life. "Piccadilly and green pastures" — London and Ottawa. Brilliancy, art, culture, and caste — and a crude little city, struggling in the chaos of newness and the doubt of permanency. And I fall to wondering what her feelings were that bleak November day, when she drove, just at nightfall, under the dripping and leafless trees, up to the door of Rideau Hall. Velvet lawns had been exchanged for a soaked meadow turf, and a palace for a comfortable, roomy, old-fashioned home. The life she was leaving behind her had filled her aesthetic nature, and the one to which she was coming could only have as its greatest merit, in her eyes, novelty.

It would not be very strange if she were not happy here, for if we look back over the two years she has spent with us, enough has happened to associate sorrow with Canada. The death of her favourite sister, the Princess Alice, which followed closely her coming, filled the first months of her stay with grief. Of course she was surrounded with an atmosphere of sympathy, but, after all, she was separated from those who felt the grief in all its bitterness around her. But even this was only allowed to very briefly interrupt the gayeties at the Government House. She assumed these duties, and bravely performed them in spite of the mourning of which her face attested the sincerity. Then came the shocking accident which almost cost her her life, and which has left her in a state against which a continual struggle must be made to prevent her sinking into confirmed invalidism. Of late she has been trying the effect of travel. During her absence Lord Lorne has to a great extent supported her role as well as his own, and during the winter just passed society has not wanted for entertainment at the Hall.

Royalty is so hedged in by etiquette, that you can only approach it through certain openings, and in Ottawa, as elsewhere, these openings do not frequently occur. Since her Royal Highness has resided at Rideau Hall, even that society which the popular voice calls "the best," has not had as free access there as formerly. In Lady Dufferin's time the doors swung open easily and often. Of course then, as now, there was always the intimate circle of friends. This, Lady Dufferin chose from Ottawa society. Now it is chosen from England, and comprises the ladies of her household and transient guests. These, almost without an exception, have been artists. Amongst these has been the gifted Miss Montalba, who is making such an enviable reputation in England, and, indeed, through out Europe. She left as a souvenir of her visit a bust of Lord Lorne, which is strong and masterly. It has been cut into bronze, and now stands in the main corridor.

The hospitalities of Rideau Hall which are extended to the general public may be enjoyed by observing the following rules. In Ottawa the political, judiciary, military, and clerical dignitaries have official precedence, while, under the head of "prominent citizens," clergymen, lawyers, doctors, bankers, and heads of large business firms, lumbering and mining interests, take rank with the officers of the civil service in society, and amongst these the chiefs of departments take the lead.

To enjoy the hospitalities of Rideau Hall — that is, to get your name upon the lists — you must go and register your name in one book for the Princess Louise, and in another for the Governor-General, and you will do well to leave a separate card for each lady and gentleman making up the Governor's family. In acknowledgment of this civility, you will have your call returned by card by those for whom you have left yours, and from the Marquis and Marchioness of Lorne you will receive invitations to the various entertainments as they occur.

These entertainments have one peculiarity which would impress an American observer: they are nearly all out-of-doors, perchance lawn tennis inaugurating the season. Some softly bright October day, such as comes in perfection in our Northern climate, the gardens and lawns surrounding the Hall are brilliant with gay people in afternoon dress. Even the usual gloom of male attire does not stand out *en bloc*, as it broken into by the uniforms of the Governor's aides-de-camp, which gleam here and there through the crowd. At such a time, and upon such a day, I can imagine with what delight an artist — Raimend de Madrazo, for instance — would study the scene. Detail and accessories are all there. Imagine this: Vaguely showing through the autumnal glow, over a mile away, is the background formed by the beautiful pile of government buildings resting upon the bold bluff which overhangs the Ottawa River. Nearer, the fringe of trees bordering the grounds, and looking like a procession with triumphal banners floating in the hazy atmosphere. Beneath these, across the lawn, and amid the richest and last floral offering of summer, promenade the guests. The band of the Governor-General's Foot-Guards is stationed near the house, and their red coats and flashing instruments harmonize with the whole. On the broad gallery stand groups of visitors, while through the open windows you see a few irrepressible dancers in the parlor.

After it is too late for lawn tennis and croquet, the skating and toboggan parties come, and at these young Canada is in its element. Then the daring of Canadian attire reaches it climax. No color is too brillant and no garment too fantastic to be worn. The toboggan slide and vicinity fairly blossoms with the merry, romping company. Surplus dignity is thrown to the winds, along with streamers of ribbons, tassels, and bright-hued scarfs. A pretty Canadian girl never looks prettier than when clad in her cloak made of a fleecy white blanket (its gay border carefully reserved as a trimming), a red or blue *tuque* perched coquettishly upon her abundant hair, its saucy-looking tassel bobbing about at its own sweet will and a bright-colored skirt just showing between her cloak and moccasined feet. Put now a toboggan and two or three beaux at her disposal, and she is happy. She will slide all afternoon, leaving, perhaps, just a margin for a skim over the ice, and then scamper into the house, replace her moccasins, or skating boots, with slippers, throw aside her cloak, and dance until the stern law of etiquette, or the equally stern command of her chaperon, who, although kind and discreet as a chaperon should be, feels at last the *ennui* and the interest in the approaching dinner hour natural to her age. These afternoon parties never last later than six o'clock, and a few minutes before that time the last guest in usually gone.

"And does the Princess Louise take part in these sliding parties?"

Yes, to a certain extent, though, knowing her character, you can readily understand that she only does so *à la princesse*. I have never seen her guide her own toboggan, a feat seemingly easy enough of accomplishment when you see it done by a Canadian girl, but which, after a trial or two, the lately arrived Briton or American is very shy of undertaking.

Lately there has been built a little log-cabin under the tall natural growth of pines, well off to one side of the Hall. It overlooks the skating rink, and is divided into two rooms, into which the skaters can retire for rest, warmth, or preparation. It is very comfortable, and doubtless serves the purpose for which it was designed, if that purpose was not picturesqueness. It is so hopelessly unlike the genuine log-cabin that one expects to see a stage peasant step out from its door and soliloquize upon its platform. On this platform chairs are arranged for the distinguished guests to rest and watch the skaters when they do not care to be of them.

For the amusement of the Governor-General and his gentleman friends there is a fine curling rink, where the lovers of "the roarin' game" very often congregate. Likewise there is a foot-ball and cricket ground for them; but as this is a pre-eminently feminine piece of literature, I decline to go outside of my province, and so say nothing about the entertainments intended only for gentlemen.

Balls are not of very frequent occurence, but I can assure those who are interested upon that point, that when they are given, they are "perfectly lovely." You are bidden one to two weeks in advance by a card of impressive dimensions, bearing the monogram of the house, and which reads as follows:

The Aide-de-Camp in waiting is commanded by
His Excellency The Governor-General
and Her Royal Highness the Princess Louise
to invite
Mrs. and Mrs._____
to a Ball on _____,
the_____, at 9 o'clock.
An answer is requested to the A.D.C. in waiting.

On the appointed night the road to New Edinburgh is lined with sleighs, and by the time the gate is reached, so dense is the crowd of vehicles that the remainder of your drive is likely to occupy more time than did that part of it from the city out. Once more inside the Hall, the scene which greets you is indeed charming. Up and down the stairs, along the brilliantly lighted corridors, into the leafy shade of the conservatory, in and out of the several handsome rooms thrown open for the occasion, throng the elegantly dressed guests. The ball-room is packed to suffocation, and it is a terrible pilgrimage to make to the further end, where the Governor-General and the Princess Louise are receiving their guests. When the dancing begins, the pilgrimage becomes an impossibility, and the only thing left for you to do is to gaze hopelessly in their direction. The dressing at one of these grand balls is elegant, and, as a rule, graceful, but when compared with that seen upon a similar occasion at the White House, for instance, is inexpensive. There are handsome silks, satins, and velvets, and a few costly laces, but very few diamonds are to be seen. As a rule, the ladies are *décolletées*, but there are amongst them a good many who are dressed in "the American fashion," as the high-necked full dress is here described.

The ball-room is a large and handsome apartment, occupying the wing to the left of the entrance. The walls are tinted in a soft dark shade, which shows off a brilliantly dressed company to the best advantage. The wood is finished in white and gold, and the window drapery is crimson. On ball nights the tennis-court, in the wing to the right of the entrance, is used for a supper-room. Its walls and ceilings are lined with red and white bunting to simulate a tent. It, as well as the ball-room, was added in Lord Dufferin's administration, and at his request. About midnight the piper is heard piping along the corridor, and the supper-room is thrown open. Into it the vice-regal party lead the way, followed by five or six hundred of their guests, as only about that number can conveniently be served at once. The vice-regal party sit, and the rest stand.

Dinners are far fewer than formerly, and the diners are chosen rather more exclusively. Of course these dinners are the most ceremonious entertainments which take place. The guests enter the reception room with the right hand bare, although they are not received by the Princess before dinner. She enters just as dinner is announced, and is escorted to the table by the gentleman who takes rank amongst the guests, the Marquis offering his arm to one of the ladies. If they are thus in company with French Canadians, they enter into conversation in French, as both speak it well and fluently. After dinner, when the company returns to the drawing-room, the Princess passes about amongst her guests, speaking to all. It is not proper to sit when the Princess does not, and whenever she has occasion to rise, the entire company does the same, and remains standing until she is again seated.

In these days of ceramic achievements it is quite allowable to peep into other people's china closets, so I may say something of the china displayed at Rideau Hall. Much of it is beautiful, but by no means exceptionally rare. Neither is the plate of unusual magnificence, though rich and handsome, and gold enters freely into the furnishing of the table. Of course the family plate of Argyll is not yet inherited, so abundant is the supply that it is hardly missed.

Of all the entertainments given at the Government House none are more popular than the theatricals, and invitations to them are eagerly sought. The ball-room is so constructed that it can easily be converted into a theatre. The platform upon which the musicians have sat for one occasion is now, by an ingeneous contrivance for enlarging it, turned into an exquisitely appointed stage. Of late years Rideau Hall has been fortunate in having within its walls most excellent amateur talent. Lady Dufferin was a most charming actress, and in the present household one of the aides-de-camp has the reputation of being the finest amateur actor in England. He certainly plays to perfection — that is, non-professional perfection. The ladies and gentlemen taking part in the theatricals are usually from Ottawa, and the Princess does not act. And just here I am reminded to say that the announcment that the Princess has written a play founded upon scenes and amongst the fisherman of Gaspé Bay is quite untrue. No such play has ever been written, or, at least, not by her Royal Highness. The theatricals are full-dress occasions, and the ballroom on these nights presents a brilliant appearance. The plays are always put upon the stage with all the elegance of which they admit, or taste or money can supply. Flowers are used in profusion, and their arrangement calls forth the greatest admiration. New scenery has been painted, under the supervision of the Princess, and altogether the stage is a little gem.

The most public appearance of the Princess in Ottawa society is upon the evening after the opening of Parliament, when she holds a "Drawing-room" in the Senate-chamber. This reception is also a full-dress affair, and whoever wishes may attend. The Governor-General and his wife stand upon the dias at one end of the chamber, and the guests approach and are introduced by one aide-de-camp, who has had the name read to him by another from the card with which each guest is provided. As the name is pronounced, the Princess and Marquis simply bow, unless it should belong to some person of sufficient distinction, when they offer their hands and speak a few words with him. After the intro-duction the guests pass out by a door to the right of the apartment without turning their backs upon royalty - a thing which is, of course, never done. The "Drawing-room" is usually over by ten o'clock. Formerly there were afternoon receptions, somewhat similar to those at the White House, which could be attended by any one who wished. These have been discontinued, and all parties are now formed of invited guests. This change is solely owing to the increasing numbers who now early come to Ottawa.

Some idea of the number of guests entertained in various ways at Rideau Hall since Lord Lorne has been Governor-General may be gained by the following figures:

At dinner parties in 1879	904
At dinner parties in 1880	688
At dinner parties in 1881	627
At balls in 1879	1000
At balls in 1881	1600
At "At Homes" each year	900
At skating and tobogganing parties, each year	2000
At theatricals, each year	1300

On New-Year's Day the Governor-General follows the custom of his predecessors in receiving all who come to wish him a happy New Year, and these receptions are quite as informal as those of the President at the White House. He is also always willing to see any one who asks to see him on business at any time, and so cordial is his manner in these interviews, and so delightful a talker is he, that occasionally his caller loses sight of business in friendly chat.

While Parliament is sitting, the Princess often occupies a chair near the Speaker on the floor of the House of Commons, an interested listener to the debate on some important bill. At such times she offers her hand and chats cordially with those members who approach to speak to her. She is always attended by a lady in waiting and an aide-de-camp.

She is, like so many English women, a good walker and a fair rider, and during her first winter here she could be met almost any day miles away from her home. She "did" much of the vicinity of Ottawa on foot, always *sensibly* shod and dressed, and in slippery weather carrying a cane. Almost invariably she wears a veil. It has been the subject of much comment, and the curious often complain that the public never sees her face. Her reason for wearing it probably lies as much in the fact that she suffers terribly from neuralgia as from any wish to thwart the curious gaze. Both the Princess and Marquis readily adopted winter sports, and many a merry snow-shoe tramp was organized from the Government House; and when the spring opened, and the rafts from Upper Ottawa began to come down by hundreds, they enjoyed the grand and exciting fun of running the rapids above the Chaudiere Falls, and coming down through the "slides" upon these log rafts.

From this slight glimpse into it you see that Rideau Hall is by no means a Castle of Indolence. The Princess is a busy woman, and her range of duties is a very wide one. Her artistic pursuits are, without doubt, nearest her heart, and you often see her abroad with her sketch-book, filling it with souvenirs of her Canadian home. She has a snug little sketching box, which can be whisked about from place to place as she desires it. Fortunately for one of her artistic nature she lives in a region surrounded by the loveliest views, and whichever way the eye turns, it is gladdened by some picture never to be forgotten.

The Princess is a communicant at St. Bartholomew's, the little English church at New Edinburgh, which stands near the grounds (the rector of which is chaplain for Rideau Hall), while the Marquis of Lorne comes into the city, and is a regular attendant at "the kirk." Her Royal Highness has always taken an active interest in church affairs, and to her the little church is indebted for a fine chime of bells. The children of the Sunday-school are regularly entertained at the Hall with a Christmas tree and party. She visits hospitals, schools, and convents, and carries on all the work of a charitable lady in private life. Much of her good work is done in a quiet, unostentatious manner, which fully carries out the Biblical injunction; but a princess can not hide from the public the work of one hand, even if she can keep it a secret from the other, and so we from time to time catch a glimpse of her true, kind heart.

All of these public duties do not interfere with those of a more domestic character. She, of course, has a small army of servants. There is a *chef*, and *un garçon de chef*, and I would be afraid to say how many more *pour faire la cuisine*; there are maid-servants and men-servants for each particular kind of work, and a housekeeper to oversee them all. But, in spite of much aid, the Marchioness of Lorne is at the head of her establishment. She does not think it beneath her dignity to go into the laundry amd instruct the maids concerning their duties, or to give an occasional eye to the marketing when it is brought in. A story I have just heard about her makes her quite rival in housewifely attainments the queen of the good King Stephen, who, from the "peck o' barley meal," concocted that historical pudding so well known to the student of Mother Goose. A friend of mine was lately dining at Rideau Hall, and during the dinner she remarked upon the excellence of the oyster *patés* to one of the ladies in waiting to the Princess. "Yes," she replied; "they were made by her Royal Highness."

The immediate household at Government House consists of two or three ladies in waiting and several aides-de-camp. The military secretary and his wife occupy a handsome house nearby, where the Princess often calls informally, or takes a five-o'clock "school-room tea" with the secretary's children.

Rideau Hall in every part shows itself to be the home of an artist and a poet. An air of culture and refinement pervades it, and whichever way you turn you are delighted by some pretty conceit, or tasteful fancy successfully carried out. Here are old tapestry hangings, as rich with history and associations as color and skill. Exquisite ornaments are scattered about in profusion, but not with that riotous plenty which simply suggests money. The "blue parlor" is, to my taste, one of the most charming rooms I can recall. It is a large and handsome apartment, and is furnished upon the happy meeting ground of classical severity and elegant luxuriousness. It is essentially feminine in its taste, and you at once say to yourself, "It is the expression of the *artist*." About you you feel much of its presiding genius. Here is a panel of flowers, and here a door decorated by her own brush; an unfinished study hangs in one corner, and rare paintings glow upon the walls. Sitting before the bright coal fire on a winter day, you can look out through the warmly draped windows upon a driving snow-storm, or, if you turn slightly, you can look into the fairy-land of flowers, for the conservatory opens from this room.

Next to the parlor is the library, a snug and rather surprising library, with none of the conventional solidity of furnishing which one naturally associates with books. It is pretty and simple, in white and green.

With the exception of perhaps these two rooms the color throughout the Hall is crimson. Perhaps no better could be chosen. It is a stately color, and glows with a perpetual warmth which our long Canadian winters make acceptable.

I have only written of that life in which the gay world is interested; but there is another and higher life lived at Rideau Hall, and I doubt if either the Marquis of Lorne or her Royal Highness knows how wide-spread its influence is. Its spirit does more toward awakening a desire for mental improvement than anything else could. Years ago we knew our present Governor-General as a writer who did not have to call his rank to his aid to gain admittance to the literary world, and before him we had learned the character of the house of Argyll. While the Princess Louise we knew better as a clever artist than as a princess. So we were prepared, in anticipating their coming, for a more exalted and refined life than Canadian society had yet known, and our anticipations have not been disappointed.

Two years is a short time, but it has been long enough to establish upon a substantial foundation a national academy of arts and several art schools in Canada, and what is, perhaps, still more to the point, to implant a respect for mental superiority in all departments. Like all people who are true to their tastes, and who are happy enough to have the means, they have opened and smoothed ways in which to advance those who are less fortunately placed. They have sent young artists abroad, generously patronized those already before the public, and fostered education in many ways. With this kindly spirit and good work the present Governor-General and his wife will have marked their stay in Canada with a characteristic influence which will be felt for many years to come.

Lady Agnes Macdonald

Lady Susan Agnes Macdonald was the second wife of Sir John A. Macdonald, Canada's first and perhaps best-known Prime Minister (1867-73, 1878-91). She was born in 1836 in Jamaica to British parents who had gone there to become landlords; she was thus well educated and well schooled in the social graces. She met the widowed Prime Minister in Canada where she had gone to live with her brother, and in February of 1867 she married him in London, England, where the final Confederation negotiations were being discussed. Some twenty years Sir John's junior, and little acquainted with politics, she nevertheless plunged into her official duties, delighting (from what her diaries tell us) in the social activities of Ottawa and in travelling with her husband. One of these trips, an official one along the CPR with her husband in 1886, she described in vivid and witty fashion, and published it in Murray's Magazine *1 (1887): 215-35, 296-311. The following is an abbreviated version of that essay.*

By Car and Cowcatcher

The evening is warm and moonlit, the wide Ottawa's dark water glides swiftly between high wooded banks; the pale foam of a rapid gleams in mid-distance; the Chaudière Falls break the silence with their muffled roar, and above them, in dim outline, on a cedar-covered cliff, stand the tall towers of the stately building where Parliament assembles in the Dominion of Canada.

It is the 10th of July — long anticipated as the day of our departure for the Pacific coast, and now everything is ready and the hour is at hand. All sorts of luggage, necessary for convenience and comfort, during a journey extending over many thousand miles, is already on its way to the Ottawa station of the Canadian Pacific Railway, and our party, six in number, is only waiting for coffee and the evening papers before bringing up the rear. All day long each intending traveller has been diligently employed in making special packing arrangements suited to his or her particular taste, and while the writer, in capacity of general manager, has given particular care to hampers and grocery lists, others of the party have selected new books, illustrated papers, maps, games, and embroidery, mindful that for at least three weeks during our absence we shall have no home but the railway car.

Off at last! a town clock is striking eleven, and the moon, unsteady with moving clouds, lights us to the station. There a long row of gleaming lamps marks out the whereabouts of our "Special," which, five minutes after we have stepped on board, has glided out among the soft shadows of a summer night, and is bearing us swiftly westward.

How pleasant it is to recall the sense of novelty and of freedom which delighted at least one of our party as we walked through the length of the train and inspected our accommodation. The "Special" (consisting of a large private car named the "Jamaica," a Pullman and a baggage car, with engine and tender complete) looked very cosy. In the baggage car our larger trunks were neatly set in rows; and in the brightly lighted Pullman, curtained bed-places alternated with velvet-cushioned seats, while travelling bags, writing cases, small portmanteaus, and alas! tobacco-boxes too, were symmetrically arranged on small fixed tables. In the rear end a separate enclosure looked very like a smoking-room, and a tell-tale embroidered cap already graced a peg.

The "Jamaica" — her large fixed lamps brightening each little sitting-room — had a very homelike effect. Baskets of flowers stood on the narrow tables, already heaped with books and newspapers; comfortable sofas lined her polished sides, and wide arm-chairs stood on either side of the entrance-doors. In a tiny kitchen the white-aproned cook stood superintending the stowage of sundry useful packages into a neat little cupboard fitted behind two cosy bedrooms placed *dos à dos* in the centre of the car, with a door opening into each parlour. These small apartments contained excellent beds, good washing apparatus, with taps for hot and cold water connecting with the kitchen-stove and a tank overhead — all somewhat resembling the cabin of a fine ship, everything being as richly coloured and effective as black walnut and gilding could make it.

Eighty feet over all, and wide in proportion, smoothly painted and varnished outside of a deep golden brown colour, the "Jamaica," though more spacious and certainly safer in its accommodations than the "Cowcatcher" of days to come, was, as will be seen in the sequel, not half so much fun! But that glorious ride through the wild passes of the mighty mountains, round curving bends of magnificent rivers, under towering snow-tipped peaks, and amid the rich green gloom of endless valleys — surrounded on all sides by scenery of striking grandeur and beauty — was a thing of the future, for twenty-three hundred miles of woodland, river, rock, lake, and prairie lay between us and the eastern base of the Rocky Mountains, where the soft ineffable beauty of those blue and white summits shall first gladden our longing eyes.

★ ★ ★

We are [at last] among the "Foot hills," or lowest range of the Rockies — great, mound-like, smooth, softly-tinted hills that swelled into many a lovely curved shape, holding in their wide folds winding blue rivers and great stretches of fine grazing land, over which, as the sweet morning air stirred through the grass, little billows of pale green seemed to pass. These are some of the cattle ranches of which we have "heard tell" so often lately.

As we travel slowly onward — slowly, so as to enjoy all to the fullest extent — these plains widen and stretch away into flat quiet distances, soft and misty, lying below farther hills outlined against the sky. Sharper risings and rougher edges appear. By and by the wide valleys change into broken ravines, and lo! through an opening in mist made rosy with early sunlight, we see far away up in the sky, its delicate pearly tip clear against the blue, a single snow-peak of the Rocky Mountains! There is a general rush to see it; — perhaps general disappointment. Surely that fragile, almost quivering point rising so high over the pink drapery that sweeps to the valley below, can have nothing to do with the rugged heights and mountains we have come to see!

Our coarse natures cannot at first appreciate the exquisite aerial grace of that solitary peak that seems on its way to heaven; but as we look, its fading, gauzy mist passes over, and it has vanished.

On again we go, now through long stretches of park-like country, now near great mountain shoulders, half-misty, half- defined, with occasional gleams of snowy peaks far away before us like kisses on the morning sky.

The Kananaskis River flows directly across the pass that leads into the mountains which here begin to close in around us. We stopped at the Kananaskis Station, and walking across a meadow, behold the wide river a mass of foam leaping over ledges of rocks into the plains below.

We reach Canmore, — sixty-eight miles from Calgary. Here the pass we are travelling through has narrowed suddenly to four miles, and as mists float upwards and away, we see great masses of scarred rock rising on each side — ranges towering one above another. Very striking and magnificent grows the prospect as we penetrate into the mountains at last, each curve of the line bringing fresh vistas of endless peaks, rolling away before and around us, all tinted rose, and blush pink, and silver, as the sun lights their snowy tips. Every turn becomes a fresh mystery, for some huge mountain seems to stand right across our way, barring it for miles, with a stern face frowning down upon us; and yet a few minutes later we find the giant has been encircled and conquered, and soon lies far away in another direction.

Mount Cascade is perhaps one of the most remarkable of these peaks. Approaching its perpendicular massive precipice-front, streaked with a thousand colours which glow in the sunshine, we half shrink from what seems an inevitable crash! but no; a few minutes later Mount Cascade has mysteriously moved away to the right, and its silver waterfall soon gleams in the distance.

Many of the mountains were skirted with low dark forests. Some had a vegetation of small evergreens marking out wide ledges; but beyond a certain height, fissured rock, in which tiny glaciers and snow-beds found a resting place, rose alone into the sky. Sometimes this bristling beard of rugged trees was sharply defined against great walls of white and grey above, with crags and peaks and ledges, in all sorts of fantastic forms, breaking the outline. Below, all was in deep shade, but above, sunlight fell in a sharp, bright line across those mighty walls, and glistened, with beauty inconceivable, upon fairy-like points in the sky.

At Banff, six miles from Canmore, sulphur springs of great medicinal value had been only lately discovered; but already, from our car window, we can see the timbers for an hotel awaiting transportation up the winding road to the springs. One of our party informs us that the Government has reserved 20,000 acres for a public park in this beautiful place, and that arrangements are already being made to render it available for this purpose. It is an enchanting spot, encircled by mountains — said to contain many more valuable springs — the air fragrant with sweet odours from low spruce-trees clothing their sides.

Here the Bow River, which we have skirted since leaving Calgary, winds through the wide green plateau, its waters of a dull China blue. About five miles farther on Castle Mountain is before us, standing a sheer precipice 5000 feet high — a giant's "keep," with turrets, bastions, and battlements complete, reared against the sky.

As we rise toward the summit, near Stephen, about thirty-five miles farther on, the railway's grade gets steeper, tall forests gather round us, and a curious effect is produced by glimpses of snowy spurs and crests peeping through the trees, and of which, though apparently near us, we see no base. This conveyed to me an idea of our elevation, and it was delightful to think of oneself among those solitary mountains, even for a few short hours, with all the troubles and worries of life left in noisy bustling cities far away!

At the Laggan Station, more than thirty miles from the summit, a huge engine — in curious black contrast to a small white house near by — stood on a siding with all steam up, waiting for our train. I then learned that this monster is necessary for the steep grades, both ascending and descending, over which we have to go.

The General Superintendent (whom I have already mentioned as having joined our party at Winnipeg — Mr. E —) in an unlucky moment suggested I should walk forward, examine this big "mountain" engine, and see its heavy proportions and fine machinery. I say "unlucky," because from the instant my eyes rested on the broad shining surface of its buffer-beam and cowcatcher, over which a bright little flag waved from a glossy brass pole, I decided to travel there and nowhere else for the remaining 600 miles of my journey!

When I announced my desire to travel on the cowcatcher, Mr. E seemed to think that a very bad job indeed. To a sensible, level-headed man as he is, such an innovation on all general rules of travelling decorum was no doubt very startling. He used many ineffectual persuasions to induce me to abandon the idea, and almost said I should not run so great a risk; but at last, being a man of few words, and seeing time was nearly up, he so far relented as to ask what I proposed using as a seat. Glancing round the platform I beheld a small empty candle-box lying near, and at once declared that was "just the thing." Before Mr. E could expostulate further, I had asked a brakesman to place the candle-box on the buffer-beam, and was on my way to the "Jamaica" to ask the Chief's permission. The Chief, seated on a low chair on the rear platform of the car, with a rug over his knees and a magazine in his hand, looked very comfortable and content. Hearing my request, after a moment's thought, he pronounced the idea "rather ridiculous," then remembered it was dangerous as well, and finally asked if I was sure I could hold on. Before the words were well out of his lips, and taking permission for granted by the question, I was again standing by the cowcatcher, admiring the position of the candle-box, and anxiously asking to be helped on.

Before I take my seat, let me try, briefly, to describe the "Cowcatcher." Of course every one knows that the buffer-beam is that narrow, heavy iron platform, with the sides scooped out, as it were, on the very fore-front of the engine over which the headlight glares, and in the corner of which a little flag is generally placed. In English engines, I believe, the buffers proper project from the front of this beam. In Canadian engines another sort of attachment is arranged, immediately below the beam, by which the engine can draw trains backwards as well as forwards. The beam is about eight feet across, at the widest part, and about three feet deep. The description of a cowcatcher is less easy. To begin with, it is misnamed, for it catches no cows at all. Sometimes, I understand, it throws up on the buffer-beam whatever maimed or mangled animal it has struck, but in most cases it clears the line by shoving forward, or tossing aside, any removable obstruction. It is best described as a sort of barred iron beak, about six feet long, projecting close over the track in a V shape, and attached to the buffer-beam by very strong bolts. It is sometimes sheathed with thin iron plates in winter, and acts then as a small snow-plough.

Behold me now, enthroned on the candle-box, with a soft felt hat well over my eyes, and a linen carriage-cover tucked round me from waist to foot. Mr. E had seated himself on the other side of the headlight. He had succumbed to the inevitable, ceased further expostulation, disclaimed all responsibility, and, like the jewel of a Superintendent he was, had decided on sharing my peril! I turn to him, peeping round the headlight, with my best smile. "This is *lovely*," I triumphantly announce, seeing that a word of comfort is necessary, "*quite lovely*; I shall travel on this cowcatcher from summit to sea!"

Mr. Superintendent, in his turn, peeps round the headlight and surveys me with solemn and resigned surprise. "I — suppose — you — will," he says slowly, and I see that he is hoping, at any rate, that I shall live to do it!

With a mighty snort, a terribly big throb, and shrieking whistle, No. 374 moves slowly forward. The very small population of Laggan have all come out to see. They stand in the hot sunshine, and shade their eyes as the stately engine moves on. "It is an awful thing to do!" I hear a voice say, as the little group lean forward; and for a moment I feel a thrill that is very like fear; but it is gone at once, and I can think of nothing but the novelty, the excitement, and the fun of this mad ride in glorious sunshine and intoxicating air, with magnificent mountains before and around me, their lofty peaks smiling down on us, and never a frown on their grand faces!

The pace quickens gradually, surely, swiftly, and then we are rushing up to the summit. We soon stand on the "Great Divide" — 5300 feet above sea-level — between the two great oceans. As we pass, Mr E by a gesture, points out a small river (called Bath Creek, I think) which, issuing from a lake on the narrow summit-level, winds near the track. I look, and lo! the water, flowing *eastward* towards the Atlantic side, turns in a moment as the Divide is passed, and pours *westward* down the Pacific slope!

Another moment and a strange silence has fallen round us. With steam shut off and brakes down, the 60-ton engine, by its own weight and impetus alone, glides into the pass of the Kicking Horse River, and begins a descent of 2800 feet in twelve miles. We rush onward through the vast valley stretching before us, bristling with lofty forests, dark and deep, that, clinging to the mountain side, are reared up into the sky. The river, widening, grows white with dashing foam, and rushes downwards with tremendous force. Sunlight flashes on glaciers, into gorges, and athwart huge, towering masses of rock crowned with magnificent tree crests that rise all round us of every size and shape. Breathless — almost awe-stricken — but with a wild triumph in my heart, I look from farthest mountain peak, lifted high before me, to the shining pebbles at my feet! Warm wind rushes past; a thousand sunshine colours dance in the air. With a firm right hand grasping the iron stanchion, and my feet planted on the buffer beam, there was not a yard of that descent in which I faltered for a moment. If I had, then assuredly in the wild valley of the Kicking Horse River, on the western slope of the Rocky Mountains, a life had gone out that day! I did not think of danger, or remember what a giddy post I had. I could only gaze at the glaciers that the mountains held so closely, 5000 feet above us, at the trace of snow avalanches which had left a space a hundred feet wide massed with torn and prostrate trees; on the shadows that played over the distant peaks; and on a hundred rainbows made by the foaming, dashing river, which swirls with tremendous rapidity down the gorge on its way to the Columbia in the valley below.

We have left the North-West Territories, and are now in the Province of British Columbia. Field — Ottertail — Leanchoile flit past us. Steam has been up for ten miles now; we have left the Kicking Horse pass behind us and are gliding into the wide Columbia Valley, full of rich, new beauty, of green tall waving grass and blue water. A lower range of Rockies, streaked and capped with snow, stretches away on either side. The roadway is very level, and the rails gleam before us, narrowing in a distant point to a silver thread. I hear the engineer piling in fuel, and whistle with shrillest note. Then, with trebly quickened pace, we dart along in the sunshine. For a second only I feel a quickening of the heart-pulse, and a hot colour mounts to my face, but it is gone in a moment, and I am none the worse for that "spurt" at the rate of fifty miles an hour.

Halted at Palliser. The Chief and his friends walked up to the cowcatcher to make a morning call. I felt a little "superior" and was rather condescending. Somewhat flushed with excitement, but still anxious to be polite, I asked "would the Chief step up and take a drive?" To the horror of the bystanders he carelessly consented, and in another moment had taken the place of Mr. E, the latter seating himself at our feet on the buffer-beam. There was a general consternation among our little group of friends and the few inhabitants of Palliser — the Chief rushing through the flats of the Columbia on a cowcatcher! and, worse still, possibly even among the wild Selkirk Mountains — those mountains of which scarcely three years before, in his charming book, 'From Old Westminster to New,' my friend Mr. Sandford Fleming had said, "no one had been through the western slope of the Selkirks"! Every one is horrified. It is a comfort to the other occupant of the buffer to find some one else wilful, and as we steamed away towards Donald, at the eastern base of the Selkirks, I felt not so bad after all!

Following the valley of the Eagle River, we wind gaily through the cedar forests of the Gold Range, gemmed with lakes blue and shining, its tall, darkly clothed summits often lit by small cascades gleaming through the trees. Crossing and recrossing the Eagle River seven or eight times, we reach the Sicamous Narrows, into which its dark hurrying waters are emptied. We presently sweep into an immense valley, through which, for many miles, the line skirts beautiful stretching lakes — grand sheets of blue water, glacier fed, lying in the folds of the Gold Range. These lakes close, as it were, into the south branch of the Thompson River. Many tunnels lie in our way as we rush by them, and during a halt I am told one of the tunnels is "wet." This being interpreted, means that the arching rock is full springs, which pour on the train as it passes. An umbrella and waterproof are therefore necessary for me — now sole occupant of the cowcatcher; and with praiseworthy economy I take off my hat, tuck it safely under my wraps, and prepare to encounter the "wet" tunnel thus equipped! We plunge into a few moments' darkness — water splashing and dripping on every side; and as we emerge into sunlight again, and stop just beyond the tunnel, I see a party of young English sportsmen standing near the roadside. They have evidently just climbed the bank, guns in hand, leaving a large canoe with two Indian paddlers on the lake below. Fine, tall young Saxons they are, in sporting attire somewhat the worse for long travel, but very conventional in style notwithstanding. Just imagine the feelings with which these well-regulated young men beheld a lady, bareheaded, and with an umbrella, seated in front of an engine, at the mouth of a tunnel in the Gold Range of British Columbia! I am sorely afraid I laughed outright at the blank amazement of their rosy faces, and longed to tell them what fun it was; but not being "introduced, you know," I contented myself with acknowledging their presence by a solemn little bow — which was quite irresistible under the circumstances!

On we go, speeding forward to the coast, meeting the sweet breath of ocean mingled with rich scent of pine boughs, their delicate tips waving welcome as we pass — on, on, steadily, swiftly down to the sea! Now nearly 3000 miles from our starting-point, Ottawa, we are nearing Port Moody on Burrard Inlet, where, alas! I must bid good-bye to candle-box and cowcatcher, and content myself with an easy-chair on the deck of a steamer bound for Victoria.

John Donkin

*John Donkin, a thirty-year-old veteran of the British military, left Eng-
land in 1884 with, as he puts it, "no very definite idea as to where my
zigzag wanderings would end." After a brief stint at farming in Brandon,
Manitoba, he joined the Northwest Mounted Police (in whose ranks were
many ex-British servicemen). Donkin left the police force in 1888, immediately wrote a book about his experiences, but failed to make it a success
and died in a London workhouse in 1890. The following passage is Chapter XVI of* Trooper and Redskin in the Far North-West *(London:
Low, Marston, 1889).*

The Hanging of Louis Riel

The irrepressible ego has caused me to neglect for some time our
friend Louis Riel, who was bewailing the failure of his ambitious
schemes, in the seclusion of a guard-room at Regina. A few Indians
and half-breeds, who had been sentenced to minor terms of impris-
onment, were here also. Big Bear, Poundmaker, and One Arrow
had been packed off to Stony Mountain Penitentiary, in Manitoba,
for three years. They, along with a number of others, were amnes-
tied in 1886.

The mounted police guard-rooms were the only prisons in the
territory. The place of durance vile attached to the one in the Regina
barracks had been extended a considerable distance to the rear, and a
yard with a high stockade had also been added. It was a matter of
common superstition that Riel would be eventually pardoned, and
in all probability pensioned, so that he did not receive at first the
many delicate attentions which were subsequently lavished upon
him. There was only the ordinary barrack-guard on duty. *Le petit
Napoleon* used daily to go for an hour's exercise in the square, under
the escort of two constables with loaded Winchesters. These weapons of the guard were always filled with three rounds of ball cartridge. Monsieur Riel was also adorned with a ball and chain, whenever he left his cell. Now to describe, as far as my feeble ability will
allow me, this terror of Red River and Saskatchewan notoriety. He
was a man about five feet seven inches in height, with a pale, flabby

face, dark grey eyes closely set together, restless in their expression. His nose was slightly aquiline, his hair and beard were reddish in hue, his lips were thick, and his neck long. He spoke invariably in a low and gentle tone.

The Wood Mountain Division, the men from Southern Manitoba, and all those who had been engaged in watching the International Boundary were in barracks at the end of October. Forty recruits had also arrived recently. As soon as the parties had come in from summer duty on the plains the guard was considerably increased. Things had begun to look very serious for Riel. His appeal was considered shaky; and experts had pronounced him sane. It was at last expected that, in spite of all the hysterical yelling of the French Canadians, in spite of all the political thimble-rigging, that he would have to "swing." The Government was on the horns of a dilemma. The people of Ontario and the North-West clamoured for his execution, the Catholics of Lower Canada enshrined him as a martyr. However, as will be seen, he was doomed.

Duty began to be heavy now. An officer took command of the guard, and, in addition, there was a sergeant and corporal. The officer of the guard, and four troopers under a corporal, always accompanied Riel in his walks abroad. Two sentries were on duty, night and day, in the corridors of the prison, the whole length of which could be commanded from the guard-room. The reorganization of the force went on apace; and there were now three full troops, of one hundred men each, at Regina. There were continual muster and mounted parades....

The weather at this season was considerably milder than that of the corresponding period in 1884. We had much rain, and the barracks square and the approaches to the stables were indescribable. A man had no need to go through the formalities laid down in the Dominion Land Act to acquire a free grant of 160 acres of "rich agrillaceous mould." He had merely to walk from the barrack-gate to his room, and he had the legalized quantity attached to each foot. You mounted guard in all the pomp and circumstance of brilliant spurs and shining boots; but when you entered the guard-room your spurs were invisible beneath hideous geological formations on either heel. Mounted patrols were now established, and a couple of these were on duty in the daytime riding round the barracks, with orders to detain all suspicious-looking persons. This patrol was posted at reveillé and was taken off at retreat. At night a perfect cordon of sentries surrounded the place.

I was away on special service under a sergeant one evening, and I returned, leading his horse, at one o'clock in the morning. I was in a rough "costume," wearing a slouch hat. On my approach I was challenged by three sentries at once. The lead horse and the head-gear, looming through the darkness, looked very fishy. Evidently I was a "breed," from Montana, who had turned up to aid Riel to escape. I could just see the gleam of the barrels as the carbines came to the "ready."

"Halt! Who goes there?"

"Friend."

"Stand, friend, and give the countersign."

"Hang the countersign! Haven't got it. Policeman on duty. Call the non com."

How this *contretemps* might have ended I know not, for some zealous youth might have potted me. However, someone on the guard-room verandah recognized my voice, and I was allowed to advance.

I was now on continuous duty; when not on mounted patrol, on guard. The barrack-guard mounted at 2 p.m., and I only enjoyed the luxury of going to bed every second night. The sentries were posted, as the guard numbered off. Thus the even numbers would find themselves placed inside the prison one day; and probably the odd numbers the next. It was very frequently my lot to find myself stationed inside.

My first experience of taking care of the rebel leader was as follows. I was marched into the corridor, and given my orders by the corporal. Then the provost sergeant, who is responsible for the discipline of the prison, came to me, and impressed upon me that I was to keep a particular eye upon Riel, and see that, under no circumstances did he communicate with, or speak to, any of the other prisoners.

"He is sitting warming himself by the stove just now, and you can turn him into his cell after a little while."

The stove stood in the centre, between two blocks of cells. The passages ran down the front of the cells from both sides of the guard-room. Every door could be fastened simultaneously by a lever worked from the latter place. Each of the little apartments possessed an open grating in the centre of its wooden door, which was the only space through which light could penetrate. There were windows along the opposite walls, which at night were hung with lamps with powerful reflectors.

I found Riel clad in a dark tweed suit, wearing a blue knitted tuque upon his head. There were a number of other prisoners, including a few troopers, "in" for breaches of discipline, standing around him. He was sitting on a wooden stool, with his feet up against the stove. It was necessary for him to move, that I might pass. "Excuse me, Mr. Riel, I wish to pass; sorry to trouble you."

"Oh! no troo-bell at all. If that was all the troo-bell, it would be well."

This was said with a pleasant smile, French accent, and a soft tone of voice. He was always most studiously polite, and painfully deferential.

He occupied the cell next to the guard-room, on the left-hand side. Writing was his continual employment, when he was not praying or at exercise. A shelf formed his bed, and a small table stood alongside. In front of him was a metal statuette of St. Joseph; and when he was telling his beads he would carry this little image in his hands, and hug it. His countenance usually displayed a calm composure, and his grey eyes were nearly always bent on the ground, as though he were wrapt in contemplation and study. The literary work on which he was engaged was supposed to be a sort of *Apologia pro vita sua*. He commenced spouting French vigorously, one night; reading aloud from his manuscript. This brought the sergeant very briskly to the wicket; he ordered me to "tell Riel to stop that racket!"

I did so, and after he had subsided into silence, he came to his peep-hole and beckoned to me.

"I tell you — but, for the others — No!" he exclaimed in a hurried *staccato*. "I *must* read. The Spirit tells me — I *must*. I tell you — for fifteen years — it is since — that I have been a prophet on the Saskatchewan." This of course was a fable, and I knew it.

His confessor, Père André, was a constant visitor, with his unkempt beard and greasy cassock. This priest had left Brittany when quite young, to lead a hard life of exile amid far-off savages. His manners had become abrupt from much contact with the wily redskins. He was the very antithesis to the courtly abbé, of the glowing land of his youth.

A Medical Commission had been appointed to examine Riel as to the insanity alleged by his friends. When these gentlemen arrived, he was marched daily to the orderly-room, where the inquiry was conducted in private. Every one knows the result. I was standing by the open door of the cell, when Dr. Jukes, the principal medical officer of the mounted police, had a protracted interview with him. The doctor sat beside him for fully an hour, listening with exemplary patience to a random list of visions vouchsafed to the Metis apostle, which utterly eclipsed any of the mystic ecstasies of any ascetic of the Middle Ages. The doctor cross-examined him with considerable acumen; and it was amusing to note his skill in inveigling the astute Riel into contradictons. This arch-rebel, among a host of similar revelations, stated that St. Peter had appeared to him in the church of St. James at Washington, District of Columbia, and had ordered him to undertake his mission. This I heard him say.

I must say his conduct in prison was most exemplary, and he gave no trouble. Every request he made was most courteously worded. At 1:30 a.m., upon a certain Saturday, he requested me to endeavour to procure him some meat. Up till midnight he had fasted, as it was *un jour maigre*. Now, to look for meat in a prison during the small hours is about as forlorn a hope as to expect to find holy water in an Orange Lodge. However, I foraged among the cupboards in the corridor, and discovered a plate of hash, which I suppose to have been put away for some unfortunate to serve as a *bonne bouche* at some needed moment.

On the Sunday previous to his execution I was on guard, and formed one of the escort when he was taken out for exercise. On this occasion we proceeded to the square patch of ground between the orderly room and the guard-room. The officer strolled about on the side-walk, while we stood at ease, one at each corner. Riel walked between us in a diagonal direction. A covered-in platform had been put up in the yard, at the rear of the prison, with all the grim accessories of the coming ceremony. Presently he asked me, pointing, —

"Is that the scaffold?"

I said it was.

"Thank God!" he exclaimed theatrically, "I do not fear the scaffold."

Then he grew excited, and appealed to the officers to send a telegram to his wife, who was at St. Boniface, the French suburb of Winnipeg. I remember the scene well: the figure holding the ball and chain on one arm, and gesticulating wildly with the disengaged hand.

Mass had been said every Sunday at a temporary altar in the prison; Riel and the other Metis were always present. The guard at this time was very strict, and the walls of the place were hung with boards, each bearing a whole string of commands. The guard-room was terribly overcrowded every night, after the picquet mounted. It was very small, and resembled any other such building anywhere. There were guard-beds on either side, with racks for the carbines at their head. A stove was in the centre. A table stood opposite the entrance, with pen and ink, and a book to record the visits of the orderly officer and the surgeon. Above the table was a shelf, and over the latter ticked an ancient clock, which was a perpetual curse to all the watches in barracks. The bugler sounded the calls by this official timepiece, which either lost or gained one hour in the twenty-four.

The steeds which we were obliged to ride on patrol at this time were execrable. They were a lot about to be cast. We were not allowed to take our own troopers, and every man had a fresh mount on each succeeding occasion. At last the date of execution was definitely fixed, and extraordinary precautions to prevent an expected rescue were taken. Dismounted bodies of men marched round the barracks at stated intervals through the night. Strong patrols, mounted, were continually scouring the surrounding prairie. The date of this historical event was set down as the 16th of November, 1885....

It was bitterly cold and densely dark when we turned out at half-past three on the eventful morning, and stumbled over half-asleep to the stables, where a dingy lantern was flashing about. We saddled our horses in silence. Early as it was, Colonel Irvine was here to inspect us, after we had mounted. The only road from the town, now, came past the rear of Government House, as the other bridge had been destroyed. We were ordered to proceed to Mr. Dewdney's residence and take up our station on the trail at that point, and to allow no one to approach the barracks who did not possess a pass properly signed. We rode in half-sections past the guard-room and out into the gloom of the prairie. On our way to the bridge across the creek, we met the two priests, who were to attend upon Riel during his last moments, driving from town in a buckboard. The frost was very keen this morning, and our feet, in boots and spurs, suffered severely. When dawn stole gently over the plain, everything was white with hoar-frost. It was a magnificent sunrise! And on this heavenly morning, Louis David Riel was to look his last upon these prairies which he had loved so well. We rode quietly up and down, and whenever any object appeared we made it an excuse for a stirring gallop. When the sun had risen, we could see the polished arms of the sentries — a perfect ring — around the barracks. Scouts were out in every direction, trotting off in the distance. Bugle-calls rang out in the clear air. An inner cordon of fifty men was posted around the guard-room at seven, and at the same hour a party of forty men, mounted, drew up at the end of the bridge opposite to us.

A crowd of people could now be seen advancing along the level plain from Regina, whose white houses were bright in the sunshine. Men on foot, on horseback, in buckboards, buggies, and "democrats," hurried along. There were visitors from Montreal, Toronto, Ottawa, and Winnipeg, and even from British Columbia. Those who were without passports were turned back, and we drew our horses across the trail, while the non-com examined the papers. There was a good deal of pleasant chaff, and the voice of the great Nicholas Flood Davin, now member for Assiniboia, in the Dominion House — more power to his elbow! — was heard in the land; the brogue of the emerald isle sounding rich and racy. After the crowd had cleared away, a great silence seemed to have filled the air, save for the horses champing their bits and pawing the hard ground.

The *Regina Leader* gave the most minute description of the final scene in this drama, which has been of such importance in the history of the young Dominion.

Mr. Gibson, the deputy-sheriff, entered the condemned cell a few minutes before eight, and informed Riel that his hour had come. The latter turned ashy pale as soon as he realized his position, but braced himself together as well as he could. The procession was now formed. Riel was placed between Father McWilliams, who was first, and Père André, who was behind him. Mr. Gibson led the way. After this, Mr. White Fraser, who was our orderly officer, and ten men of the guard followed. Colonel Irvine and other officers of the mounted police, Dr. Jukes, and four members of the press brought up the rear. They ascended by steps to a room above the guard-room, which ran the entire length of the building. At the far end was a window, and through this was the scaffold. As they passed along, Riel exclaimed, *"courage, mon père!"*

The hangman was Jack Henderson, who had been a former prisoner of Riel at Fort Garry in 1869. Verily the tables were turned with a vengeance! He was waiting on the platform. Before stepping out upon this, the priests and the prisoner knelt down in prayer; all, except the guard, removing their hats. Riel made the responses in a firm voice. His whole demeanour betokened suppressed excitement; his brow was covered with beads of perspiration, while he held a crucifix which had been lent to him by Madame Forget, the wife of the clerk to the N.W. Council. At twenty-six minutes past eight, the deputy-sheriff touched father McWilliams on the shoulder, as an intimation that the time was up. Père André told Riel that they must cease. They all rose, and Père André asked the doomed man if he were at peace with all men. Riel answered in the affirmative.

"Do you forgive all your enemies?"

"Yes."

Riel then asked if he might speak, but he was advised not to do so. He then received the kiss of peace from both priests, and Father André exclaimed —

"Alors, allez au ciel!"

While conversation was in progress, Henderson had been engaged in pinioning the prisoner's arms. Dr. Jukes, Colonel Irvine, with the two priests, and two of the newspaper-men went out upon the platform. Riel was placed upon the drop, where his legs were pinioned and the rope adjusted. His last words were to say good-bye to Dr. Jukes and to thank him for his kindness, and, just before the white cap was pulled over his face, he said —

"Remerciez Madame Forget."

While he was praying the trap was pulled. Death was instantaneous. His pulse ceased beating four minutes after the trap-door fell. Thus ended the man who had inaugurated and carried out two rebellions.

Harriet Jephson

Lady Harriet Julia (Campbell) Jephson, who had spent much of her early life in Canada, was an inveterate traveller and commentator on the British Empire. A staunch imperialist, she contributed articles to many British magazines, this one appearing in National Review, *21 (1893): 51-57.*

The French Canadian Habitant

There is no peasant so much attached to tradition as the French Canadian. He finds himself on a continent whose moving spirit is that
of progression. The rest of the American world is more or less given
up to electric-tramway cars, elevated railways, and other abomina-
tions. Factory chimneys belch forth their disfiguring smoke, and
saw-mills rend the air with hideous noises, within touch, almost, of
the quaint picturesque French villages which lie nestling to the south
of the St. Lawrence. The contiguity of progress and push, of manufacture and wealth, in no wise affects the unambitious *habitant*. He
teems with contentment and philosophy. Has he not a decent farm, a
tidy cottage, a good wife, an enormous progeny, and a *curé* to help
him on his road to heaven? Is it not possible, also, to put by a little
money each year towards his old age — enough to procure for him
and his a decent burial, and to pay for masses, in the sad by-and-by?
What more can a man want? Jacques Bonhomme has a supreme belief in himself and his belongings, in his country and its constitution.
A poor *habitant* (so the story goes) went to Quebec, and was taken by
a friendly priest to see the sights of the city. In a convent church he
saw a large painting of David and Goliath. Jacques fixed his gaze ad-
miringly on Goliath. "Ah!" said he, "what a fine man!" "Yes," said
the *curé*: "it is a fine man." "Magnificent!" said Jacques; then paused.
"I suppose he was a French Canadian?" "*Bien, oui!*" retorted the
priest, not liking to disappoint the patriot. "O, yes! Goliath was a
French Canadian."

This strikes the key-note of the French Canadian character.
Where people are self-complacent enough to believe themselves
perfect, they do not need to seek improvement, nor do they strain
after higher ideals. The *habitant* sees no reason to complain of himself

or of his position: he believes implicitly in the wisdom of his fore-fathers, and remains the most picturesque and only historical figure on the continent of North America. He farms his own acres, owes allegiance to no man besides his priest, builds his cottage on the ancient Norman model, and looks upon all new-fangled inventions (such as steam-ploughs and threshing-machines) as creations of the Devil. Although more than a century has elapsed since the British standard was unfurled in the Citadel of Quebec, the *habitant* remains as French as his ancestors were the day they left their country. This, too, on a continent where the English, the Irish, and the Scotch, merge their national characteristics in the course of thirty years into those of the ubiquitous Yankee. Jacques, happy in coming under the rule of a generous conqueror, has preserved his language, his laws, and his religion, intact; and he has gratitude enough to value the liberty given him by his English rulers and to make him the strongest opponent of Annexation in Canada.

The French Canadian peasantry are descendants of the hardy men brought to American shores by Champlain over 200 years ago. Their forefathers were, for the most part, mariners, and the French Canadian of today retains traces of his origin in his peculiar phraseology. No true-born *habitant* would use the verb *monter* as applied to a *voiture*: *embarquer* would be his word: and there are many idioms in hourly use which are essentially and strangely nautical. The *patois* of the French Canadian peasant has long been the subject of discussion and research; but there seems little reason to doubt that it is the dialect spoken by his Norman ancestors 200 years ago. Conservative in this, as in all else, the French Canadian has preserved the dialect of his forefathers; whilst his French cousin of today has kept pace with the times and drifted into more modern forms of speech. The *habitant*'s accent leaves much to be desired as regards beauty, and in this respect he shares the fate of his compatriot the English Canadian. American air does not seem to favour the cultivation of soft voices and graceful modes of speech. Our good friend Jacques has a shrill voice, and ugly forms of expression: he calls his wife a "*créature*" and his daughter a "*figue.*"

The *habitants* of Canada are chiefly confined to the Province of Quebec, by far the elder province in point of colonization, and assuredly the more interesting as regards physical beauty and historical association. From the Gulf, all the way up the wonderful St. Lawrence, the river's banks are dotted with innumerable white houses and villages. Enter any of these, and you find yourself transported to old-world and time-honoured institutions. Here are veritable Norman cottages, steep-roofed, with dormer windows, wide and deep chimneys, picturesque rafters. Cross the road and you see an oven of ancient construction; hard by, a wayside cross, before which the devout peasant kneels in prayer for a good harvest. In the middle of the village stands the church, severely whitewashed, with a red-tiled roof and a picturesque steeple. Glance behind it and you see the *curé's* neat cottage, and his reverence (arrayed in black *soutane*) pacing his garden-walk. Stiff rows of holly-hocks, dahlias, and sunflowers, delight his soul, and are not out of harmony with his prim exterior. Be sure that a convent lurks somewhere near: convents and seminaries are the only educational establishments approved by the orthodox French Canadian. A glimpse over a fence reveals demure nuns super- intending the recreation of convent-bred misses, and the white goffered caps and black robes make us breathe the atmosphere of Old France. The avenues of poplar trees planted by the early settlers in memory of their beloved country help the illusion. On all sides we have evidence of the deep love for his mother country, the reverence for tradition, the piety, and the extreme contentment, which mark the French Canadian character. The *habitant* lives longer than his ambitious, restless neighbour over the border; his digestion lasts; his temperament is placid, and his temper is good. When he sins, he wipes out his transgression by comfortable penance, and when he falls ill he makes a pilgrimage to "La bonne Ste. Anne."

The *habitant* works hard all summer in the fields, and when the winter's snow covers his land he sets to with a will to make boots of cured bullocks' hide (with uppers of sheepskin) for his numerous family. A skilful mechanic, he makes his own hay-carts and rakes, turns out his own furniture, cures the tobacco grown in his garden, salts his own pork, and builds his own house. Curiously enough, gardening is the one pursuit considered derogatory by the French Canadian. It is thought fit only for his women and children. Vegetables are not much cultivated for home consumption, and are usually intended for market purposes. The *habitant* lives chiefly on rye-bread, sour milk, fat pork, and potatoes. Maple sugar, eggs, and fish are appreciated; but fresh meat is little in demand. Omelettes and pancakes, as in France, are reserved for high days and holidays; and, although the present race of French Canadian women possess infinitely less skill or knowledge in cookery than their French sisters, they can generally toss a pancake with the best of them.

All good *habitants* marry young. Edwin is not usually more than twenty when he woos his Angela of seventeen. Enormous families follow; but they are looked upon as blessings in these lands of vast acreage, and Jacques' bitterest taunt is reserved for the luckless wight cursed with the empty cradle. Owing to the prevalence of Canadian cholera, infant mortality in Canada during the hot summer is great; and thus the tendency to over-population is somewhat balanced.

The good wife is no drone in the *habitant* hive. She spins and weaves, making cloth and flannel for her children's clothes, and putting by blankets, sheets, and rough towelling for her daughters' *dot*. She dries rushes, and during the long winter evenings she plaits hats for her family. She knits wool of her own spinning into socks and stockings, and shapes and makes the simple skirts and jackets which her girls wear, and the loose trousers and shirts which clothe her lads. In point of thrift she is not behind her ancestors. Living amid an improvident, extravagant English population, she remains as careful and economical as ever. If an English family come to spend a summer in a French Canadian cottage, Jeanne turns out with all her children into a sort of *dépendance*, taking her spinning-wheel and cradles with her. She petitions the cook for tea-leaves, set apart otherwise for the dust-heap, dries them, and stores them gainst the winter. She asks for the cast-off and useless clothes, tears them into rags, dips them in home-made dyes, and weaves the strips together, by means of a strong twine, into a firm and useful carpet, called "catalan". Her instincts, if immature, are artistic. There is no attempt at tawdry ornament nor gaudy cheapness, no terrible antimacassar. The walls of the kitchen (which is also the living-room) are of pitch-pine, and the ceiling is made picturesque by rafters. Generally a little staircase, painted deep-red, leads from one corner of the kitchen to the rooms above. The fireplace is open, and much what one sees in Norman cottages. The chairs, severe but suitable, are made of unpainted wood, which by constant use has assumed a rich tone and polish. The spinning-wheel and distaff gives an air of quaintness to the room, and two rocking-chairs lend the one touch of comfort. Underneath the table is a strip of bright "catalan"; over the chimney-piece is a black wooden cross; near it, a print of Ste. Veronica's Veil. Pio Nono's portrait is in every good French Canadian's house. He has not yet seemed to grasp the fact that another man sits in the chair of St. Peter. The bedrooms are usually small, carpeted with "cata-lan," curtained with homespun material, and having huge four-posters with feather beds and bolsters of great height.

Compared with most peasantry, the French Canadians are won-derfully clean in their houses and persons. Unlike most peasantry, they nearly all ride in their own carriages. On market-days those liv-ing outside towns jog long distances in their carts to sell their pro-duce. There can scarce be a more picturesque sight (be it even the Piazza dell' Erba at Verona or the Campo del Fiori at Rome) than the old Quebec market-place as it was a few years ago, with its rows of covered carts drawn up side-by-side, and filled with little bright-eyed French women offering their wares for sale. Lamb, butter, eggs, cheese, maple sugar, syrup, homespun cloth, and home-grown vegetables form the staple commodities of the *habitant*.

The ambition of every well-to-do farmer is to have an *avocat* in his family, or a priest; and where enough money can be scraped together to send an olive-branch to a seminary, great are the rejoicings of these simple people. All French Canadians are deeply religious. As a rule their priests are singularly pure in their lives, and wholesome in their doctrines. They are often men of deep learning, and not infre-quently of cultivated tastes. They are not devoid of humour. A trou-blesome parishioner roused his *curé* at uncanonical hours to baptize his new-born child. The *habitant* (Gouin by name) had driven some distance in order to have his baby received without delay into the bosom of Mother Church, and was not to be baulked. The *curé* de-murred, grumbled, and at last consented, on the condition that he should name the child. Gouin was enchanted, and heard with com-placence the name of *"Marin"* given to his baby. As he jogged home-wards he coupled the names together: "Marin Gouin, Marin Gouin." "*Sacre bleu!*' cried he: "he has christened my child '*Mos-quito*'!" Many have journeyed once in their lives to Rome, and brought back the memory of experiences which last all their lives, and furnish many a tale to amaze "the gazing rustics ranged around." They are all intensely patriotic, and pride themselves on the immeas-urable superiority of Canada, in point of scenery, climate, and con-stitution, to the rest of the world. In time of cholera or of fever the priests have proved themselves worthy successors of the heroic band of Recollet fathers who bore the toil and burden of the day two hun-dred years ago.

The chief religious *fête* is that of St. Jean Baptiste. Not even in Papal Italy is the procession more picturesque. Emblematic cars and various bands playing the air of *"A la Claire Fontaine"* for part of the procession; but all the interest centres in St. John, who is personated by a small lad wearing a golden wig, dressed in sheepskins, carrying a crook, and accompanied in his car by a lamb. Another great day is that of *Fête de Dieu*, in which the Host is carried through the streets to various stations, all prostrating themselves before it. Very picturesque, too, are the ceremonies in connection with the first Communion. Troops of little girls in white muslin frocks, wearing white gloves, and caps covered with white veils, are to be seen, accompanied by proud mothers and fathers, walking about the streets.

Poor as he is, the French Canadian is not without his national literature, which takes the form of songs. Every *habitant* loves his fiddle, and in fiddling finds his chief amusement when the labours of the day are over. These lays are often curiously Baccanalian: in contrast with the habits of those who sing them. In M. de Gaspé's valuable book, *Les Anciens Canadiens*, I find two good examples of the style I mean. —

> "Oui! j'aime à boire, moi:
> C'est là ma manie
> J'en conviens de bonne foi.
> Chacun a sa folie:
> Un buveur vit sans chagrin
> Et sans inquiètude:
> Bien fêter le dieu du vin,
> Voilà sa seule étude," etc.

Another, better known than any I have here quoted, begins as

> "Derrier chez nous, ya-t-un étang,
> En roulant ma boule,"

And the montonous refrain is

> "En roulant ma boule, roulant."

The manners of the French Canadian are superior to those of his English compatriot in the same rank of life. He condescends on occasions to say "Monsieur" and "Madame"; but he is also absolutely devoid of any feeling of social inferiority, and merely gives these titles from a sense of politeness, and as he would do to his equals. Without the slightest taint of Republicanism or of Communism, the *habitant's* views find expression in John Bull's lines:

"When Adam dolve and Eve span,
Who was then the gentleman?"

In a country where all men work, the only distinction between classes, recognizable to him, is that of wealth and poverty, which he understands. With all his simplicity, M. Jacques is keenly alive to the advantages of money, and no Jew can drive a better bargain.

With the upper class of French Canadians (descendants of the *ancienne noblesse* who fled from the horrors of the guillotine and Reign of Terror) it is not within the province of this article to deal. I may say, however, without undue digression, that there are many French Canadian *seigneurs* who received their lands earlier than the French Revolution, under charters of Louis XIV and Louis XV; and life and death were placed in their power.

The *habitant*, however, is menaced with a change from his idyllic stagnation. The overflow of French Canadian population is gradually finding its way to the broad lands of Manitoba. Here a struggle for supremacy between the English and the French recently began. The *habitant* wished to apply his limited views of life. He insisted, besides, on a dual language, and that French should be taught in the schools. Fearful lest the priesthood should become all-powerful, as in the Province of Quebec, and the laws be framed exclusively for the French population, the English Canadian resisted. In the end the Englishman triumphed; but time alone can show how far the French Canadian transplanted to Manitoba will assimilate with English ways. In the province of Quebec he stands alone as

"One in whom persuasion and belief
Have ripened into faith, and faith become
A passionate intuition: — "

faith in his God, faith in his forefathers, faith in himself, in his country, and his belongings. Where, in this doubting, sneering age, can you find a more unique personality?

Georgina Binnie-Clark

Born in 1871, in Dorset, England, and a journalist by trade, Georgina Binnie-Clark emigrated to Fort Qu'Appelle, Saskatchewan in 1905 to join some of her family who had become farmers. She created somewhat of a sensation, however, by the fact that, not contented to merely be a man's helper, she became a farmer. Equally sensational was the fact that she wrote about her experiences as a woman-farmer in A Summer on the Canadian Prairie *(1910) and* Wheat and Woman *(1914). And thankful we are that she did. For her memoirs are among the most enlightening and entertaining of their kind. Other females had written of homesteading life but usually in subservient roles; Binnie-Clark's memoirs are those of a landowner and farmer with all their attendant problems, to which are added those of being a female. The following extract is from* Wheat and Woman.*

Threshing

"Have you made any arrangements about threshing?' inquired our neighbour. "Because if you have not, Guy Mazey will take on your job and mine as soon as he has finished his own. It's only a small outfit, but he is a reliable chap and will thresh our crops as carefully as his own. Russell Haynes wants him to go there, but if you agree he will come straight through to us after he has threshed himself out, and then go on to Haynes and finish. I don't think you will do better. There aren't many outfits round this year."

I closed at once with this offer, and, with one's usual way of waving away the detail of responsibility, I considered the threshing arrangement made, and that I need think nothing more of it until the engine and gang came in at the gate. But there is a certain etiquette to be observed in the ceremony of threshing in Canada. Some eight days later I got belated on my way home from South Qu'Appelle and lost my way utterly and completely in the neighbourhood of home, until Charles Edward literally fell up against Guy Mazey's fence, and, guided by the barking of many dogs and a bright light, I came step by step to the comfortable cheer of Mrs. Mazey's kitchen. In the process of conversation I found that it was quite news to him that he was to thresh out the crop. It is probable in the dazzling brightness of the kitchen my greenness, standing out from the background of the pathetic darkness in which I had lost my way, stood me in good stead, since among the entire threshing-gang only one tittered audibly at my amazed discomfiture, and he was promptly shut up. I gladly shared the evening meal, and before Charles Edward and I were set upon the right road I had asked my host if he would be kind enough to thresh for me, and he had most graciously consented.

The charge was to be four cents a bushel for oats, and five cents for wheat; and he found all the stook teams. So that if one or both my teams were in the field he was due to pay me for the use of them; and the same law held good with the neighbours. But we were all more casual about payment in those days when threshing terms were comparatively low. In due course the engine arrived at my neighbour's, and Hilaria and I went over to make acquaintance with the Mazey family, who were always in the trail of their father, always choosing some form or another of work for play, and always happy. At that time they only numbered eight of the present eleven, and each seemed to have arrived within easy distance of the other. The eldest girl was driving a stook team, the eldest boy was fireman, the third girl had stooked from dawn till dark through the gathering of the harvest, and was still busy at one thing or another in the threshing field, whilst the second girl was at home preparing meals for the gang of fifteen men, and all the younger branches took care of themselves and each other. They were a healthy, jolly, friendly group, and in time we grew to know each other well. On that occasion I remember taking their photograph on my new camera, which to this day seldom registers a success.

Hilaria and I had more than one offer of help in the entertainment of our threshing party, but the only one she would hear of was Ella Carroll, the daughter of our neighbour, — the farmer and postmaster, Sam Carroll of Strathcarrol. We liked her because she was pretty, and we stood in no awe of her because she was only sixteen. Hilaria presided over the cook-stove, and Ella Carroll made scones by the hundred and raisin pies, apple pies, lemon pies, and all sorts and conditions of cakes just as casually and quickly as the average Englishwoman sits down and sews on buttons with an air of rest. I was henchman to Hilaria, and usually dispatched to fetch the meat and merchandise in the morning, and more meat and all the other things that had been forgotten from Fort Qu'Appelle in the afternoon.

For a day and a half all went merrily. The sun was generous indeed that year, and in October it was as deliciously warm by day as is the Riviera in April, and with bright, keen, moonlit, frost-kissed nights. The two new granaries had been drawn up side by side in the centre of the eighty-acre wheat-patch. The wheat was of excellent quality, plump, and of a deep gold colour, and hard as the shell of ripe nuts. In the bliss of ignorance we were unaware that it was freely sprinkled with wild oats.

"There must be three thousand bushels of grain," said Lal. "We have nearly filled the first granary, and that patch of cleared land looks to be barely one-tenth of the field."

But the fact was that those two granaries never contained a thousand bushels of grain. There is a simple table in Canadian farm statistics by which one can calculate, through the number of pounds of grain due to a bushel, the amount of grain in a granary by measuring the amount of space it takes up. The rule is to multiply length by breadth by height by eight, and cut off the final figure. Thus a granary measuring fourteen feet by fourteen by seven should contain one thousand and ninety-seven bushels of wheat. Oats and barley take up more space in relation to weight. As oats weigh but thirty-five pounds to the bushel and barley forty-five against the sixty pounds which should find place in the orthodox bushel of wheat, thus the threshing-charge for the coarser grains is nominally less, but really higher, than the charge for wheat, and the Canadian plan of feeding oats in sheaf saves the cost of threshing and renders the winter chore of stock-feeding considerably lighter as the beasts consume first the oats and then the more appetizing portions of the oat-straw, but there is always a considerable amount left over for ready-to-hand bedding. However, some farmers think that the waste which is entailed through the shelling of the oats in stack out-weighs the cost of threshing, and the greater number put aside sufficient sheaves for threshing to yield at least three hundred bushels. Wheat badly frozen or cut on the green side will fall below the average standard of weight to the bushel, but on the whole the method works out well, and its rule should be securely fixed in the memory of the grain-farmer. My ignorance cost me a considerable sum in more seasons than one, although I levelled up in one year through the ignorance or carelessness of the thresher-man. A new granary had been unsoundly built, and it broke down on its first journey out. It leaned slightly on its right side on an incline, and to its care was confided the grain drawn from a newly broken sixteen-acre field. The thresher-man debited me with three hundred and fifty bushels in that granary, but afterwards when I had sold three hundred and fifty bushels there remained between eighty and a hundred bushels, which I treasured for seed. The grain was sold on the street, and the dealers at the local elevator are the last in the world to err on the wrong side. The grain, too, was very fine, and perfectly ripe; but it must have weighed out at the rate of eighty-five pounds to the bushel to have accounted for the margin.

Apropos of the newly built granaries of my first harvest a story in connexion with bulk and space will serve to show how, among other things, stories grow on the prairie. A neighbour who had been working for Guy Mazey at that first threshing, and between then and now has managed to become the possessor of three farms, was driving his own stook team at my harvest of 1911.

The weather was fiendishly cold. Many of the gang were standing by one of the two granaries waiting for something in connexion with the engine to thaw out, and the topic of conversation was, as is usual at threshing-time, the quality and quantity of the grain.

"D'you mind the first year you came to the place, and Guy Mazey threshed you out, and charged you at the rate of a thousand bushels to each of them two granaries, an' you paid it?" he inquired.

"Not he nor I," I answered. "I'm not likely to forget my first year for many reasons, but, as a matter of fact, the grain was not measured at all. I paid Guy Mazey a hundred dollars spot cash on account, and he took my figure of weight from the return bills of the elevator net — not even *gross*. When it was all sold we calculated what was left for seed, and in the following spring I paid him the balance."

"Took the figures from the elevator weigh-bills! Golly! I wish all the threshing outfits would work out their sums that way. My returns ain't never once been quite up to the level of the threshing bill. Well now, if that ain't news to me! I've always heard tell that he charged you a thousand bushels each for them two granaries — an' that you paid it. Any you fellows heard the same?" he demanded.

"Sure thing! That's right," came the chorus.

To return to the threshing of 1905. On the second day down came a snowstorm.

"It's horribly annoying for you," said our neighbour, "but Guy means to shut down and pull over to Haynes. They have their wheat stacked, so it will thresh out all right in spite of the snow. But he is quite right not to risk this. We shall probably get the Indian summer after the snowstorm, which means six or eight weeks of very hot weather, so that if the grain passed into the granary in a moist condition it would probably shoot, which would be ruinous. He will pull in again directly he has finished with Haynes. But it's hard luck having the bother twice over as it were in your first experience of threshers."

"I don't know that I am so very sorry," said Hilaria. "It's a respite at least. And they are all very kind and nice, and really no trouble. As for bucking wood and drawing water, why two of them bucked enough for a week in an hour. And when I think of those harvest worthies looking on with their hands in their pockets, I feel one can't be too decent to them."

"Oh, they are pleasant enough," I allowed, "but it's the eternal cooking and smell of cooking. And then one's so awfully afraid that there shouldn't be enough when they come trooping in. Lal says it's a point of honour to do them magnificently — the farmers' wives do anything to outrival the reputation of each other. Every kind of iced cake beneath the sun — stewed fruit — canned fruit — whipped cream — junket and heaven knows what!"

"Don't take the slightest notice of Lal's fussiness," advised Hilaria. "He is either 'pulling our leg' or doesn't know anymore than we do. Yesterday just half an hour before dinner he came in with the tale that three of the men were Jews and wouldn't touch pork under any condition. I had two joints of pork in the oven, and of course there was no more room, so I had to draw on the beefsteak I had in reserve for supper — to say nothing of the extra annoyance and trouble at the last moment. And to crown it all — did *not* those three Jews eat pork? You should have seen them!"

The Indian summer followed the snowstorm, and in three days back came the threshing outfit. The little engine took things easily, and Guy Mazey had decreased the number of his gang, so that it was four days before they finished, but they were a quiet, well-behaved group of men, although drawn from many nations, and, barring the inevitable drudgery attached to the washing-up as well as the cooking of three heavy meals a day, they were no trouble.

It was on the last afternoon that I went down to the Fort to replenish our store of sausages for the final breakfast, and, taking the pace at the lazy will of Charles Edward, I only reached home just before supper. Hilaria met me on the veranda with cheeks aflame, and wrath in her blue eyes, which always seemed the bluer in the nearness of her blue overall.

"It is quite too bad of you not to have managed to get home before," she said resentfully. "There have been callers — troops of them! The first contingent arrived in quite the jolliest car just after I had finished laying the table for supper, and the last just as I was hoping the others were intending to depart. Cooking beefsteak for a dozen men is hardly a merely temporary occupation. Oh, it was humiliating! This beastly country — how I loathe it! My feet are sore with walking over the stubble last Sunday, and then standing for ever and ever on that greasy kitchen floor. And I had put on the hideous pair of shoes we bought at Lipton when we were waiting for the lost baggage. That was not enough — the threshers had left the basin that twelve of them had washed their hands in on the veranda just outside the front door. — And alongside were their towels. — You know their towels!"

"It does sound a little appalling," I allowed. "Never mind — I hope you gave them tea."

"Oh, I gave them tea, and they only stayed about half an hour, but it felt like eternity. They said they wouldn't have come had they known it was threshing, and that kind of thing, and I've no doubt they understood. But there was a man with them. And my blue overall, a skirt shorter than a petticoat — and those awful shoes!"

"You needn't worry about the overall," I consoled her. "I should never wear anything else if I were you."

"It's all very well for you to say nice things," she said ungratefully. "You weren't there."

"Who was the late arrival?" I inquired.

"Oh, Mrs. Dugald Bertie. She's charming!"

"Really! How?"

"Beautiful eyes. And at this loose end of the world *bien soignée*. She stayed quite a while after the others had gone, and was quite nice. I could almost have poured out to her about the shoes. Her gloves were most fasky — the Indians made them. She is coming again, and she wants me — that is, of course, *us* — to go down."

"If there are to be callers and so forth, I suppose we shall have to buy chairs and that kind of thing, shan't we?" I suggested.

"Oh, I don't know. There was no hint of 'Pleased to make your acquaintance' in the quite natural way in which they attached themselves to the bench and Tate's sugar boxes. I suppose the cheque-book having swallowed so many extraordinary camels lately has indigestion at the mere thought of the gnat-like proportions of tables and chairs."

"Go for a long walk," I recommended, "and for once let me finish getting supper, wash up, and prepare the breakfast. Did they come early for Ella?"

"Yes; she is going to a box-social. And if you don't mind I would rather hold on to my own chores this last night. But I really am getting a little played out."

Before noon of the next day the last bag from the last load of oats had been emptied into one end of the old granary. There seemed to be oats enough to last for ever, but our neighbour looked ominous.

"Not more than two hundred and fifty bushels," he said. "I'm afraid you will have to be buying in the spring. With so little hay this amount of oats won't tide you over. The old man never grew many oats, but he was the finest hay and wood gatherer in these parts. There is quite a good stack of oat-straw, which you must keep for feed, and just use the wheat-straw for bedding."

Guy Mazey departed in the trail of his outfit. He told me he was coming back to measure the grain, but he didn't come, and it was in this way I sent him a cheque for one hundred dollars on account, and suggested that he should take the weight returns from the weigh-bills received at the elevator, and I would pay him the balance. He accepted the suggestion in his quiet even way without even a lurking smile, and I hadn't the smallest idea it was a little unusual.

It was my brother's suggestion that we should start hauling at once, and, as everybody seemed to be waiting for all the money I could get, I agreed. It was chiefly owing to this that no work was done on the land that autumn, and what hay there was remained cocked in the sloughs. Meanwhile, every morning the wagon-load of wheat went into the elevator, and afterwards we cheerfully counted dollars.

Satirical and Humorous Sketches

Satirical and Humorous Sketches

Commentary

Canada is not now, nor ever has been, the overwhelmingly staid, serious-minded, self-conscious country that many observers, especially some vistors like Oscar Wilde and Charles Dickens, have made it out to be. Just as now we laugh at ourselves in the cartoons of Yardley Jones or the spoofs of Charlie Farquharson, so we have always, though perhaps less willingly, smiled at our pretentiousness in the humorous and satirical sketches of many excellent writers. Indeed, satirical writing, as all literary historians acknowledge, was what first put Canada on the literary map of the world. Thomas Chandler Haliburton, whose "Sam Slick" rivalled Dickens's Little Dorrit in contemporary popularity, was called and still retains the title, "Father of American humour"; his international popularity as humorist and satirist was only equalled (perhaps even surpassed) almost a hundred years later by another Canadian, Stephen Butler Leacock.

Both achieved their monumental success in much the same way: through original ideas and memorable characters, and by their skill in making local customs convey universal truths. In "Sam Slick" and his "soft sawder," and in Deacon Drone and Mariposa, Haliburton and Leacock created new and captivating situations and caricatures which, though set in early Nova Scotia and smalltown Ontario, evoked, in a gentle, non-threatening satirical mode, a familar aspect of human behaviour for readers far removed from the local setting. Sam and the Deacon were the kind of people whom readers were certain they knew, or had friends who knew them, in the flesh. And many modern readers still think so as well. Though some of Haliburton's satirical thrusts, in the context of "old colony" (Nova Scotia) Tory politics, "low" and "high" church wrangles, and social hierarchy, are now somewhat obscure, the general gullibility of his neighbours and the sly witticisms of his Yankee pedlar, Sam Slick, are as funny and relevant now as they were in the 1840s. Leacock, too, though sometimes impeded by an out-dated sexism and old-fashioned conservatism, vivifies human foibles and creates burlesque situations that still make us think and laugh.

When literary historians comment on Haliburton and Leacock they see them always as "humorists" or "satirists" — sometimes calling them "professional humorists" as they would Mark Twain. They are, in fact, the only two writers from this anthology's era to be consistently regarded as such. There were many other writers, however, who wrote occasional humorous stories and sketches or who, when writing novels and short stories, employed a humorous or satirical mode. They are what we might call (for want of a better term) "incidental" humorists.

Thomas McCulloch, for example, a Presbyterian minister and principal of Pictou Academy in Nova Scotia in the 1820s, contributed his *Letters of Mephibosheth Stepsure* to the *Acadian Recorder* in an incidental manner — not to become famous as a satirist but to chide his flock into submission and his renegade parishioners into repentance. His cleverness at caricature and his almost Swiftian satire gained him a readership beyond his immediate confines and well into the century, influencing even Haliburton himself. At the other extreme is Frances Brooke, who did set out to become a "literary lioness" and wrote what is considered the first Canadian novel. For her, wit and satire were part of a larger novelistic design; but they — especially in the chief character's tongue-in-cheek comments on Canadian society — are what gave (and still gives) it its greatest appeal. Frances Brooke was a cleverly facetious writer.

In between are three lesser-known writers whose occasional ventures into humour enrich the literature as a whole. E.W. Thompson was a prolific short-story writer, published voluminously in American magazines, the best of which, nearly always set in the Ottawa valley, are born out of his penchant for the "comic" situation. Robert Barr, even more prolific as a writer of romantic fiction, also gained considerable recognition as a satirist, both through his association with Jerome K. Jerome, editor of *The Idler* (a satirical magazine) and through a few short stories in which he departed from his usual plot-controlled fiction. All in all, whether we consider the contributions of our professional humorists or the many kinds of incidental humour produced in other forms, the field is ripe for enjoyment and discussion.

Further Reading

Fred Cogswell, "Haliburton," in Carl F. Klinck, ed., *The Literary History of Canada*, Vol. I. (Toronto: U. of T. Press, 1976), 107-15.

Gerald Lynch, *Stephen Leacock: Humour and Humanity*. Kingston: McGill-Queen's University Press, 1988.

Robert L. McDougall, Introduction to T.C. Haliburton's *The Clockmaker*. Toronto: McClelland & Stewart, 1967. ix-xvi.

Stanley E. McMullen, ed. "Thomas Chandler Haliburton," in *Canadian Writers and Their Works*. Vol. II. (Toronto: ECW Press, 1989), 26-76.

David Staines, ed. *Stephen Leacock: A Reappraisal*. Ottawa: University of Ottawa Press, 1986.

Frank Tierney, ed. *The Thomas Chandler Haliburton Symposium*. Ottawa: University of Ottawa Press, 1985.

Frances Brooke

Frances Brooke, who was born and died in England, lived in Canada for five years, 1763-68, while her husband was a military chaplain at Quebec. While there she compiled notes for what became the first novel to come out of North America: The History of Emily Montague *(London: Dodsley, 1769). She had already written several pseudo-novels in England and was, according to literary historians, "a literary lion of a minor order." Among the guests attending her farewell-to-Canada party were such celebrities as Hannah More, Miss Seward, Dr. Johnson, and James Boswell. It is her Canadian novel, however, that is now best known — mainly because it is the first of its kind. Epistolary in style — a series of letters to and from various fictitious people — it is both witty and subtly satirical, and reveals a great deal about Canadian society.*

The History of Emily Montague

LETTER 10
Silleri, August 24.

I have been a month arrived, my dear, without having seen your brother, who is at Montreal, but I am told is expected to-day. I have spent my time however very agreeably. I know not what the winter may be, but I am enchanted with the beauty of this country in summer; bold, picturesque, romantic, nature reigns here in all her wanton luxuriance, adorned by a thousand wild graces which mock the cultivated beauties of Europe. The scenery about the town is infinitely lovely; the prospect extensive, and diversified by a variety of hills, woods, rivers, cascades, intermingled with smiling farms and cottages, and bounded by distant mountains which seem to scale the very Heavens.

The days are much hotter here than in England, but the heat is more supportable from the breezes which always spring up about noon; and the evenings are charming beyond expression. We have much thunder and lightning, but very few instances of their being fatal: the thunder is more magnificent and aweful than in Europe, and the lightning brighter and more beautiful; I have even seen it of a clear pale purple, resembling the gay tints of the morning.

The verdure is equal to that of England, and in the evening acquires an unspeakable beauty from the lucid splendor of the fire-flies sparkling like a thousand little stars on the trees and on the grass.

There are two very noble falls of water near Quebec, la Chaudiere and Montmorenci: the former is a prodigious sheet of water, rushing over the wildest rocks, and forming a scene grotesque, irregular, astonishing: the latter, less wild, less irregular, but more pleasing and more majestic, falls from an immense height, down the side of a romantic mountain, into the river St. Lawrence, opposite the most smiling part of the island of Orleans, to the cultivated charms of which it forms the most striking and agreeable contrast.

The river of the same name, which supplies the cascade of Montmorenci, is the most lovely of all inanimate objects: but why do I call it inanimate? It almost breathes; I no longer wonder at the enthusiasm of Greece and Rome; twas from objects resembling this their mythology took its rise; it seems the residence of a thousand deities.

Paint to yourself a stupendous rock burst as it were in sunder by the hands of nature, to give passage to a small, but very deep and beautiful river; and forming on each side a regular and magnificent wall, crowned with the noblest woods that can be imagined; the sides of these romantic walls adorned with a variety of the gayest flowers, and in many places little streams of the purest water gushing through, and losing themselves in the river below: a thousand natural grottoes in the rock make you suppose yourself in the abode of the Nereids; as a little island, covered with flowering shrubs, about a mile above the falls, where the river enlarges itself as if to give it room, seems intended for the throne of the river goddess. Beyond this, the rapids, formed by the irregular projections of the rock, which in some places seem almost to meet, rival in beauty, as they excel in variety, the cascade itself, and close this little world of enchantment. In short, the loveliness of this fairy scene alone more than pays the fatigues of my voyage; and, if I ever murmur at having crossed the Atlantic, remind me that I have seen the river Montmorenci.

I can give you a very imperfect account of the people here; I have only examined the landscape about Quebec, and have given very little attention to the figures; the French ladies are handsome, but as to the beaux, they appear to me not at all dangerous, and one might safely walk in a wood by moonlight with the most agreeable French-man here. I am not surprized the Canadian ladies take such pains to seduce our men from us; but I think it a little hard we have no temp-tation to make reprisals.

I am at present at an extreme pretty farm on the banks of the river St. Lawrence; the house stands at the foot of a steep mountain cov-ered with a variety of trees, forming a verdant sloping wall, which rises in a kind of regular confusion,

"Shade above shade, a woody theatre,"

and has in front this noble river, on which the ships continually pass-ing present to the delighted eye the most charming moving picture imaginable; I never saw a place so formed to inspire that pleasing las-situde, that divine inclination to saunter, which may not improperly be called, the luxurious indolence of the country. I intend to build a temple here to the charming goddess of laziness.

A gentleman is just coming down the winding path on the side of the hill, whom by his air I take to be your brother. Adieu! I must receive him: my father is at Quebec.

Yours, Arabella Fermor

LETTER II
Silleri, Jan. 1

To Miss Rivers, Clarges Street.

It is with difficulty I breathe, my dear; the cold is so amazingly in-tense as almost totally to stop respiration. I have business, the busi-ness of pleasure, at Quebec; but have not courage to stir from the stove.

We have had five days, the severity of which none of the natives remember to have ever seen equaled: 'tis said, the cold is beyond all the thermometers here, tho' intended for the climate.

The strongest wine freezes in a room which has a stove in it; even brandy is thickened to the consistence of oil: the largest wood fire, in a wide chimney, does not throw out its heat a quarter of a yard.

I must venture to Quebec to-morrow, or have company at home: amusements are here necessary to life; we must be jovial, or the blood will freeze in our veins.

I no longer wonder the elegant arts are unknown here; the rigour of the climate suspends the very powers of the understanding; what then must become of those of the imagination? Those who expect to see

"A new Athens rising near the pole,"

will find themselves extremely disappointed. Genius will never mount high, where the faculties of the mind are benumbed half the year.

'Tis sufficient employment for the most lively spirit here to contrive how to preserve an existence, of which there are moments that one is hardly conscious: the cold really sometimes brings on a sort of stupefaction.

We had a million of beaux here yesterday, notwithstanding the severe cold: 'tis the Canadian custom, calculated I suppose for the climate, to visit all the ladies on New-year's-day, who sit dressed in form to be kissed: I assure you, however, our kisses could not warm them; but we were obliged, to our eternal disgrace, to call in raspberry brandy as an auxiliary.

You would have died to see the men; they look just like so many bears in their open carrioles, all wrapped in furs from head to foot; you see nothing of the human form appear, but the tip of a nose.

They have entire coats of beaver skin, exactly like Friday's in Robinson Crusoe, and casques on their heads like the old knights errant in romance; you never saw such tremendous figures; but without this kind of clothing it would be impossible to stir out at present.

The ladies are equally covered up, tho' in a less unbecoming style; they have long cloth cloaks with loose hoods, like those worn by the market-women in the north of England. I have one in scarlet, the hood lined with sable, the prettiest ever seen here, in which I assure you I look amazingly handsome; the men think so, and call me the *Little red riding-hood*; a name which becomes me as well as the hood.

The Canadian ladies wear these cloaks in India silk in summer, which, fluttering in the wind, look really graceful on a fine woman.

Besides our riding-hoods, when we go out, we have a large buffalo's skin under our feet, which turns up, and wraps round us almost to our shoulders; so that, upon the whole, we are pretty well guarded from the weather as well as the men.

Our covered carrioles too have not only canvas windows (we dare not have glass, because we often overturn), but cloth curtains to draw all round us; the extreme swiftness of these carriages also, which dart along like lightning, helps to keep one warm, by promoting the circulation of the blood.

I pity the Fitz; no tiger was ever so hard-hearted as I am this weather: the little god has taken his flight, like the swallows. I say nothing, but cruelty is no virtue in Canada; at least at this season.

I suppose Pygmalion's statue was some frozen Canadian gentlewoman, and a sudden warm day thawed her. I love to expound ancient fables, and I think no exposition can be more natural than this.

Would you know what makes me chatter so this morning? Papa has made me take some excellent *liquer*, 'tis the mode here; all the Canadian ladies take a little, which makes them so coquet and agreable. Certainly brandy makes a woman talk like an angel. Adieu!

Yours,
A. Fermor

Thomas McCulloch

Between December 22, 1821 and May 11, 1822 The Acadian Re-corder of Pictou, Nova Scotia, carried a series of satirical sketches which gained considerable popularity at the time and were reprinted in 1862 as The Letters of Mephibosheth Stepsure. *Their author was Thomas McCulloch, an unorthodox Presbyterian minister, who later became the first president of Dalhousie University. His* Stepsure Letters *anticipates the later humour of Thomas Haliburton, exhibiting a sure control of subtle understatement. In them the foibles of the Pictou people are laid bare and often delineated with a sure Swiftian touch.*

The Letters of Mephibosheth Stepsure

To the Editors of the Acadian Recorder,

Gentlemen,

Since I wrote you last, I stepped over one afternoon to converse an hour with my neighbour Saunders; who, as you may perceive, does not want rough good sense. Upon the same day, Puff's farm happened to be sold by Mr. Ledger. Puff is one of our great folks; and, as he says himself, has done a great deal to keep up the credit of the town. Indeed, few among us carried their heads higher than the Puff family; or expended so much upon dress, chaises, and other sorts of finery. But Mr. Ledger, who has also the credit of our town very much at heart, took a different view of the subject; and, by foreclos-ing the mortgage upon Puff's farm, interrupted his exertions to make us a respectable people.

When I was sitting with Saunders, the neighbours were returning from the sale in very gallant style; some in sleighs, and others on horseback; and all hurrying to Tipple's or some other public place in order to enjoy themselves a little, before they returned to domestic life. As they were galloping past my neighbour's one of his little boys, who was wonderfully delighted with their appearance, came running in, and asked his father to buy him a horse. Saunders, though a good natured man, is a little hasty; and withal, a deadly enemy to our townsmen's general practice of riding in chariots and upon horses; which he calls the abomination of the Egyptians. All at once, therefore, his hand was raised high for correcting uses: but, in looking at the size of the little chap, he forgot that he had been angry, and brought it down gently over his head; telling him to be a good boy till spring, and when Mortar the mason came to build the chimneys of his new house, he would get him a mare. At the same time Saunders observed, that, though I had written a great deal about the management of my farm, the chronicles of our town would be incomplete, if they did not contain an account of the management of my children. Many fine young families among us, he said, were ruined through the thoughtless folly and ill conduct of their parents. The youth of this country, he added, are acute and active; and, if they were only brought up as they ought to be, they would become judicious and respectable men: but many of their parents were fools; and their children, as might be expected, turned out to be rogues and vagabonds.

You must not, however, imagine that all our young people are wickedly inclined. Miss Clippit, though formerly a miserable sinner, is now, as she says herself, a very religious young woman. In her own opinion, she knows more about experiences and marks of grace, than parson Drone himself; and some of those who have attended her ministrations, even say that she can preach a better sermon. I could also mention many others, who, when they have no opportunity to frolic or play at cards, very punctually attend those night meetings where miserable sinners like Miss Clippit, all at once become uncommonly religious people: And, you may depend upon it, they do not attend without profit; for, when they go to Tipple's, which they do very often, they sing so many hymns over their grog that he frequently declares his own house to be as uncomfortable to him as parson Drone's church upon Sunday.

Indeed, our people do a great deal for the instruction of youth. All the Cribbage family, as soon as they are able to crawl about, acquire the first principles of arithmetic, the art of castle-building, and a world of ingenuity of different kinds, by means of the cards. The Sippits, too, as soon as they can handle a cup, are initiated into the mysteries of genteel life, by having tea parties and frolics for their little companions. When our youth get a little farther on, the boys are taught to saddle the mare and go errands; and also, to read and write a little under the tuition of Mr. Pat O'Rafferty or some other teacher as good. As for the girls, they are intrusted to Mrs. McCackle, who, I assure you, does ample justice to their education. Though this lady has never been at court; nor, indeed, farther into what is called the world, than to edge in at Sippit's of an evening, she knows all about fashionable life; and can teach our young ladies to talk as glibly, to sit as uprightly, and to walk as much according to rule, as any boarding school mistress can teach a boarding school miss. Besides, she gives them many other accomplishments no less valuable. When they return home to get husbands and manage families, they can paint flowers and make filligree work to admiration. They can also sing and dance delightfully; and some of them can even play upon the piano forte so well, that in frolicking times old Driddle is occasionally out of employment. As for cookery and other things connected with housekeeping, Mrs. McCackle and her pupils are careful to leave them to vulgar folks. Indeed, to act otherwise would be a violation of common sense; for were any rational person to see one of our fine young ladies in her Canton crapes, stooping over a tub, scrubbing a floor, or cooking a dinner; it would not appear less contrary to nature, than the sight of one of our genteel young farmers in his superfine, longtailed coat, ploughing or harrowing on a fine summers day.

With respect to the religious instruction of youth, also, our town is provided with a variety of means. Our old parson upon Sundays, preaches to all who are willing to hear him; and, indeed, upon other days too, he labours among us as much as the care of his own cattle and pigs will permit. Mrs. Sham and Miss Clippit, as I said before, are likewise labourers in word and doctrine. In addition to these, our town enjoys the ministrations of parson Howl; and also of young Yelpit, who lately converted and called himself to the preaching of the gospel; so that, upon the whole, our youth are by no means destitute of religious instructors. Mr. Drone, it is true, does not seem to relish the assistance of these helpers in the word; and Tipple, who dislikes the parson, says, that our clergyman has been all his life praying that labourers might be sent into the vineyard; and now when they are come, he is not satisfied. But my neighbour Saunders, who, since his conversion failed, holds them in utter abhorrence, declares that the whole seed and generation of them, are under the delusions of Satan; and no better than Muckle John Gib and Mrs. Buchan, who, with their ravings and nonsense, tried to lead silly people off their feet in Scotland: And that providence has sent them and their erroneous doctrine into our town, not for the improvement, but for the destruction of youth. Old fools, he says, gallop about the country, after them and their meetings; and, in the mean time, their children at home have liberty to run into every kind of mischief. And young people, too, who follow them, get into a notion that they are converted; when they are only lazy, idle vagabonds, fit for nothing else but singing hymns and cheating. That, if he had got his will, when Mrs. Sham bit her husband's thumb to the bone, he would have made her eat her own tongue to the root: And that, as for Howl and Yelpit, fellows as ignorant as his stots, he would send them to the house of correction; where, if they did not learn some sense, they would at least get the laziness squeezed out of them, and be of some use in the world.

How far Saunders' views and plans are correct, I shall not pretend to affirm. Nor, indeed, will any of your readers be well qualified to judge; till they peruse that part of the chronicles of our town, which directly records the life and ministrations of parson Drone and his helpers. From what I have stated, however, they will all perceive, that, if our youth be not very religious, it is not for want of public instructors.

In addition to these means of knowledge, many of our young people receive also reproof and correction in abundance. Some parents, it is true, do not flog their children at home; nor would they permit Mr. Pat O'Rafferty to correct them. And, indeed, no wonder; for when Pat was giving Judy her schooling, it cost her many a pair of black eyes. Puff and others of our gentlemen frequently say, that the poor little dears are not sent to a teacher to be scolded and beaten, but to get on with their education. It is certain, however, that all our youth do not serve such an easy apprenticeship. In Mrs. Grumble's family and among all her connexions, every thing begins with a grudge and ends with a scolding. When Mrs. Sham, too, returns from her meetings, her girls, as they well deserve, receive both scolding and beating for their neglect of family affairs: and Trot's sons, who always left the work when he went after the news, were, at his return, sure of a good pounding.

With some of these means of education our old parson was never well satisfied. For the cards in particular, he was at no time an advocate. In discussing this point he has frequently told us, that, before a religious man admit them into his house, he should be sure that their admission originates in a degree of good sense and piety, superior to the principles of those who have reprobated cards, as an amusement unfriendly alike to personal religion and sober education of youth. And, also, that, before any parent employ them as a domestic recreation, he should ask himself, if, along with them, he be willing to grapple with his share of that misery which they have entailed upon the world.

How it is with you in Halifax, I do not know; but the experience of our townsmen presents no encouragement to any rational man to be a great player at cards. Cribbage and a number of our gentlemen have frequent evening parties in each other's houses by rotation; where they empty the pockets of each other with much apparent good humour upon all sides. But the losers invariably return home in a rage; abusing the winners, and declaring that they had been invited, merely for the purpose of swindling them out of their money, in order to pay for their supper. Not that any of our genteel people are swindlers; for, you know, a cardplayer may fleece and even ruin his neighbour, and yet be as honest and honourable as any other gentleman like himself. But losses beget ill humour; and some how or other, ill humour discovers successful gamesters to be rogues. In our town, also, Swap, Truck, and other chaps of the same sort, are great hands for the cards; and between their amusement and drinking, swearing and fighting, frequently spend whole nights in Tipple's. But, though the happiness of a life of this kind be great, it is at times exposed to unexpected interruptions. Not long ago, it was reported among us, that, in the heat of one of their broils, the devil himself was so scandalised at their conduct, that he appeared personally to command the peace. The poor fellows, of course, were dreadfully alarmed; and talked of going to parson Howl to get themselves converted. But it turned out to be the brother of Mr. Gosling's black wench; who happened to be going past pretty early in the morning, and hearing the noise, looked in at the window to see what was the matter. When the truth spunked out, the chaps returned to their cards; and deferred their conversion, till they would be more at leisure.

With the frolicking part of the education of youth, our old parson was always displeased. In adverting to this point he has frequently said to us, "Young people need amusement; but both the nature and extent of their pleasures should be carefully watched. The youthful mind pants for enjoyment; and what it desires, it is prone to consider as the grand object of life. But in the present stage of human existence, beside enjoyment, there is much duty to be performed and adversity to be endured. Parents, therefore, by their own reason and experience, should correct the views and regulate the passions of youth; not mislead and inflame their minds, by the overweening indulgence of injudicious affection. Amusements ought not to be withheld from children: but every parent who loves his offspring so as to consult their happiness, will study to render their youthful pleasures subservient to the duties of life, and to that rational enjoyment for which life is designed. Parents who act in any other way, are the worst enemies to the happiness of their offspring; and their children will repay them with retributions of misery. It grieves me to say, that, in the experience of many of you, truth speaks for itself. What are those whose youth has passed away in frolicking amusements? Have they arrived at religion? at respectability in life? at the enjoyment of happiness? They are the idle, wandering, drinking, bundling part of the town; in youth, characterised by their follies; in old age, loaded with contempt and misery."

Though our people enjoy many a comfortable nap at church; whenever the parson preached upon this topic, almost every one imagined that Mr. Drone was pointing at him, and not preaching to other people only, as in ordinary cases; and, on this account, anger set all disposition to nod at defiance. To vindicate their own conduct, also, they would abuse the parson, as by far too hard upon young people. The Sippit family in particular, never failed to revile him for a bigot; whose narrow contracted mind made no allowance for the sprightliness of youth. He was of no use in the town, they said; except to give young people a dislike to religion: for he was never satisfied unless they were praying or poring over their Bibles. Religion, they would add, was not intended to make men miserable: And, accordingly, to show that they knew better than the parson, and would not be priest-ridden; when Mr. Drone preached upon training up children, the Sippits improved his doctrine by a tea party and frolic, which usually concluded with a bundling.

When the remarks of the Sippits were repeated to the parson; he would merely reply, that, perhaps, he might be a bigot: but that the point for them to consider, was, whether he had told them the truth; and whether, when they were misrepresenting him, they might not be cheating themselves out of that religion which they would find very necessary when affliction or death knocked at their door: "And let me tell you farther," he would say, "that a great deal of frolicking and a life such as human beings ought to lead, are utterly incompatible. Those who give the heart to pleasure are not lovers of God; and so it fares with them. They take the frolicking first; and leave their poring upon the bible and their prayers till a period, when these may afford them neither the improvement nor peace which their situation needs:" And sure enough, when Miss Sippit was lately attacked with the pleurisy, there was a sad to do in the family.

I formerly told you that Miss Dinah Gosling began to droop after Miss Sippit's tea party and frolic. This young lady, too, by dancing and bustling about to make her company comfortable, had overheated herself; and was in consequence seized with a cold, which terminated in a pleuritic affection. At that time, along with the disease, the thoughts of dying naturally occurred. Now, the person who contemplates the grave, endeavours also to look beyond it; and from a consideration of the future, insensibly turns to the recollection of the past. But to poor Miss Sippit the remembrance of frolicking times did not link itself with the grateful and desireable hope of future enjoyment. Her pleasures had perished with the using; and their place was occupied by a variety of thoughts, which neither brightened her prospects nor soothed her mind. Gladly she would have turned to evidences of her religious improvement; but memory interposed, and supplied her with the recollection of times in which a view of religion, as the essence of life and a preparation for death, made her miserable; and as a rude intruder, was banished by amusement: And though she had formerly supposed, that dying persons have only to be sorry for their sins, receive forgiveness, and then leave the world; now, she was very sorry indeed, and yet a stranger to hope.

Old Mr. Sippit, who is an indulgent parent, perceiving his daughter in this state of mind and upon the brink of the grave, was very much grieved. He told her not to distress herself: that she had always been a dutiful child; and was now going to a merciful father, from whom she had nothing to fear. But her own judgment marked her out, as a lover of pleasure, and not a lover of God: and though of religion in general her conceptions were crude; some how or other, she perceived distinctly, that death introduces retributions of justice, which are not blended with the forgiving fondness of doting affection. On this account, the cheering consolations of her father were administered in vain.

To relieve her mind, therefore, he next proposed to read to her the Bible. This, indeed, was an employment of which he was not very fond; for, when a boy, he had experienced that it always made him dull and melancholy. But he had heard that it was of use to persons who are dying; and though he did not exactly see how it could cheer up the mind of his daughter, he was very willing to try it, however disagreeable to himself. From what I have stated, you will perceive that the old gentleman was not very well qualified to make an appropriate selection of parts; and, indeed, when he was going to begin, he found himself puzzled. He recollected, however, that, when he and his friends had occasionally discussed religion over their wine after dinner, it was frequently remarked that the book of Proverbs contains a large fund of sound morality. It occurred to him, therefore, that, as his daughter was perplexed about her sins, he could not do better than teach her about her duty; and, accordingly, as an introduction to spiritual relief, he read to her the first chapter.

It is not necessary to tell your readers what the first chapter of the Proverbs contains; for, as they are not going to die soon like Miss Sippit, they do not need to be instructed. Besides, I am not sure, that any of them have the least curiosity to know. I can assure them, however, that, as the old gentleman proceeded, his daughter listened with increasing eagerness; and when he had concluded the lesson, he found that all the long speeches of Job's three comforters, did not produce so much misery, as the simple reading of the first chapter of the Proverbs, had planted in the breast of his child. She told him that it marked her character and sealed her doom. "I never," said she, "attended to the instructions of Mr. Drone: I am falling into the hands of the living God."

When matters were in this state; though the Sippits do not like the parson, they were glad to send for him: and, indeed, I may say, that, in our town, all who revile Mr. Drone, are very anxious to enjoy his presence, when adversity or death visits their families. By means of his instructions, the poor girl's mind became considerably composed. She was very penitent for the past, and hopeful for the future; and firmly resolved, that, if providence spared her, she would live in a very different manner. In a short time, her disease assumed a favourable appearance, and she began to recover. The parson then told her, that he had always viewed a death bed repentance, as a suspicious kind of religion; and now it became her to prove that her penitence had not been forced out by fear. The young lady's mind was in that chastened state which every person feels, when the cessation of severe affliction administers relief. She was, therefore, profuse in her professions and promises. At last, complete health returned, and with it the absence of all those gloomy thoughts which had alarmed her mind; and tonight, she is going to have a large tea party and frolic, to celebrate her recovery. Our old parson does not seem to be much disappointed. On mentioning to him the result of his labours, he only said, *Education which begins with frolicking, is not likely to terminate in godliness. But, though frolickers should live an hundred years, and rejoice in them all, let them remember the days of darkness; for they shall be many.*

With respect to my own children I would only observe, that I have always endeavoured to conduct their education, according to the directions of our worthy old parson; on which account, as well as for other reasons that were formerly stated, our townsmen consider me as rather an odd sort of man. The most of our people keep Mr. Drone, not to instruct them, but to preach to them upon Sundays; and except when they are sick or dying, they take special good care, I assure you, that he attend to his own duty, without interfering with any part of their management. I, on the other hand, have always been anxious to receive from him instruction as well as preaching; and I must say for our parson, that, in following his advice about the management of youth, I have every reason to be satisfied with the result. My children, though not perhaps as white as the old crow imagined her brood to be, are strangers to those habits which have forced many of our people to accept the sympathy of the sheriff; and from their general conduct, my spouse and I derive as much satisfaction, as reasonable parents should expect from youth. What instructions our clergyman occasionally gave me upon the subject of education, I may probably, at some future period, put upon record in the chronicles of our town.

Mephibosheth Stepsure

Thomas Chandler Haliburton

"Sam Slick" is perhaps the best-known fictional character in Canadian literature. His creator, Thomas Chandler Haliburton, was labelled by Artemus Ward "the father of American humour." Haliburton, born in Windsor, Nova Scotia, in 1796, was the first Canadian (indeed the first colonial) to be honoured by Oxford University for his literary achievement.

The "Clockmaker" series (twenty-two instalments) first appeared in Joseph Howe's Novascotian *in 1835 and 1836 before appearing in book form in 1836. It was followed by a second and third series in 1838 and 1840, all of which were combined in a single edition in 1849. The series went through some seventy editions in the nineteenth century, being very popular in the United States and Great Britain.*

The Clockmaker

I had heard of Yankee clock pedlars, tin pedlars, and Bible pedlars, especially of him who sold Polyglot Bibles (all in English) to the amount of sixteen thousand pounds. The house of every substantial farmer had three substantial ornaments, a wooden clock, a tin reflector, and a Polyglot Bible. How is it that an American can sell his wares, at whatever price he pleases, where a blue-nose would fail to make a sale at all? I will enquire of the Clockmaker the secret of his success.

"What a pity it is, Mr. Slick," (for such was his name) "what a pity it is," said I, "that you, who are so successful in teaching these people the value of clocks, could not also teach them the value of time." "I guess," said he, "they have got that ring to grow on their horns yet, which every four year old has in our country. We reckon hours and minutes to be dollars and cents. They do nothin' in these parts, but eat, drink, smoke, sleep, ride about, lounge at taverns, make speeches at temperance meetings, and talk about '*House of Assembly.*' If a man don't hoe his corn, and he don't get a crop, he says it is all owin' to the Bank; and if he runs into debt and is sued, why he says lawyers are a cuss to the country. They are a most idle set of folks, I tell *you*."

"But how is it," said I, "that you manage to sell such an immense number of clocks, (which certainly cannot be called necessary articles) among a people with whom there seems to be so great a scarcity of money?"

Mr. Slick paused, as if considering the propriety of answering the question, and looking me in the face, said, in a confidential tone, "Why, I don't care if I do tell you, for the market is glutted, and I shall quit this circuit. It is done by a knowledge of *soft sawder* and *human natur'*. But here is Deacon Flint's," said he, "I have but one clock left, and I guess I will sell it to him."

At the gate of a most comfortable looking farm house stood Deacon Flint, a respectable old man, who had understood the value of time better than most of his neighbours, if one might judge from the appearance of every thing about him. After the usual salutation, an invitation to "alight" was accepted by Mr. Slick, who said, he wished to take leave of Mrs. Flint before he left Colchester.

We had hardly entered the house, before the Clockmaker pointed to the view from the window, and addressing himself to me, said, "if I was to tell them in Connecticut, there was such a farm as this away down east here in Nova Scotia, they wouldn't believe me — why there ain't such a location in all New England. The deacon has a hundred acres of dyke — " "Seventy," said the deacon, "only seventy." "Well, seventy; but then there is your fine deep bottom, why I could run a ramrod into it — " "Interval, we call it," said the Deacon, who, though evidently pleased at this eulogium, seemed to wish the experiment of the ramrod to be tried in the right place — "Well, interval if you please, (though Professor Eleazer Cumstick, in his work on Ohio, calls them bottoms), is just as good as dyke. Then there is that water privilege, worth 3,000 or 4,000 dollars, twice as good as what Governor Cass paid 15,000 dollars for. I wonder, Deacon, you don't put up a carding mill on it: the same works would carry a turning lathe, a shingle machine, a circular saw, grind bark, and — " "Too old," said the Deacon, "too old for all those speculations" — "Old," repeated the Clockmaker, "not you; why you are worth half a dozen of the young men we see, now a-days, you are young enough to have — " here he said something in a lower tone of voice, which I did not distinctly hear; but whatever it was, the Deacon was pleased, he smiled and said he did not think of such things now.

"But your beasts, dear me, your beasts must be put in and have a feed;" saying which, he went out to order them to be taken to the stable.

As the old gentleman closed the door after him, Mr. Slick drew near to me, and said in an under tone, "now that is what I call *soft sawder*. An Englishman would pass that man as a sheep passes a hog in a pastur', without lookin' at him; or," said he, looking rather archly, "if he was mounted on a pretty smart horse, I guess he'd trot away, if he could. Now I find — " Here his lecture on *soft sawder* was cut short by the entrance of Mrs. Flint. "Jist come to say good bye, Mrs. Flint." "What, have you sold all your clocks?" "Yes, and very low, too, for money is scarce, and I wished to close the concarn; no, I am wrong in saying all, for I have jist one left. Neighbour Steel's wife asked to have the refusal of it, but I guess I won't sell it; I had but two of them, this one and the feller of it that I sold Governor Lincoln. General Green, the Secretary of State for Maine, said he'd give me 50 dollars for this here one — it has composition wheels and patent axles, it is a beautiful article — a real first chop — no mistake, genuine superfine, but I guess I'll take it back; and beside, Squire Hawk might think kinder harder that I didn't give him the offer." "Dear me," said Mrs. Flint, "I should like to see it; where is it?" "It is in a chist of mine over the way, at Tom Tape's store. I guess he can slip it on to Eastport." "That's a good man," said Mrs. Flint, "Jist let's look at it."

Mr. Slick, willing to oblige, yielded to these entreaties, and soon produced the clock — a gawdy, highly varnished, trumpery looking affair. He placed it on the chimney-piece where its beauties were pointed out and duly appreciated by Mrs. Flint, whose admiration was about ending in a proposal, when Mr. Flint returned from giving his directions about the care of the horses. The Deacon praised the clock, he too thought it a handsome one; but the Deacon was a prudent man, he had a watch — he was sorry, but he had no occasion for a clock. "I guess you're in the wrong furrow this time, Deacon, it ain't for sale," said Mr. Slick; "and if it was, I reckon neighbour Steel's wife would have it, for she gives me no peace about it." Mrs. Flint said, that Mr. Steel had enough to do, poor man, to pay his interest, without buying clocks for his wife. "It's no concarn of mine," said Mr. Slick, "so long as he pays me, what he has to do, but I guess I don't want to sell it, and besides it comes too high; that clock can't be made at Rhode Island under 40 dollars. Why it ain't possible," said the Clockmaker, in apparent surprise, looking at his watch, "why as I'm alive it is 4 o'clock, and if I hav'nt been two blessed hours here — how on airth shall I reach River Philip to-night? I'll tell you what, Mrs. Flint, I'll leave the clock in your care till I return on my way to the States — I'll set it a going and put it to the right time."

As soon as this operation was performed, he delivered the key to the Deacon with a sort of serio-comic injunction to wind up the clock every Saturday night, which Mrs. Flint said she would take care should be done, and promised to remind her husband of it, in case he should chance to forget it.

"That," said the Clockmaker, as soon as we were mounted, "that I call 'human natur'! Now that clock is sold for 40 dollars — it cost me jist 6 dollars and 50 cents. Mrs. Flint will never let Mrs. Steel have the refusal — nor will the Deacon larn until I call for the clock that having once indulged in the use of a superfluity, how difficult it is to give it up. We can do without any article of luxury we have never had, but when once obtained, it isn't in human natur' to surrender it voluntarily. Of fifteen thousand sold by myself and partners in this province, twelve thousand were left in this mannner, and only ten clocks were ever returned — when we called for them they invariably bought them. We trust to 'soft sawder' to get them into the house, and to 'human natur' that they never come out of it."

E.W. Thomson

Edward William Thomson was a prolific writer, much of his work being of the journalistic kind (stemming from his editorship of the Toronto Globe*) and much more being for juvenile readers. He was editor of the American juvenile magazine* Youth's Companion *and produced hundreds of stories for that magazine and others like it. He published only one book of fiction for adults,* Old Man Savarin and Other Stories *(1895), but that brought him literary acclaim. He was praised for being a master of the short story form and a pioneer of literary realism in Canada. The following story is from* Harper's Weekly *35 (July 25, 1891): 558.*

The Privilege of the Limits

"Yes, indeed, my grandfather wass once in jail," said old Mrs. McTavish, of the county of Glengarry, in Ontario, Canada; "but that wass for debt, and he wass a ferry honest man whateffer, and he would not broke his promise — no, not for all the money in Canada. If you will listen to me, I will tell chust exactly a true story about that debt, to show you what an honest man my grandfather wass.

"One time Tougal Stewart, him that wass the poy's grandfather that keeps the same store in Cornwall to this day, sold a plough to my grandfather, and my grandfather said he would pay half the plough in October, and the other half whateffer time he felt able to pay the money. Yes, indeed, that was the very promise my grandfather gave.

"So he was at Tougal Stewart's store on the first of October early in the morning before the shutters wass taken off, and he paid half chust exactly to keep his word. Then the crop wass ferry bad next year, and the year after that one of his horses was killed by lightning, and the next year his brother, that wass not rich and had a big family, died, and do you think wass my grandfather to let the family be disgraced without a big funeral? No, indeed. So my grandfather paid for the funeral, and there wass at it plenty of meat and drink for everybody, as wass the right Hielan' custom those days; and after the funeral my grandfather did not feel chust exactly able to pay the other half for the plough that year either.

"So, then, Tougal Stewart met my grandfather in Cornwall next day after the funeral, and asked him if he had some money to spare.

"'Wass you in need of help, Mr. Stewart?' says my grandfather, kindly. 'For if it's in any want you are, Tugal,' says my grandfather, 'I will sell the coat off my back, if there is no other way to lend you a loan'; for that wass always the way of my grandfather with all his friends, and a bigger-hearted man there never wass in all Glengarry, or in Stormont, or in Dundas, moreofer.

"'In want!' says Tougal — 'in want, Mr. Mactavish!' says he, very high. 'Would you wish to insult a gentleman, and him of the name of Stewart, that's the name of princes of the world?' he said, so he did.

"Seeing Tougal had his temper up, my grandfather spoke softly, being a quiet, peaceable man, and in wonder what he had said to offend Tougal.

"'Mr. Stewart,' says my grandfather, 'it wass not in my mind to anger you whatefer. Only I thought, from your asking me if I had some money, that you might be looking fir a wee bit of a loan, as many a gentleman has to do at times, and no shame to him at all,' said my grandfather.

"'A loan?' says Tougal, sneering. 'A loan, is it? Where's your memory, Mr. McTavish! Are you not owing me half the price of the plough you've had these three years?'

"'And wass you asking me for money for the other half of the plough?' says my grandfather, very astonished.

"'Just that,' says Tougal.

"'Have you no shame or honour in you?' says my grandfather, firing up. 'How could I feel able to pay that now, and me chust yesterday been giving my poor brother a funeral fit for the McTavishes' own grandnephew, that wass as good chentleman's plood as any Stewart in Glengarry. You saw the expense I wass at, for there you wass, and I thank you for the politeness of coming, Mr. Stewart,' says my grandfather, ending mild, for the anger would never stay in him more than a minute, so kind was the nature he had.

"'If you can spend money on a funeral like that, you can pay me for my plough,' says Stewart; for with buying and selling he wass become a poor creature, and the heart of a Hielan' man wass half gone out of him, for all he wass so proud of his name of monarchs and kings.

"My grandfather had a mind to strike him down on the spot, so he often said; but he thought of the time when he hit Hamish Cochrane in anger, and he minded the penances the priest put on him for breaking the silly man's jaw with that blow, so he smothered the heat that wass in him, and turned away in scorn. With that Tougal went to court, and sued my grandfather, puir mean creature.

"You might think that Judge Jones — him that wass judge in Cornwall before Judge Jarvis that's dead — would do justice. But no, he made the law that my grandfather must pay at once, though Tougal Stewart could not deny what the bargain wass.

"'Your honour,' says my grandfather, 'I said I'd pay when I felt able. And do I feel able now? No, I do not.' says he. 'It's a disgrace to Tougal Stewart to ask me, and himself telling you what the bargain wass,' said my grandfather. But Judge Jones said that he must pay, for all that he did not feel able.

"'I will nefer pay one copper til I feel able,' says my grandfather; 'but I'll keep my Hielan' promise to my dying day, as I always done,' says he.

"And with that the old judge laughed, and said he would have to give judgment. And so he did; and after that Tougal Stewart got out an execution. But not the worth of a handful of oatmeal could the bailiff lay hands on, because my grandfather had chust exactly taken the precaution to give a bill of sale on his gear to his neighbour, Alexander Frazer, that could be trusted to do what was right after the law play was over.

"The whole settlement had great contempt for Tougal Stewart's conduct; but he wass a headstrong body, and once he begun to do wrong against my grandfather, he held on, for all that his trade fell away; and finally he had my grandfather arrested for debt, though you'll understand, sir, that he was owing Stewart nothing that he ought to pay when he didn't feel able.

"In those times prisoners for debt wass taken to jail in Cornwall, and if they had friends to give bail that they would not go beyond the posts that wass around the sixteen acres nearest the jail walls, the prisoners could go where they liked on that ground. This was called 'the privilege of the limits.' The limits, you'll understand, was marked by cedar posts painted white about the size of hitching-posts.

"The whole settlement wass ready to go bail for my grandfather if he wanted it, and for the health of him he needed to be in the open air, and so he gave Tuncan Macdonnell of the Greenfields, and Aeneas Macdonald of the Sandfields, for his bail, and he promised, on his Hielan' word of honour, not to go beyond the posts. With that he went where he pleased, only taking care that he never put even the toe of his foot beyond a post, for all that some prisoners of the limits would chump ofer them and back again, or maybe swing round them, holding by their hands.

"Efery day the neighbours would go into Cornwall to give my grandfather the good word, and they would offer to pay Tougal Stewart for the other half of the plough, only that vexed my grandfather, for he wass too proud to borrow, and, of course, every day he felt less and less able to pay on account of him having to hire a man to be doing the spring ploughing and seeding and making the kaleyard.

"All this time, you'll mind, Tougal Stewart had to pay five shillings for my grandfather's keep, the law being so that if the debtor swore he had not five pounds' worth of property to his name, then the creditor had to pay the five shillings, and, of course, my grandfather had nothing to his name after he gave the bill of sale to Alexander Frazer. A great diversion it was to my grandfather to be reckoning up that if he lived as long as his father, that was hale and strong at ninety-six, Tougal would need to pay five or six hundred pounds for him, and there was only two pounds ten shillings to be paid on the plough.

"So it was like that all summer, my grandfather keeping heartsome, with the neighbours coming in so steady to bring him the news of the settlement. There he would sit, just inside one of the posts, for to pass his jokes, and tell what he wished the family to be doing next. This way it might have kept going on for forty years, only it came about that my grandfather's youngest child — him that was my father — fell sick, and seemed like to die.

"Well, when my grandfather heard that bad news, he wass in a terrible way, to be sure, for he would be longing to hold the child in his arms, so that his heart was sore and like to break. Eat he could not, sleep he could not: all night he would be groaning, and all day he would be walking around by the posts, wishing that he had not passed his Hielan' word of honour not to go beyond a post; for he thought how he could have broken out like a chentleman, and gone to see his sick child, if he had stayed inside the jail wall. So it went on three days and three nights before the wise thought came into my grandfather's head to show him how he need not go beyond the posts to see his little sick boy. With that he went straight to one of the white cedar posts, and pulled it out of the hole, and started for home, taking great care to carry it in his hands before him, so he would not be beyond it one bit.

"My grandfather wass not half a mile out of Cornwall, which was only a little place in those days, when two of the turnkeys came after him.

"'Stop, Mr. McTavish,' says the turnkeys.

"'What for would I stop?' says my grandfather.

"'You have broke your bail,' says they.

"'It's a lie for you,' says my grandfather, for his temper flared up for anybody to say he would broke his bail. 'Am I beyond the post?' says my grandfather.

"With that they run in on him, only that he knocked the two of them over with the post, and went on rejoicing, like an honest man should, at keeping his word and overcoming them that would slander his good name. The only thing besides thoughts of the child that troubled him was questioning whether he had been strictly right in turning round for to use the post to defend himself in such a way that it was nearer the jail than he wass. But he remembered how the jailer never complained of prisoners of the limits chumping ofer the posts, if so they chumped back again in a moment, the trouble went out of his mind.

"Pretty soon after that he met Tuncan Macdonnell of Greenfields, coming into Cornwall with the wagon.

"'And how is this Glengatchie?' says Tuncan. 'For you were never the man to broke your bail.'

"Glengatchie, you'll understand, sir, is the name of my grandfather's farm.

"'Never fear Greenfields,' says my grandfather, 'for I'm not beyond the post.'

"So Greenfields looked at the post, and he looked at my grandfather, and he scratched his head a wee, and he seen it was so; and then he fell into a great admiration entirely.

"'Get in with me, Glengatchie — it's proud I'll be to carry you home'; and he turned his team around. My grandfather did so, taking great care to keep the post in front of him all the time; and that way he reached home. Out comes my grandmother running to embrace him; but she had to throw her arms around the post and my grandfather's neck at the same time, he was that strict to be within his promise. Pefore going ben the house, he went to the back end of the kale-yard which was farthest from the jail, and there he stuck the post; and then he went back to see his sick child, while all the neighbours that came round was glad to see what a wise thought the saints had put into his mind to save his bail and his promise.

"So there he stayed a week till my father got well. Of course the constables came after my grandfather, but the settlement would not let the creatures come within a mile of Glengatchie. You might think, sir, that my grandfather would have stayed with his wife and weans, seeing the post was all the time in the kale-yard, and him careful not to go beyond it; but he was putting the settlement to a great deal of trouble day and night to keep the constables off, and he was fearful that they might take the post away, if ever they got to Glengatchie, and give him the name of false, which no McTavish ever had. So Tuncan Greenfields and Aeneas Sandfield drove my grandfather back to jail, him with the post behind him in the wagon, so as he would be between it and the jail. Of course Tougal Stewart tried his best to have the bail declared forfeited; but old Judge Jones only laughed, and said my grandfather was a Hielan' gentleman, with a very nice sense of honour, and that was chust exactly the truth.

"How did my grandfather get free in the end? Oh, then, that was because of Tougal Stewart being careless — him that thought he knew so much of the law. The law was, you will mind, that Tougal had to pay five shillings a week for keeping my grandfather in the limits. The money was to be paid efery Monday, and it was to be paid in lawful money of Canada, too. Well, would you belief that Tougal paid in four shillings in silver one Monday, and one shilling in coppers, for he took up the collection in church the day pefore, and it was not till Tougal had gone away that the jailer saw that one of the coppers was a Brock copper — a medal, you will understand, made at General Brock's death, and not lawful money of Canada at all. With that the jailer came out to my grandfather.

"'Mr. McTavish,' says he, taking off his hat, 'you are a free man, and I'm glad of it.' Then he told him what Tougal had done.

"'I hope you will not have any hard feelings toward me, Mr. McTavish,' said the jailer; and a decent man he wass, for all that there wass not a drop of Hielan' blood in him. 'I hope you will not think hard of me for not being hospitable to you, sir,' he says; 'but it's against the rules and regulations for the jailer to be offering the best he can command to the prisoners. Now that you are free, Mr. McTavish,' says the jailer, 'I would be a proud man if Mr. McTavish of Glengatchie would do me the honour of taking supper with me this night. I will be asking your leave to invite some of the gentlemen of the place, if you will say the word, Mr. McTavish,' says he.

"Well, my grandfather could never bear malice, the kind man he wass, and he seen how bad the jailer felt, so he consented, and a great company came in, to be sure, to celebrate the occasion.

"Did my grandfather pay the balance on the plough? What for should you suspicion, sir, that my grandfather would refuse his honest debt? Of course he paid for the plough, for the crop was good that fall.

"'I would be paying you the other half of the plough now, Mr. Stewart,' says my grandfather, comin' in when the store was full.

"'Hoicch, but YOU are the honest McTavish,' says Tougal, sneering.

"But my grandfather made no answer to the creature, for he thought it would be unkind to mention how Tougal had paid out six pounds four shillings and eleven pence to keep him on account of a debt of two pounds five that never was due till it was paid.

Stephen Leacock

In the 1920s through to the 1930s, Stephen Butler Leacock was one of the most popular and most critically-acclaimed humorists in the world. The acclaim began in 1910 with the publication of Literary Lapses *(a series of sketches that were published in periodicals as early as 1899) and was consolidated with* Sunshine Sketches of a Little Town *(1912). In a mixture of burlesque and social satire Leacock entertained and mildly chastised many thousands of readers around the world.*

Leacock was born in Swanmoor, England, in 1869, came to Canada as a boy of seven, was educated at Upper Canada College, the University of Toronto, and the University of Chicago. From the last institution he received a PhD in economics, which is what he taught at McGill for the rest of his life. But it was as a humorist-satirist that Leacock achieved a lasting fame. "Borrowing a Match" was first printed in Truth, *16 (Apr 22, 1897): 6; "My Financial Career" in* Life *25 (Apr 11, 1895): 238-39.*

Borrowing a Match

You might think that borrowing a match upon the street is a simple thing. But any man who has ever tried it will assure you that it is not, and will be prepared to swear on oath to the truth of my experience of the other evening.

I was standing on the corner of the street with a cigar that I wanted to light. I had no match. I waited till a decent, ordinary man came along. Then I said:

"Excuse me, sir, but could you oblige me with the loan of a match?"

"A match?" he said, "why certainly." Then he unbuttoned his overcoat and put his hand in the pocket of his waistcoat. "I know I have one," he went on, "and I'd almost swear it's in the bottom pocket — or, hold on, though, I guess it may be in the top — just wait till I put these parcels down on the sidewalk."

"Oh, don't trouble," I said, "It's really of no consequence."

"Oh, it's no trouble, I'll have it in a minute; I know there must be one in here somewhere" — he was digging his fingers into his pockets as he spoke — "but you see this isn't the coat I generally…"

I saw that the man was getting excited about it. "Well, never mind," I protested; "if that isn't the waistcoat you generally — why, it doesn't matter."

"Hold on, now, hold on!" the man said. "I've got one of the cursed things in here somewhere. I guess it must be with my watch. No, it's not there either. Wait till I try my coat. If that confounded tailor only knew enough to make a pocket so that a man could get at it!"

He was getting pretty well worked up now. He had thrown down his walking stick and was plunging at his pockets with his teeth set. "It's that cursed young boy of mine," he hissed; "this comes of his fooling with my pockets. By Gad! perhaps I won't harm him when I get home. Say, I'll bet that it's in my hip-pocket. You just hold up the tail of my overcoat a second till I..."

"No, no," I protested again, "please don't take all this trouble, it really doesn't matter. I'm sure you needn't take off your overcoat, and oh, pray don't throw away your letters and things in the snow like that, and tear out your pockets by the roots! Please, please don't trample over your overcoat and put your feet through the parcels. I do hate to hear you swearing at your little boy, with that peculiar whine in your voice. Don't — please don't tear your clothes so savagely."

Suddenly the man gave a grunt of exultation, and drew his hand up from inside the lining of his coat.

"I've got it," he cried. "Here you are!" Then he brought it out under the light.

It was a toothpick.

Yielding to the impulse of the moment I pushed him under the wheels of a trolley-car and ran.

My Financial Career

When I go into a bank I get rattled. The clerks rattle me; the wickets rattle me; the sight of the money rattles me; everything rattles me.

The moment I cross the threshold of a bank and attempt to transact business there, I become an irresponsible idiot.

I knew this beforehand, but my salary had been raised to fifty dollars a month and I felt that the bank was the only place for it.

So I shambled in and looked timidly round at the clerks. I had an idea that a person about to open an account must needs consult the manager.

I went up to a wicket marked "Accountant." The accountant was a tall, cool devil. The very sight of him rattled me. My voice was sepulchral.

"Can I see the manager?" I said, and added solemnly, "alone." I don't know why I said "alone."

"Certainly," said the accountant, and fetched him.

The manager was a grave, calm man. I held my fifty-six dollars clutched in a crumpled ball in my pocket.

"Are you the manager?" I said. God knows I didn't doubt it.

"Yes," he said.

"Can I see you," I asked, "alone?" I didn't want to say "alone" again, but without it the thing seemed self-evident.

The manager looked at me in some alarm. He felt that I had an awful secret to reveal.

"Come in here," he said, and led the way to a private room. He turned the key in the lock.

"We are safe from interruption here," he said. "Sit down."

We both sat down and looked at each other. I found no voice to speak.

"You are one of Pinkerton's men, I presume," he said.

He had gathered from my mysterious manner that I was a detective. I knew what he was thinking, and it made me worse.

"No, not from Pinkerton's," I said, seeming to imply that I came from a rival agency.

"To tell the truth," I went on, as if I had been prompted to lie about it, "I am not a detective at all. I have come to open an account. I intend to keep all my money in this bank."

The manager looked relieved but still serious; he concluded now that I was a son of Baron Rothschild or a young Gould.

"A large account, I suppose," he said.

"Fairly large," I whispered. "I propose to deposit fifty-six dollars now and fifty dollars a month regularly."

The manager got up and opened the door. He called to the accountant.

"Mr. Montgomery," he said unkindly loud, "this gentleman is opening an account, he will deposit fifty-six dollars. Good morning."

I rose.

A big iron door stood open at the side of the room.

"Good morning," I said, and stepped into the safe.

"Come out," said the manager coldly, and showed me the other way.

I went up to the accountant's wicket and poked the ball of money at him with a quick convulsive movement as if I were doing a conjuring trick.

My face was ghastly pale.

"Here," I said, "deposit it." The tone of the words seemed to mean, "Let us do this painful thing while the fit is on us."

He took the money and gave it to another clerk.

He made me write sum on a slip and sign my name in a book. I no longer knew what I was doing. The bank swam before my eyes.

"Is it deposited?" I asked in a hollow, vibrating voice.

"It is," said the accountant.

"Then I want to draw a cheque."

My idea was to draw out six dollars of it for present use. Someone gave me a cheque-book through a wicket and someone else began telling me how to write it out. The people in the bank had the impression that I was an invalid millionaire. I wrote something on the cheque and thrust it in at the clerk. He looked at it.

"What! you are drawing it all out again?" he asked in surprise. Then I realized that I had written fifty-six instead of six. I was too far gone to reason now. I had a feeling that it was impossible to explain the thing. All the clerks had stopped writing to look at me.

Reckless with misery, I made a plunge.

"Yes, the whole thing."

"You withdraw your money from the bank?"

"Every cent of it."

"Are you not going to deposit any more?" said the clerk, astonished.

"Never."

An idiot hope struck me that they might think something had insulted me while I was writing the cheque and that I had changed my mind. I made a wretched attempt to look like a man with a fearfully quick temper.

The clerk prepared to pay the money.

"How will you have it?" he said.

"What?"

"How will you have it?"

"Oh" — I caught his meaning and answered without even trying to think — "in fifties."

He gave me a fifty-dollar bill.

"And the six?" he asked dryly.

"In sixes," I said.

He gave it me and I rushed out.

As the big door swung behind me I caught the echo of a roar of laughter that went up to the ceiling of the bank. Since then I bank no more. I keep my money in cash in my trousers pocket and my savings in silver dollars in a sock.

Robert Barr

Robert Barr was born in Scotland in 1850, was brought to Canada as a very young boy, and lived there for nearly thirty years before moving to the United States where, for a few years, he pursued a career as a humorist with the Detroit Free Press. *He finally settled in England where he continued to write fiction and continued a career in humour by being associated with Jerome K. Jerome and* The Idler. *Though most of Barr's fiction is of the "social" kind (involving socialites in business and love affairs), much of it is written in a light-hearted vein, and is often satirical and sometimes very funny. His only Canadian novel,* The Measure of the Rule *(1907), is perhaps his best, the first chapter of which shows a deft satirical touch. The humorous story below is from* The Canadian Magazine *42 (1914): 267-72.*

How Finley McGillis Held the Pier

This is a story of war's alarms, and the agony that comes through man's inhumanity to man. It is generally supposed that it is upon the common soldier that the brunt of battle falls, but very often highly-placed officers are called upon to suffer for their country, and it is the pathetic tale of one of these war-dogs that I now set myself to relate, hoping that his heroism may thus retain a place in the annals of the land. If Madame History, after listening to my tale of woe, reserves a modest niche in the temple of fame for Captain Angus McKerricher, I shall be more than satisfied.

Of course, being the privileged historian of McKerricher, I should by rights keep silence regarding my own military exploits, but few of us are entirely unselfish, and so, having the opportunity, I may casually mention, seeing that no one else is likely to do so, that I fell gloriously in the defence of the Empire, yet no medal has been awarded me. As it is not yet too late to remedy this neglect of one of our bravest men, I may be forgiven for dwelling on this personal incident. The "Fenian Scare," as it was called, caused much expenditure of money and pine lumber. There arose all over our part of Canada, and doubtless in other portions as well, huge drillsheds whose style of architecture more nearly resembled the Country Fair building of later days, than it did the White City of the Chicago Exhibition. As I remember, the cost was defrayed somewhat in this way: any town or municipality patriotic enough to yearn for one of these military erections, got up part of the money and the general Government furnished the remainder. The township council pressed the button, and Parliament did the rest.

The drill-sheds were great oblong buildings made of pine, covered by a wide-spreading shingled roof. The floor was the original soil of Canada, which the building was constructed to defend. Under the ample roof, a regiment might have gone through its evolutions. Few of these drill-sheds now remain standing, although none, so far as I can learn, were destroyed by the valiant Fenians, the most terrible warriors with their mouths who ever struck panic into a peaceful people. The expanding roof (of the drill-sheds, not of the Fenians' mouths) offered too tempting a mark for the amateur cyclone roaming over the land, and thus there came a stormy day when the component parts of the building were distributed with impartiality among the taxpayers of that and the adjoining county, furnishing superb kindling wood for all the farmers to the leeward of the original site. So scatters military glory. I helped to build several of these historic structures, and one fine day fell from the apex of the one in Iona, Elgin County, my fall being happily broken and soothed by a pile of brick on which I came down, with the debris of a scaffold on top of me. When, today, people who know me confidently predict that I shall end on the scaffold, they little realise how near their prophecy came to being forestalled. Would it be believed that, up to date, Iona has put up no stone on the spot, with the inscription; "Here fell Barr in the defence of his country?" I mention this incident, not in hope of recognition or even with an eye towards a pension, but because it was through that fall that I am now the humble historian of McKerricher, for after coming out of the doctor's hands I came to the conclusion that carpentering was too exciting a business for a nervous person like myself, so I took to the literary life, and here I am.

It must not be supposed that we in Western Canada were not a military people even before the drill-sheds spread over the land either through my building or with the aid of the cyclones. We were always a blood-thirsty gang, and our military system has since been plagiarised by Germany and France. Service in the ranks was compulsory, and one whole day in the year was devoted to drill, the consumption of stimulants, and the making of effete Europe tremble. This memorable annual festival was the 24th of May, the birthday of the Queen. Unless a day in the middle of harvest had been chosen, no more inopportune time could have been selected than the 24th of May, so far as the farmers were concerned. The leaves were just out on the trees, the roads were becoming passable again through the drying of the mud, and spring work was at its height. It was therefore extremely inconvenient for farmers to turn their plow-shares into muzzle-loaders and go from three to thirteen miles to the village and revel in gore, yet the law made attendance compulsory. For years the rigour of military discipline had been mitigated by a well-known device. Some neighbour, at the reading of the roll, would shout "Here" when an absentee's name was called, and so the reports that went into the Government always showed the most marvellously constant attendance on duty that has ever gone on record. No wonder the Queen sat securely on her throne and was unafraid.

Thus the Empire ran serenely on until Angus McKerricher was made captain of the militia. I don't know why he was appointed, but I think it was because he was the only man in the district who owned a sword, which had descended to him from his Highland ancestry, doubtless escaping confiscation by the English soldiery, and was thus preserved to become the chief support to the British throne — certainly a change from its use in younger days. I was a small boy when Angus first took command, but I well remember the dismay his action spread over the district. Angus knew personally every man in the county, which, to parody Gilbert, was

A fact they hadn't counted upon
When they first put their uniform on.

The Captain's uniform consisted of his ordinary clothes rendered warlike by a scarlet sash looped over the left shoulder and tied in a sanguinary knot under the right arm, or "oxter," as Angus termed that portion of his body. But what added perturbation to the feelings of the crowd assembled on the parade ground was the long claymore held perpendicularly up the rigid right arm, the hilt almost down at the knee, the point extending above the head, as Angus stood erect with heels together and chin held high. Even the dullest of us could perceive that the slovenliness of our former captains, in happy-go-lucky style of deportment, was a thing of the past. We were now face to face with the real terrors of war, in the person of Captain Angus McKerricher.

The stout yeomanry were all drawn up in line, and beside the statue-like figure of the captain stood the town clerk, or whatever the official was who kept the roll of able-bodied citizens between the ages of eighteen and forty-five who were liable to military service. The day began with the calling of the names.

"Peter McAlpine."

"Here."

"John Finleyson."

"Here."

"Dugald McMillan."

"Here."

"Sandy McCallum"

"Here."

"Baldy McVannell."

"Present."

At this juncture the suddenly up-lifted sword of the captain stopped the reading of the roll.

"Baldy McVannell, step forward from the ranks!" was the sharp command of the armed officer. There was a moment's apprehensive silence, but no one stepped from the ranks, which was not to be wondered at, for Baldy was at that moment peacefully plowing his fields seven good miles away, and "Present" had been answered by his friend and relative, McCallum, who had varied the word from his own answer, "Here," the better to escape notice, a plan which had always been successful before. Deep was the scowl on the Captain's face.

"Put him down fur a fine," he said to the clerk.

"He's over the aadge," cried McCallum, who felt that he had to stand by his absent friend.

"He's neither over nor under the aadge, Sandy," cried the Captain with decision; "he's between thirty and forty, and he should be here this day, as he very well knows. Put him down fur a fine — a dollar."

An ignored law suddenly enforced carries consternation into any community. The infliction of these fines made a greater financial panic in our district than the failure of the Upper Canada Bank. More than two-thirds of the effective warriors of the township proved to be absent, and the commercial stringency caused by this unexpected clapping on of fines penetrated to the farthest bounds of the municipality. A dollar was indeed a dollar in those days, and not to be lightly parted with. However, such was the law, and there was no help for it; but the inflicting of the penalty did nothing towards increasing the popularity of the Captain, although it did increase the attendance on parade for many a year after. Vengeance came swiftly. It had been anticipated that it would take the form of a fight between McKerricher and one of the indignant friends of an absentee, as soon as parade was over and the friend had taken on board sufficient whiskey to make him quarrelsome, which was not as large a quantity as some of our temperance friends might imagine. There was Celtic blood in the locality and it flowed freely from punched noses on less momentous occasions than the day of the grand muster. After the dismissal of the troops, the Captain kept his good sword in his hand, and it was still too early in the afternoon for any to have courage enough to attack him with bare fists. That was expected later, for it takes time to reach the proper pitch even with potent Canadian malt. However, revenge presented itself to the Captain in strictly legal guise. A villager, learned in the law, engineered the matter, and the constable arrested McKerricher on the charge of carrying a knife with a blade longer than the statutes allowed. About that time there had become prevalent a villainous-looking dirk with a long sharply-pointed blade, which shut up like an ordinary jack-knife, but which had at the back of the handle a catch which held the blade rigid, once opened. This weapon had in more than one row, which would in ordinary circumstance have been innocent enough, proved disastrous, and a law had been passed to suppress it. No man was allowed to carry, concealed or in sight, any knife with a blade more than six inches long, and there must be no device that held the blade rigid. It was alleged that McKerricher's sword violated this ordinance, and that he had paraded the town with this illegal instrument in plain sight, to the terror and dismay of Her Majesty's faithful subjects, be the same more or less, in the case made and provided, &c., &c., in fact, I do not remember the exact legal phraseology of the indictment, but anyhow it was in words to that effect. In vain the Captain pleaded that the sword was a necessary implement of his new trade as militia officer, and that the peace and comfort of the realm had not been visibly interfered with through his carrying of it, but it was easily proved that he had retained his sword while not on duty, and that said instrument was knife within the meaning of the Act, its blade being more than six inches in length, firmly affixed to the handle aforesaid. The magistrate fined him five dollars, and administered a solemn warning from the bench.

"Cot pless her," exclaimed an indignant Northerner when the verdict was made known, "if she waants ta lah, let her have awl ta lah!"

In other words, if the law against absentees was to be enforced, let us also set the law regarding jack-knives in motion.

But it was the Fenian scare that brought out the superb Napoleonic qualities of Captain McKerricher, as great crises always develop the latent genius of notable men. "To arms!" was the cry, and everything that would shoot, except the blacksmith's anvil with which he used to celebrate the Queen's birthday, was brought into requisition. Shot guns, muskets and rifles were brought down from their wooden pegs along the hewn halls of the log houses. We youngsters were set at moulding bullets, and it was great fun. Every house possessed bullet moulds, iron arrangements like a pair of pinchers with metal cups at the business end, where a small hole at the junction of the closed cups enabled you to pour in the melted lead. There was also a couple of sharp blades forming part of the handles, which, working on the principle of nut-crackers, enabled you to clip off the lead protuberance and leave a perfectly moulded bullet which would kill a man as effectively as if it had been cast by the Government. Mounted men had rushed galloping up the main roads from the lake and along the concession lines, shouting as they passed, "The Fenians are coming!" pausing for no comment, but hurrying forward with the news. It needed no other warning to cause every man who could shoulder a gun to make his way as quickly as possible, with whatever weapon he had, to the village which he knew would be the rendezvous. It seems funny to look back on this commotion, for there was no more chance of the Fenians coming to our part of the country than there was of the Russians, nevertheless we did not stop to think about that until later; and if invaders had come, I am willing to risk an even dollar that they would have wished themselves safe once more in Buffalo saloons, in spite of the justly celebrated reputation of our own brands of liquor, for they would have come into a peaceful community that would rather fight than eat. Few of us knew anything about the merits of the Irish question at that day; our attention being absorbed in politics that pertained to the talismanic names of "John A." or "George Brown." Still if invasion came, we were all willing to fight first and inquire into the case afterwards, which was only natural.

The northern shore of Lake Erie, at least that part with which I am acquainted, is a coast perfect as a defence. High perpendicular clay walls, quite unscalable, form a barrier which no enemy of sense would care to encounter. It must not be supposed that I am accusing the Fenians of having been men of sense, for I have no such intention, but even they would hesitate to attempt the clay walls of Western Ontario. However, the eagle eye of the commander at once viewed the weak point in our defence with an unerring instinct worthy of Von Moltke. This was the pier. A creek flowed into the lake, and a road to the shore ran along the banks of this creek. At the terminus of the road had been built a pier jutting out into the lake some hundreds of feet in length. Here, in peaceful times, schooners from Cleveland, Erie, or Buffalo, had loaded themselves with oaken staves or prime wheat. Captain McKerricher saw that once the pier was captured, the Empire fell. He therefore massed his force on either bank of the ravine, so that a withering cross fire would discommode the enemy as he came up the valley; not at all a bad formation either. Thus the embattled farmers stood prepared to fire a shot which, if not heard round the world, would at least echo to the village two miles sway. As evening drew on, preparations were made for camping out all night on these heights and guards were set on the pier, Finley McGillis at the post of danger, the end nearest to the Fenians, while McCallum and McVannell held down the shore end, all three prepared to wade in blood should any miscreant attempt to kidnap the pier, except the limited liability company which rightfully owned it. Sentries were placed round the camp inland, and outposts farther off. Never was there more firm discipline exacted from any body of soldiers. The rigour of the British army was as nothing compared with the martinet character of the regulations of this camp. Captain McKerricher in person visited every sentinel and informed him that this was no 24th of May parade, but real war, and that any sentinel caught asleep would be forthwith shot instead of being fined a dollar, and that if a man lit his pipe he would spend the rest of his life in Kingston Penitentiary.

But the invincibility of a camp is unknown until it is tested. The Captain resolved to put the firmness of his sentinels to the proof. He took no one into his confidence, and here again his likeness to Napoleon is evidenced; he never let any of his subordinate officers know what the next move on the board was to be. There was a small skiff in the creek, and, the evening darkening early because of a coming storm, the Captain pushed out the boat unobserved and rowed some distance to the west, then turned south and out into the lake, finally coming north again toward the end of the pier. The night was black, relieved by an occasional glimmer of lightning on the surface of the lake, and the wind was rising. McKerricher's quest was getting to be an unpleasant one, for he was essentially a landsman, and the increasing motion of the boat was disagreeable, but what will a man not do and dare for his country's sake? It is probable that he descried the form of Finley McGillis against the dark sky before the sentinel caught any indication of the boat on the murky water. Finley said afterwards that he was just wondering whether he dare risk a smoke in his isolated position and trust to putting his pipe out if he heard a step coming up the pier, when he was startled by a voice from the lake —

"Surrender! Drop your gun and save your life. Surrender in the name of the Fenian Brotherhood!"

McGillis made no reply, and the Captain began to think he had caught his chief sentry asleep, but as the wabbling boat became dimly visible to the man on the end of the pier, Finley said slowly, "I can see ye now. If ye move hand or fut I'll blow ye out of the wat'ter."

"That's all right," said the Captain hastily, "I'm glad to note that you are on the alert. I'm Captain McKerricher."

"A likely story," replied McGillis contemptuously. "The Keptin's no a mahn to risk himself in a bit shallop like that, an' a storm comin up. Yer ma preesoner, an' ye'll be a deed mahn in another meenit if ye pit hand to oar."

"You fool," cried the angered voyager, "how could I know about McKerricher if I were a Fenian?"

"Oh, it's easy enough to hear aboot McKerricher, and it's verra weel ken't in the Auld Country an' in the States that he's oor Keptin. Yer a wolf in sheep's clothing, that's what ye are, and jist listen ta me. There's a ball nearly an inch thick in this musket, an' that'll be through you before ye can say 'click' if you don't do whut I tell ye. Then in this shotgun at ma feet there's a load of slugs, that'll rive yer boat to bits if ye attempt ta mak' aff. Is there a rope in that boat?"

"Yes."

"Then throw it ta me if it's lang enough."

This was done, and Finley tied the end of it to one of the upright piles. "Hand you up they oars. That's right. Now yer ta the windward o' the pier, an' nice an' comfortable fur the nicht."

"You are surely not going to keep me here all night, and the rain coming?"

"The rain's no warse fur you than fur me. A buddy munna be ower parteecular in time of war. If it should be that yer the Keptin, I'll make my apologies in the mornin'; if yer the Fenian ye said ye were, then Aang'as 'll hang ye fur yer impidence in takin' his name."

"Fire one gun in the air; and call the officers. You have two, so there's no risk. Disobey your Captain at your peril, and I'll have you court-martialled in the morning."

"I'll fire aff naething avaw. I'm not gaun to waste a shot an' poother sa dear. If I fire, it will be at you, and besides if I did fire, the whole camp would be shootin' at once from the heights in this direction, an' while I'm compelled ta risk being shot by the Fenians, it's no in the bargain that I should stand fire from ma own friens, an' a bullit fra the north kills as readily as yen fra the sooth."

The wind rose, the boat rocked and the rain came on.

"Give me the oars, at least," implored the captive, "that rope will break and then I'll be adrift and helpless."

"The win't doon the lake, so if it breaks, ye'll jist come ashore aboot Long Point."

But the rope did not break, and very soon the Captain was past the point where conversation is a pleasure, for however brave he might be on land, he had never been intended for the navy.

"Yer no used ta a boat," commented the sentinel, who had been a fisherman in the Highlands.

"It's unca hard at the time, they tell me, but yell be a' the better fur it in the mornin'."

When day broke Finley McGillis expressed the utmost consternation and surprise to find that his prisoner was really his captain. "Man! Wha wud ha' beleeved that!" he cried in amazement.

The subordinate officers who helped their haggard captain out of the boat, advised him strongly to say nothing about the incident. This, so far as I know, was the only naval encounter that occurred at the time of the Fenian Raid, and it goes to show, as I said in the beginning, that those who devote themselves to the cause of their country, suffer unrecorded hardships for which, alas, medals are not given. Even this section of history is futile, for, as what I have set down is strictly true, I could not give real names, because I have had no opportunity of consulting with either captain or sentinel, and do not know but one or other might object to the revelation of their identity.

Animal
Stories

Animal Stories

Commentary

Up until this century the animal story was grounded in the fabulist tradition. From Aesop's fox to Anna Sewell's Black Beauty, fictional animals were anthropomorphic to the core, existing either as moral embodiments of human behaviour or as antagonists to human heroes. In the 1890s, however, two Canadian writers — Charles G.D. Roberts and Ernest Thompson Seton — altered that state of affairs forever by writing what are now regarded as the first realistic/naturalistic animal stories in English. They attempted, with a great deal of popular success, to tell their stories from the animal's point of view and to accurately depict its natural imperatives — the need to hunt, protect its young, and deal with predators. As Roberts put it, they attempted to write "psychological" romances "constructed on a framework of natural science." When there were humans in their stories (in Seton's more often than in Roberts's) they were subject to the same natural imperatives as the animals themselves.

As natural scientists, both Roberts and Seton were self-taught: Roberts in a casual, though competent, manner through close observation of animal behaviour while living in the backwoods of New Brunswick; Seton in a more professional manner while preparing for his career as a naturalist-artist, his paintings of animals gaining considerable fame in Europe. As far as their animal stories are concerned, therefore, it is generally conceded that Seton is the more scientifically accurate and Roberts more artistically satisfying, though it might be pointed out that both ascribe to animals a kind of "reasoning" that bothered some early naturalists (such as Theodore Roosevelt) who favoured the "pure instinct" approach.

Roberts's animal stories are very similar in design to short stories — though he does write animal biographies and nature sketches — whereas Seton's tend more often to be animal biographies. This partly stems from their relative expertise as naturalists, but moreso from the fact that Roberts, poet and novelist, is the more gifted writer. Thus, whereas Seton's stories are more likely to be simply "true tales," uncomplicated and unencumbered by tonal shifts, Roberts's will challenge the reader to respond to the moods, setting, structure, and ironies.

Together, however, these two writers took the world by storm. By the end of the first decade of the twentieth century they had produced several hundred "animal" stories, publishing them in the best popular magazines of the day, and following up with numerous collections of such stories. Seton's *Wild Animals I Have Known* (1898) became an international bestseller and soon writers were enthralling readers around the world with a new kind of animal story. And, though the animal story's popularity waned shortly after Roberts and Seton ceased writing, the genre began to flourish again somewhat later, both internationally and, with great credit to the two "fathers" of the genre, very strongly in Canada where it has been perpetuated and perfected in the work of such well-known writers as Grey Owl, Sheila Burnford, Roderick Haig-Brown, and Farley Mowat.

Further Reading

John Coldwell Adams, *Sir Charles God Damn: The Life of Sir Charles G.D. Roberts*. Toronto: U. of T. Press, 1986.
Betty Keller, *Black Wolf: The Life of Ernest Thompson Seton*. Vancouver: Douglas & McIntyre, 1984.
Alec Lucas, "Nature Writers" in Carl F. Klinck, ed., *Literary History of Canada* 2nd ed., Vol. I. Toronto: U. of T. Press, 1976. 380-404.

Charles G.D. Roberts

Born on January 10, 1860, near Fredericton, New Brunswick, Roberts, after graduating with degrees in philosophy and political economy, began his adult life as a teacher. This he gave up in 1883 to become editor of The Week. *Thereafter, between 1885 and 1895, he became a professor of English at King's College, from which he resigned to become a full-time writer. His creative output was prodigious: thousands of poems (in periodicals and in eighteen collections), nine novels and novelettes, and more than twenty collections of stories. While his influence as poet is immeasurable — he was, after all, the "father of Canadian literature"— it is now being realized that his great genius was as a writer of animal/nature stories. The stories below are from* Harper's Magazine *86 (1892-93): 120-23, and* Windsor Magazine *20 (1904): 33-38.*

Do Seek their Meat from God

One side of the ravine was in darkness. The darkness was soft and rich, suggesting thick foliage. Along the crest of the slope tree-tops came into view — great pines and hemlocks of the ancient unviolated forest — revealed against the orange disk of a full moon just rising. The low rays slanting through the moveless tops lit strangely the upper portion of the opposite steep, the western wall of the ravine, barren, unlike its fellow, bossed with great rocky projections, and harsh with stunted junipers. Out of the sluggish dark that lay along the ravine as in a trough, rose the brawl of a swollen, obstructed stream.

Out of a shadowy hollow behind a long white rock, on the lower edge of that part of the steep which lay in the moonlight, came softly a great panther. In common daylight his coat would have shown a warm fulvous hue, but in the elvish decolorizing rays of that half hidden moon he seemed to wear a sort of spectral gray. He lifted his smooth round head to gaze on the increasing flame, which presently he greeted with a shrill cry. That terrible cry, at once plaintive and menacing, with an undertone like the fierce protestations of a saw beneath the file, was a summons to his mate, telling her that the hour had come when they should seek their prey. From the lair behind the rock, where the cubs were being suckled by their dam, came no immediate answer. Only a pair of crows, that had their nest in a giant fir-tree across the gulf, woke up and croaked harshly their indignation. These three summers past they had built in the same spot, and had been nightly awakened to vent the same rasping complaints.

The panther walked restlessly up and down, half a score of paces each way, along the edge of the shadow, keeping his wide-open green eyes upon the rising light. His short, muscular tail twitched impatiently, but he made no sound. Soon the breadth of confused brightness had spread itself further down the steep, disclosing the foot of the white rock, and the bones and antlers of a deer which had been dragged thither and devoured.

By this time the cubs had made their meal, and their dam was ready for such enterprise as must be accomplished ere her own hunger, now grown savage, could hope to be assuaged. She glided supplely forth into the glimmer, raised her head, and screamed at the moon in a voice as terrible as her mate's. Again the crows stirred, croaking harshly; and the two beasts, noiselessly mounting the steep, stole into the shadows of the forest that clothed the high plateau.

The panthers were fierce with hunger. These two days past their hunting had been wellnigh fruitless. What scant prey they had slain had for the most part been devoured by the female; for had she not those small blind cubs at home to nourish, who soon must suffer at any lack of hers? The settlements of late had been making great inroads on the world of ancient forest, driving before them the deer and smaller game. Hence the sharp hunger of the panther parents, and hence it came that on this night they hunted together. They purposed to steal upon the settlements in their sleep, and take tribute of the enemies' flocks.

Through the dark of the thick woods, here and there pierced by the moonlight, they moved swiftly and silently. Now and again a dry twig would snap beneath the discreet and padded footfalls. Now and again, as they rustled some low tree, a pewee or a nuthatch would give a startled chirp. For an hour the noiseless journeying continued, and ever and anon the two gray, sinuous shapes would come for a moment into the view of the now well-risen moon. Suddenly there fell upon their ears, far off and faint, but clearly defined against the vast stillness of the Northern forest, a sound which made those stealthy hunters pause and lift their heads. It was the voice of a child crying, — crying long and loud, hopelessly, as if there were no one by to comfort it. The panthers turned aside from their former course and glided toward the sound. They were not yet come to the outskirts of the settlement, but they knew of a solitary cabin lying in the thick of the woods a mile and more from the nearest neighbor. Thither they bent their way, fired with fierce hope. Soon would they break their bitter fast.

Up to noon of the previous day the lonely cabin had been occupied. Then its owner, a shiftless fellow, who spent his days for the most part at the corner tavern three miles distant, had suddenly grown disgusted with a land wherein one must work to live, and had betaken himself with his seven-year-old boy to seek some more indolent clime. During the long lonely days when his father was away at the tavern the little boy had been wont to visit the house of the next neighbor, to play with a child of some five summers, who had no other playmate. The next neighbor was a prosperous pioneer, being master of a substantial frame house in the midst of a large and well-tilled clearing. At times, though rarely, because it was forbidden, the younger child would make his way by a rough wood road to visit his poor little disreputable playmate. At length it had appeared that the five-year-old was learning unsavory language from the elder boy, who rarely had an opportunity of hearing speech more desirable. To the bitter grief of both children, the companionship had at length been stopped by unalterable decree of the master of the frame house.

Hence it had come to pass that the little boy was unaware of his comrade's departure. Yielding at last to an eager longing for that comrade, he had stolen away late in the afternoon, traversed with endless misgivings the lonely stretch of wood road, and reached the cabin only to find it empty. The door, on its leathern hinges, swung idly open. The one room had been stripped of its few poor furnishings. After looking in the rickety shed, whence darted two wild and hawklike chickens, the child had seated himself on the hacked threshold, and sobbed passionately with a grief that he did not fully comprehend. Then seeing the shadows lengthen across the tiny clearing, he had grown afraid to start for home. As the dusk gathered, he had crept trembling into the cabin, whose door would not stay shut. When it grew quite dark, he crouched in the inmost corner of the room, desperate with fear and loneliness, and lifted up his voice piteously. From time to time his lamentations would be choked by sobs, or he would grow breathless, and in the terrifying silence would listen hard to hear if any one or anything were coming. Then again would the shrill childish wailings arise, startling the unexpectant night, and piercing the forest depths, even to the ears of those great beasts which had set forth to seek their meat from God.

The lonely cabin stood some distance, perhaps a quarter of a mile, back from the highway connecting the settlements. Along this main road a man was plodding wearily. All day he had been walking, and now as he neared home his steps began to quicken with anticipation of rest. Over his shoulder projected a double-barrelled fowling-piece, from which was slung a bundle of such necessities as he had purchased in town that morning. It was the prosperous settler, the master of the frame house. His mare being with foal, he had chosen to make the tedious journey on foot.

The settler passed the mouth of the wood road leading to the cabin. He had gone perhaps a furlong beyond, when his ears were startled by the sound of a child crying in the woods. He stopped, lowered his burden to the road, and stood straining ears and eyes in the direction of the sound. It was just at this time that the two panthers also stopped, and lifted their heads to listen. Their ears were keener than those of the man, and the sound had reached them at a greater distance.

Presently the settler realized whence the cries were coming. He called to mind the cabin; but he did not know the cabin's owner had departed. He cherished a hearty contempt for the drunken squatter; and on the drunken squatter's child he looked with small favor, especially as a playmate for his own boy. Nevertheless he hesitated before resuming his journey.

"Poor little devil!" he muttered, half in wrath. "I reckon his precious father's drunk down at 'the Corners,' and him crying for loneliness!" Then he reshouldered his burden and strode on doggedly.

But louder, shriller, more hopeless and more appealing, arose the childish voice, and the settler paused again, irresolute, and with deepening indignation. In his fancy he saw the steaming supper his wife would have awaiting him. He loathed the thought of retracing his steps, and then stumbling a quarter of a mile through the stumps and bog of the wood road. He was foot-sore as well as hungry, and he cursed the vagabond squatter with serious emphasis; but in that wailing was a terror which would not let him go on. He thought of his own little one left in such a position, and straightway his heart melted. He turned, dropped his bundle behind some bushes, grasped his gun, and made speed back of the cabin.

"Who knows," he said to himself, "but that drunken idiot has left his youngster without a bite to eat in the whole miserable shanty. Or maybe he's locked out, and the poor little beggar's half scared to death. *Sounds* as if he was scared"; and at this thought the settler quickened his pace.

As the hungry panthers drew near the cabin, and the cries of the lonely child grew clearer, they hastened their steps, and their eyes opened to a wider circle, flaming with a greener fire. It would be thoughtless superstition to say the beasts were cruel. They were simply keen with hunger, and alive with the eager passion of the chase. They were not ferocious with any anticipation of battle, for they knew the voice was the voice of a child, and something in the voice told them the child was solitary. Theirs was no hideous or unnatural rage, as it is the custom to describe it. They were but seeking with the strength, the cunning, the deadly swiftness given them to that end, the food convenient for them. On their success in accomplishing that for which nature had so exquisitely designed them depended not only their own, but the lives of their blind and helpless young, now whimpering in the cave on the slope of the moon-lit ravine. They crept through a wet alder thicket, bounded lightly over the ragged brush fence, and paused to reconnoitre on the edge of the clearing, in the full glare of the moon. At the same moment the settler emerged from the darkness of the wood-road on the opposite side of the clearing. He saw the two great beasts, heads down and snouts thrust forward, gliding toward the open cabin door.

For a few moments the child had been silent. Now his voice rose again in pitiful appeal, a very ecstasy of loneliness and terror. There was a note in the cry that shook the settler's soul. He had a vision of his own boy, at home with his mother, safe-guarded from even the thought of peril. And here was this little one left to the wild beasts! "Thank God! Thank God I came!" murmured the settler, as he dropped on one knee to take a surer aim. There was a loud report (not like the sharp crack of a rifle), and the female panther, shot through the loins, fell in a heap, snarling furiously and striking with her fore-paws.

The male walked around her in fierce and anxious amazement. Presently, as the smoke lifted, he discerned the settler kneeling for a second shot. With a high screech of fury, the lithe brute sprang upon his enemy, taking a bullet full in his chest without seeming to know he was hit. Ere the man could slip in another cartridge the beast was upon him, bearing him to the ground and fixing keen fangs in his shoulder. Without a word, the man set his strong fingers desperately into the brute's throat, wrenched himself partly free, and was struggling to rise, when the panther's body collapsed upon him all at once, a dead weight which he easily flung aside. The bullet had done its work just in time.

Quivering from the swift and dreadful contest, bleeding profusely from his mangled shoulder, the settler stepped up to the cabin door and peered in. He heard sobs in the darkness.

"Don't be scared, sonny," he said, in a reassuring voice. "I'm going to take you home along with me. Poor little lad, *I'll* look after you if folks that ought to don't."

Out of the dark corner came a shout of delight, in a voice which made the settler's heart stand still. "*Daddy*, daddy," it said, "I *knew* you'd come. I was so frightened when it got dark!" And a little figure launched itself into the settler's arms, and clung to him trembling. The man sat down on the threshold and strained the child to his breast. He remembered how near he had been to disregarding the far-off cries, and great beads of sweat broke out upon his forehead.

Not many weeks afterwards the settler was following the fresh trail of a bear which had killed his sheep. The trail led him at last along the slope of a deep ravine, from whose bottom came the brawl of a swollen and obstructed stream. In the ravine he found a shallow cave, behind a great white rock. The cave was plainly a wild beast's lair, and he entered circumspectly. There were bones scattered about, and on some dry herbage in the deepest corner of the den, he found the dead bodies, now rapidly decaying, of two small panther cubs.

The Master of the Golden Pool

The shore of the pool was a spacious sweeping curve of the sward, dotted with clumps of blue flag-flowers. From the green fringes of this shore the bottom sloped away softly over a sand so deep and glowing in its hue of orange-yellow as to give the pool the rich name by which it was known for miles up and down the hurrying Clearwater. The other shore was a high, overhanging bank, from whose top drooped a varied leafage of birch, ash, poplar, and hemlock. Under this bank the water was deep and dark, a translucent black with trembling streaks and glints of amber. Fifty yards upstream a low fall roared musically; but before reaching the fresh tranquillity of the pool, the current bore no signs of its disturbance save a few softly whirling foam clusters. Light airs, perfumed with birch and balsam and warm scents of the sun-steeped sward, drew over the pool from time to time, wrinkling and clouding its glassy surface. Birds flew over it, catching the small flies to whom its sheen was a ceaseless lure. And huge dragon-flies, with long, iridescent bodies and great jewelled, sinister eyes, danced and darted above it.

The cool black depths under the bank retained their coolness through the fiercest heats of summer, because just here the brook was joined by the waters of an icy spring stealing down through a crevice of the rocks; and here in the deepest recess, exacting toll of all the varied life that passed his domain, the master of Golden Pool made his home.

For several years the great trout had held his post in the pool, defying every lure of the crafty fisherman. The Clearwater was a protected stream; being leased to a rich fishing club; and the master of the pool was therefore secure against the treacherous assaults of net or dynamite. Many times each season fishermen would come and pit their skill against his cunning; but never a fly could tempt him, never a silvery, trolled minnow or whirling spoon deceive him to the fatal rush. At some new lure he would rise lazily once in a while, revealing his bulk to the ambitious angler, but never to take hold. Contemptuously he would flout the cheat with his broad flukes, and go down again with a grand swirl to his lair under the rock.

It was only to the outside world — to the dragon-fly, and the bird, and the chattering red squirrel in the overhanging hemlock — that the deep water under the bank looked black. To the trout in his lair, looking upward toward the sunlight, the whole pool had a golden glow. His favourite position was a narrow place between two stones, where he lay with head upstream and belly about two inches from the sandy bottom, gently fanning the water with his party-coloured fins, and opening and closing his rosy gill-fringes as he breathed. In length he was something over twenty inches, with a thick, deep body tapering finely to the powerful tail. Like all the trout of the Clearwater, he was silver-bellied with a light pink flush, the yellow and brown markings on his sides light in tone, and his spots of the most high, intense vermilion. His great lower jaw was thrust forward in a way that gave a kind of bulldog ferocity to his expression.

The sky of the big trout's world was the flat surface of Golden Pool. From the unknown place beyond that sky there came to his eyes but moving shadows, arrangements of light and dark. He could not see out and through into the air unobstructedly, as one looks forth from a window into the world. Most of these moving shadows he understood very well. When broad and vague, they did not, as a rule, greatly interest him; but when they got small, and sharply black, he knew they might at any instant break through with a splash and become real, coloured things, probably good to eat. A certain slim little shadow was always of interest to him unless he was feeling gorged. Experience had taught him that when it actually touched the shining surface above, and lay there sprawling helplessly with wet wings, it would prove to be a May fly, which he liked. Having no rivals to get ahead of him, there was no need of haste. He would sail up with dignity, open his great jaws, and take in the tiny morsel.

Sometimes the moving shadows were large and of a slower motion, and these, if they chanced to break through, would prove to be bright-coloured moths or butterflies, or glittering beetles, or fat black and yellow bumblebees, or lean black and yellow wasps. If he was hungry, all these things were good for food, and his bony, many-toothed mouth cared nothing for stings. Sometimes when he was not at all hungry, but merely playful, he would rise with a rush at anything breaking the sheen of his roof, slap it with his tail, then seize it between his hard lips and carry it down with him, only to drop it a moment later as a child might drop a toy. Once in a while, either in hunger or in sport, he would rise swiftly at the claws or wing-tips of a dipping swallow; but he never managed to catch the nimble bird. Had he, by any chance, succeeded, he would probably have found the feathers no obstacle to his enjoyment of the novel fare.

At times it was not a shadow, but a splash, that would attract his attention to the shining roof of his world. A grasshopper would fall in, and kick grotesquely till he rose to end its troubles. Or a misguided frog, pursued perhaps by some enemy on land, would dive in and swim by with long, webbed toes. At this sight the master of the pool would dart from his lair like a bolt from a catapult. Frogs were much to his taste. And once in a long time even a wood-mouse, hard pressed and panic-stricken, would leap in to swim across to the meadow shore. The first time this occurred the trout had risen slowly, and followed below the swimmer till assured that there was no peril concealed in the tempting phenomenon. After that, however, he always went at such prey with a ferocious rush, hurling himself half out of the water in his eagerness.

But it was not only to his translucent sky that the master of the pool looked for his meat. A large part of it came down upon the current of the brook. Bugs, grubs, and worms, of land and water, some dead, others disabled or bewildered by their passage through the falls, contributed to his feasting. Above all, there were the smaller fish who were so reckless or uninformed as to try to pass through Golden Pool. They might be chub, or suckers, or red-fin; they might be — and more often were — kith and kin of his own. It was all the same to the big trout, who knew as well as any gourmet that trout were royal fare. His wide jaws and capacious gullet were big enough to accommodate a cousin a full third of his own size, if swallowed properly, head first. His speed was so great that any smaller fish which he pursued was doomed, unless fortunate enough to be within instant reach of shoal water. Of course, it must not be imagined that the great trout was able to keep his domain quite inviolate. When he was full fed, or sulking, then the finny wanderers passed up and down freely, — always, however, giving wide berth to the lair under the bank. In the bright shallows over against the other shore, the scurrying shoals of pin-fish played safely in the sun. Once in a long while a fish would pass, up or down, so big that the master of the pool was willing to let him go unchallenged. And sometimes a muskrat, swimming with powerful strokes of his hind legs, his tiny forepaws gathered childishly under his chin, would take his way over the pool to the meadow of the blue flag-flowers. The master of the pool would turn up a fierce eye, and watch the swimmer's progress breaking the golden surface into long, parabolic ripples; but he was too wise to court a trial of the muskrat's long, chisel-like teeth.

There were two occasions, never to be effaced from his sluggish memory, on which the master of the pool had been temporarily routed from his mastership and driven in a panic from his domain. Of these the less important had seemed to him by far the more appalling.

Once, on a summer noonday, when the pool was all of a quiver with golden light, and he lay with slow-waving fins close to the coldest up-gushing of the spring which cooled his lair, the shining roof of his realm had been shattered and upheaved with a tremendous splash. A long, whitish body, many times his own length, had plunged in and dived almost to the bottom. This creature swam with wide-sprawling limbs, like a frog, beating the water, and leaping, and uttering strange sounds; and the disturbance of its antics was a very cataclysm to the utmost corners of the pool. The trout had not stayed to investigate the horrifying phenomenon, but had darted madly downstream for half a mile, through fall and eddy, rapid and shale low, to pause at last, with throbbing sides and panting gills, in a little black pool behind a tree root. Not till hours after the man had finished his bath, and put on his clothes, and strode away whistling up the shore, did the big trout venture back to his stronghold. He found it already occupied by a smaller trout, whom he fell upon and devoured, to the assuaging of his appetite and the salving of his wounded dignity. But for days he was tremulously watchful, and ready to dart away if any unusually large shadow passed over his amber ceiling. He was expecting a return of the great, white, sprawling visitor.

His second experience was one which he remembered with cunning wariness rather than with actual terror. Yet this had been a real peril, one of the gravest with which he could be confronted in the guarded precincts of Golden Pool. One day he saw a little lithe black body swimming rapidly at the surface, — its head above the water. It was about ten feet away from his lair, and headed up-stream. The strange creature swam with legs, like a muskrat, instead of with fins like a fish, but it was longer and slenderer than a muskrat; and something in its sinister shape and motion, or else some stirring of an inherited instinct, filled the big trout with apprehension as he looked. Suddenly the stranger's head dipped under the surface, and the stranger's eyes sought him out, far down in his yellow gloom. That narrow-nosed, triangular head with its pointed fangs, those bright, cruel, undeceivable eyes, smote the trout with instant alarm. Here was an enemy to be avoided. The mink had dived at once, going through the water with the swiftness and precision of a fish. Few trout could have escaped. But the master of the pool, as we have seen, was no ordinary trout. The promptness of his cunning had got him under way in time. The power of his broad and muscular tail shot him forth from his lair just before the mink got there. And before the baffled enemy could change his direction, the trout was many feet away, heading up for the broken water of the rapids. The mink followed vindictively, but in the foamy stretch below the falls he lost all track of the fugitive. Angry and disappointed he scrambled ashore, and, finding a dead sucker beside his runway, seized it savagely. As he did so, there was a smart click, and the jaws of a steel trap, snapping upon his throat, rid the wilderness of one of its most bloodthirsty and implacable marauders. A half-hour later the master of the pool was back in his lair, waving his delicate, gay-coloured fins over the yellow sand, and lazily swallowing a large crayfish. One claw of the crayfish projected beyond his black jaw; and, being thus comfortably occupied, he turned an indifferent eye upon the frightened swimming of a small green frog, which had just then fallen in and disturbed the sheen of his amber roof.

Very early one morning, when all his world was of a silvery gray, and over the glassy pallor of his roof thin gleams of pink were mingled with ghostly, swirling mist-shadows, a strange fly touched the surface, directly above him. It had a slender, scarlet, curving body, with long hairs of yellow and black about its neck, and brown and white wings. It fell upon the water with the daintiest possible splash, just enough to catch his attention. Being utterly unlike anything he had ever seen before, it aroused his interest, and he slanted slowly upward. A moment later a second fly touched the water, a light gray, mottled thing, with a yellow body, and pink and green hairs fringing its neck. This, too, was strange to him. He rolled a foot higher, not with any immediate idea of trying them, but under his usual vague impulse to investigate everything pertaining to his pool. Just then the mist-swirls lifted slightly, and the light grew stronger, and against the smooth surface he detected a fine, almost invisible, thread leading from the head of each fly. With a derisive flirt of his tail he sank back to the bottom of his lair. Right well he knew the significance of that fine thread.

The strange flies skipped lightly over the surface of the pool, in a manner that to most trout would have seemed very alluring. They moved away toward a phenomenon which he just noticed for the first time, a pair of dark, pillar-like objects standing where the water was about two feet deep, over toward the further shore. These dark objects moved a little, gently. Then the strange flies disappeared. A moment later they dropped again, and went through the same performance. This was repeated several times, the big trout watching with interest mingled with contempt. There was no peril for him in such gauds.

Presently the flies disappeared for good. A few minutes later two others came in their place, — one a tiny, white, moth-like thing, the other a big, bristling bunch of crimson hairs. The latter stirred, far back in his dull memory, an association of pain and fear, and he backed deeper into his watery den. It was a red hackle; and in his early days, when he was about eight inches long and frequented the tail of a shallow, foamy rapid, he had had experience of its sharp allurements. The little moth he ignored, but he kept an eye on the red hackle as it trailed and danced hither and thither across the pool. Once, near the other side, he saw a misguided fingerling dart from under a stone in the shallow water and seize the gay morsel. The fingerling rose, with a jerk, from the water, and was no more seen. It vanished into the unknown air; and the master of the pool quailed as he marked its fate. After this, the pair of dark, pillar-like objects moved away to the shore, no longer careful, but making a huge, splashing noise. No more strange flies appeared; and the gold light of full day stole down to the depths of the pool. Soon, flies which the master well knew, with no fine threads attached to them, began to speck the surface over him, and he fed, in his lazy way, without misgiving. The big trout had good reason for his dread of the angler's lure. His experience with the red hackle had given him the wisdom which had enabled him to live through all the perils of a well-known trout-stream and grow to his present fame and stature. Behind that red hackle which hooked him in his youth had been a good rod, a crafty head, and a skilful wrist. His hour had sounded then and there, but for a fortunate flaw in the tackle. The leader had parted just at the drop, and the terrified trout (he had taken the tail fly) had darted away frantically through the rapids with three feet of fine gut trailing from his jaw. For several weeks he trailed that hampering thread, and carried that red hackle in the cartilage of his upper jaw; and he had time to get very familiar with them. He grew thin and slab-sided under the fret of it before he succeeded, by much nosing in gravel and sand, in wearing away the cartilage and rubbing his jaw clear of the encumbrance. From that day forward he had scrutinized all unfamiliar baits or lures to see if they carried any threadlike attachment.

When any individual of the wild kindreds, furred, feathered, or finned, achieves the distinction of baffling man's efforts to undo him, his doom may be considered sealed. There is no beast, bird, or fish so crafty or so powerful but some one man can worst him, and will take the trouble to do it if the game seems to be worth while. Some lure would doubtless have been found, some scheme devised for the hiding of the line, whereby the big trout's cunning would have been made foolishness. Some swimming frog, some terrified, hurrying mouse, or some great night-moth flopping down upon the dim water of a moonless night, would have lulled his suspicions and concealed the inescapable barb; and the master of the pool would have gone to swell the record of an ingenious conqueror. He would have been stuffed, and mounted, and hung upon the walls of the club-house, down at the mouth of the Clearwater. But it pleased the secret and inscrutable deities of the woods that the end of the lordly trout should come in another fashion.

It is an unusual thing, an unfortunate and pitiful thing, when death comes to the wild kindred by the long-drawn, tragic way of overripeness. When the powers begin to fail, the powers which enabled them to conquer, or to flee from, or to outwit their innumerable foes, — then life becomes a miserable thing for them. But that is not for long. Fate meets them in the forest trails or the flowing water-paths; and they have grown too dull to see, too heavy to flee, too indifferent to contend. So they are spared the anguish of slow, uncomprehending decrepitude.

But to the master of Golden Pool Fate came while he was yet master unchallenged, and balked the hopes of many crafty fishermen. It came in a manner not unworthy of the great trout's dignity and fame, giving him over to swell no adversary's triumph, betraying him to no contemptible foe.

One crisp autumn morning, when leaves were falling all over the surface of the pool, and insects were few, and a fresh tang in the water was making him active and hungry, the big trout was swimming hither and thither about his domain instead of lying lazily in his deep lair. He chanced to be over in the shallows near the grassy shore, when he saw, at the upper end of the pool, a long, dark body slip noiselessly into the water. It was not unlike the mink in form, but several times larger. It swam with a swift movement of its forefeet, while its hind legs, stretched out behind with the tail, twisted powerfully, like a big sculling-oar. Its method, indeed, combined the advantages of that of the quadruped and that of the fish. The trout saw at once that here was a foe to be dreaded, and he lay quite still against a stone, trusting to escape the bright eyes of the stranger.

But the stranger, as it happened, was hunting, and the stranger was an otter. The big trout was just such quarry as he sought, and his bright eyes, peering restlessly on every side, left no corner of the pool uninvestigated. They caught sight of the master's silver and vermilion sides, his softly waving, gay-coloured fins.

With a dart like that of the swiftest of fish, the stranger shot across the pool. The trout darted madly toward his lair. The otter was close upon him, missing him by a fin's breadth. Frantic now with terror, the trout shot up-stream toward the broken water. But the otter, driven not only by his forefeet but by that great combined propeller of his hind legs and tail, working like a screw, swam faster. Just at the edge of the broken water he overtook his prey. A set of long, white teeth went through the trout's backbone. There was one convulsive twist, and the gay-coloured fins lay still, the silver and vermilion body hung limp from the captor's jaws.

For many days thereafter, Golden Pool lay empty under its dropping crimson and purple leaves, its slow sailing foam flakes. Then, by twos and threes, small trout strayed in, and found the new region a good place to inhabit. When, in the following spring, the fishermen came back to the Clearwater, they reported the pool swarming with pan-fish, hardly big enough to make it worth while throwing a fly. Then word went up and down the Clearwater that the master of the pool was gone, and the glory of the pool, for that generation of fishermen, went with him.

Ernest Thompson Seton

Born Ernest Evan Thompson in South Shields, England, on August 14, 1860, Seton (who legally changed his named in 1901), emigrated in 1866 with his family to Lindsay, Ontario. He was later educated at the Ontario College of Art, and continued his art studies in London, Paris, and New York. In 1882 he settled in Manitoba, to study its wildlife, later became the government naturalist for that province, and in 1891 published The Birds of Manitoba. *In 1896, he moved to the United States, continued his wildlife painting, and became one of its best-known naturalist-writers, his* Wild Animals I Have Known *(1898) becoming an international best-seller. The following selection — slightly abridged — comes from that book.*

The Biography of a Grizzly

Part I: The Cubhood of Wahb

He was born over a score of years ago, away up in the wildest part of the Wild West, on the head of the Little Piney, above where the Palette Ranch is now.

His mother was just an ordinary Silvertip, living the quiet life that all Bears prefer, minding her own business and doing her duty by her family, asking no favours of any one excepting to let her alone.

It was July before she took her remarkable family down the Little Piney to the Graybull, and showed them what strawberries were, and where to find them.

Notwithstanding their Mother's deep conviction, the cubs were not remarkably big or bright; yet they were a remarkable family, for there were four of them, and it is not often a Grizzly Mother can boast of more than two.

The woolly-coated little creatures were having a fine time, and revelled in the lovely mountain summer and the abundance of good things. Their Mother turned over each log and flat stone they came to, and the moment it was lifted they all rushed under it like a lot of little pigs to lick up the ants and grubs there hidden.

It never once occurred to them that Mammy's strength might fail sometime, and let the great rock drop just as they got under it; nor would any one have thought so that might have chanced to see that huge arm and that shoulder sliding about under the great yellow robe she wore. No, no; that arm could never fail. The little ones were quite right. So they hustled and tumbled one another at each fresh log in their haste to be first, and squealed little squeals, and growled little growls, as if each was a pig, a pup, and a kitten all rolled into one.

They were well acquainted with the common little brown ants that harbour under logs in the uplands, but now they came for the first time on one of the hills of the great, fat, luscious Wood-ant, and they all crowded around to lick up those that ran out. But they soon found that they were licking up more cactus-prickles and sand than ants, till their Mother said in Grizzly, "Let me show you how."

She knocked off the top of the hill, then laid her great paw flat on it for a few moments, and as the angry ants swarmed on to it she licked them up with one lick, and got a good rich mouthful to crunch, without a grain of sand or a cactus-stinger in it. The cubs soon learned. Each put up both his little brown paws, so that there was a ring of paws all around the ant-hill, and there they sat, like children playing 'hands,' and each licked first the right and then the left paw, or one cuffed his brother's ears for licking a paw that was not his own, till the ant-hill was cleared out and they were ready for a change. Ants are sour food and made the Bears thirsty, so the old one led down to the river. After they had drunk as much as they wanted, and dabbled their feet, they walked down the bank to a pool, where the old one's keen eye caught sight of a number of Buffalo-fish basking on the bottom. The water was very low, mere pebbly rapids between these deep holes, so Mammy said to the little ones: "Now you all sit there on the bank and learn something new."

First she went to the lower end of the pool and stirred up a cloud of mud which hung in the still water, and sent a long tail floating like a curtain over the rapids just below. Then she went quietly round by land, and sprang into the upper end of the pool with all the noise she could. The fish had crowded to that end, but this sudden attack sent them off in a panic, and they dashed blindly into the mud-cloud. Out of fifty fish there is always a good chance of some being fools, and half a dozen of these dashed through the darkened water into the current, and before they knew it they were struggling over the shingly shallow. The old Grizzly jerked them out to the bank, and the little ones rushed noisily on these funny, short snakes that could not get away, and gobbled and gorged till their little bellies looked like balloons.

They had eaten so much now, and the sun was so hot, that all were quite sleepy. So the Mother-bear led them to a quiet little nook, and as soon as she lay down, though they were puffing with heat, they all snuggled around her and went to sleep, with their little brown paws curled in, and their little black noses tucked into their wool as though it were a very cold day.

After an hour or two they began to yawn and stretch themselves, except little Fuzz, the smallest; she poked out her sharp nose for a moment, then snuggled back between her Mother's great arms, for she was a gentle, petted little thing. The largest, the one afterward known as Wahb, sprawled over on his back and began to worry a root that stuck up, grumbling to himself as he chewed it, or slapped it with his paw for not staying where he wanted it. Presently, Mooney, the mischief, began tugging at Frizzle's ears, and got his own well boxed. They clenched for a tussle; then, locked in a tight, little grizzly yellow ball, they sprawled over and over on the grass, and, before they knew it, down a bank, and away out of sight toward the river.

Almost immediately there was an outcry of yells for help from the little wrestlers. There could be no mistaking the real terror in their voices. Some dreadful danger was threatening.

Up jumped the gentle Mother, changed into a perfect demon, and over the bank in time to see a huge Range-bull make a deadly charge at what he doubtless took for a yellow dog. In a moment all would have been over with Frizzle, for he had missed his footing on the bank; but there was a thumping of heavy feet, a roar that startled even the great bull, and, like a huge bounding ball of yellow fur, Mother Grizzly was upon him. Him! the monarch of the herd, the master of all these plains, what had he to fear? He bellowed his deep war-cry, and charged to pin the old one to the bank; but as he bent to tear her with his shining horns, she dealt him a stunning blow, and before he could recover she was on his shoulders, raking the flesh from his ribs with sweep after sweep of her terrific claws.

The bull roared with rage, and plunged and reared, dragging Mother Grizzly with him; then, as he hurled heavily off the slope, she let go to save herself, and the Bull rolled down into the river.

This was a lucky thing for him, for the Grizzly did not want to follow him there; so he waded out on the other side, and bellowing with fury and pain, slunk off to join the herd to which he belonged.

II

Old Colonel Pickett, the cattle king, was out riding the range. The night before, he had seen the new moon descending over the white cone of Pickett's Peak.

"I saw the last moon over Frank's Peak," said he, "and the luck was against me for a month; now I reckon it's my turn."

Next morning his luck began. A letter came from Washington granting his request that a post-office be established at his ranch, and contained the polite enquiry, "What name do you suggest for the new post-office?"

The Colonel took down his new rifle, a 45-90 repeater. "May as well," he said; "this is my month"; and he rode up the Graybull to see how the cattle were doing.

As he passed under the Rimrock Mountain he heard a far-away roaring as of bulls fighting, but thought nothing of it till he rounded the point and saw on the flat below a lot of his cattle pawing the dust and bellowing as they always do when they smell the blood of one of their number. He soon saw that the Great Bull, 'the boss of the bunch,' was covered with blood. His back and sides were torn as by a Mountain-lion, and his head was battered as by another Bull.

"Grizzly," growled the Colonel, for he knew the mountains. He quickly noted the general direction of the Bull's back trail, then rode toward a high bank that offered a view. This was across the gravelly ford of the Graybull, near the mouth of the Piney. His horse splashed through the cold water and began jerkily to climb the other bank.

As soon as the rider's head rose above the bank his hand grabbed the rifle, for there in full sight were five Grizzly Bears, an old one and four cubs.

"Run for the woods," growled the Mother Grizzly, for she knew that men carried guns. Not that she feared for herself; but the idea of such things among her darlings was too horrible to think of. She set off to guide them to the timber-tangle on the Lower Piney. But an awful, murderous fusillade began.

Bang! and Mother Grizzly felt a deadly pang.

Bang! and poor little Fuzz rolled over with a scream of pain and lay still.

With a roar of hate and fury Mother Grizzly turned to attack the enemy.

Bang! and she fell paralyzed and dying with a high shoulder shot. And the three little cubs, not knowing what to do, ran back to their Mother.

Bang! bang! and Mooney and Frizzle sank in dying agonies beside her, and Wahb, terrified and stupefied, ran in a circle about them. Then, hardly knowing why, he turned and dashed into the timber-tangle, and disappeared as a last bang left him with a stinging pain and a useless, broken hind paw.

That is why the post-office was called "Four-Bears." The Colonel seemed pleased with what he had done; indeed, he told of it himself.

But away up in the woods of Anderson's Peak that night a little lame Grizzly might have been seen wandering, limping along, leaving a bloody spot each time he tried to set down his hind paw; whining and whimpering, "Mother! Mother! Oh, Mother, where are you?" for he was cold and hungry, and had such a pain in his foot. But there was no Mother to come to him, and he dared not go back where he had left her, so he wandered aimlessly about among the pines.

Then he smelt some strange animal smell and heard heavy footsteps; and not knowing what else to do, he climbed a tree. Presently a band of great, long-necked, slim-legged animals, taller than his Mother, came by under the tree. He had seen such once before and had not been afraid of them then, because he had been with his Mother. But now he kept very quiet in the tree, and the big creatures stopped picking the grass when they were near him, and blowing their noses, ran out of sight.

He stayed in the tree till near morning, and then he was so stiff with cold that he could scarcely get down. But the warm sun came up, and he felt better as he sought about for berries and ants, for he was very hungry. Then he went back to the Piney and put his wounded foot in the ice-cold water.

He wanted to get back to the mountains again, but still he felt he must go to where he had left his Mother and brothers. When the afternoon grew warm, he went limping down the stream through the timber, and down on the banks of the Graybull till he came to the place where yesterday they had had the fish-feast; and he eagerly crunched the heads and remains that he found. But there was an odd and horrid smell on the wind. It frightened him, and as he went down to where he last had seen his Mother the smell grew worse. He peeped out cautiously at the place, and saw there a lot of Coyotes, tearing at something. What it was he did not know; but he saw no Mother, and the smell that sickened and terrified him was worse than ever, so he quietly turned back toward the timber-tangle of the Lower Piney, and nevermore came back to look for his lost family. He wanted his Mother as much as ever, but something told him it was no use.

As cold night came down, he missed her more and more again, and he whimpered as he limped along, a miserable, lonely, little, motherless Bear — not lost in the mountains, for he had no home to seek, but so sick and lonely, and with such a pain in his foot, and in his stomach a craving for the drip that would never more be his. That night he found a hollow log, and crawling in, he tried to dream that his Mother's great, furry arms were around him, and he snuffled himself to sleep.

III

Wahb had always been a gloomy little Bear; and the string of misfortunes that came on him just as his mind was forming made him more than ever sullen and morose.

It seemed as though every one were against him. He tried to keep out of sight in the upper woods of the Piney, seeking his food by day and resting at night in the hollow log. But one evening he found it occupied by a Porcupine as big as himself and as bad as a cactus-bush. Wahb could do nothing with him. He had to give up the log and seek another nest.

One day he went down on the Graybull flat to dig some roots that his Mother had taught him were good. But before he had well begun, a greyish-looking animal came out of a hole in the ground and rushed at him, hissing and growling. Wahb did not know it was a Badger, but he saw it was a fierce animal as big as himself. He was sick, and lame too, so he limped away and never stopped till he was on a ridge in the next canyon. Here a Coyote saw him, and came bounding after him, calling at the same time to another to come and join in the fun. Wahb was near a tree, so he scrambled up to the branches. The Coyotes came bounding and yelping below, but their noses told them that this was a young Grizzly they had chased, and they soon decided that a young Grizzly in a tree means a Mother Grizzly not far away, and they had better let him alone.

After they had sneaked off Wahb came down and returned to the Piney. There was better feeding on the Graybull, but every one seemed against him there now that his loving guardian was gone, while on the Piney he had peace at least sometimes, and there were plenty of trees that he could climb when an enemy came.

His broken foot was a long time in healing; indeed, it never got quite well. The wound healed and the soreness wore off, but it left a stiffness that gave him a slight limp, and the sole-balls grew together quite unlike those of the other foot. It particularly annoyed him when he had to climb a tree or run fast from his enemies; and of them he found no end, though never once did a friend cross his path. When he lost his Mother he lost his best and only friend. She would have taught him much that he had to learn by bitter experience, and would have saved him from most of the ills that befell him in his cub-hood — ills so many and so dire that but for his native sturdiness he never could have passed through alive.

The pinons bore plentifully that year, and the winds began to shower down the ripe, rich nuts. Life was becoming a little easier for Wahb. He was gaining in health and strength, and the creatures he daily met now let him alone. But as he feasted on the pinons one morning after a gale, a great Black-bear came marching down the hill. "No one meets a friend in the woods" was a byword that Wahb had learned already. He swung up the nearest tree. At first the Black-bear was scared, for he smelt the smell of Grizzly; but when he saw it was only a cub, he took courage and came growling at Wahb. He could climb as well as the little Grizzly, or better, and high as Wahb went, the Black-bear followed, and when Wahb got out on the smallest and highest twig that would carry him, the Black-bear cruelly shook him off, so that he was thrown to the ground, bruised and shaken and half-stunned. He limped away moaning, and the only thing that kept the Black-bear from following him up and perhaps killing him was the fear that the old Grizzly might be about. So Wahb was driven away down the creek from all the good pinon woods.

There was not much food on the Graybull now. The berries were nearly all gone; there were no fish or ants to get, and Wahb, hurt, lonely, and miserable, wandered on and on, till he was away down toward the Meteetsee. A Coyote came bounding and barking through the sage-brush after him. Wahb tried to run, but it was no use; the Coyote was soon up with him. Then with a sudden rush of desperate courage Wahb turned and charged his foe. The astonished Coyote gave a scared yowl or two, and fled with his tail between his legs. Thus Wahb learnt that war is the price of peace. But the forage was poor here; there were too many cattle; and Wahb was making for a far-away pinon wood in the Meteetsee Canyon when he saw a man, just like the one he had seen on that day of sorrow. At the same moment he heard a *bang*, and some sage-brush rattled and fell just over his back. All the dreadful smells and dangers of that day came back to his memory, and Wahb ran as he never had run before.

He soon got into a gully and followed it into the canyon. An opening between two cliffs seemed to offer shelter, but as he ran toward it a Range-cow came trotting between, shaking her head at him and snorting threats against his life.

He leaped aside upon a long log that led up a bank, but at once a savage Bobcat appeared on the other end and warned him to go back. It was no time to quarrel. Bitterly Wahb felt that the world was full of enemies. But he turned and scrambled up a rocky bank into the pinon woods that border the benches of the Meteetsee. The Pine Squirrels seemed to resent his coming, and barked furiously. They were thinking about their pinon-nuts. They knew that this Bear was coming to steal their provisions, and they followed him overhead to scold and abuse him, with such an outcry that an enemy might have followed him by their noise, which was exactly what they intended.

There was no one following, but it made Wahb uneasy and nervous. So he kept on till he reached the timber line, where both food and foes were scarce, and here on the edge of the Mountain-sheep land at last he got a chance to rest.

IV

Wahb never was sweet-tempered like his baby sister, and the perse-
cutions by his numerous foes were making him more and more sour.
Why could not they let him alone in his misery? Why was every one
against him? If only he had his Mother back! If he could only have
killed that Black-bear that had driven him from his woods! It did not
occur to him that some day he himself would be big. And that spite-
full Bobcat, that took advantage of him; and the man that had tried to
kill him. He did not forget any of them, and he hated them all.

Wahb found his new range fairly good, because it was a good nut
year. He learned just what the Squirrels feared he would, for his nose
directed him to the little granaries where they had stored up great
quantities of nuts for winter's use. It was hard on the Squirrels, but it
was good luck for Wahb, for the nuts were delicious food. And
when the days shortened and the nights began to be frosty, he had
grown fat and well favoured.

He travelled over all parts of the canyon now, living mostly in the
higher woods, but coming down at times to forage almost as far as
the river. One night as he wandered by the deep water a peculiar
smell reached his nose. It was quite pleasant, so he followed it up to
the water's edge. It seemed to come from a sunken log. As he
reached over toward this, there was a sudden *clank*, and one of his
paws was caught in a strong, steel Beaver-trap.

Wahb yelled and jerked back with all his strength, and tore up the
stake that held the trap. He tried to shake it off, then ran away
through the bushes trailing it. He tore at it with his teeth; but there it
hung, quiet, cold, strong, and immovable. Every little while he tore
at it with his teeth and claws or beat it against the ground. He buried
it in the earth, then climbed a low tree, hoping to leave it behind; but
still it clung, biting into his flesh. He made for his own woods, and sat
down to try to puzzle it out. He did not know what it was, but his
little green-brown eyes glared with a mixture of pain, fright, and
fury as he tried to understand his new enemy.

He lay down under the bushes, and, intent on deliberately crushing the thing, he held it down with one paw while he tightened his
teeth on the other end, and bearing down as it slid away, the trap
jaws opened and the foot was free. It was mere chance, of course,
that led him to squeeze both springs at once. He did not understand

it, but he did not forget it, and he got these not very clear ideas: "There is a dreadful little enemy that hides by the water and waits for one. It has an odd smell. It bites one's paws and is too hard for one to bite. But it can be got off by hard squeezing."

For a week or more the little Grizzly had another sore paw, but it was not very bad if he did not do any climbing.

It was now the season when the Elk were bugling on the mountains. Wahb heard them all night, and once or twice had to climb to get away from one of the big-antlered Bulls. It was also the season when the trappers were coming into the mountains, and the Wild Geese were honking overhead. There were several quite new smells in the woods, too. Wahb followed one of these up, and it led to a place where were some small logs piled together; then, mixed with the smell that had drawn him, was one that he hated — he remembered it from the time when he had lost his Mother. He sniffed about carefully, for it was not very strong, and learned that this hateful smell was on a log in front, and the sweet smell that made his mouth water was under some brush behind. So he went around, pulled away the brush till he got the prize, a piece of meat, and as he grabbed it, the log in front went down with a heavy *chock*.

It made Wahb jump; but he got away all right with the meat and some new ideas, and with one old idea made stronger, and that was: "When that hateful smell is around it always means trouble."

As the weather grew colder, Wahb became very sleepy; he slept all day when it was frosty. He had not any fixed place to sleep in; he knew a number of dry ledges for sunny weather, and one or two sheltered nooks for stormy days. He had a very comfortable nest under a root, and one day, as it began to blow and snow, he crawled into this and curled up to sleep. The storm howled without. The snow fell deeper and deeper. It draped the pine-trees till they bowed, then shook themselves clear to be draped anew. It drifted over the mountains and poured down the funnel-like ravines, blowing off the peaks and ridges, and filling up the hollows level with their rims. It piled up over Wahb's den, shutting out the cold of the winter, shutting out itself: and Wahb slept and slept.

Part II: The Days of His Strength

Wahb's third summer had brought him the stature of a large-sized Bear, though not nearly the bulk and power that in time were his. He was very light-coloured now, and this was why Spahwat, a Shoshone Indian who more than once hunted him, called him the Whitebear, or Wahb.

Spahwat was a good hunter, and as soon as he saw the rubbing-tree on the Upper Meteetsee he knew that he was on the range of a big Grizzly. He bushwhacked the whole valley, and spent many days before he found a chance to shoot; then Wahb got a stinging flesh-wound in the shoulder. He growled horribly, but it had seemed to take the fight out of him; he scrambled up the valley and over the lower hills till he reached a quiet haunt, where he lay down.

His knowledge of healing was wholly instinctive. He licked the wound and all around it, and sought to be quiet. The licking re-moved the dirt, and by massage reduced the inflammation, and it plastered the hair down as a sort of dressing over the wound to keep out the air, dirt, and microbes. There could be no better treatment.

But the Indian was on his trail. Before long the smell warned Wahb that a foe was coming, so he quietly climbed farther up the mountain to another resting-place. But again he sensed the Indian's approach, and made off. Several times this happened, and at length there was a second shot and another galling wound. Wahb was furious now. There was nothing that really frightened him but that horrible odour of man, iron, and guns, that he remembered from the day when he lost his Mother; but now all fear of these left him. He heaved painfully up the mountain again, and along under a six-foot ledge, then up and back to the top of the bank, where he lay flat. On came the Indian, armed with knife and gun; deftly, swiftly keeping on the trail; gloating joyfully over each bloody print that meant such anguish to the hunted Bear. Straight up the slide of broken rock he came, where Wahb, ferocious with pain, was waiting on the ledge. On sneaked the dogged hunter; his eye still scanned the bloody slots or swept the woods ahead, but never was raised to glance above the ledge. And Wahb, as he saw this shape of Death relentless on his track, and smelt the hated smell, poised his bulk at heavy cost upon his quivering mangled arm, there held until the proper instant came, then to his sound arm's matchless native force he added all the weight of desperate hate as down he struck one fearful, crushing blow. The Indian sank without a cry, and then dropped out of sight. Wahb rose, and sought again a quiet nook where he might nurse his wounds. Thus he learned that one must fight for peace; for he never saw that Indian again, and he had time to rest and recover.

II

The years went on as before, except that each winter Wahb slept less soundly, and each spring he came out earlier and was a bigger Grizzly, with fewer enemies that dared to face him. When his sixth year came he was a very big, strong, sullen Bear, with neither friendship nor love in his life since that evil day on the Lower Piney.

No one ever heard of Wahb's mate. No one believes that he ever had one. The love-season of Bears came and went year after year, but left him alone in his prime as he had been in his youth. It is not good for a Bear to be alone; it is bad for him in every way. His habitual moroseness grew with his strength, and any one chancing to meet him now would have called him a dangerous Grizzly.

He had lived in the Meteetsee Valley since first he betook himself there, and his character had been shaped by many little adventures with traps and his wild rivals of the mountains. But there was none of the latter that he now feared, and he knew enough to avoid the first, for that penetrating odour of man and iron was a never-failing warning, especially after an experience which befell him in his sixth year.

His ever-reliable nose told him that there was a dead Elk down among the timber.

He went up the wind, and there, sure enough, was the great delicious carcass, already torn open at the the very best place. True, there was that terrible man-and-iron taint, but it was so slight and the feast so tempting that after circling around and inspecting the carcass from his eight feet of stature, as he stood erect, he went cautiously forward, and at once was caught by his left paw in an enormous Bear-trap. He roared with pain and slashed about in a fury. But this was no Beaver-trap; it was a big forty-pound Bear-catcher, and he was surely caught.

Wahb fairly foamed with rage, and madly grit his teeth upon the trap. Then he remembered his former experiences. He placed the trap between his hind legs, with a hind paw on each spring, and pressed down with all his weight. But it was not enough. He dragged off the trap and its clog, and went clanking up the mountain. Again and again he tried to free his foot, but in vain, till he came where a great trunk crossed the trail a few feet from the ground. By chance, or happy thought, he reared again under this and made a new attempt. With a hind foot on each spring and his mighty shoulders underneath the tree, he bore down with his titanic strength: the great steel springs gave way, the jaws relaxed, and he tore out his foot. So Wahb was free again, though he left behind a great toe which had been nearly severed by the first snap of the steel.

Again Wahb had a painful wound to nurse, and as he was a left-handed Bear — that is, when he wished to turn a rock over he stood on the right paw and turned with the left — the result of this disablement was to rob him for a time of all those dainty foods that are found under rocks or logs. The wound healed at last, but he never forgot that experience, and thenceforth the pungent smell of man and iron, even without the gun smell, never failed to enrage him.

Many experiences had taught him that it is better to run if he only smelt the hunter or heard him far away, but to fight desperately if the man was close at hand. And the cowboys soon came to know that the Upper Meteetsee was the range of a Bear that was better let alone.

III

Wahb was getting well past his youth now, and he began to have pains in the hind leg that had been wounded so often. After a cold night or a long time of wet weather he could scarcely use that leg, and one day, while thus crippled, the west wind came down the canyon with an odd message to his nose. Wahb could not clearly read the message, but it seemed to say, "Come," and something within him said, "Go." The smell of food will draw a hungry creature and disgust a gorged one. We do not know why, and all that any one can learn is that the desire springs from a need of the body. So Wahb felt drawn by what had long disgusted him, and he slouched up the mountain path, grumbling to himself and slapping savagely back at branches that chanced to switch his face.

The odd odour grew very strong; it led him where he had never been before — up a bank of whitish sand to a bench of the same colour, where there was unhealthy-looking water running down, and a kind of fog coming out of a hole. Wahb threw up his nose suspiciously — such a peculiar smell! He climbed the bench.

A snake wriggled across the sand in front. Wahb crushed it with a blow that made the near trees shiver and sent a balanced boulder toppling down, and he growled a growl that rumbled up the valley like distant thunder. Then he came to the foggy hole. It was full of water that moved gently and steamed. Wahb put in his foot, and found that it was quite warm and that it felt pleasantly on his skin. He put in both feet, and little by little went in farther, causing the pool to overflow on all sides, till he was lying at full length in the warm, almost hot, sulphur-spring, and sweltering in the greenish water, while the wind drifted the steam about overhead.

There are plenty of these sulphur-springs in the Rockies, but this chanced to be the only one on Wahb's range. He lay in it for over an hour; then, feeling that he had had enough, he heaved his huge bulk up on the bank, and realized that he was feeling remarkably well and supple. The stiffness of his hind leg was gone.

He shook the water from his shaggy coat. A broad ledge in full sun-heat invited him to stretch himself out and dry. But first he reared against the nearest tree and left a mark that none could mistake. True, there were plenty of signs of other animals using the sulphur-bath for their ills; but what of it? Thenceforth that tree bore this inscription, in a language of mud, hair, and smell, that every mountain creature could read:

My bath. Keep away!
(Signed) WAHB.

Wahb lay on his belly till his back was dry, then turned on his broad back and squirmed about in a ponderous way till the broiling sun had wholly dried him. He realized that he was really feeling very well now. He did not say to himself, "I am troubled with that unpleasant disease called rheumatism, and sulphur-bath treatment is the thing to cure it." But what he did know was, "I have dreadful pains; I feel better when I am in this stinking pool." So thenceforth he came back whenever the pains began again, and each time he was cured.

Part III: The Waning

Years went by. Wahb grew no bigger — there was no need for that — but he got whiter, crosser, and more dangerous. He really had an enormous range now. Each spring, after the winter storms had removed his notice-boards, he went around and renewed them. It was natural to do so, for, first of all, the scarcity of food compelled him to travel all over the range. There were lots of clay wallows at that season, and the itching of his skin, as the winter coat began to shed, made the dressing of cool, wet clay very pleasant, and the exquisite pain of a good scratching was one of the finest pleasures he knew. So whatever his motive, the result was the same: the signs were renewed each spring.

At length the Palette Ranch outfit appeared on the Lower Piney, and the men got acquainted with the "ugly old fellow." The cowpunchers when they saw him, decided they "hadn't lost any Bears and they had better keep out of his way and let him mind his business."

II

Every one knows that a Bitter-root Grizzly is a bad Bear. The Bitter-root Range is the roughest part of the mountains. The ground is everywhere cut up with deep ravines and overgrown with dense and tangled underbrush.

It is an impossible country for horses, and difficult for gunners, and there is any amount of good Bear-pasture. So there are plenty of Bears and plenty of trappers.

The Roachbacks, as the Bitter-root Grizzlies are called, are a cunning and desperate race. An old Roachback knows more about traps than half a dozen ordinary trappers; he knows more about plants and roots than a whole college of botanists. He can tell to a certainty just when and where to find each kind of grub and worm, and he knows by a whiff whether the hunter on his trail a mile away is working with guns, poison, dogs, traps, or all of them together. And he has one general rule, which is an endless puzzle to the hunter: "Whatever you decide to do, do it quickly and follow it right up." So when a trapper and a Roachback meet, the Bear at once makes up his mind to run away as hard as he can, or to rush at the man and fight to a finish.

The Grizzlies of the Bad Lands did not do this: they used to stand on their dignity and growl like a thunderstorm, and so gave the hunters a chance to play their deadly lightning; and lightning is worse than thunder any day. Men can get used to growls that rumble along the ground and up one's legs to the little house where one's courage lives; but Bears cannot get used to 45-90 soft-nosed bullets, and that is why the Grizzlies of the Bad Lands were all killed off.

So the hunters have learned that they never know what a Roachback will do; but they do know that he is going to be quick about it.

Altogether these Bitter-root Grizzlies have solved very well the problem of life, in spite of white men, and are therefore increasing in their own wild mountains.

Of course a range will hold only so many Bears, and the increase is crowded out; so that when that slim young Bald-faced Roachback found he could not hold the range he wanted, he went out perforce to seek his fortune in the world.

He was not a big Bear, or he would not have been crowded out; but he had been trained in a good school, so that he was cunning enough to get on very well elsewhere. How he wandered down to the Salmon River Mountains and did not like them; how he travelled till he got among the barbed-wire fences of the Snake Plains and of course could not stay there; how he made for the Snake River Mountains and found more hunters than berries; how he crossed into the Tetons and looked down with disgust on the teeming man colony of Jackson's Hole, does not belong to this history of Wahb. But when Baldy Roachback crossed the Gros Ventre Range and over the Wind River Divide to the head of the Graybull, he does come into the story, just as he did into the country and the life of the Meteetsee Grizzly.

The Roachback had not found a man-sign since he left Jackson's Hole, and here he was in a land of plenty of food. He feasted on all the delicacies of the season, and enjoyed the easy, brushless country till he came on one of Wahb's sign-posts.

"Trespassers beware!" it said in the plainest manner. The Roachback reared up against it.

"Thunder what a Bear!" The nose-mark was a head and neck above Baldy's highest reach. Now, a simple Bear would have gone quietly away after this discovery; but Baldy felt that the mountains owed him a living, and here was a good one if he could keep out of the way of the big fellow. He nosed about the place, kept a sharp lookout for the present owner, and went on feeding wherever he ran across a good thing.

A step or two from this ominous tree was an old pine stump. In the Bitter-roots there are often mice-nests under such stumps, and Baldy jerked it over to see. There was nothing. The stump rolled over against the sign-post. Baldy had not yet made up his mind about it; but a new notion came into his cunning brain. He turned his head on this side, then on that. He looked at the stump, then at the sign, with his little pig-like eyes. Then he deliberately stood up on the pine root, with his back to the tree, and put his mark away up, a head at least above that of Wahb. He rubbed his back long and hard, and he sought some mud to smear his head and shoulders, then came back and made the mark so big, so strong, and so high, and emphasized it with such claw-gashes in the bark, that it could be read only in one way — a challenge to the present claimant from some monstrous invader, who was ready, nay anxious, to fight to a finish for this desirable range.

Maybe it was accident and maybe design, but when the Roach-back jumped from the root it rolled to one side. Baldy went on down the canyon, keeping the keenest lookout for his enemy.

It was not long before Wahb found the trail of the interloper, and all the ferocity of his nature was aroused.

He followed the trail for miles on more than one occasion. But the small Bear was quick-footed as well as quick-witted, and never showed himself. He made a point, however, of calling at each sign-post, and if there was any means of cheating, so that his mark might be put higher, he did it with a vim, and left a big, showy record. But if there was no chance for any but a fair register, he would not go near the tree but looked for a fresh tree near by with some log or side-ledge to reach from.

Thus Wahb soon found the interloper's marks towering far above his own — a monstrous Bear evidently, that even he could not be sure of mastering. But Wahb was no coward. He was ready to fight to a finish any one that might come; and he hunted the range for that invader. Day after day Wahb sought for him and held himself ready to fight. He found his trail daily, and more and more often he found that towering record far above his own. He often smelt him on the wind; but he never saw him, for the old Grizzly's eyes had grown very dim of late years; things but a little way off were mere blurs to him. The continual menace could not but fill Wahb with uneasiness, for he was not young now, and his teeth and claws were worn and blunted. He was more than ever troubled with pains in his old wounds, and though he could have risen on the spur of the moment to fight any number of Grizzlies of any size, still the continual apprehension, the knowledge that he must hold himself ready at any moment to fight this young monster, weighed on his spirits and began to tell on his general health.

III

The Roachback's life was one of continual vigilance, always ready to run, doubling and shifting to avoid the encounter that must mean instant death to him. Many a time from some hiding-place he watched the great Bear, and trembled lest the wind should betray him. Several times his very impudence saved him, and more than once he was nearly cornered in a box canyon. Once he escaped only by climbing up a long crack in a cliff, which Wahb's huge frame could not have entered. But still, in a mad persistence, he kept on marking the trees farther into the range.

At last he scented and followed up the sulphur bath. He did not understand it at all. It had no appeal to him, but hereabouts were the treks of the owner. In a spirit of mischief the Roachback scratched dirt into the spring, and then seeing the rubbing-tree, he stood sidewise on the rocky ledge, and was thus able to put his mark fully five feet above that of Wahb. Then he nervously jumped down, and was running about, defiling the bath and keeping a sharp lookout, when he heard a noise in the woods below. Instantly he was all alert. The sound drew near, then the wind brought the sure proof and the Roachback, in terror, turned and fled into the woods.

It was Wahb. He had been failing in health of late; his old pains were on him again, and, as well as his hind leg, had seized his right shoulder, where were still lodged two rifle-balls. He was feeling very ill, and crippled with pain. He came up the familiar bank at a jerky limp, and there caught the odour of the foe; then he saw the track in the mud — his eyes said the track of a small Bear, but his eyes were dim now, and his nose, his unerring, nose, said, "This is the track of the huge invader." Then he noticed the tree with his sign on it, and there beyond doubt was the stranger's mark far above his own. His eyes and nose were agreed on this; and more, they told him that the foe was close at hand, might at any moment come.

Wahb was feeling ill and weak with pain. He was in no mood for a desperate fight. A battle against such odds would be madness now. So, without taking the treatment, he turned and swung along the bench away from the direction taken by the stranger — the first time since his cubhood that he had declined to fight.

That was a turning-point in Wahb's life. If he had followed up the stranger he would have found the miserable little craven trembling, cowering, in an agony of terror, behind a log in a natural trap, a walled-in glade only fifty yards away, and would surely have crushed him. Had he even taken the bath, his strength and courage would have been renewed, and if not, then at least in time he would have met his foe, and his afterlife would have been different. But he had turned. This was the fork in the trail, but he had no means of knowing it.

He limped along, skirting the lower spurs of the Shoshones, and soon came on that horrid smell that he had known for years, but never followed up or understood. It was right in his road, and he traced it to a small, barren ravine that was strewn over with skeletons and dark objects, and Wahb, as he passed, smelt a smell of many different animals, and knew by its quality that they were lying dead in this treeless, grassless hollow. For there was a cleft in the rocks at the upper end, whence poured a deadly gas; invisible but heavy, it filled the little gulch like a brimming poison bowl, and at the lower end there was a steady overflow. But Wahb knew only that the air that poured from it as he passed made him dizzy and sleepy, and repelled him, so that he got quickly away from it and was glad once more to breathe the piny wind.

Once Wahb decided to retreat, it was all too easy to do so next time; and the result worked double disaster. For, since the big stranger was allowed possession of the sulphur-spring, Wahb felt that he would rather not go there. Sometimes when he came across the traces of his foe, a spurt of his old courage would come back. He would rumble that thunder-growl as of old, and go painfully lumbering along the trail to settle the thing right then and there. But he never overtook the mysterious giant, and his rheumatism, growing worse now that he was barred from the cure, soon made him daily less capable of either running or fighting.

Sometimes Wahb would sense his foe's approach when he was in a bad place for fighting, and, without really running, he would yield to a wish to be on a better footing, where he would have a fair chance. This better footing never led him nearer the enemy, for it is well known that the one awaiting has the advantage.

Some days Wahb felt so ill that it would have been madness to have staked everything on a fight, and when he felt well or a little better, the stranger seemed to keep away.

Wahb soon found that the stranger's track was most often on the Warhouse and the west slope of the Piney, the very best feeding-grounds. To avoid these when he did not feel equal to fighting was only natural, and as he was always in more or less pain now it amounted to abandoning to the stranger the best part of the range.

Weeks went by. Wahb had meant to go back to his bath, but he never did. His pains grew worse; he was now crippled in his right shoulder as well as in his hind leg.

The long strain of waiting for the fight begot anxiety, that grew to be apprehension, which, with the sapping of his strength, was breaking down his courage, as it always must when courage is founded on muscular force. His daily care now was not to meet and fight the invader, but to avoid him till he felt better.

Thus that first little retreat grew into one long retreat. Wahb had to go farther and farther down the Piney to avoid an encounter. He was daily worse fed, and as the weeks went by was daily less able to crush a foe.

He was living and hiding at last on the Lower Piney — the very place where once his Mother had brought him with his little brothers. The life he led now was much like the one he had led after that dark day. Perhaps for the same reason. If he had had a family of his own all might have been different. As he limped along one morning, seeking among the barren aspen groves for a few roots, or the wormy partridge-berries that were too poor to interest the Squirrel and the Grouse, he heard a stone rattle down the western slope into the woods, and, a little later on the wind was borne the dreaded taint. He waded through the ice-cold Piney — once he would have leaped it — and the chill water sent through and up each great hairy limb keen pains that seemed to reach his very life. He was retreating again —

which way? There seemed but one way now — toward the new ranch-house.

But there were signs of stir about it long before he was near enough to be seen. His nose, his trustiest friend, said, "Turn, turn and seek the hills," and turn he did, even at the risk of meeting there the dreadful foe. He limped painfully along the north bank of the Piney, keeping in the hollows and among the trees. He tried to climb a cliff that of old he had often bounded up at full speed. When half-way up his footing gave way, and down he rolled to the bottom. A long way round was now the only road, for onward he must go — on — on. But where? There seemed no choice now but to abandon the whole range to the terrible stranger.

And feeling, as far as a Bear can feel, that he is fallen, defeated, de-throned at last, that he is driven from his ancient range by a Bear too strong for him to face, he turned up the west fork, and the lot was drawn. The strength and speed were gone from his once mighty limbs; he took three times as long as he once would to mount each well-known ridge, and as he went he glanced backward from time to time to know if he were pursued. Away up the head of the little branch were the Shoshones, bleak, forbidding; no enemies were there, and the Park was beyond it all — on, on he must go. But as he climbed with shaky limbs, and short uncertain steps, the west wind brought the odour of Death Gulch, that fearful little valley where everything was dead, where the very air was deadly. It used to disgust him and drive him away, but now Wahb felt that it had a message for him; he was drawn by it. It was in his line of flight, and he hobbled slowly toward the place. He went nearer, nearer, until he stood upon the entering ledge. A Vulture that had descended to feed on one of the victims was slowly going to sleep on the untouched car-cass. Wahb swung his great grizzled muzzle and his long white beard in the wind. The odour that he once had hated was attractive now. There was a strange biting quality in the air. His body craved it. For it seemed to numb his pain and it promised sleep, as it did that day when first he saw the place.

Far below him, to the right and to the left and on and on as far as the eye could reach, was the great kingdom that once had been his; where he had lived for years in the glory of his strength; where none had dared to meet him face to face. The whole earth could show no view more beautiful. But Wahb had no thought of its beauty; he only knew that it was a good land to live in; that it had been his, but that now it was gone, for his strength was gone, and he was flying to seek a place where he could rest and be at peace.

Away over the Shoshones, indeed, was the road to the Park, but it was far, far away, with a doubtful end to the long, doubtful journey. But why so far? Here in this little gulch was all he sought; here were peace and painless sleep. He knew it; for his nose, his never-erring nose, said, "*Here! here now!*"

He paused a moment at the gate, and as he stood the wind-borne fumes began their subtle work. Five were the faithful wardens of his life, and the best and trustiest of them all flung open wide the door he long had kept. A moment still Wahb stood in doubt. His lifelong guide was silent now, had given up his post. But another sense he felt within. The Angel of the Wild Things was standing there, beckoning, in the little vale. Wahb did not understand. He had no eyes to see the tear in the Angel's eyes, nor the pitying smile that was surely on his lips. He could not even see the Angel. But he *felt* him beckoning, beckoning.

A rush of his ancient courage surged in the Grizzly's rugged breast. He turned aside into the little gulch. The deadly vapours entered in, filled his huge chest and tingled in his vast, heroic limbs as he calmly lay down on the rocky, herbless floor and as gently went to sleep, as he did that day in his Mother's arms by the Graybull, long ago.

Short Stories

Short Stories

Commentary

"Short stories broke out everywhere." That was how H.G. Wells characterized the chief literary activity of the last three decades of the nineteenth century. It was indeed, in both America and Britain, the "age of the short story." And it coincided with — some would insist was brought about by — the emergence of the popular periodical. In magazines such as *Argosy, Cassell's, Longman's, Good Housekeeping, Cosmopolitan, Saturday Evening Post, Strand, Scribner's, Munsey's, McClure's,* and *Everybody's* short-story writers found their readiest reception and their largest audience. There were, even discounting the many hundreds of parochial and ephemeral journals in existence, more than a hundred weekly and monthly magazines which a reader could buy and in them there were published more than fifty thousand short stories in the three-decade period.

An impressive proportion of those stories were written by Canadians — some of whom had moved to the United States or Great Britain to better avail themselves of the literary opportunities open to them; and some who remained in Canada, writing for both a domestic and foreign market. And, judging by the quality of the magazines in which they appeared and the frequency of appearance, these Canadian writers were as popular (in as great demand) as some of their international contemporaries — H.G. Wells, Robert Louis Stevenson, Brete Harte, Israel Zangwill, H.H. Munro and others. Robert Barr, for example (who is presented in the section on Humour), published more than two hundred short stories in magazines. Marjorie Pickthall was hailed by her magazine publisher as being perhaps the best (and certainly the most popular) short-story writer of her day. Similarly, other Canadians such as Roger Pocock, James Macdonald Oxley, Lily Dougall, Gilbert Parker, Charles G.D. Roberts, Arthur Stringer, Norman Duncan, Sara Jeannette Duncan, Theodore Roberts, and L.M. Montgomery were extremely prolific and were popular with magazine readers throughout the English-speaking world.

The short stories written by Canadians before World War I (a sampling of which is offered here) are representative of the genre as a whole. That is, whereas the traditional story — with its emphasis on plot and character conflict, and its romantic dénouement — dominates, there are some which, given the interest in human psychology that was transforming all writing, are quite modern-looking in their realism and psychological verisimilitude. Thus, while Gilbert Parker still embraces romantic notions of the hero and conveys that in a stereotypical style, Marjorie Pickthall attempts a kind of psychological thriller in a less conventional way. The distinction, however, is not always that clear. In fact, in the stories offered here, and in a great many stories at the turn of the century, one can, within the stories themselves, see evidence of the transition between traditional and modern — a sentimental plot with a realistic style, an open-ended outcome to a conventional story, and so forth. The point is, Canadian writers were aware of what was happening to their craft, were experimenting and transforming, and were successfully competing in a very large and demanding market.

Further Reading

Clare Hanson, *Short Stories and Short Fictions 1880-1980*. London: Macmillan, 1985.

Desmond Pacey, Introduction to A Book of Canadian Stories. Toronto: Ryerson, 1947. xi-xxxviii.

Gordon Roper, "New Forces: New Fiction 1880-1920" in Carl F. Klinck, ed., *Literary History of Canada* 2nd ed., Vol. I. Toronto: U of T Press, 1976. 274-97.

Gilbert Parker

Like a number of other writers (Sara Jeannette Duncan and Robert Barr, for example), Gilbert Parker, born in Camden East, Ontario, only became successful after leaving Canada. Parker, like the hero of one of his novels, set out to prove that a colonial could assume the role of an English gentleman: he became a member of the British Parliament, was knighted in 1902, was made a member of the Privy Council, and published more than thirty works of fiction, many of which are collections of short stories. The following is from Pierre and His People *(1893) one of Parker's many "Canadian" stories.*

The Patrol of the Cypress Hills

"He's too ha'sh," said old Alexander Windsor, as he shut the creaking door of the store after a vanishing figure, and turned to the big iron stove with out-stretched hands; hands that were cold both summer and winter. He was of lean and frigid make.

"Sergeant Fones is too ha'sh," he repeated, as he pulled out the damper and cleared away the ashes with the iron poker.

Pretty Pierre blew a quick, straight column of cigarette smoke into the air, tilted his chair back, and said: "I do not know what you mean by "ha'sh," but he is the devil. Eh, well, there was more than one devil made sometime in the North West." He laughed softly.

"That gives you a chance in history, Pretty Pierre," said a voice from behind a pile of woollen goods and buffalo skins in the centre of the floor. The owner of the voice then walked to the window. He scratched some frost from the pane and looked out to where the trooper in dog-skin coat, gauntlets and cap, was mounting his broncho. The old man came and stood near the young man, — the owner of the voice, — and said again: "He's too ha'sh."

"*Harsh* you mean, father," added the other.

"Yes, *harsh* you mean, Old Brown Windsor, — quite harsh," said Pierre.

Alexander Windsor, storekeeper and general dealer, was sometimes called "Old Brown Windsor" and sometimes "Old Aleck," to distinguish him from his son, who was known as "Young Aleck."

As the old man walked back again to the stove to warm his hands, Young Aleck continued: "He does his duty, that's all. If he doesn't wear kid gloves while at it, it's his choice. He doesn't go beyond his duty. You can bank on that. It would be hard to exceed that way out here."

"True, Young Aleck, so true; but then he wears gloves of iron, of ice. That is not good. Sometime the glove will be too hard and cold on a man's shoulder, and then! — Well, I should like to be there," said Pierre, showing his white teeth.

Old Aleck shivered, and held his fingers where the stove was red hot.

The young man did not hear this speech; from the window he was watching Sergeant Fones as he rode towards the Big Divide. Presently he said: "He's going towards Humphrey's place. I — " He stopped, bent his brows, caught one corner of his slight moustache between his teeth, and did not stir a muscle until the Sergeant had passed over the Divide.

Old Aleck was meanwhile dilating upon his theme before a passive listener. But Pierre was only passive outwardly. Besides hearkening to the father's complaints he was closely watching the son. Pierre was clever, and a good actor. He had learned the power of reserve and outward immobility. The Indian in him helped him there. He had heard what Young Aleck had just muttered; but to the man of the cold fingers he said: "You keep good whisky in spite of the law and the iron glove, Old Aleck." To the young man: "And you can drink it so free, eh, Young Aleck?" The half-breed looked out of the corners of his eyes at the young man, but he did not raise the peak of his fur cap in doing so, and his glances askance were not seen.

Young Aleck had been writing something with his finger-nail on the frost of the pane, over and over again. When Pierre spoke to him thus he scratched out the word he had written, with what seemed unnecessary force. But in one corner it remained: "Mab — "

Pierre added: "That is what they say at Humphrey's ranch."

"Who says that at Humphrey's? Pierre, you lie!" was the sharp and threatening reply. The significance of this last statement had been often attested on the prairies by the piercing emphasis of a six-chambered revolver. It was evident that Young Aleck was in earnest. Pierre's eyes glowed in the shadow, but he idly replied:

"I do not remember quite who said it. Well, mon ami, perhaps I lie; perhaps. Sometimes we dream things, and these dreams are true.

You call it a lie — *bien*! Sergeant Fones, he dreams perhaps Old Aleck sells whisky against the law to men you call whisky runners, sometimes to Indians and half-breeds — half-breeds like Pretty Pierre. That was a dream of Sergeant Fones; but you see he believes it true. It is good sport, eh? Will you not take — what is it? — a silent partner? Yes; a silent partner, Old Aleck. Pretty Pierre has spare time, a little, to make money for his friends and for himself, eh?"

When did not Pierre have time to spare? He was a gambler. Unlike the majority of half-breeds, he had a pronounced French manner, nonchalant and debonair. The Indian in him gave him coolness and nerve. His cheeks had a tinge of delicate red under their whiteness, like those of a woman. That was why he was called Pretty Pierre. The country had, however, felt a kind of weird menace in the name. It was used to snakes whose rattle gave notice of approach or signal of danger. But Pretty Pierre was like the death-adder, small and beautiful, silent and deadly. At one time he had made a secret of his trade, or thought he was doing so. In those days he was often to be seen at David Humphrey's home, and often in talk with Mab Humphrey; but it was there one night that the man who was ha'sh gave him his true character, with much candour and no comment. Afterwards Pierre was not seen at Humphrey's ranch. Men prophesied that he would have revenge some day on Sergeant Fones; but he did not show anything on which this opinion could be based. He took no umbrage at being called Pretty Pierre the gambler. But for all that he was possessed of a devil.

Young Aleck had inherited some money through his dead mother from his grandfather, a Hudson's Bay factor. He had been in the East for some years, and when he came back he brought his "little pile" and an impressionable heart with him. The former Pretty Pierre and his friends set about to win; the latter, Mab Humphrey won without the trying. Yet Mab gave Young Aleck as much as he gave her. More. Because her love sprang from a simple, earnest, and uncontaminated life. Her purity and affection were being played against Pierre's designs and Young Aleck's weakness. With Aleck cards and liquor went together. Pierre seldom drank.

But what of Sergeant Fones? If the man that knew him best — the Commandant — had been asked for his history, the reply would have been: "Five years in the Service, rigid disciplinarian, best non-commissioned officer on the Patrol of the Cypress Hills." That was all the Commandant knew.

A soldier-policeman's life on the frontier is rough, solitary, and severe. Active duty and responsibility are all that make it endurable. To few is it fascinating. A free and thoughtful nature would, however, find much in it, in spite of great hardships, to give interest and even pleasure. The sense of breadth and vastness, and the inspiration of pure air could be a very gospel of strength, beauty, and courage, to such an one — for a time. But was Sergeant Fones such an one? The Commandant's scornful reply to a question of the kind would have been: "He is the best soldier on the Patrol."

And so with hard gallops here and there after the refugees of crime or misfortune, or both, who fled before them like deer among the passes of the hills, and, like deer at bay, often fought like demons to the death; with border watchings, and protection and care and vigilance of the Indians; with hurried marches at sun-rise, the thermometer at fifty degrees below zero often in winter, and open camps beneath the stars, and no camp at all, as often as not, winter and summer; with rough barrack fun and parade and drill and guard of prisoners; and with chances now and then to pay homage to a woman's face, — the Mounted Force grew full of the Spirit of the West and became brown, valiant, and hardy, with wind and weather. Perhaps some of them longed to touch, oftener than they did, the hands of children, and to consider more the faces of women, — for hearts are hearts even under a belted coat of red on the Fiftieth Parallel, — but men of nerve do not blazon their feelings.

No one would have accused Sergeant Fones of having a heart. Men of keen discernment would have seen in him the little Bismarck of the Mounted Police. His name carried farther on the Cypress Hills Patrol than any other; and yet his officers could never say that he exceeded his duty or enlarged upon the orders he received. He had no sympathy with crime. Others of the force might wink at it; but his mind appeared to sit severely upright upon the cold platform of Penalty, in beholding breaches of the statutes. He would not have rained upon the unjust as the just if he had had the directing of the heavens. As Private Gellatly put it: "Sergeant Fones has the fear o' God in his heart, and the law of the land across his saddle, and the newest breech-loading at that!" He was part of the great machine of Order, the servant of Justice, the sentinel in the vestibule of Martial Law. His interpretation of duty worked upward as downward. Officers and privates were acted on by the force known as Sergeant Fones. Some people, like Old Brown Windsor, spoke hardly and

openly of this force. There were three people who never did —
Pretty Pierre, Young Aleck, and Mab Humphrey. Pierre hated him;
Young Aleck admired in him a quality lying dormant in himself —
decision; Mab Humphrey spoke unkindly of no one. Besides — but
no!

What was Sergeant Fones's country? No one knew. Where had
he come from? No one asked him more than once. He could talk
French with Pierre, — a kind of French that sometimes made the
undertone of red in the Frenchman's cheeks darker. He had been
heard to speak German to a German prisoner, and once, when a
gang of Italians were making trouble on a line of railway under construction, he arrested the leader, and, in a few swift, sharp words in
the language of the rioters, settled the business. He had no accent
that betrayed his nationality. He had been recommended for a commission. The officer in command had hinted that the Sergeant might
get a Christmas present. The officer had further said: "And if it was
something that both you and the Patrol would be the better for, you
couldn't object, Sergeant." But the Sergeant only saluted, looking
steadily into the eyes of the officer. That was his reply.

Private Gellatly, standing without, heard Sergeant Fones say, as
he passed into the open air, and slowly bared his forehead to the winter sun:

"Exactly."

And Private Gellatly cried, with revolt in his voice, "Divils me
own, the word that a't to have been full o' joy was like the clip of a
rifle-breech."

Justice in a new country is administered with promptitude and
vigour, or else not administered at all. Where an officer of the
Mounted Police-Soldiery has all the powers of a magistrate, the law's
delay and the insolence of office have little space in which to work.
One of the commonest slips of virtue in the Canadian West was selling whisky contrary to the law of prohibition which prevailed.
Whisky runners were land smugglers. Old Brown Windsor had,
somehow, got the reputation of being connected with the whisky
runners; not a very respectable business, and thought to be dangerous. Whisky runners were inclined to resent intrusion on their privacy with a touch of that biting inhospitableness which a moon-
lighter of Kentucky uses toward an inquisitive, unsympathetic
marshal. On the Cypress Hills Patrol, however, the erring servants of
Bacchus were having a hard time of it. Vigilance never slept there in

the days of which these lines bear record. Old Brown Windsor had, in words, freely espoused the cause of the sinful. To the careless spectator it seemed a charitable siding with the suffering; a proof that the old man's heart was not so cold as his hands. Sergeant Fones thought differently, and his mission had just been to warn the store-keeper that there was menacing evidence gathering against him, and that his friendship with Golden Feather, the Indian Chief, had better cease at once. Sergeant Fones had a way of putting things. Old Brown Windsor endeavoured for a moment to be sarcastic. This was the brief dialogue in the domain of sarcasm:

"I s'pose you just lit round in a friendly sort of way, hopin' that I'd kenoodle with you later."

"Exactly."

There was an unpleasant click to the word. The old man's hands got colder. He had nothing more to say.

Before leaving, the Sergeant said something quietly and quickly to Young Aleck. Pierre observed, but could not hear. Young Aleck was uneasy; Pierre was perplexed. The Sergeant turned at the door, and said in French: "What are your chances for a Merry Christmas at Pardon's Drive, Pretty Pierre?" Pierre answered nothing. He shrugged his shoulders, and as the door closed, muttered, "*Il est le diable.*" And he meant it. What should Sergeant Fones know of that intended meeting at Pardon's Drive on Christmas Day? And if he knew, what then? It was not against the law to play euchre. Still it perplexed Pierre. Before the Windsors, father and son, however, he was, as we have seen, playfully cool.

After quitting Old Brown Windsor's store, Sergeant Fones urged his stout broncho to a quicker pace than usual. The broncho was, like himself, wasteful of neither action nor affection. The Sergeant had caught him wild and independent, had brought him in, broken him, and taught him obedience. They understood each other; perhaps they loved each other. But about that even Private Gellatly had views in common with the general sentiment as to the character of Sergeant Fones. The private remarked once on this point: "Sarpints alive! the heels of the one and the law of the other is the love of them. They'll weather together like the Divil and Death."

The Sergeant was brooding; that was not like him. He was hesitating; that was less like him. He turned his broncho round as if to cross the Big Divide and to go back to Windsor's store; but he changed his mind again, and rode on toward David Humphrey's ranch. He sat as if he had been born in the saddle. His was a face for the artist, strong and clear, and having a dominant expression of force. The eyes were deepset and watchful. A kind of disdain might be traced in the curve of the short upper lip, to which the moustache was clipped close — a good fit, like his coat. The disdain was more marked this morning.

The first part of his ride had been seen by Young Aleck, the second part by Mab Humphrey. Her first thought on seeing him was one of apprehension for Young Aleck and those of Young Aleck's name. She knew that people spoke of her lover as a ne'er-do-weel; and that they associated his name freely with that of Pretty Pierre and his gang. She had a dread of Pierre, and, only the night before, she had determined to make one last great effort to save Aleck, and if he would not be saved — strange that, thinking it all over again, as she watched the figure on horseback coming nearer, her mind should swerve to what she had heard of Sergeant Fones's expected promotion. Then she fell to wondering if anyone had ever given him a real Christmas present; if he had any friends at all; if life meant anything more to him than carrying the law of the land across his saddle. Again he suddenly came to her in a new thought, free from apprehension, and as the champion of her cause to defeat the half-breed and his gang, and save Aleck from present danger or future perils. She was such a woman as prairies nurture; in spirit broad and thoughtful and full of energy; not so deep as the mountain woman, not so imaginative, but with more persistency, more daring. Youth to her was a warmth, a glory. She hated excess and lawlessness, but she could understand it. She felt sometimes as if she must go far away into the unpeopled spaces, and shriek out her soul to the stars from the fulness of too much life. She supposed men had feelings of that kind too, but that they fell to playing cards and drinking instead of crying to the stars. Still, she preferred her way.

Once, Sergeant Fones, on leaving the house, said grimly after his fashion: "Not Mab but Ariadne excuse a soldier's bluntness. . . Good-bye!" and with a brusque salute he had ridden away. What he meant she did not know and could not ask. The thought instantly came to her mind: Not Sergeant Fones; but — who? She wondered if Ariadne was born on the prairie. What knew she of the girl who helped Theseus, her lover, to slay the Minotaur? What guessed she of the Slopes of Naxos? How old was Ariadne? Twenty? — For that was Mab's age. Was Ariadne beautiful? She ran her fingers loosely through her short brown hair, waving softly about her Greek-shaped head, and reasoned that Ariadne must have been presentable, or Sergeant Fones would not have made the comparison. She hoped Ariadne could ride well, for she could.

But how white the world looked this morning, and how proud and brilliant the sky! Nothing in the plane of vision but waves of snow stretching to the Cypress Hills; far to the left a solitary house, with its tin roof flashing back the sun, and to the right the Big Divide. It was an old-fashioned winter, not one in which bare ground and sharp winds make life outdoors inhospitable. Snow is hospitable — clean, impacted snow; restful and silent. But there was one spot in the area of white, on which Mab's eyes were fixed now, with something different in them from what had been there. Again it was a memory with which Sergeant Fones was associated. One day in the summer just past she had watched him and his company put away to rest under the cool sod, where many another lay in silent company, a prairie wanderer, some outcast from a better life gone by. Afterwards, in her home, she saw the Sergeant stand at the window, looking out towards the spot where the waves in the sea of grass were more regular and greener than elsewhere, and were surmounted by a high cross. She said to him — for she of all was never shy of his stern ways: "Why is the grass always greenest there, Sergeant Fones?"

He knew what she meant, and slowly said: "It is the Barracks of the Free."

She had no views of life save those of duty and work and natural joy and loving a ne'er-do-weel, and she said: "I do not understand that."

And the Sergeant replied: "'*Free among the Dead like unto them that are wounded and lie in the grave, who are out of remembrance.*'"

But Mab said again: "I do not understand that either."

The Sergeant did not at once reply. He stepped to the door and gave a short command to some one without, and in a moment his company was mounted in line; handsome, dashing fellows; one the son of an English nobleman, one the brother of an eminent Canadian politician, one related to a celebrated English dramatist. He ran his eye along the line, then turned to Mab, raised his cap with machine-like precision, and said: "No, I suppose you do not understand that. Keep Aleck Windsor from Pretty Pierre and his gang. Good-bye."

Then he mounted and rode away. Every other man in the company looked back to where the girl stood in the doorway; he did not. Private Gellatly said, with a shake of the head, as she was lost to view: "Devils bestir me, what a widdy she'll make!" It was understood that Aleck Windsor and Mab Humphrey were to be married on the coming New Year's Day. What connection was there between the words of Sergeant Fones and those of Private Gellatly? None, perhaps.

Mab thought upon that day as she looked out, this December morning, and saw Sergeant Fones dismounting at the door. David Humphrey, who was outside, offered to put up the Sergeant's horse; but he said: "No, if you'll hold him just a moment, Mr. Humphrey, I'll ask for a drink of something warm, and move on. Miss Humphrey is inside, I suppose?"

"She'll give you a drink of the best to be had on your patrol, Sergeant," was the laughing reply.

"Thanks for that, but tea or coffee is good enough for me," said the Sergeant. Entering, the coffee was soon in the hand of the hardy soldier. Once he paused in his drinking and scanned Mab's face closely. Most people would have said the Sergeant had an affair of the law in hand, and was searching the face of a criminal; but most people are not good at interpretation. Mab was speaking to the chore-girl at the same time and did not see the look. If she could have defined her thoughts when she, in turn, glanced into the Sergeant's face, a moment afterwards, she would have said, "Austerity fills this man. Isolation marks him for its own." In the eyes were only purpose, decision, and command. Was that the look that had been fixed upon her face a moment ago? It must have been. His features had not changed a breath. Mab began their talk.

"They say you are to get a Christmas present of promotion, Sergeant Fones."

"I have not seen it gazetted," he answered enigmatically.

"You and your friends will be glad of it."

"I like the service."

"You will have more freedom with a commission."

He made no reply, but rose and walked to the window, and looked out across the snow, drawing on his gauntlets as he did so.

She saw that he was looking where the grass in summer was the greenest!

He turned and said:

"I am going to barracks now. I suppose Young Aleck will be in quarters here on Christmas Day, Miss Mab?"

"I think so," and she blushed.

"Did he say be would be here?"

"Yes."

"Exactly."

He looked toward the coffee. Then:

"Thank you... Good-bye."

"Sergeant?"

"Miss Humphrey!"

"Will you not come to us on Christmas Day?"

His eyelids closed swiftly and opened again.

"I shall be on duty."

"And promoted?"

"Perhaps."

"And merry and happy?" — she smiled to herself to think of Sergeant Fones being merry and happy.

"Exactly."

The word suited him.

He paused a moment with his fingers on the latch, and turned round as if to speak; pulled off his gauntlet, and then as quickly put it on again. Had he meant to offer his hand in good-bye? He had never been seen to take the hand of anyone except with the might of the law visible in steel.

He opened the door with the right hand, but turned round as he stepped out, so that the left held it while he faced the warmth of the room and the face of the girl.

The door closed.

Mounted, and having said good-bye to Mr. Humphrey, he turned towards the house, raised his cap with soldierly brusqueness, and rode away in the direction of the barracks.

The girl did not watch him. She was thinking of Young Aleck, and of Christmas Day, now near. The Sergeant did not look back.

Meantime the party at Windsor's store was broken up. Pretty Pierre and Young Aleck had talked together, and the old man had heard his son say:

"Remember, Pierre, it is for the last time."

Then they talked after this fashion: "Ah, I know, mon ami; for the last time! Eh, bien, you will spend Christmas Day with us too — no? You surely will not leave us on the day of good fortune? Where better can you take your pleasure — for the last time? One day is not enough for farewell. Two, three; that is the magic number. You will, eh? no? Well, well, you will come tomorrow — and — eh, mon ami, where do you go the next day? Oh, pardon, I forgot, you spend the Christmas Day — I know. And the day of the New Year? Ah, Young Aleck, that is what they say — the devil for the devil's luck. So."

"Stop that, Pierre." There was fierceness in the tone. "I spend the Christmas Day where you don't, and as I like, and the rest doesn't concern you. I drink with you, I play with you — bien! As you say yourself, bien, isn't that enough?"

"Pardon! We will not quarrel. No; we spend not the Christmas Day after the same fashion, quite. Then, to-morrow at Pardon's Drive! Adieu!"

Pretty Pierre went out of one door, a malediction between his white teeth, and Aleck went out of another door with a malediction upon his gloomy lips. But both maledictions were levelled at the same person. Poor Aleck.

"Poor Aleck!" That is the way we sometimes think of a good nature gone awry; one that has learned to say cruel maledictions to itself, and against which demons hurl their deadly maledictions too. Alas, for the ne'er-do-weel!

That night a stalwart figure passed from David Humphrey's door, carrying with him the warm atmosphere of a good woman's love. The chilly outer air of the world seemed not to touch him, Love's curtains were drawn so close. Had one stood within "the Hunter's Room," as it was called, a little while before, one would have seen a man's head bowed before a woman, and her hand smoothing back the hair from the handsome brow where dissipation had drawn some deep lines. Presently the hand raised the head until the eyes of the woman looked full into the eyes of the man.

"You will not go to Pardon's Drive again, will you, Aleck?"

"Never again after Christmas Day, Mab. But I must go to-morrow. I have given my word."

"I know. To meet Pretty Pierre and all the rest, and for what? Oh, Aleck, isn't the suspicion about your father enough, but you must put this on me as well?"

"My father must suffer for his wrongdoing if he does wrong, and I for mine."

There was a moment's silence. He bowed his head again.

"And I have done wrong to us both. Forgive me, Mab."

She leaned over and caressed his hair. "I forgive you, Aleck."

A thousand new thoughts were thrilling through him. Yet this man had given his word to do that for which he must ask forgiveness of the woman he loved. But to Pretty Pierre, forgiven or unforgiven, he would keep his word. She understood it better than most of those who read this brief record can. Every sphere has its code of honour and duty peculiar to itself.

"You will come to me on Christmas morning, Aleck?"

"I will come on Christmas morning."

"And no more after that of Pretty Pierre?"

"And no more of Pretty Pierre."

She trusted him; but neither could reckon with unknown forces.

Sergeant Fones, sitting in the barracks in talk with Private Gellatly, said at that moment in a swift silence, "Exactly."

Pretty Pierre, at Pardon's Drive, drinking a glass of brandy at that moment, said to the ceiling:

"No more of Pretty Pierre after to-morrow night, monsieur! Bien! If it is for the last time, then it is for the last time. So... so."

He smiled. His teeth were amazingly white.

The stalwart figure strode on under the stars, the white night a lens for visions of days of rejoicing to come. All evil was far from him. The dolorous tide rolled back in this hour from his life, and he revelled in the light of a new day.

"When I've played my last card to-morrow night with Pretty Pierre, I'll begin the world again," he whispered.

And Sergeant Fones in the barracks said just then, in response to a further remark of Private Gellatly,- "Exactly."

Young Aleck fell to singing:

> "Out from your vineland come
> Into the prairies wild;
> Here will we make our home,—
> Father, mother, and child;
> Come, my love, to our home,—
> Father, mother, and child,
> Father, mother, and—"

He fell to thinking again — "and child—and child," — it was in his ears and in his heart.

But Pretty Pierre was singing softly to himself in the room at Pardon's Drive:

> "Three good friends with the wine at night—
> Vive la compagnie!
> Two good friends when the sun grows bright —
> Vive la compagnie!
> Vive la, vive la, vive l'amour!
> Vive la, vive la, vive l'amour!
> Three good friends, two good friends —
> Vive la compagnie!"

What did it mean?

Private Gellatly was cousin to Idaho Jack, and Idaho Jack disliked Pretty Pierre, though he had been one of the gang. The cousins had seen each other lately, and Private Gellatly had had a talk with the man who was ha'sh. It may be that others besides Pierre had an idea of what it meant.

In the house at Pardon's Drive the next night sat eight men, of whom three were Pretty Pierre, Young Aleck, and Idaho Jack. Young Aleck's face was flushed with bad liquor and the worse excitement of play. This was one of the unreckoned forces. Was this the man that sang the tender song under the stars last night? Pretty Pierre's face was less pretty than usual; the cheeks were pallid, the eyes were hard and cold. Once he looked at his partner as if to say, "Not yet." Idaho Jack saw the look; he glanced at his watch; it was eleven o'clock. At that moment the door opened, and Sergeant Fones entered. All started to their feet, most with curses on their lips; but Sergeant Fones never seemed to hear anything that could make a feature of his face alter. Pierre's hand was on his hip, as if feeling for something. Sergeant Fones saw that; but he walked to where Aleck stood, with his unplayed cards still in his hand, and, laying a hand on his shoulder, said, "Come with me."

"Why should I go with you?" — this with a drunken man's bravado.

"You are my prisoner."

Pierre stepped forward. "What is his crime?" he exclaimed.

"How does that concern you, Pretty Pierre?"

"He is my friend."

"Is he your friend, Aleck?"

What was there in the eyes of Sergeant Fones that forced the reply, — "To-night, yes; to-morrow, no."

"Exactly. It is near to-morrow; come."

Aleck was led towards the door. Once more Pierre's hand went to
his hip; but he was looking at the prisoner, not at the Sergeant. The
Sergeant saw, and his fingers were at his belt. He opened the door.
Aleck passed out. He followed. Two horses were tied to a post. With
difficulty Aleck was mounted. Once on the way his brain began
slowly to clear, but he grew painfully cold. It was a bitter night. How
bitter it might have been for the ne'er-do-weel let the words of
Idaho Jack, spoken in a long hour's talk next day with Old Brown
Windsor, show. "Pretty Pierre, after the two were gone, said, with a
shiver of curses — 'another hour and it would have been done, and
no one to blame. He was ready for trouble. His money was nearly
finished. A little quarrel easily made, the door would open, and he
would pass out. His horse would be gone, he could not come back;
he would walk. The air is cold, quite, quite cold; and the snow is a
soft bed. He would sleep well and sound, having seen Pretty Pierre
for the last time. And now — ' The rest was French and furtive."

From that hour Idaho Jack and Pretty Pierre parted company.

Riding from Pardon's Drive, Young Aleck noticed at last that
they were not going towards the barracks.

He said: "Why do you arrest me?"

The Sergeant replied: "You will know that soon enough. You are
now going to your own home. Tomorrow you will keep your word
and go to David's place; the next day I will come for you. Which do
you choose: to ride with me to-night to the barracks and know why
you are arrested, or go, unknowing, as I bid you, and keep your
word with the girl?" Through Aleck's fevered brain, there ran the
words of the song he sang before—

> Out from your vineland come
> Into the prairies wild;
> Here will we make our home,—
> Father, mother, and child."

He could have but one answer.

At the door of his home the Sergeant left him with the words,
"Remember you are on parole."

Aleck noticed as the Sergeant rode away that the face of the sky had changed, and slight gusts of wind had come up. At any other time his mind would have dwelt upon the fact. It did not do so now.

Christmas Day came. People said that the fiercest night, since the blizzard day of 1863, had been passed. But the morning was clear and beautiful. The sun came up like a great flower expanding. First the yellow, then the purple, then the red, and then a mighty shield of roses. The world was a blanket of drift, and down, and glistening silver.

Mab Humphrey greeted her lover with such a smile as only springs to a thankful woman's lips. He had given his word and had kept it; and the path of the future seemed surer.

He was a prisoner on parole; still that did not depress him. Plans for coming days were talked of, and the laughter of many voices filled the house. The ne'er-do-weel was clothed and in his right mind. In the Hunter's Room the noblest trophy was the heart of a repentant prodigal.

In the barracks that morning a gazetted notice was posted, announcing, with such technical language as is the custom, that Sergeant Fones was promoted to be a lieutenant in the Mounted Police Force of the North West Territory. When the officer in command sent for him he could not be found. But he was found that morning; and when Private Gellatly, with a warm hand, touching the glove of "iron and ice" — that, indeed, now said: "Sergeant Fones, you are promoted, God help you!" he gave no sign. Motionless, stern, erect, he sat there upon his horse, beside a stunted larch tree. The broncho seemed to understand, for he did not stir, and had not done so for hours; — they could tell that. The bridle rein was still in the frigid fingers, and a smile was upon the face.

A smile upon the face of Sergeant Fones!

Perhaps he smiled that he was going to the Barracks of the Free—

"Free among the Dead like unto them that are wounded and lie in the grave, that are out of remembrance."

In the wild night he had lost his way, though but a few miles from the barracks.

He had done his duty rigidly in that sphere of life where he had lived so much alone among his many comrades. Had he exceeded his duty once in arresting Young Aleck?

When, the next day, Sergeant Fones lay in the barracks, over him the flag for which he had sworn to do honest service, and his promotion papers in his quiet hand, the two who loved each other stood beside him for many a throbbing minute. And one said to herself, silently: "I felt sometimes " — but no more words did she say even to herself.

Old Aleck came in, and walked to where the Sergeant slept, wrapped close in that white frosted coverlet which man wears but once. He stood for a moment silent, his fingers numbly clasped.

Private Gellatly spoke softly: "Angels betide me, it's little we knew the great of him till he wint away; the pride, and the law — and the love of him."

In the tragedy that faced them this Christmas morning one at least had seen "the love of him." Perhaps the broncho had known it before.

Old Aleck laid a palm upon the hand he had never touched when it had life. "He's-too-ha'sh," he said slowly.

Private Gellatly looked up wonderingly.

But the old man's eyes were wet.

Lily Dougall

*Born in Montreal in 1858, and educated in Scotland, Dougall spent most of her life in England (where she lived permanently after 1900). Before turning to a life of religious writing, she wrote eleven novels and many short stories, a few of which are set in Canada. She is a lively, witty writer, though often her subject (she was especially interested in religious themes) gets in the way of her plot. The following short story first appeared in At-*lantic Monthly *76 (Dec. 1895): 740-47.*

Witchcraft

A young minister was walking through the streets of a small town in the island of Cape Breton. The minister was only a theological student who had been sent to preach in this remote place during his summer holiday. The town was at once very primitive and very modern. Many log-houses still remained in it; almost all the other houses were built of wood. The little churches, which represented as many sects, looked like the churches in a child's Dutch village. The town hall had only a brick facing. On the hillsides that surrounded the town far and wide were many fields, in which the first stumps were still standing, charred by the fires that had been kindled to kill them. There were also patches of forest still to be seen among these fields, where the land had not yet been cleared. In spite of all this the town was very modern, every improvement being of the newest kind because so recently achieved. Upon huge ungainly tree-trunks, roughly erected along the streets, electric lamps hung and telephone wires crossed and recrossed one another from roof to roof. There was even an electric tram that ran straight through the town and some distance into the country on either side. The general store had a gayly dressed lay figure in its window, — a female figure, — and its gown was labeled "The latest Parisian novelty."

The theological student was going out to take tea. He was a tall, active fellow, and his long strides soon brought him to a house a little way out of the town, which was evidently the abode of some degree of taste and luxury. The house was of wood, painted in dull colors of red and brown; it had large comfortable verandas under shingled roofs. Its garden was not old-fashioned in the least; but though it aspired to trimness, the grass had not grown there long enough to make a good lawn, so the ribbon flower-beds and plaster vases of flowers lacked the green velvet setting that would have made them appear better. The student was the less likely to criticise the lawn because a very nice, fresh-looking girl met him at the gate.

She was really a fine girl. Her dress showed rather more effort at fashion than was quite in keeping with her very rural surroundings, and her speech and accent betrayed a childhood spent among uneducated folk, and only overlaid by more recent schooling. Her face had the best parts of beauty; health and good sense were written there, also flashes of humor and an habitual sweet seriousness. She had chanced to be at the gate gathering flowers. Her reception of the student was frank, and yet there was just a touch of blushing dignity about it which suggested that she took a special interest in him. The student, also, it would appear, took an interest in her, for, on their way to the house, he made a variety of remarks upon the weather which proved that he was a little excited, and unable to observe that he was talking nonsense.

In a little while the family were gathered round the tea-table. Miss Torrance sat at the head of the table. Her father was a banker and insurance agent. He sat opposite his eldest daughter, and did the honors of the meal with the utmost hospitality, yet with reserve of manner caused by his evident consciousness that his grammar and manners were not equal to those of his children and their guest. There were several daughters and two sons younger than Miss Torrance. They talked with vivacity.

The conversation soon turned upon the fact that the abundant supply of cream to which the family were accustomed was not forthcoming. Strawberries were being served with the tea; some sort of cold pudding was also on the table: and all this to be eaten without cream! These young people might have been asked to go without their supper, so indignant they were.

Now, Mr. Torrance had been decorously trying to talk of the young minister's last sermon, and of the affairs of the small Scotch church of which he was an elder; and Miss Torrance was ably seconding his effort by comparing the sentiments of the sermon with a recent magazine article, but against her will she was forced to attend to the young people's clamor about the cream.

It seemed that Trilium, the cow, had recently refused to give her milk. Mary Torrance was about eighteen: she suddenly gave it as her opinion that Trilium was bewitched; there was no other explanation, she said, no other possible explanation of Trilium's extraordinary conduct.

A flush mounted over Miss Torrance's face; she frowned at her sister when the student was not looking.

"It's wonderful, the amount of witchcraft we have about here, Mr. Howitt," said the master of the house tentatively to the minister.

Howitt had taken Mary's words in jest. He gave his smooth-shaven face the twist that with him always expressed ideas wonderful or grotesque. It was a strong, thin face, full of intelligence.

"I never could have conceived anything like it," said he. "I come across witch tales here, there, everywhere; and the marvelous thing is, some of the people really seem to believe them."

The younger members of the Torrance family fixed their eyes upon him with apprehensive stare.

"You can't imagine anything more degrading," continued the student, who came from afar.

"Degrading, of course." Mr. Torrance sipped his tea hastily. "The Cape Breton people are superstitious, I believe."

An expression that might have betokened a new and noble resolution appeared upon the fine face of the eldest daughter.

"We are Cape Breton people, father," she said, with dignified reproach. "I hope"— here a timid glance as if imploring support — "I hope we know better than to place any real faith in these degrading superstitions."

Howitt observed nothing but the fine face and the words that appeared to him natural. Torrance looked at them both with the air of an honest man who was still made somewhat cowardly by new-fashioned propriety.

"I never put much o' my faith in these things myself," he said at last in broad accents; "still," — an honest shake of the head, — "there's queer things happens."

"It is like going back to the Middle ages" — Howitt was still impervious — "to hear some of these poor creatures talk. I never thought it would be my lot to come across anything so delightfully absurd."

"Perhaps, for the sake of the ministry, ye'd better be careful how ye say your mind about it," suggested Mr. Torrance; "in the hearing of the poor and uneducated, of course, I mean. But if ye like to make a study o' that sort of thing, I'd advise ye to go and have a talk with Mistress Betty McLeod. She's got a great repertory of tales, has Mistress Betty."

Mary spoke again. Mary was a young woman who had the courage of her opinions. "And if you go to Mistress McLeod, Mr. Howitt, will you just be kind enough to ask her how to cure poor Trilium? And don't forget anything of what she says."

Miss Torrance gave her sister a word of reproof. There was still upon her face the fine glow born of her resolution never again to listen to a word of witchcraft.

As for Howitt, there came across his clever face the whimsical look which denoted that he understood Mary perfectly. "I will go tomorrow!" he exclaimed. "When the wise woman has told me who has bewitched Trilium, we will make a waxen figure and stick pins in it."

The next day Howitt went over the hills in search of Mistress Betty McLeod. The lake of the Bras d'Or held the sheen of the western sun in its breast. The student walked upon green slopes far above the water, and watched the outline of the hills on the other side of the inlet, and thought upon many things. He thought upon religion and philosophy, for he was religious and studious; he thought upon practical details of his present work, for he was anxious for the welfare of the souls under his charge; but on whatever subject his thoughts dwelt, they came back at easy intervals to the fair, dignified face of his new friend, Miss Torrance.

"There's a fine girl for you," he said to himself repeatedly, with boyish enthusiasm. He thought, too, how nobly her life would be spent if she chose to be the helpmeet of a Christian minister. He wondered whether Mary could take her sister's place in the home circle. Yet with all this he made no decision as to his own course. He was discreet, and in minds like his decisions upon important matters are fruits of slow growth.

He came at last to a farm, — a very goodly farm for so hilly a district. It lay, a fertile flat, in a notch of the green hillside. When he reached the houseyard, he asked for Mistress Betty McLeod, and was led to her presence. The old dame sat at her spinning-wheel in a farm kitchen. Her white hair was drawn closely, like a thin veil, down the sides of her head and pinned at the back. Her features were small, her eyes bright; she was not unlike a squirrel in her sharp little movements and quick glances. She wore a small shawl pinned around her bare shoulders. Her skirts fell upon the treadle of the spinning-wheel. The kitchen in which she sat was unused; there was no fire in the stove. The brick floor, the utensils hanging on the walls, had the appearance of undisturbed rest. Doors and windows were open to the view of the green slopes and the golden sea beneath them.

"You come from Canada?" said the old dame. She left her spinning with a certain interested formality of manner.

"From Montreal," he replied.

"That's the same. Canada is a terrible way off."

"And now," he said, "I hear there are witches in this part of the land." Whereupon he smiled in an incredulous, cultured way.

She nodded her head as if she had gauged his thought. "Ay, there's many a minister believes in them, if they don't let on they do. I mind"—

"Yes," said he.

"I mind how my sister went out early one morning, and saw a witch milking one of our cows."

"How did you know she was a witch?"

"Och, she was a neighbor we knew to be a witch real well. My sister didn't anger her. It's terrible unlucky to vex them. But would you believe it? as long as we had that cow her cream gave no butter. We had to sell her and get another. And one time — it was years ago, when Donald and me was young — the first sacrament came round"—

"Yes," said he, looking sober.

"And all the milk of our cows would give hardly any butter for a whole year! And at house-cleaning time, there, above the milk shelves, what did they find but a bit of hair rope! Cows' and horses' hair it was. Oh, it was terrible knotted, and knotted just like anything! So then, of course, we knew."

"Knew what?"

"Why, that the milk was bewitched. We took the rope away. Well, that very day more butter came at the churning, and from that time on, more, but still not so much as ought by rights to have come. Then, one day, I thought to unknot the rope, and I undid, and undid, and undid. Well, when I had got it undone, that day the butter came as it should!"

"But what about the sacrament?" asked he.

"That was the time of the year it was. Oh, but I could tell you a sad, sad story of the wickedness of witches. When Donald and me was young, and had a farm up over on the other hill — well, there was a poor widow with seven daughters. It was hard times then for us all, but for her, she only had a bit of flat land with some bushes, and four cows and some sheep, and you see she sold butter to put meat in the children's mouths. Butter was all she could sell.

"Well, there came to live near her on the hill an awful wicked old man and woman. I'll tell you who their daughter is: she's married to Mr. McCurdy, who keeps the store. The old man and his wife were awful wicked to the widow and the fatherless. I'll tell you what they did. Well the widow's butter failed. Not one bit more could she get. The milk was just the same, but not one bit of butter. 'Oh,' said she, 'it's a hard world, and me a widow!' But she was a brave woman, bound to get along some way. So now that she had nothing to sell to buy meal, she made curds of the milk, and fed the children on that.

"Well, one day the old man came in to see her in a neighboring way, and she, being a good woman, — oh, but she was a good woman! — set a dish of curds before him. 'Oh,' said he, 'these are very fine curds!' So he went away, and next day she put the rennet in the milk, and not a bit would the curd come. 'Oh,' said she, 'but I must put something in the children's mouths!' She was a fine woman, she was. So she kept the lambs from the sheep all night, and next morning she milked the sheep. Sheep's milk is rich, and she put rennet in that, and fed the children on curd.

"So one day the old man came in again. He was a wicked one; he was dreadful selfish; and as he was there, she, being a hospitable woman, gave him some of the curd. 'That's good curd,' said he. Next day she put the rennet in the sheep's milk, and not a bit would the curd come. She felt it bitterly, poor woman; but she had a fine spirit, and she fed the children on a few bits of potato she had growing.

"Well, one day the eldest daughter got up very early to spin, — in the twilight of the dawn it was; and she looked out, and there was the old woman coming from her house on the hill, with a shawl over her head and a tub in her arms. Oh, but she was a really wicked one, for I'll tell you what she did. Well, the girl watched and wondered, and in the twilight of the dawn she saw the old woman crouch down by one of the alder bushes, and put her tub under it, and go milking with her hands; and after a bit she lifted her tub, that seemed to have something in it, and set it over against another alder bush, and went milking with her hands again. So the girl said, 'Mother, mother, wake up, and see what the neighbor woman is doing!' So the mother looked out, and there, in the twilight of the dawn, she saw her four cows in the bit of land among the alder bushes, and the old neighbor woman milking away at a bush. And then the old woman moved her tub likewise to another bush, and likewise, and likewise, until she had milked four bushes; and she took up her tub, and it seemed awful heavy, and she had her shawl over it, and was going up the hill.

"So the mother said to the girl, 'Run, run, and see what she has got in it.' For they weren't up to the ways of witches, and they were astonished like. But the girl, she said, 'Oh, mother, I don't like!' Well, she was timid, anyway, the eldest girl. But the second girl was a romping thing, not afraid of anything, so they sent her. By this time the wicked old woman was high on the hill; so she ran and ran, but she could not catch her before she was in at her own door. But that second girl, she was not afraid of anything, so she runs in at the door, too. Now, in those days they used to have sailing-chests that lock up; they had iron bars over them, so you could keep anything in that was a secret. They got them from the ships, and this old woman kept her milk in hers. So when the girl bounced in at the door, there she saw that wicked old woman pouring milk out of the tub into her chest, and the chest half full of milk, and the old man looking on! So then, of course, they knew where the good of their milk had gone."

The story was finished. The old dame looked at the student and nodded her head, with eyes that awaited some outburst of his righteous indignation.

"What did they know?" asked he.

"Know! Oh, why, that the old woman was an awful wicked witch, and she'd taken the good of their milk."

"Oh, indeed!" said the student; and then, "But what became of the widow and the seven daughters?"

"Well, of course she had to sell her cows and get others, and then it was all right. But that old man and his wife were that selfish they'd not have cared if she'd starved. And I tell you, it's one of the things witches can do to take the good out of food, if they've an eye to it; they can take every bit of nouriture out of it that's in it. There were two young men that went from here to the States, — that's Boston, ye know. Well, pretty soon one, that was named McPherson, came back, looking so white like and ill that nothing would do him any good. He drooped and he died. Well, years after, the other, whose name was McVey, came back. He was of the same wicked stock as the old folks I've been telling ye of. Well, one day he was in low spirits like, and he chanced to be talking to my father, and says he, 'It's one of the sins I'll have to 'count for at the judgment that I took the good out of McPherson's food till he died. I sat opposite to him at the table when we was at Boston together, and I took the good out of his food, and it's the blackest sin I done,' said he.

"Oh, they're awful wicked people, these witches! One of them offered to teach my sister how to take the good out of food, but my sister was too honest; she said, 'I'll learn to keep the good of my own, if ye like.' However, the witch wouldn't teach her that because she wouldn't learn the other. Oh, but I cheated a witch once. Donald, he brought me a pound of tea. 'Twasn't always we got tea in those days, so I put it in the tin box; and there was just a little over, so I was forced to leave that in the paper bag. Well, that day a neighbor came in from over the hill. I knew fine she was a witch; so we sat and gossiped a bit. She was a real pleasant woman, and she sat and sat, and the time of day went by. So I made her a cup of tea, her and me; but I used the drawing that was in the paper bag. Said she, 'I just dropped in to borrow a bit of tea going home, but if that's all ye have' — Oh, but I could see her eying round; so I was too sharp for her, and I says, 'Well, I've no more in the paper just now, but if ye'll wait till Donald comes, maybe he'll bring some.' So she saw I was too sharp for her, and away she went. If I'd as much as opened the tin she'd have had every grain of good out of it with her eyes."

At first the student had had the grave and righteous intention of denouncing the superstition, but gradually he had perceived that to do so would be futile. The artistic soul of him was caught by the curious recital. He remembered now the bidding of Mary Torrance, and thought with pleasure that he would go back and repeat these strange stories to Miss Torrance, and smile at them in her company.

"Now, for instance," he said aloud, "if a good cow, that is a great pet in the family, should suddenly cease to give her milk, how would you set about curing her?"

The dame's small bright eyes grew keener. She moved to her spinning-wheel, and gave it a turn. "Ay," she said, "and whose is the cow?"

He was not without a genuine curiosity. "What would you do for any cow in that case?"

"And is it Torrance's cow?" asked Mistress Betty. "Och, but I know it's Torrance's cow that ye're speiring for."

The young minister was recalled to a sense of his duty. He rose up with brisk dignity. "I only asked you to see what you would say. I do not believe the stories you have been telling me."

She nodded her head, taking his assertion as a matter of course. "But I'll tell you exactly what they must do," she said. "Ye can tell Miss Torrance she must get a pound of pins."

"A pound of pins!" said he.

"Ay, it's a large quantity, but they'll have them at the store, for it's more than sometimes they're wanted, — a time here, a time there, against the witches. And she's to boil them in whatever milk the cow gives, and she's to pour them boiling hot into a hole in the ground; and when she's put the earth over them, and the sod over that, she's to tether the animal there and milk it there, and the milk will come right enough."

While the student was making his way home along the hillside, through field and forest, the long arm of the sea turned to red and gold in the light of the clouds which the sun had left behind when it sank down over the distant region that the Cape Breton folk call Canada.

The minister meditated upon what he had heard, but not for long. He could not bring his mind into such attitude towards the witch-tales as to conceive of belief in them as an actual part of normal human experience. Insanity, or the love of making a good story out of notions which have never been seriously entertained, was, he supposed, the warp and woof of the fabric of such strange imaginings. It is thus we account for most experiences we do not understand.

The next evening the Torrance family were walking to meeting. The student joined himself to Miss Torrance. He greeted her with the whimsical look of grave humor. "You are to take a pound of pins," he said.

"I do not believe it would do any good," she interrupted eagerly.

It struck him as very curious that she should assert her unbelief. He was too nonplused to go on immediately. Then he supposed it was part of the joke, and proceeded to give the other details.

"Mr. Howitt," — a tremulous pause, — "it is very strange about poor Trilium, she has always been such a good, dear cow; the children are very fond of her, and my mother was very fond of her when she was a heifer. The last summer before she died, Trilium fed out of mother's hand, and now — she's in perfect health as far as we can see, but father says that if she keeps on refusing to give her milk he will be obliged to sell her."

Miss Torrance, who was usually strong and dignified, spoke now in an appealing voice.

"Couldn't you get an old farmer to look at her, or a vet?"

"But why do you think she has suddenly stopped giving milk?" persisted the girl.

"I am very sorry, but I really don't know anything about animals," said he.

"Oh, then, if you don't know anything about them "- She paused. There had been such an evident tone of relief in her voice that he wondered much what could be coming next. In a moment she said, "I quite agreed with you, the other night, when you said that the superstition about witchcraft was degrading."

"No one could think otherwise." He was much puzzled at the turn of her thought.

"Still, of course, *about animals* old people like Mistress Betty McLeod may know something."

As they talked they were walking down the street in the calm of the summer evening to the prayer-meeting. The student's mind was intent upon his duties, for, as they neared the little white-washed church, many groups were seen coming from all sides across the grassy space in which it stood. He was an earnest man, and his mind now became occupied with the thought of the spiritual needs of these others who were flocking to hear him preach and pray.

Inside the meeting-room, unshaded oil lamps flared upon a congregation most serious and devout. The student felt that their earnestness and devotion laid upon him the greater responsibility; he also felt much hindered in his speech because of their ignorance and remote ways of thought. It was a comfort to him to feel that there was at least one family among his hearers whose education would enable them to understand him clearly. He looked with satisfaction at the bench where Mr. Torrance sat with his children. He looked with more satisfaction to where Miss Torrance sat at the little organ. She presided over it with dignity and sweet seriousness. She drew music even out of its squeaking keys.

A few days after that prayer-meeting the student happened to be in the post office. It was a small, rough place; a wooden partition shut off the public from the postmistress and her helpers. He was waiting for some information for which he had asked; he was forced to stand outside the little window in this partition. He listened to women's voices speaking on the other side, as one listens to that which in no way concerns himself.

"It's just like her, stuck up as she is since she came from school, setting herself and her family up to be better than other folks."

"Perhaps they were out of them at the store," said a gentler voice.

"Oh, don't tell me. It's on the sly she's doing it, and then pretending to be grander than other folks."

Then the postmistress came to the window with the required information. When she saw who was there, she said something else also.

"There's a parcel come for Miss Torrance, if you happen to be going up that way," she simpered.

The student became aware for the first time that his friendship with Miss Torrance was a matter of public interest. He was not entirely displeased. "I will take the parcel," he said.

As he went along the sunny road, he felt so light-hearted that, hardly thinking what he did, he began throwing up the parcel and catching it again in his hands. It was not large, and it was very tightly done up in thick paper, and had an ironmonger's label attached; so that, though he paid small attention, it did not impress him as a thing that could be easily injured. Something, however, did soon make a sharp impression upon him: once as he caught the parcel he felt his hand deeply pricked. Looking closely, he saw that a pin was working its way through the thick paper. After that he walked more soberly, and did not play ball. He remembered what he had heard at the post office. The parcel was certainly addressed to Miss Torrance. It was very strange. He remembered now with displeasure the assumption of the postmistress that he would be glad to carry this parcel.

He delivered the pound of pins at the door without making a call. His own mind had never come to any decision as regarded his feeling for Miss Torrance, and now he was more undecided than ever. He was full of curiosity about the pins. He found it hard to believe that they were to be used for a base purpose, but suspicion had entered his mind. The knowledge that the eyes of the little public were upon him made him realize that he could not continue to frequent the house merely to satisfy his curiosity.

He was destined to know more.

That night, long after dark, he was called to visit a dying man, and the messenger led him somewhat out of the town.

He performed his duty to the dying with wistful eagerness. The spirit passed from earth while he yet knelt beside the bed. When he was returning home alone in the darkness, he felt his soul open to the power of unseen spirit, and to him the power of the spiritual unseen was the power of God.

Walking on the soft, quiet road, he came near the house where he had lately loved to visit, and his eye was arrested by seeing a lantern twinkling in the paddock where Trilium grazed. He saw the forms of two women moving in its little circle of light; they were digging in the ground.

He felt that he had a right to make sure of the thing he suspected. The two women were not far from a fence by which he could pass; and he did pass that way, looking and looking till a beam of the lantern fell full on the bending faces. When he saw that Miss Torrance was actually there, he went on without speaking.

After that two facts became known in the village, each much discussed in its own way; yet they were not connected with each other in the common mind. One was that the young minister had ceased to call frequently upon Miss Torrance; the other, that Trilium, the cow, was giving her milk.

Duncan Campbell Scott

Scott is best-known as a descriptive poet — one of the Confederation poets — who, along with Roberts, Carman, Campbell, and Lampman, became the first internationally recognized "Canadian" writers by celebrating Canada's wilderness. Scott also wrote some very fine "Indian" poems which derive from his experience as head of the Department of Indian Affairs at Ottawa. He wrote one novel which is unmemorable and a book of short stories which should be better known. The following story is from his collection of short stories The Village of Viger *(1896).*

Paul Farlotte

Near the outskirts of Viger, to the west, far away from the Blanche, but having a Country outlook of their own, and a glimpse of a shadowy range of hills, stood two houses which would have attracted attention by their contrast, if for no other reason. One was a low cottage, surrounded by a garden, and covered with roses, which formed jalousies for the encircling veranda. The garden was laid out with the care and completeness that told of a master hand. The cottage itself had the air of having been secured from the inroads of time as thoroughly as paint and a nail in the right place at the right time could effect that end. The other was a large gaunt-looking house, narrow and high, with many windows, some of which were boarded up, as if there was no further use for the chambers into which they had once admitted light. Standing on a rough piece of ground it seemed given over to the rudeness of decay. It appeared to have been the intention of its builder to veneer it with brick; but it stood there a wooden shell, discoloured by the weather, disjointed by the frost, and with the wind fluttering the rags of tar-paper which had been intended as a protection against the cold, but which now hung in patches and ribbons. But despite this dilapidation it had a sort of martial air about it, and seemed to watch over its embowered companion, warding off tempests and gradually falling to pieces on guard, like a faithful soldier who suffers at his post. In the road, just between the two, stood a beautiful Lombardy poplar. Its shadow fell upon the little cottage in the morning, and travelled across the garden, and in the evening touched the corner of the tall house, and faded out with the sun, only to float there again in the moonlight, or to commence the journey next morning with the dawn. This shadow seemed, with its constant movement, to figure the connection that existed between the two houses.

The garden of the cottage was a marvel; there the finest roses in the parish grew, roses which people came miles to see, and parterres of old-fashioned flowers, the seed of which came from France, and which in consequence seemed to blow with a rarer colour and more delicate perfume. This garden was a striking contrast to the stony ground about the neighbouring house, where only the commonest weeds grew unregarded; but its master had been a gardener, just as another man is born a musician or a poet. There was a superstition in the village that all he had to do was to put anything, even a dry stick, into the ground, and it would grow. He was the village schoolmaster, and Madame Laroque would remark spitefully enough that if Monsieur Paul Farlotte had been as successful in planting knowledge in the heads of his scholars as he was in planting roses in his garden Viger would have been celebrated the world over. But he was born a gardener, not a teacher; and he made the best of the fate which compelled him to depend for his living on something he disliked. He looked almost as dry as one of his own hyacinth bulbs; but like it he had life at his heart. He was a very small man, and frail, and looked older than he was. It was strange, but you rarely seemed to see his face; for he was bent with weeding and digging, and it seemed an effort for him to raise his head and look at you with the full glance of his eye. But when he did, you saw the eye was honest and full of light. He was not careful of his personal appearance, clinging to his old garments with a fondness which often laid him open to ridicule, which he was willing to bear for the sake of the comfort of an old pair of shoes, or a hat which had accommodated itself to the irregularities of his head. On the street he wore a curious skirt-coat that seemed to be made of some indestructible material, for he had worn it for years, and might be buried in it. It received an extra brush for Sundays and holidays, and always looked as good as new. He made a quaint picture, as he came down the road from the school. He had a hesitating walk, and constantly stopped and looked behind him; for he always fancied he heard a voice calling him by his name. He would be working in his flower-beds when he would hear it over his shoulder, "Paul"; or when he went to draw water from his well, "Paul"; or when he was reading by his fire, someone calling him softly, "Paul, Paul"; or in the dead of night, when nothing moved in his cottage he would hear it out of the dark, "Paul." So it came to be a sort of companionship for him, this haunting voice; and sometimes one could have seen him in his garden stretch out his hand and smile, as if he were welcoming an invisible guest. Sometimes the guest was not invisible, but took body and shape, and was a real presence; and often Paul was greeted with visions of things that had been, or that would be, and saw figures where, for other eyes, hung only the impalpable air.

He had one other passion besides his garden, and that was Montaigne. He delved in one in the summer, in the other in the winter. With his feet on his stove he would become so absorbed with his author that he would burn his slippers and come to himself disturbed by the smell of the singed leather. He had only one great ambition, that was to return to France to see his mother before she died; and he had for years been trying to save enough money to take the journey. People who did not know him called him stingy, and said the saving for his journey was only a pretext to cover his miserly habits. It was strange, he had been saving for years, and yet he had not saved enough. Whenever anyone would ask him, "Well, Monsieur Farlotte, when do you go to France?" he would answer, "Next year — next year." So when he announced one spring that he was actually going, and when people saw that he was not making his garden with his accustomed care, it became the talk of the village: "Monsieur Farlotte is going to France"; "Monsieur Farlotte has saved enough money, true, true, he is going to France."

His proposed visit gave no one so much pleasure as it gave his neighbours in the gaunt, unkempt house which seemed to watch over his own; and no one would have imagined what a joy it was to Marie St. Denis, the tall girl who was mother to her orphan brothers and sisters, to hear Monsieur Farlotte say, "When I am in France"; for she knew what none of the villagers knew, that, if it had not been for her and her troubles, Monsieur Farlotte would have seen France many years before. How often she would recall the time when her father, who was in the employ of the great match factory near Viger, used to drive about collecting the little paper match-boxes which were made by hundreds of women in the village and the country around; how he had conceived the idea of making a machine in which a strip of paper would go in at one end, and the completed match-boxes would fall out at the other; how he had given up his situation and devoted his whole time and energy to the invention of this machine; how he had failed time and again, but continued with a perseverance which at last became a frantic passion; and how, to keep the family together, her mother, herself, and the children joined that army of workers which was making the match-boxes by hand. She would think of what would have happened to them then if Monsieur Farlotte had not been there with his help, or what would have happened when her mother died, worn out, and her father, overcome with disappointment, gave up his life and his task together, in despair. But whenever she would try to speak of these things Monsieur Farlotte would prevent her with a gesture, "Well, but what would you have me do — besides, I will go some day— now who knows, next year, perhaps." So here was the "next year," which she had so longed to see, and Monsieur Farlotte was giving her a daily lecture on how to treat the tulips after they had done flowering, preluding everything he had to say with, "When I am in France," for his heart was already there.

He had two places to visit, one was his old home, the other was the birthplace of his beloved Montaigne. He had often described to Marie the little cottage where he was born, with the vine arbours and the long garden walks, the lilac-bushes, with their cool dark-green leaves, the white eaves where the swallows nested, and the poplar, sentinel over all. "You see," he would say, "I have tried to make this little place like it; and my memory may have played me a trick, but I often fancy myself at home. That poplar and this long walk and the vines on the arbour — sometimes when I see the tulips by the border I fancy it is all in France."

Marie was going over his scant wardrobe, mending with her skil-ful fingers, putting a stitch in the trusty old coat, and securing its but-tons. She was anxious that Monsieur Farlotte should get a new suit before he went on his journey; but he would not hear of it. "Not a bit of it," he would say, "if I made my appearance in a new suit, they would think I had been making money; and when they would find out that I had not enough to buy cabbage for the soup there would be a disappointment." She could not get him to write that he was coming. "No, no," he would say, "if I do that they will expect me." "Well, and why not — why not?" "Well, they would think about it — in ten days Paul comes home, then in five days Paul comes home, and then when I came they would set the dogs on me. No, I will just walk in — so — and when they are staring at my old coat I will just sit down in a corner and my old mother will commence to cry. Oh, I have it all arranged."

So Marie let him have his own way; but she was fixed on having her way in some things. To save Monsieur Farlotte the heavier work, and allow him to keep his strength for the journey, she would make her brother Guy do the spading in the garden, much to his disgust, and that of Monsieur Farlotte, who would stand by and interfere, taking the spade into his own hands with infinite satisfaction. "See," he would say, "go deeper and turn it over so." And when Guy would dig in his own clumsy way, he would go off in despair, with the words, "God help us, nothing will grow there."

When Monsieur Farlotte insisted on taking his clothes in an old box covered with raw-hide, with his initials in brass tacks on the cover, Marie would not consent to it, and made Guy carry off the box without his knowledge and hide it. She had a good tin trunk which had belonged to her mother, which she knew where to find in the attic and which would contain everything Monsieur Farlotte had to carry. Poor Marie never went into this attic without a shudder, for occupying most of the space was her father's work bench, and that complicated wheel, the model of his invention, which he had tried so hard to perfect, and which stood there like a monument of his failure. She had made Guy promise never to move it, fearing lest he might be tempted to finish what his father had begun — a fear that was almost an apprehension, so like him was he growing. He was tall and large-boned, with a dark restless eye, set under an overhanging forehead. He had long arms, out of proportion to his height, and he hung his head when he walked. His likeness to his father made him seem a man before his time. He felt himself a man; for he had a good position in the match factory, and was like a father to his little brothers and sisters.

Although the model had always had a strange fascination for him, the lad had kept his promise to his sister, and had never touched the mechanism which had literally taken his father's life. Often when he went into the attic he would stand and gaze at the model and wonder why it had not succeeded, and recall his father bending over his work, with his compass and pencil. But he had a dread of it, too, and sometimes would hurry away, afraid lest its fascination would conquer him.

Monsieur Farlotte was to leave as soon as his school closed, but weeks before that he had everything ready, and could enjoy his roses in peace. After school hours he would walk in his garden, to and fro, to and fro, with his hands behind his back, and his eyes upon the ground, meditating; and once in a while he would pause and smile, or look over his shoulder when the haunting voice would call his name. His scholars had commenced to view him with additional interest, now that he was going to take such a prodigious journey; and two or three of them could always be seen peering through the palings, watching him as he walked up and down the path; and Marie would watch him, too, and wonder what he would say when he found that his trunk had disappeared. He missed it fully a month before he could expect to start; but he had resolved to pack that very evening. "But there is plenty of time," remonstrated Marie.

"That's always the way," he answered. "Would you expect me to leave everything until the last moment?"

"But, Monsieur Farlotte, in ten minutes everything goes into the trunk."

"So, and in the same ten minutes something is left out of the trunk, and I am in France, and my shoes are in Viger, that will be the end of it."

So, to pacify him, she had to ask Guy to bring down the trunk from the attic. It was not yet dark there; the sunset threw a great colour into the room, touching all the familiar objects with transfiguring light, and giving the shadows a rich depth. Guy saw the model glowing like some magic golden wheel, the metal points upon it gleaming like jewels in the light. As he passed he touched it, and with a musical click something dropped from it. He picked it up: it was one of the little paper match-boxes, but the defect that he remembered to have heard talked of was there. He held it in his hand and examined it; then he pulled it apart and spread it out. "Ah," he said to himself, "the fault was in the cutting." Then he turned the wheel, and one by one the imperfect boxes dropped out, until the strip of paper was exhausted. "But why," — the question rose in his mind — "why could not that little difficulty be overcome?"

He took the trunk down to Marie, who at last persuaded Monsieur Farlotte to let her pack his clothes in it. He did so with a protestation, "Well, I know how it will be with a fine box like that, some fellow will whip it off when I am looking the other way, and that will be the end of it."

As soon as he could do so without attracting Marie's attention Guy returned to the attic with a lamp. When Marie had finished packing Monsieur Farlotte's wardrobe, she went home to put her children to bed; but when she saw that light in the attic window she nearly fainted from apprehension. When she pushed open the door of that room which she had entered so often with the scant meals she used to bring her father, she saw Guy bending over the model, examining every part of it. "Guy," she said, trying to command her voice, "you have broken your promise." He looked up quickly. "Marie, I am going to find it out — I can understand it — there is just one thing, if I can get that we will make a fortune out of it."

"Guy, don't delude yourself; those were father's words, and day after day I brought him his meals here, when he was too busy even to come downstairs; but nothing came of it, and while he was trying to make a machine for the boxes, we were making them with our fingers. O Guy," she cried, with her voice rising into a sob, "remember those days, remember what Monsieur Farlotte did for us, and what he would have to do again if you lost your place."

"That's all nonsense, Marie. Two weeks will do it, and after that I could send Monsieur Farlotte home with a pocket full of gold."

"Guy, you are making a terrible mistake. That wheel was our curse, and it will follow us if you don't leave it alone. And think of Monsieur Farlotte; if he finds out what you are working at he will not go to France — I know him; he will believe it his duty to stay here and help us, as he did when father was alive. Guy, Guy, listen to me!"

But Guy was bending over the model, absorbed in its labyrinths. In vain did Marie argue with him, try to persuade him, and threaten him; she attempted to lock the attic door and keep him out, but he twisted the lock off, and after that the door was always open. Then she resolved to break the wheel into a thousand pieces; but when she went upstairs, when Guy was away, she could not strike it with the axe she held. It seemed like a human thing that cried out with a hundred tongues against the murder she would do; and she could only sink down sobbing, and pray. Then failing everything else she simulated an interest in the thing, and tried to lead Guy to work at it moderately, and not to give up his whole time to it.

But he seemed to take up his father's passion where he had laid it down. Marie could do nothing with him; and the younger children, at first hanging around the attic door, as if he were their father come back again, gradually ventured into the room, and whispered to-gether as they watched their rapt and unobservant brother working at his task. Marie's one thought was to devise a means of keeping the fact from Monsieur Farlotte; and she told him blankly that Guy had been sent away on business, and would not be back for six weeks. She hoped that by that time Monsieur Farlotte would be safely started on his journey. But night after night he saw a light in the attic window. In the past years it had been constant there, and he could only connect it with one cause. But he could get no answer from Marie when he asked her the reason; and the next night the dis-tracted girl draped the window so that no ray of light could find its way out into the night. But Monsieur Farlotte was not satisfied; and a few evenings afterwards, as it was growing dusk, he went quietly into the house, and upstairs into the attic. There he saw Guy stretched along the work bench, his head in his hands, using the last light to ponder over a sketch he was making, and beside him, figured very clearly in the thick gold air of the sunset, the form of his father, bending over him, with the old eager, haggard look in his eyes. Monsieur Farlotte watched the two figures for a moment as they glowed in their rich atmosphere; then the apparition turned his head slowly, and warned him away with a motion of his hand.

All night long Monsieur Farlotte walked in his garden, patient and undisturbed, fixing his duty so that nothing could root it out. He found the comfort that comes to those who give up some exceeding deep desire of the heart, and when next morning the market-gar-dener from St. Valerie, driving by as the matin bell was clanging from St. Joseph's, and seeing the old teacher as if he were taking an early look at his growing roses, asked him, "Well, Monsieur Far-lotte, when do you go to France?" he was able to answer cheerfully, "Next year — next year."

Marie could not unfix his determination. "No," he said, "they do not expect me. No one will be disappointed. I am too old to travel. I might be lost in the sea. Until Guy makes his invention we must not be apart."

At first the villagers thought that he was only joking, and that they would some morning wake up and find him gone; but when the holidays came, and when enough time had elapsed for him to make his journey twice over they began to think he was in earnest. When they knew that Guy St. Denis was chained to his father's invention, and when they saw that Marie and the children had commenced to make match-boxes again, they shook their heads. Some of them at least seemed to understand why Monsieur Farlotte had not gone to France.

But he never repined. He took up his garden again, was as contented as ever, and comforted himself with the wisdom of Montaigne. The people dropped the old question, "When are you going to France?" Only his companion voice called him more loudly, and more often he saw figures in the air that no one else could see.

Early one morning, as he was working in his garden around a growing pear-tree, he fell into a sort of stupor, and sinking down quietly on his knees he leaned against the slender stem for support. He saw a garden much like his own, flooded with the clear sunlight, in the shade of an arbour an old woman in a white cap was leaning back in a wheeled chair, her eyes were closed, she seemed asleep. A young woman was seated beside her holding her hand. Suddenly the old woman smiled, a childish smile, as if she were well pleased. "Paul," she murmured, "Paul, Paul." A moment later her companion started up with a cry; but she did not move, she was silent and tranquil. Then the young woman fell on her knees and wept, hiding her face. But the aged face was inexpressibly calm in the shadow, with the smile lingering upon it, fixed by the deeper sleep into which she had fallen.

Gradually the vision faded away, and Paul Farlotte found himself leaning against his pear-tree, which was almost too young as yet to support his weight. The bell was ringing from St. Joseph's, and had shaken the swallows from their nests in the steeple into the clear air. He heard their cries as they flew into his garden, and he heard the voices of his neighbour children as they played around the house.

Later in the day he told Marie that his mother had died that morning, and she wondered how he knew.

Norman Duncan

Born in Ontario in 1871, Norman Duncan became a journalist in the United States, working for such prestigious newspapers and magazines as New York Evening Post *and* McClure's Magazine. *This work took him to many parts of the world and his descriptive writing became extremely popular. Around 1901 he went to Newfoundland to do a series of articles on the Grenfell Mission; he fell in love with the island people, went back for several summers, and eventually wrote several books about his adventures there. These are Duncan's best and best-loved stories. The following is from* The Way of the Sea *(1903).*

The Fruits of Toil

Now the wilderness, savage and remote, yields to the strength of men. A generation strips it of tree and rock, a generation tames it and tills it, a generation passes into the evening shadows as into rest in a garden, and thereafter the children of that place possess it in peace and plenty, through succeeding generations, without end, and shall to the end of the world. But the sea is tameless: as it was in the beginning, it is now, and shall ever be — mighty, savage, dreaded, infinitely treacherous and hateful, yielding only that which is wrested from it, snarling, raging, snatching lives, spoiling souls of their graces. The tiller of the soil sows in peace, and in a yellow, hazy peace he reaps; he passes his hand over a field, and, lo, in good season he gathers a harvest, for the earth rejoices to serve him. The deep is not thus subdued; the toiler of the sea — the Newfoundlander of the upper shore — is born to conflict, ceaseless and deadly, and, in the dawn of all the days, he puts forth anew to wage it, as his father did, and his father's father, and as his children must, and his children's children, to the last of them; nor from day to day can he foresee the issue, nor from season to season foretell the worth of the spoil, which is what chance allows. Thus laboriously, precariously, he slips through life: he follows hope through the toilsome years; and past summers are a black regret and bitterness to him, but summers to come are all rosy with new promise.

Long ago, when young Luke Dart, the Boot Bay trader, was ambitious for Shore patronage, he said to Solomon Stride, of Ragged Harbour, a punt fisherman: "Solomon, b'y, an you be willin', I'll trust you with twine for a cod-trap. An you trade with me, b'y, I'll trade with you, come good times or bad." Solomon was young and lusty, a mighty youth in bone and seasoned muscle, lunged like a blast furnace, courageous and finely sanguine. Said he: "An you trust me with twine for a trap, skipper, I'll deal fair by you, come good times or bad. I'll pay for un, skipper, with the first fish I cotches." Said Luke Dart: "When I trust, b'y, I trust. You pays for un when you can." It was a compact, so, at the end of the season, Solomon builded a cottage under the Man-o'-War, Broad Cove way, and married a maid of the place. In five months of that winter he made the trap, every net of it, leader and all, with his own hands, that he might know that the work was good, to the last knot and splice. In the spring, he put up the stage and the flake, and made the skiff; which done, he waited for a sign of fish. When the tempered days came, he hung the net on the horse, where it could be seen from the threshold of the cottage. In the evenings he sat with Priscilla on the bench at the door, and dreamed great dreams, while the red sun went down in the sea, and the shadows crept out of the wilderness.

"Woman, dear," said this young Solomon Stride, with a slap of his great thigh, "'twill be a gran' season for fish this year."

"Sure, b'y," said Priscilla, tenderly; "'twill be a gran' season for fish."

"Ay," Solomon sighed, "'twill that — this year."

The gloaming shadows gathered over the harbour water, and hung, sullenly, between the great rocks, rising all round about.

"'Tis handy t' three hundred and fifty dollars I owes Luke Dart for the twine," mused Solomon.

"'Tis a hape of money t'owe," said Priscilla.

"Hut!" growled Solomon, deep in his chest, "'Tis like nothin'."

"'Tis not much," said Priscilla, smiling, "when you has a trap."

Dusk and a clammy mist chased the glory from the hills; the rocks turned black, and a wind, black and cold, swept out of the wilderness and ran to sea.

"Us'll pay un all up this year," said Solomon. "Oh," he added loftily, "'twill be easy. 'Tis to be a gran' season!"

"Sure," said she, echoing his confidence.

Night filled the cloudy heavens overhead. It drove the flush of pink in upon the sun, and, following fast and overwhelmingly, thrust the flaring red and gold over the rim of the sea; and it was dark.

"Us'll pay un for a trap, dear," chuckled Solomon, "an' have enough left over t' buy a —"

"Oh," she cried with an ecstatic gasp, "a sewin' machine!"

"Iss," he roared. "Sure, girl!"

But, in the beginning of that season, when the first fish ran in for the caplin and the nets were set out, the ice was still hanging off shore, drifting vagrantly with the wind; and there came a gale in the night, springing from the northeast — a great, vicious wind, which gathered the ice in a pack and drove it swiftly in upon the land. Solomon Stride put off in a punt, in a sea tossing and white, to loose the trap from its moorings. Three times, while the pack swept nearer, crunching and horribly groaning, as though lashed to cruel speed by the gale, the wind beat him back through the tickle; and, upon the fourth essay, when his strength was breaking, the ice ran over the place where the trap was, and chased the punt into the harhour, frothing upon its flank. When, three days thereafter, a west wind carried the ice to sea, Solomon dragged the trap from the bottom. Great holes were bruised in the nets, head rope and span line were ground to pulp, the anchors were lost. Thirty-seven days and nights it took to make the nets whole again, and in that time the great spring run of cod passed by. So, in the next spring, Solomon was deeper in the debt of sympathetic Luke Dart — for the new twine and for the winter's food he had eaten; but, of an evening, when he sat on the bench with Priscilla, he looked through the gloaming shadows gathered over the harbour water and hanging between the great rocks, to the golden summer approaching, and dreamed gloriously of the fish he would catch in his trap.

"Priscilla, dear," said Solomon Stride, slapping his iron thigh, "they be a fine sign of fish down the coast. 'Twill be a gran' season, I'm thinkin'."

"Sure, b'y," Priscilla agreed; "'twill be a gran' cotch o' fish you'll have this year."

Dusk and the mist touched the hills, and, in the dreamful silence, their glory faded; the rocks turned black, and the wind from the wilderness ruffled the water beyond the flake.

"Us'll pay Luke Dart this year, I tells you," said Solomon, like a boastful boy. "Us'll pay un twice over."

"'Twill be fine to have the machane," said she, with shining eyes.

"An' the calico t'use un on," said he.

And so, while the night spread overhead, these two simple folk feasted upon all the sweets of life; and all that they desired they possessed, as fast as fancy could form wishes, just as though the bench were a bit of magic furniture, to bring dreams true — until the night, advancing, thrust the red and gold of the sunset clouds over the rim of the sea, and it was dark.

"Leave us goa in," said Priscilla.

"This year," said Solomon, rising, "I be goaing to cotch three hundred quintals of fish. Sure, I be — this year."

"'Twill be fine," said she.

It chanced in that year that the fish failed utterly; hence, in the winter following, Ragged Harbour fell upon days of distress; and three women and one old man starved to death — and five children, of whom one was the infant son of Solomon Stride. Neither in that season, nor in any one of the thirteen years coming after, did this man catch three hundred quintals of cod in his trap. In pure might of body — in plenitude and quality of strength — in the full, eager power of brawn — he was great as the men of any time, a towering glory to the whole race, here hidden; but he could not catch three hundred quintals of cod. In spirit — in patience, hope, courage, and the fine will for toil — he was great; but, good season or bad, he could not catch three hundred quintals of cod. He met night, cold, fog, wind, and the fury of waves, in their craft, in their swift assault, in their slow, crushing descent; but all the cod he could wrest from the sea, being given into the hands of Luke Dart, an honest man, yielded only sufficient provision for food and clothing for himself and Priscilla — only enough to keep their bodies warm and still the crying of their stomachs. Thus, while the nets of the trap rotted, and Solomon came near to middle age, the debt swung from seven hundred dollars to seven, and back to seventy-three, which it was in an evening in spring, when he sat with Priscilla on the sunken bench at the door, and dreamed great dreams as he watched the shadows gather over the harbour water and sullenly hang between the great rocks, rising all round about.

"I wonder, b'y," said Priscilla, "if 'twill be a good season — this year."

"Oh, sure!" exclaimed Solomon. "Sure!"

"D'ye think it, b'y?" wistfully.

"Woman," said he impressively, "us'll cotch a hape o' fish in the trap this year. They be millions o' fish t' the say," he went on excitedly; "millions o' fish t' the say. They be there, woman. 'Tis oan'y for us t' take un out. I be goain' t' wark hard this year."

"You be a great warker, Solomon," said she; "my, but you be!"

Priscilla smiled, and Solomon smiled; and it was as though all the labour and peril of the season were past, and the stage was full to the roof with salt cod. In the happiness of this dream they smiled again, and turned their eyes to the hills, from which the glory of purple and yellow was departing to make way for the misty dusk.

"Skipper Luke Dart says t' me," said Solomon, "that 'tis the luxuries that keep folks poor."

Priscilla said nothing at all.

"They be nine dollars agin me in seven years for crame o' tartar," said Solomon. "Think o' that!"

"My," said she, "but 'tis a lot! But we be used to un now, Solomon, and we can't get along without un."

"Sure," said he, "'tis good we're not poor like some folk." Night drove the flush of pink in upon the sun and followed the red and gold of the horizon over the rim of the sea.

"'Tis growin' cold," said she. "Leave us goa in," said he.

In thirty years after that time, Solomon Stride put to sea ten thousand times. Ten thousand times he passed through the tickle rocks to the free, heaving deep for salmon and cod, thereto compelled by the inland waste, which contributes nothing to the sustenance of the men of that coast. Hunger, lurking in the shadows of days to come, inexorably drove him into the chances of the conflict. Perforce he matched himself ten thousand times against the restless might of the sea, immeasurable and unrestrained, surviving the gamut of its moods, because he was great in strength, fearlessness, and cunning. He weathered four hundred gales, from the grey gusts which come down between Quid Nunc and the Man-o'-War, leaping upon the fleet, to the summer tempests, swift and black, and the first blizzards of winter. He was wrecked off the Mull, off the Three Poor Sisters, on the Pancake Rock, and again off the Mull. Seven times he was swept to sea by the off-shore wind. Eighteen times he was frozen to the seat of his punt; and of these, eight times his feet were frozen, and thrice his festered right hand. All this he suffered, and more, of which I may set down six separate periods of starvation, in which thirty-eight men, women, and children died — all this, with all the toil, cold, despair, loneliness, hunger, peril, and disappointment therein contained. And so he came down to old age — with a bent back, shrunken arms, and filmy eyes — old Solomon Stride, now prey for the young sea. But, of an evening in spring, he sat with Priscilla on the sunken bench at the door, and talked hopefully of the fish he would catch from his punt.

"Priscilla, dear," said he, rubbing his hand over his weazened thigh, "I be thinkin' us punt fishermen'll have a —"

Priscilla was not attending; she was looking into the shadows above the harbour water, dreaming deeply of a mystery of the Book, which had long puzzled her; so, in silence, Solomon, too, watched the shadows rise and sullenly hang between the great rocks.

"Solomon, b'y," she whispered, "I wonder what the seven thunders uttered?"

"'Tis quare, that — what the seven thunders uttered," said Solomon. "My, woman, but 'tis!"

"'An' he set his right foot upon the sea,'" she repeated, staring over the greying water to the clouds which flamed gloriously at the edge of the world, "'an' his left foot on the earth — '"

"'An' cried with a loud voice,'" said he, whispering in awe, "'as when a lion roareth; an' when he had cried, *seven thunders uttered their voices.*'"

"'Seven thunders uttered their voices,'" said she; "'an' when the seven thunders had uttered their voices, I was about to write, an' I heard a voice from heaven sayin' unto me, Seal up those things which the seven thunders uttered, and write them not.'"

The wind from the wilderness, cold and black, covered the hills with mist; the dusk fell, and the glory faded from the heights.

"Oh, Solomon," she said, clasping her hands, "I wonder what the seven thunders uttered! Think you, b'y, 'twas the kind o' sins that can't be forgiven?"

"'Tis the seven mysteries!"

"I wonder what they be," said she.

"Sh-h-h, dear," he said, patting her grey head; "thinkin' on they things'll capsize you an you don't look out."

The night had driven all the colour from the sky; it had descended upon the red and gold of the cloudy west, and covered them. It was cold and dark.

"'An' seven thunders uttered their voices,'" she said, dreamily.

"Sh-h-h, dear!" said he. "Leave us goa in."

Twenty-one years longer old Solomon Stride fished out of Ragged Harbour. He put to sea five thousand times more, weathered two hundred more gales, survived five more famines — all in the toil for salmon and cod. He was a punt fisherman again, was old Solomon; for the nets of the trap had rotted, had been renewed six times, strand by strand, and had rotted at last beyond repair. What with the weather he dared not pit his failing strength against, the return of fish to Luke Dart fell off from year to year; but, as Solomon said to Luke, "livin' expenses kep' up wonderful," notwithstanding.

"I be so used t' luxuries," he went on, running his hand through his long grey hair, "that 'twould be hard t' come down t' common livin'. Sure, 'tis sugar I wants t' me tea — not black-strap. 'Tis what I l'arned," he added proudly, "when I were a trap fisherman."

"'Tis all right, Solomon," said Luke. "Many's the quintal o' fish you traded with me."

"Sure," Solomon chuckled, "'twould take a year t' count un."

In course of time it came to the end of Solomon's last season — those days of it when, as the folk of the coast say, the sea is hungry for lives — and the man was eighty-one years old, and the debt to Luke Dart had crept up to $230.80. The off-shore wind, rising suddenly, with a blizzard in its train, caught him alone on the Grappling Hook grounds. He was old, very old — old and feeble and dull: the cold numbed him; the snow blinded him; the wind made sport of the strength of his arms. He was carried out to sea, rowing doggedly, thinking all the time that he was drawing near the harbour tickle; for it did not occur to him then that the last of eight hundred gales could be too great for him. He was carried out from the sea, where the strength of his youth had been spent, to the Deep, which had been a mystery to him all his days. That night he passed on a pan of ice, where he burned his boat, splinter by splinter, to keep warm. At dawn he lay down to die. The snow ceased, the wind changed; the ice was carried to Ragged Harbour. Eleazar Manuel spied the body of Solomon from the lookout, and put out and brought him in — revived him and took him home to Priscilla. Through the winter the old man doddered about the Harbour, dying of consumption. When the tempered days came — the days of balmy sunshine and cold evening winds — he came quickly to the pass of glittering visions, which, for such as die of the lung trouble, come at the end of life.

In the spring, when the *Lucky Star*, three days out from Boot Bay, put into Ragged Harbour to trade for the first catch, old Skipper

Luke Dart was aboard, making his last voyage to the Shore; for he was very old, and longed once more to see the rocks of all that coast before he made ready to die. When he came ashore, Eleazar Manuel told him that Solomon Stride lay dying at home; so the skipper went to the cottage under the Man-o'-War to say good-bye to his old customer and friend —and there found him, propped up in bed, staring at the sea.

"Skipper Luke," Solomon quavered, in deep excitement, "be you just come in, b'y?"

"Iss — but an hour gone."

"What be the big craft hangin' off shoare? Eh — what be she, b'y?"

There had been no craft in sight when the *Lucky Star* beat in. "Were she a fore-an'-after, Solomon?" said Luke, evasively.

"Sure, noa, b'y!" cried Solomon. "She were a square-rigged craft, with all sail set—a great, gran' craft — a quare craft, b'y — like she were made o' glass, canvas an' hull an' all; an' she had shinin' ropes, an' she were shinin' all over. Sure, they be a star t' the tip o' her bowsprit, b'y, an' a star t' the peak o' her mainmast — seven stars they be, in all. Oh, she were a gran' sight!"

"Hem-m !" said Luke, stroking his beard. "She've not come in yet."

"A gran' craft!" said Solomon.

"'Tis according," said Luke, "t' whether you be sot on oak bottoms or glass ones."

"She were bound down north t' the Labrador," Solomon went on quickly, "an' when she made the Grapplin' Hook grounds she come about an' headed for the tickle, with her sails squared. Sure she ran right over the Pancake, b'y, like he weren't there at all, an' — How's the wind, b'y?"

"Dead off shore from the tickle."

Solomon stared at Luke. "She were comin' straight in agin the wind," he said, hoarsely. "Maybe, skipper," he went on, with a little laugh, "she do be the ship for souls. They be many things strong men knows nothin' about. What think you?"

"Ay — maybe; maybe she be."

"Maybe — maybe — she do be invisible t' mortal eyes. Maybe, skipper, you hasn't seed her; maybe 'tis that my eyes do be opened t' such sights. Maybe she've turned in — for me. "

The men turned their faces to the window again, and gazed long and intently at the sea, which a storm cloud had turned black. Solomon dozed for a moment, and when he awoke, Luke Dart was still staring dreamily out to sea.

"Skipper Luke," said Solomon, with a smile as of one in an enviable situation, "'tis fine t' have nothin' agin you on the books when you comes t' die."

"Sure, b'y," said Luke, hesitating not at all, though he knew to a cent what was on the books against Solomon's name, "'tis fine to be free o' debt."

"Ah," said Solomon, the smile broadening gloriously, "'tis fine, I tells you! 'Twas the three hundred quintal I cotched last season that paid un all up. 'Twas a gran cotch — last year. Ah," he sighed, "'twas a gran' cotch o' fish."

"Iss — you be free o' debt now, b'y."

"What be the balance t' my credit, skipper? Sure I forget."

"Hem-m," the skipper coughed, pausing to form a guess which might be within Solomon's dream; then he ventured: "Fifty dollars?"

"Iss," said Solomon, "fifty an' moare, skipper. Sure, you has forgot the eighty cents."

"Fifty-eighty," said the skipper, positively. "'Tis that. I call un t' mind now. 'Tis fifty-eighty — iss, sure. Did you get a receipt for un, Solomon?"

"I doan't mind me now."

"Um-m-m-well," said the skipper, "I'll send un t' the woman the night — an order on the *Lucky Star*."

"Fifty-eighty for the woman!" said Solomon. "Twill kape her off the Gov'ment for three years, an she be savin'. 'Tis fine — that!"

When the skipper had gone, Priscilla crept in, and sat at the head of the bed, holding Solomon's hand; and they were silent for a long time, while the evening approached.

"I be goain' t' die the night, dear," said Solomon at last. "Iss, b'y," she answered; "you be goain' t' die." Solomon was feverish now; and, thereafter, when he talked, his utterance was thick and fast.

"'Tis not hard," said Solomon. "Sh-h-h," he whispered, as though about to impart a secret. "The ship that's hangin' off shoare, waitin' for me soul, do be a fine craft — with shinin' canvas an' ropes. Sh-h! She do be t'other side o' Mad Mull now — waitin'."

Priscilla trembled, for Solomon had come to the time of visions — when the words of the dying are the words of prophets, and contain revelations. What of the utterings of the seven thunders?

"Sure the Lard he've blessed us, Priscilla," said Solomon, rational again. "Goodness an' marcy has followed us all the days o' our lives. Our cup runneth over.

"Praise the Lard," said Priscilla.

"Sure," Solomon went on, smiling like a little child, "We've had but eleven famines, an' we've had the means o' grace pretty reg'lar, which is what they hasn't t' Round 'Arbour. We've had one little baby for a little while. Iss — one de-ear little baby, Priscilla; an' there's them that's had none o' their own, at all. Sure we've had enough t' eat when there wasn't a famine — an' bakin' powder, an' 'raisins, an' all they things, an' sugar, an' rale good tea. An' you had a merino dress, an I had a suit o' rale tweed — come straight from England. We hasn't seed a railroad train, dear, but we've seed a steamer, an' we've heard tell o' the quare things they be t' St. John's. Ah, the Lard he've favoured us above our deserts. He've been good t' us, Priscilla. But, oh, you hasn't had the sewin' machane, an' you hasn't had the peachstone t' plant in the garden. 'Tis my fault, dear — 'tis not the Lard's. I should 'a' got you the peach-stone from St. John's, you did want un so much — oh, so much! 'Tis that I be sorry for, now, dear; but 'tis all over, an' I can't help it. It wouldn't 'a' growed anyway, I know it wouldn't; but you thought it would, an' I wisht I'd got un for you."

"'Tis nothin', Solomon," she sobbed. "Sure, I was joakin' all the time. 'Twouldn't 'a' growed."

"Ah," he cried, radiant, "was you joakin'?"

"Sure," she said.

"We've not been poor, Priscilla," said he, continuing, "an' they be many folk that's poor. I be past me labour now," he went on, talking with rising effort, for it was at the sinking of the sun, "An' 'tis time for me t' die. 'Tis time — for I be past me labour."

Priscilla held his hand a long time after that — a long, silent time, in which the soul of the man struggled to release itself, until it was held but by a thread.

"Solomon!"

The old man seemed not to hear.

"Solomon, b'y!" she cried.

"Iss?" faintly.

She leaned over him to whisper in his ear, "Does you see the gates o' heaven?" she said. "Oh, does you?"

"Sure, dear; heaven do be — "

Solomon had not strength enough to complete the sentence.

"B'y! B'y!"

He opened his eyes and turned them to her face. There was the gleam of a tender smile in them.

"The seven thunders," she said. "The utterin's of the seven thunders — what was they, b'y?"

"An' the seven thunders uttered their voices," he mumbled, "'an' — '"

She waited, rigid, listening, to hear the rest; but no words came to her ears.

"Does you hear me, b'y?" she said.

"'An' seven — thunders — uttered their voices,'" he gasped, "'an' the seven thunders — said — said — '"

The light failed; all the light and golden glory went out of the sky, for the first cloud of a tempest had curtained the sun.

"'An' said — '" she prompted.

"'An' uttered — an' said — an' said — '"

"Oh, what?" she moaned.

Now, in that night, when the body of old Solomon Stride, a worn-out hulk, aged and wrecked in the toil of the deep, fell into the hands of Death, the sea, like a lusty youth, raged furiously in those parts. The ribs of many schooners, slimy and rotten, and the white bones of men in the off-shore depths, know of its strength in that hour — of its black, hard wrath, in gust and wave and breaker. Eternal in might and malignance is the sea! It groweth not old with the men who toil from its coasts. Generation upon the heels of generation, infinitely arising, go forth in hope against it, continuing for a space, and returning spent to the dust. They age and crumble and vanish, each in its turn, and the wretchedness of the first is the wretchedness of the last. Ay, the sea has measured the strength of the dust in old graves, and, in this day, contends with the sons of dust, whose sons will follow to the fight for an hundred generations, and thereafter, until harvests may be gathered from rocks. As it is written, the life of a man is a shadow, swiftly passing, and the days of his strength are less; but the sea shall endure in the might of youth to the wreck of the world.

Sara Jeannette Duncan

*Born in Brantford, Ontario in December, 1861, Duncan became a news-
paper journalist (with the* Toronto Globe, The Week *and the* Washington Post*), an occupation which gave her the opportunity to see the
world. Her travels, in turn, provided her with enough material for a dozen
novels and a few travel books. In 1888 she moved to India, where she met
her husband and lived for the next twenty-five years. In those years she
achieved international acclaim as a fiction writer. Her last years, before her
death in 1922, were spent in England. A very cosmopolitan writer, only
one of her novels and a few of her short stories are set in Canada. This
story first appeared in* Harper's Magazine *110 (March 1905): 625-31.*

The Heir Apparent

"I like the shape of his head," Miss Garratt said. We were talking of
Randal Cope, and there was more than approval in Miss Garratt's
words; there was barely suppressed enthusiasm. We three — Miss
Garratt, her niece, Ida Chamier, and I — were sitting on the veranda
of a private hotel in Toronto. Randal Cope was just visible in the
smoking-room; his head, indeed, with a pipe attached, was the sali-
ent feature of the window. It was a night of warm June; the maple-
trees hung heavily in their clustering sprays around the house. The
air held an expanded sense that the day had been got through with,
and we sat sharing it with all the city, watching the electric cars flash
up and down.

"I like the shape of his head," said Miss Garratt.

"It is a head," I responded, "plainly made to carry a great deal."

Ida looked languidly round at the silhouette in the window. "If it
carries its own traditions," she began.

"It will have enough to do?" I suggested. "Oh, well, we expect
more than that."

"Yes indeed," explained Ida's aunt, with that agreeable Southern
enunciation that runs the two words into one emphasis. "We expect, don't we, an immense amount?"

It was partly, no doubt, due to the enervating atmosphere that
Miss Garratt stopped short of the catalogue of what we did expect;

but none of us, of course, would have been able to make it with confidence and facility. The immense amount that we expected was naturally almost as vague as it was vivid; there were so many possibilities, all of them dramatic in the sense of leaping achievement, and never so much as a sign, as yet, to tell us which way to look. Without other indication the gaze upon Randal Cope enthusiastically travelled back to the chivalric statesman who was his grandfather, and to Mrs. Robert Cope, who was his mother. Either of them by himself or herself would have been an antecedent to build upon, but both! Charles Randal, whose personality had stood even with his power in every capital of Europe, whose moral standards still shone plain above politics: classicist, dialectician, all but artist — and to this great shade his daughter, who was simply in the world of the ideal and its numbered symbols alone a force and a current — here was a Valhalla for a nursery! It contained, so unusually, both the general and the particular. There was not an eye in the great republic so neighboring to us on Miss Lucas's veranda that would not light with a kind of proprietorship in his doctrines at the name of Charles Randal; his was one of those rare circles that widen across the Atlantic and strike effectively upon its still half-hostile farther shore. And to those smaller, more peculiar groups who propose to themselves initiation, what priestess ever stood, with one finger on the curtain and another on her lip, more honored in function than Margaret Cope? Verily we left our shoes outside. Poet and essayist she was, moulding life with her hands; delicate truth she sounded upon a chord lifted and mystic. Critic and scholar, she measured the world from a height; but in her verse she walked among us and saw all our sad horizons, and beyond.

So that this young man had merely to write his name to make a double appeal, to the heart and to the imagination. He seemed to be aware of this, for he wrote the whole of it and suffered himself to be introduced by the whole of it — "Mr. Randal Cope." On the other hand, he wrote it badly, with cramped carefulness, and he was awkward in acknowledging the eager salutations which the world had for him. We of the boundless expectations had such things to go upon — that he came into a room magnificently and went out of it almost sideways; that he had an immense distinction of appearance, which he wore like a tiresome necessary diadem; that he had taken, at Oxford, a degree even more brilliant than his grandfather's — a reflection which gave us an instant's thrill of sympathy with Oxford upon the high ground of prophecy. These were simple threads, but we found at Miss Lucas's that they could be woven into patterns of quite extraordinary complexity. It is satisfying to think that if he had known we were weaving them he could not have retired himself more completely from the field of observation. We saw him before us every day, and to the fact that his splendid head was the ornament of a commanding person we could add that he was rather slovenly in his dress, with an opulent taste in neckties. There was also the general understanding that he was "out here" on an imperialistic mission for one of the leading English magazines. That was all we knew, all we seemed likely to know, and it was so little that one could understand its constituting, for Miss Garratt, a grievance.

We felt the weight of trifles when, a moment or two later, Mr. Cope joined us on the veranda. His hesitation in the French window from the drawing-room was so palpable, his decision in our favor so obvious, that we could not help apprehending that he did nothing lightly. He sat down beside us — not quite beside us, but near enough to form a communicable part of our group — I speak for Miss Garratt and myself; Ida barely lifted her eyelids. Miss Garratt and I were conscious of excitement; I am afraid in our attitudes of alert encouragement we betrayed it; Miss Garratt even twisted her chair a little to bring Mr. Cope's within an arc of welcome. And it was Miss Garratt naturally who addressed him.

"Well, Mr. Cope," said she, "and what do you think of this *al fresco* life?"

The young man looked at her with distant deference. "This-?"

"Oh, this emancipation all about you, this sitting on verandas in the public of the moon, these airs of the forest in the city streets. But no; I shouldn't ask. These impressions are precisely — aren't they? — what you've come so far to dig out of yourself. They are, of course, valuable, and you keep them, or you ought to keep them, locked up. But you can at least tell us if you don't think it very hot."

It seems absurd to say that Miss Garratt's speech had the force of an assault upon a citadel. Its object seemed literally to gather himself into himself; he visibly receded, shrank into some fastness, from which he still looked out, startled, troubled, and insecure.

"I do indeed find it hot. But — but very delightful also — Miss Garratt."

There was a peculiar charm in his hesitation before uttering her name, and the way his voice dropped in saying it. Certainly deference was his personal note, his note of intercourse. One's imagination flew to his mother and his grandfather — my imagination and Miss Garratt's. And Ida looked up.

"One mustn't press, I know," Miss Garratt went on. "All the same, it would be fascinating to compare notes — what you see with what we see. We too have brought virgin imaginations to this part of the empire; we haven't been here before, either. And we come from Mississippi."

Mr. Cope looked at her seriously and hesitated, seeming to revolve many replies. One saw a young man in a rather rigid attitude of attention, with eyes in which expression struggled to be born, pulling — as if that would help — at his mustache. One noticed a hand of extraordinary shapeliness — the modern, beautifully nervous kind; a hand, one thought, to grasp its inheritance.

"I suppose," he said, finally, "it is even warmer in Mississippi — just now."

"It is quite impossibly warm there," Miss Garratt replied, and I saw her make, and arrest, a movement toward the lorgnette that hung in the folds of her dress. Ida, where she sat, on the edge of the veranda, made half a movement of her head toward her aunt, in which Miss Garratt might have detected something like protest.

"Have you been penetrated by our national anthem, Mr. Cope?" I inquired.

"'The maple leaf, our emblem dear,
The maple leaf forever.'
In two or three hundred years it will gather sentiment enough to turn it into music. Meanwhile these are all maples, round the house, all that aren't chestnuts."

Mr. Cope started slightly in my direction, as if toward a new emergency. "I have not seen it, I am afraid," he said. His gravity really rendered him culpable. "I must look it up at once."

"I know two more lines," Ida suddenly declared, "if you would like to hear them."

"May I?"

She swung round on the palm of one hand and lifted the clear oval of her face in the shadows.

"'God save the King, and Heaven bless
The maple leaf forever!'"

she sang, with enthusiasm and submission. It was a simple, gay, impersonal note she sounded, with a touch of extravagance, half mocking, in which her young Americanism must needs declare itself; and it took absolutely no account, except the most adventitious, of Mr. Randal Cope as her listener. It was then that I saw, for the first time, his wonderful flash and smile. It was one thing, the sudden happy torch that lightened and deepened in his eyes and the way his upper lip lifted and turned down at the corners, — a demonstration so vivid, a sign so plain, that one threw with a delightful impulse a votive flower to Margaret Cope in the moonlight.

"The maple seems — doesn't it? — to have more leaves than rhymes," he said to Ida, drawing himself back as it were for the effort, which came from him at once audacious and shy, with the oddest effect of old-fashioned prankishness in the way he went on smiling at her from under his eyebrows, very courteous and conceding. It must have been thus, we thought, that he had seen his grandfather address ladies when he was very young.

I suppose Ida Chamier found something to say, but there is no doubt that she looked back at him, felt the release in him, took the smile from his eyes. This one saw in a swift instant pass straight into the soul of her, whence she gave as quickly something back to him that also sped on a smile. It happened then, just then — the story; and a moment's silence followed it, while the moon moved thoughtfully to a better point of view. Presently Ida sprang up and put on her hat. She was going to post a letter, she said, and she would like to go herself, — thanks. When Randal Cope stepped, rather awkwardly, along the wooden walk by her side, Miss Garratt and I exchanged glances which confessed, startled and contrite, our hateful presence where the moon should have been the only one. Then we saw that he went but to open the gate, and felt relief. He closed the gate, indeed, with quite a contrasting deliberateness, and came slowly back to the house, reaching his rooms by another door.

I looked with more interest than ever at Ida's photograph that night. Her aunt had given it to me; when Miss Garratt became fond of anybody she gave her Ida's photograph. It was a fortunate portrait; it yielded Miss Chamier's personality as well as her beauty; it suggested her fastidiousness as well as her grace, and was as true to her easy distinction as it could not help being to her charming clothes. No doubt, as Miss Garratt said, she was immensely clever — I glanced again at the sonnet the elder lady had lent me — no doubt she shared her aunt's passionate interest in human forms of genius. If one did not see the critical worshipping eye, it was, Miss Garratt declared, because in the arrogance of youth she hid her fire, which nevertheless burned fiercely, and nowhere with more ardent dedication, I had been assured, than upon the altar of Margaret Cope.

"You *must* find it," Miss Garratt charged me a week later. "You must. It's too maddening."

What Miss Garratt so peremptorily demanded that I should find ought by now, we both vaguely felt, to be a matter of daily quiet evidence, — the vision and the power, to put it concisely, that with such brilliant confidence we had predicated of him. And it was not; oh, assuredly it was not. How clever we were, how stimulating, how adventurous! How we danced before him with lutes into the realm of the imagination, always, alas! to look back and see him seated upon the verge, with a pipe! Everything worth reading he had read, everybody worth meeting he had met — the latter invariably at his mother's, at lunch, — but his consciousness seemed a deep receptive pool into which these things simply disappeared, leaving an untroubled surface. Now and then at the lifting of an eyelid one caught a reflection; it was always true and just, and sometimes it was charming. It gave one vividly the idea that this life upon which he had been able to draw so largely had contributed very really to a fund, somewhere stored up in him, of right thinking and exquisite taste. But the depths were black and the indication most inadequate. We could both point to half a dozen men who abounded in the testimony we sought without producing a tenth of the belief we had already.

"With her," said Miss Garratt, "it would be so entirely a matter of that."

We were convinced that it would. "That" was especially and peremptorily what Ida Chamier would require, and require not in hypothesis, but in demonstration. Nothing else in a mate would claim her, Miss Garratt declared; she knew Ida; and she cited Teddy Farnham with his millions, and Arthur Rennick with his political future, as if their rejected addresses might illustrate her point, but were by no means necessary to prove it. Miss Garratt's own idea was very clear. Ida had a spark of genius. I had long since learned its family history. Another spark might bring it to a flame. There was something sacred about such a trust, primarily reposed in Ida and secondarily in her aunt, and though hitherto Miss Garratt had been content to interpret her share of it in the duty of vestal virgin fanning at the altar, the advent of Randal Cope had widened both her solicitude and her responsibility.

"Did I tell you he had written her some verses?" Gussie went on, with dejection.

"No!" I said. "How did you know?"

"Oh, she showed them to me. She well might — they were *in Latin!*"

"Good heavens!"

"She said they were very good, very witty. She knows, you know. But when she translated them I couldn't see the wit."

"One never can, in translations," I soothed her. "It's a matter of the use of the gerund, or the conjunction *ut*. They probably *were* good."

"Oh, I dare say — I mean, of course they were. How could he produce anything that wasn't? He simply radiates quality," she went on, looking at me anxiously; "and for fibre, hear him speak — look at his hands."

"You're not trying to convince *me!*" I protested. "But here she comes. Shall I be bold?"

Miss Garratt sent me a frightened glance, which I ignored.

"We were talking about Randal Cope," I said, as Ida joined us.

The faintest look of displeasure showed, for an instant, between her eyebrows. Then she laughed.

"No!" she exclaimed, railing at us, as if we were always doing it.

"We simply cannot make up our minds," I continued.

"Make up your minds?" It was an excellent effect of wondering indifference, and Miss Chamier sat down to the piano.

"Whether one is safe, after all, in predicating great things of him."

She struck two or three chords, into which, I fancied, thought passed. "Why predicate anything?" she said. "Why not wait?"

"That's so difficult," I sighed, "when one is dying to foretell and be gloriously vindicated. We complain, your aunt Gussie and I, that he gives us nothing to go upon but our instincts."

"I am out of temper with him," said Miss Garratt, taking up a book.

Ida glanced from one to the other of us. "I don't see that it matters," she said. "I don't see what right you have — any of us have — to expect him to please *us*."

"That view," I said, with infinite guile, "simply shows you non-speculative, dear. Or perhaps not so deeply interested as your aunt and I are in his mother. We want to see Mrs. Cope fulfilled in her son, and he seems somehow to present a baffling front to his destiny. It's absurd, as you justly remark, to be irritated, but we both are."

"Oh, his mother!" exclaimed Miss Chamier, and fell to the brilliant execution of the "Appassionata." She paused abruptly to say, "He seems to take a good deal for granted about his mother."

"Not too much, surely."

"Well, he is always telling one what she thinks or what she does."

"How delightful of him! I wish he would tell me."

"Doesn't he?"

"Never a word. He tells me little stories, usually about bishops."

"He suggests having always lived among them," put in Miss Garratt, with an air of mournful detachment. "Bishops and high-thinking men. But he is the enviable inheritor of all the great traditions, isn't he? In letters and morals and politics."

"And there's something in him," I contributed, "so hoarded, so precious, so absolutely the last expression, that its inaccessibility —"

I stopped. Ida had left the piano, and waited, looking at me oddly, with her hand upon the door. She broke almost passionately upon my hesitation.

"I can't think," she said, "why you and Aunt Gussie talk about him so much! I can't think!" Then she went quickly out.

"And now," demanded Miss Garratt, in low tones of panic — "and now what have you done?"

Well, we could wait. After all, it came to that, and her aunt and I made all, I venture, that could be made out of the fact that this obvious course was Ida's own suggestion. Meanwhile a leading magazine published another of her Italian sketches, which she immediately locked up in a drawer. I did not hear of it till long afterwards.

Mr. Cope's commission was from the *Period*. His reticence could only be described as protective, but so much he had divulged, not being able to help it, since Miss Garratt asked him point-blank. The *Period*, we agreed, was precisely the medium through which a Randal Cope could show his essential quality to the world. You found, as your great grandfather had found, the best thought in England in the *Period*; and one could imagine its welcome to young Randal. They had given him generous imperial range; I understood he was only beginning with Canada; and he seemed to me to be almost hampered with facilities. The name of the Lieutenant-Governor of the province came up between us.

"I know Sir George," he said. "He was kind enough to ask me to stay there."

"And you didn't?" I queried.

"Well, no. I think a fellow had better keep out of Government Houses. He's a bit too much in the middle of it there, I find."

"How are you getting on?" I asked, looking out of the window. "I believe it will rain, after all."

"Oh — thank you — there's immense material, isn't there? I — I've sent them something."

Presently he turned and looked at me with directness, a simple and sudden regard. The rain struck softly on the trees and murmured over the grass. The quiet breath of it came into the room.

"You know I ought to do something," he said, and in his eyes, with almost a pang, I saw the problem that had been perplexing us all.

"But you will. You can hardly" — I hesitated — "help it."

"That's just it." He paused appreciably, and then added, "It seems to me that I've got — more or less — to trust to that. I hope one may. One has dreams."

He gave me a look full of courage and patience and nice feeling, but he had come to the end of his confidence.

"I'll walk out to the Hunt Club, I think," he said; "it's such a jolly day."

He brought it to me himself; the August *Period*, on the veranda, while there was still light enough to read. I remember thinking, as one notes trifles at great moments, that the *Period* had never approved of undignified anticipation; when the time came you got your *Period*, and not in the third week of the previous month. Almost at the same moment the gate clicked, and Ida came quickly up the path. She went to her room without a glance at us, and she carried a book-seller's parcel.

My eye fled down the list of contents on the cover. There it was, the fourth article: "Canada and the Empire. — I. By Randal Cope."

My eye fled over the first sentence, lost itself in the middle of the next paragraph, and dashed back to take the task seriously, with powers collected. The queer premonitory shiver that sprang upon me I paused to denounce as foolish, premature; but the very rebuke revealed its apprehension. I tried to soothe a jumping pulse with the assurance that this was a matter with which, after all, my concern was remote; what was it, indeed, to me though Randal Cope spoke with the tongue of men and of angels and had not imagination? Then I set out to read the opening paragraph, deliberately, and quite in vain. It was concerned, I perceived, with facts of the first importance in the balance of political science, but their category escapes me now as then; the character of the thing, its quality, its significance beyond its meaning, leaped out from it and obscured the words. Presently I gave up the effort and looked at it, just looked, and at the next paragraph, and the next.

Then, hastily, I regarded the article by pages, from top to bottom, from beginning to end; it bulked very respectably among the contents of the *Period*. The eye could take it in that way, I realized in my dismay; its lines and proportions stood square and plain; it had formal definition; it was instantly realizable, in scope, intention, achievement. And we who thought to ponder it, to wonder and exclaim! To be confounded by directness and set at naught by exactitude was perhaps in the nature of proper chastening, but the structure proffered also the consideration of material, and there was no escape from the dejected conviction that it was all built of bricks.

Closer examination here and there showed the bricks substantial, with plenty of straw, but when one had looked for a marble palace! Irreproachable bricks, set with precision, and what would have been, in any other material, a certain dignity of sequence and design, a great subject in ground-plan, and an eminence like a railway station. And curiously colorless and withdrawn, never the flush of a prejudice, never the flash of a mistake! I dropped the thing in my lap. "*How* they have taught him!" I almost groaned aloud. At that very instant I saw Gussie Garratt from her retreat by the drawing-room window pounce upon the postman, who delivered to her the magazine in its unmistakable wrapper. As she scuttled across the end of the veranda with it I waved my copy at her. "Never — never — never!" I cried. She gave me a frightened glance and sped on. Then Randal Cope came back and dropped into a chair. His face was still bright with the pleasure and excitement of it. He had won his spurs, and there they were, for my intelligent consideration. I turned them over. There was plenty to say in honest praise; one had only to forget the signature.

We talked for a while, and presently a vagueness grew upon him.

"Would you be so good as to show the article to — to Miss Chamier?" he said elaborately at last, poor dear boy. "She has kindly expressed a wish to see it." And I went upstairs, feigning to consent, well knowing that Miss Chamier, alone in her room, had long since considered the article in its fullest import.

I do not know what induced me to throw the publication across the room; it was quite a disproportionate display of feeling; but I did, and there it was lying, face downwards, when Ida Chamier, with barely a knock, walked in.

"I came," she said, with an odd challenge in her voice, "to show you Mr. Cope's paper in the *Period*." She put it before me and stood looking over my shoulder. "It's quite excellent, I think — wonderfully sound" — and then her eyes caught the dishevelled thing on the floor. "But you've seen it already!" She walked over and picked up the insulted magazine, smoothing out its ruffled leaves and sending me, on a glance, a full charge of indignation. "What did you do this to it for?" she demanded; and there was nothing else for it, so I said out of my pure wonder,

"I was disappointed with it."

"Of course you were! And Aunt Gussie — no doubt she's 'disappointed' too! You both expected something different, something from his mother or his grandfather. His mother is a poet and an essayist — well and good, very charming. His grandfather was just a great Englishman, and there are lots of them. And he is himself!"

Her eyes were bright with excitement; she was really talking very impulsively.

"Just a big, strong, splendid man, his own stamp and his own pattern — "

"My *dear* Ida!" I expostulated.

"You had no *earthly* business to be disappointed," she went on, undaunted. "Can't he inherit all that — that you thought of — in his most" — she seemed to seek, in the magnificence of her concession, for words that should hold nothing back — "his most lovable and princely nature? Can't he himself be the sole person to benefit — and perhaps the particularly happy woman whom he marries? Imagine any individuality that is worth its salt condescending to take the mould that is prescribed for it! But of course there was always the danger — and I was so afraid he might be some sort of repetition. I don't think anybody could permanently l-like a man who was only that."

"Ida! You don't — you're not going to — "

"But I do — and I just am! He doesn't know what I waited for, but I don't mind telling you it was this. I wanted to be quite sure.

And I wish you'd say," she went on, with beguilement, "that you think it's a good article."

"If I were in love with him," I retorted, "I should think it a splendid article;" at which Miss Chamier pressed her lips together with immense self-control and left me. "You and Aunt Gussie," she put her head back in the door to say, "did put one off so dreadfully!"

The book appeared in due course, and the only thing the copious reviewers never found to say of it was that the world would clearly have no share in Randal Cope's inheritance. They missed this obvious deduction, though other volumes have proved it with increasing clearness since. The younger Copes live in Westminster near the Colonial Office, where Randal has got a "job" — his wife delights, I think maliciously, to dwell upon it under that unlovely term. He is generally acknowledged to be rather good at his job. Miss Garratt, who has a flat in their neighborhood, nurses a grievance that these things should not appear to surprise the people of England. She discovers here a subtle form of ingratitude not confined to republics. And she cannot be bullied into any recantation about the shape of his head.

L. M. Montgomery

Born on Prince Edward Island on November 30, 1874, Lucy Maud Montgomery became an international celebrity with the publication of Anne of Green Gables *in 1908. She followed this up with seven "Anne" sequels and an "Emily" trilogy. Though a lesser known fact, she was also an accomplished poet (publishing about 450 poems) and short-story writer (publishing about 500). The last of these are nearly always in the romantic tradition but are characterized by clever plots, interesting complications and a great deal of wry humour. The following was first published in* Everybody's Magazine *16 (April 1907): 495-503.*

The Quarantine at Alexander Abraham's

I refused to take that Sunday-school class the first time I was asked. Not that I objected to teaching in the Sunday-school. On the contrary, I rather liked the idea; but it was the Rev. Aaron Crickett who asked me and it had always been a matter of principle with me never to do anything a man asked me to do if I could help it. It saves so much trouble and simplifies everything so beautifully. I had always disliked men. It must have been born in me, because, as far back as I can remember, an antipathy to men and dogs was one of my strongest characteristics. My experiences through life only served to deepen it. The more I saw of men, the more I cared for cats.

So of course when the Rev. Aaron asked me to take a Sunday-school class I said no in a fashion calculated to chasten him wholesomely. If he had sent his wife the first time, as he did the second, it would have been wiser.

Mrs. Crickett talked smoothly for half an hour before she mentioned Sunday-school, and paid me several compliments. Mrs. Crickett is noted for her tact. Tact is a faculty for meandering around to a given point by the longest way instead of making a bee-line. I have no tact. As soon as Mrs. Crickett's conversation came in sight of the Sunday-school I said straight out, "What class do you want me to teach?"

Mrs. Crickett was so surprised that she forgot to be tactful and answered plainly for once in her life:

"There are two classes — one of boys and one of girls. You may have your choice, Miss MacNicol."

"Then I'll take the boys," I said decidedly. "Since they have to grow up to be men it's as well to train them properly. Nuisances they are bound to become in any circumstances; but if they are taken in hand young enough they may not grow up to be such nuisances as they otherwise would, and that will be some unfortunate woman's gain."

Mrs. Crickett looked dubious. "They are a very wild set of boys," she said.

"I never knew boys who weren't," I retorted.

"I — I — think perhaps you would like the girls best," said Mrs. Crickett hesitatingly.

"It is not what I like best that must be considered, Mrs. Crickett," I said rebukingly. "It is what is best for those boys. I feel that *I* shall be best for *them*."

"Oh, I've no doubt of that, Miss MacNicol," said Mrs. Crickett. It was a fib for her, minister's wife though she was. She had doubt. She thought I would be a dismal failure as teacher of a boys' class.

But I wasn't. I am not often a dismal failure when I make up my mind to do a thing.

"It is wonderful what a reformation you have worked in that class, Miss MacNicol — wonderful," said the Rev. Mr. Crickett some weeks later. He didn't mean to show how amazing a thing he thought it that an old maid noted for being a man-hater should have managed it, but his face betrayed him.

"Where does Jimmy Fraser live?" I asked him crisply. "He came one Sunday three weeks ago and hasn't been back since. I mean to find out why."

Mr. Crickett coughed.

"I believe he is hired as handy boy with Alexander Abraham Bennett, out on the Oriental road," he said.

"Then I am going out to Alexander Abraham Bennett's on the Oriental road to see why Jimmy Fraser doesn't come to Sunday-school," I said firmly.

Mr. Crickett's eye twinkled ever so slightly.

"Possibly Mr. Bennett won't appreciate your kind interest. He has — ah! — a singular aversion to your sex, I understand. No woman has ever been known to get inside of Mr. Bennett's house since his sister died twenty years ago."

"Oh, he's the one, is he?" I said, remembering. "He is the woman-hater who threatens that if a woman comes into his yard he'll chase her out with a pitchfork. Well, he won't chase me out!"

Mr. Crickett gave a chuckle — a ministerial chuckle, but still a chuckle. It irritated me slightly because it seemed to imply that he thought Alexander Abraham Bennett would be too much for me. But I did not show Mr. Crickett that it annoyed me. It is always a big mistake to let a man see that he can vex you.

The next afternoon I harnessed my sorrel pony to the buggy and drove out to Alexander Abraham Bennett's. As usual, I took William Adolphus with me for company. He sat up on the seat beside me and looked far more like a Christian than many a man I've seen in a similar position.

Alexander Abraham's place was about three miles out from the village. I knew the house as soon as I came to it by its neglected appearance. Plainly there was no woman about *that* place. Still, it was a nice house and the barns were splendid.

"Alexander Abraham may be a woman-hater, but he evidently knows how to run a farm," I remarked to William Adolphus as I got out and tied the pony to the railing. I had driven up to the house from behind, and now I was opposite a side door opening on the veranda. I thought I might as well go to it, so I tucked William Adolphus under my arm and marched up the path. Just as I was half-way up a dog swooped around the front corner and made straight for me. He was the ugliest dog I had ever seen, and he didn't even bark — just came silently and speedily on, with a businesslike eye. I never stop to argue matters with a dog that doesn't bark. I know when discretion is the better part of valor. Firmly clasping William Adolphus I ran — not to the door, for the dog was between me and it, but to a big, low-branching cherry-tree at the back corner of the house. I reached it in time and no more. First thrusting William Adolphus on to a limb above my head, I scrambled up into that blessed tree without stopping to think how it might look to Alexander Abraham if he happened to be watching. My time for reflection came when I found myself perched half-way up the tree with William Adolphus, quite calm and unruffled, beside me. The dog was sitting on the ground below, watching us, and it was quite plain from his leisurely manner that it was not his busy day. He bared his teeth and growled when he caught my eye. "You *look* like a woman-hater's dog," I told him.

Then I set myself to solving the question, "How am I to get out of this predicament?" I decided not to scream. There was probably no one to hear me except perhaps Alexander Abraham, and I had painful doubts about his tender mercies. It was impossible to go down. Was it, then, possible to go up?

I looked up. Just above my head was an open window with a tolerably stout branch right across it. Without hesitation I picked up William Adolphus and began to climb, while the dog ran in circles about the tree and looked things not lawful to be uttered. It probably would have been a relief to him to bark if it hadn't been so against his principles.

I got in by a window easily enough, and found myself in a bedroom the like of which for disorder and dust and general awfulness I had never seen in my life. But I did not pause to gather details. With William Adolphus under my arm I marched downstairs, fervently hoping I should meet no one on the way.

I did not. The hall below was empty and dusty. I opened the first door I came to and walked boldly in. A man was sitting by the window looking out moodily. I should have known him for Alexander Abraham anywhere. He had just the same uncared-for, ragged appearance that the house had; and yet, like the house, it seemed that he would not be bad-looking if he were trimmed up a little.

His hair didn't seem ever to have been combed and his whiskers were wild in the extreme. He looked at me with blank amazement in his countenance.

"Where is Jimmy?" I demanded. "I've come to see him."

"How did that dog ever let you in?" asked the man, staring at me.

"He didn't let me in," I retorted. "He chased me all over the lawn and I only saved myself from being torn to pieces by scrambling up a tree. Then I climbed in by the window and came down-stairs. You ought to be prosecuted for keeping such a dog. Where is Jimmy?"

Instead of answering, Alexander Abraham began to laugh — not much externally, but internally, as I could see.

"Trust a woman for getting into a man's house if she's made up her mind to," he said disagreeably.

Seeing that it was his intention to vex me, I remained cool and collected.

"Oh, I wasn't particular about getting into your house, Mr. Bennett," I said calmly. "I hadn't much choice in the matter — it was get in lest a worse fate befall me. It was not you or your house I wanted to see — although I admit it's worth seeing if a person is anxious to find out how dirty a place can be. It was Jimmy. For the third and last time — where is Jimmy?"

"Jimmy is not here," said Mr. Bennett. "He left last week and hired with a man down at Prestonville."

"In that case," I said, picking up William Adolphus, who was exploring the room, "I won't disturb you any longer. I will go."

"Yes, I think it would be the wisest thing," said Alexander Abraham — not disagreeably this time, but reflectively, as if there were some doubt about the matter. "I'll let you out by the back door. Then the — ahem! — the dog will not interfere with you. Please go away quietly and quickly."

I said nothing, thinking this the most dignified course of conduct, and followed Alexander Abraham out to the kitchen. That kitchen! Even William Adolphus gave a meow of protest as we passed through. Cat though he was, he understood that there was something uncanny about such a place. Alexander Abraham opened the door, which was locked, just as a buggy containing two men drove into the yard.

"Too late!" he exclaimed in a tragic tone. I understood that something dreadful had happened, but I did not care, since, as I fondly supposed, it did not concern me. I pushed out past Alexander Abraham — who was looking strangely guilty — and came face to face with the man who had sprung from the buggy. It was old Dr. Nicholson, and he was looking at me as if he had caught me shoplifting.

"My dear Peter," he said gravely "I am very sorry to see you here — very sorry, indeed."

I admit that exasperated me. Besides, no man on earth, not even my old family doctor, has any right to "My dear Peter" me.

"There is no loud call for sorrow, doctor," I said loftily. "If a woman forty-five years of age, a member of the Presbyterian Church in good and regular standing, can't call upon one of her Sunday-school scholars without wrecking all the proprieties, how old must she be before she can?"

The doctor did not answer my question. Instead, he looked reproachfully at Alexander Abraham.

"Is this how you keep your word, Mr. Bennett?" he said. "I thought that you promised me that you would not let any one into the house."

"I didn't let her in," growled Mr. Bennett. "Good heavens, man, she climbed in at an upstairs window despite the presence on my grounds of a policeman and a dog! What's to be done with a woman like that?"

"My dear Peter," said the doctor impressively, turning to me, "this house is under quarantine for smallpox. You will have to stay here."

Smallpox! For the first and last time in my life I openly lost my temper with a man. I wheeled furiously upon Alexander Abraham.

"Why didn't you tell me?" I cried.

"Tell you!" he said, glaring at me. "When I first saw you it was too late to tell you. I thought the kindest thing I could do was to hold my tongue and let you get away in happy ignorance. This will teach you to take a man's house by storm, madam."

"Now, now, don't quarrel, my good people," interposed the doctor seriously — but I am sure I saw a grin in his eye — "you'll have to spend some time together under the same roof and you won't improve the situation by disagreeing. You see, Peter, it was this way. Mr. Bennett was in town yesterday — where, as you are aware, there is a bad outbreak of smallpox — and took dinner in a boardinghouse where one of the maids was ill. Last night she developed unmistakable symptoms of smallpox. The Board of Health at once got after all the people who were in the house yesterday, so far as they could locate them and put them under quarantine. I came out here this morning and explained the matter to Mr. Bennett and vaccinated him. I brought Jeremiah Jeffries to guard the front of the house, and Mr. Bennett gave me his word of honor he would not let any one in by the back way while I went to get another policeman and make all the necessary arrangements. I have brought Thomas Wright and have secured the services of another man to attend to Mr. Bennett's barn work and bring provisions to the house. Jacob Green and Cleophas Lee will watch at night. I don't think that there is much danger of Mr. Bennett's taking the smallpox, but until we are sure you must remain here, Peter. Have you been vaccinated?"

While listening to the doctor I had been thinking. It was the most distressing predicament that I had ever got into in my life but there was no use making it worse.

"Very well, doctor," I said calmly. "Yes, I was vaccinated a month ago when the news of the smallpox first came. When you go back to the village kindly go to Sarah Blenkhorn and ask her to live in my house during my absence and look after things, especially the cats. Tell her to give them new milk twice a day and a square inch of butter apiece once a week. Get her to put my two dark cotton wrappers, some aprons, and a change of underclothing in my third best valise and have it sent out to me. My pony is tied out there to the fence. Please take him home. That is all, I think."

"No, it isn't all," said Alexander Abraham grumpily. "Send that cat home too. I won't have a cat round the place — I'd rather have the smallpox."

I looked Alexander Abraham over gradually, beginning at his feet and traveling up to his head. Then I said gently:

"You may have both. Anyway, you'll have to have William Adolphus. He is under quarantine as well as you and I. Do you suppose I am going to have my cat ranging at large through Amberly, scattering smallpox germs among innocent people? I'll have to put up with that dog of yours. You will have to endure William Adolphus."

Alexander Abraham groaned, but I could see that the way I had looked him over had had its due effect. The doctor drove away and I went into the house, not choosing to be grinned at by Thomas Wright. I hung my coat up in the hall and laid my bonnet carefully on the sitting-room table, having first dusted a clean place for it with my handkerchief. I longed to fall upon that house at once and clean it up, but I had to wait until the doctor should come back with my wrappers. I could not clean house in my new suit and a silk shirt-waist.

Alexander Abraham was sitting on a chair looking at me. Presently he said, "I am not curious — but will you tell me why the doctor called you Peter?"

"Because that is my name, I suppose," I answered, shaking up a cushion for William Adolphus to lie on and thereby disturbing the dust of years.

Alexander Abraham coughed gently. "Isn't that a — ahem! — a rather peculiar name for a woman?"

"It is," I said, wondering how much soap, if any, there was in the house.

"I am not curious," said Alexander Abraham, "but would you mind telling me how you came to be called Peter?"

"If I had been a boy my parents intended to call me Peter in honor of a rich uncle. When I fortunately turned out to be a girl, my mother insisted that I should be called Angelina. They gave me both names and called me Angelina, but as soon as I grew old enough I determined to be called Peter. It was bad enough, but not as bad as Angelina."

"I should say it was more appropriate," said Alexander Abraham, intending, as I perceived, to be disagreeable.

"Precisely," I agreed calmly. "My last name is MacNicol and I live at Spinster's Glory in Amberly. As you are not curious, that will be all the information you will need about me."

"Ah!" Alexander Abraham looked as if light had broken in on him. "I've heard of you. You — ah — pretend to dislike men."

Pretend! Goodness only knows what would have happened to Alexander Abraham just then if a diversion had not taken place. But the door was pushed open and a dog came in — *the* dog. I suppose he had got tired of waiting under the cherry-tree. He was even uglier indoors than out.

"Ah, Mr. Riley, Mr. Riley, see what you have let me in for," said Alexander Abraham reproachfully.

But Mr. Riley — since that was the brute's name — paid no attention to Alexander Abraham. He had caught sight of William Adolphus curled up on the cushion and he started across the room to investigate him. William Adolphus sat up and began to take notice.

"Call off that dog," I said warningly to Alexander Abraham.

"Call him off yourself," he retorted. "Since you've brought that cat here you can protect him."

"Oh, it wasn't for the cat's sake I spoke," I said ominously. "William Adolphus can protect himself."

William Adolphus could and did. He humped his back, flattened his ears, swore once, and then made a flying leap for Mr. Riley, who by that time was quite close. William Adolphus landed squarely on Mr. Riley's brindled back and promptly took fast hold, spitting and clawing and caterwauling.

You never saw a more astonished dog than Mr. Riley. With a yell of terror he bolted out to the kitchen, out of the kitchen into the hall, through the hall into the room, and so into the kitchen and round again. With each circuit he went faster and faster till he looked like a brindled streak with a dash of black and white on top. Such a racket and commotion I never heard and I laughed until the tears came into my eyes. Mr. Riley flew around and around and William Adolphus held on grimly and clawed. Alexander Abraham turned purple with rage.

"Woman, call off that infernal cat before he kills my dog," he shouted above the din of yelps and yowls.

"Oh, he won't kill him," I called reassuringly, "and he's going too fast to hear me if I did call him. If you can stop the dog, Mr. Bennett, I'll guarantee to make William Adolphus listen to reason, but there's no use trying to argue with a lightning flash."

Alexander Abraham made a frantic lunge at the brindled streak as it whirled past him, with the result that he overbalanced himself and went sprawling on the floor with a crash. When he picked himself up, he said viciously, "I wish you and your fiend of a cat were in — in — "

"Amberly," I finished quickly. "So do I, Mr. Bennett, but since we are not, let us make the best of it like sensible people."

With this the end came and I was thankful, for the noise those two animals made was so terrific that I expected the policemen would be rushing in, smallpox or no smallpox, to see if Alexander Abraham and I were trying to murder each other. Mr. Riley suddenly veered in his mad course and bolted into a dark corner between the stove and the wood-box. William Adolphus let go just in time.

There was never any more trouble with Mr. Riley after that. A meeker, more thoroughly chastened dog you could not find. William Adolphus had the best of it and he kept it.

Seeing that things had calmed down and that it was five o'clock I decided to get tea. I told Alexander Abraham that I would prepare it if he would show me where the eatables were.

"You needn't mind," said Alexander Abraham viciously. "I've been in the habit of getting my own tea for twenty years."

"I dare say; but you haven't been in the habit of getting mine," I said firmly. "I wouldn't eat anything you cooked if I starved to death. If you want some occupation you'd better get some salve and anoint the scratches on that dog's back."

Alexander Abraham said something that I prudently did not hear. Seeing that he had no information to hand out I went on an exploring expedition into the pantry. The place was awful beyond description, and for the first time a vague sentiment of pity for Alexander

Abraham glimmered in my breast. When a man had to live in such surroundings the wonder was, not that he hated women, but that he didn't hate the whole human race.

But I got a supper up somehow. I made good tea and excellent toast and I found a can of peaches in the pantry, which, being bought, I wasn't afraid to eat. As for the bread, it looked decent and I took it on faith.

That tea and toast mellowed Alexander Abraham in spite of himself. He ate the last crust and didn't growl when I gave William Adolphus all the cream that was left. By this time the doctor's boy had arrived with my valise. Alexander Abraham gave me to understand that there was a spare room across the hall and that I might take possession of it, since I had to be put somewhere. I went to it and put on one of my wrappers.

"Now," I said briskly, returning to the kitchen, "I'm going to clean up and I'm going to begin with this kitchen. You'd better betake yourself to the sitting-room, Mr. Bennett, so's to be out of the way."

Alexander Abraham glared at me.

"I'm not going to have my house meddled with," he snapped. "It suits me. If you don't like it, you can leave it."

"No, I can't. That is just the trouble," I said pleasantly. "If I could leave it I shouldn't be here a minute. Since I can't it simply has to be cleaned. Go into the sitting-room."

Alexander Abraham went. As he closed the door I heard him say, "What an awful woman!"

I cleaned that kitchen and the pantry adjoining. It was ten o'clock when I finished, and Alexander Abraham had gone to bed without deigning further speech. I locked Mr. Riley in one room and William Adolphus in another and went to bed too. I never felt so dead tired in my life.

But I was up bright and early the next morning and got a tip-top breakfast, which Alexander Abraham condescended to eat. When the provision man came into the yard I called to him from the window to bring me a box of soap in the afternoon, and then I tackled the sitting-room. It took me the best part of a week to get that house in order; but I did it thoroughly, and at the end of the time it was clean from garret to cellar. Alexander Abraham made no comments on my operations, though he groaned loud and often and said caustic things to poor Mr. Riley, who hadn't the spirit to answer back after his drubbing by William Adolphus. I made allowances for Alexander Abraham because his vaccination had taken and his arm was real sore; and I cooked elegant meals, not having much else to do once I got things scoured up. The house was full of provisions - Alexander Abraham wasn't mean about such things, I will say that for him. Altogether, I was more comfortable than I had expected to be. When Alexander Abraham wouldn't talk I let him alone; and when he would, I said just as sarcastic things as he did, only I said them smiling and pleasant. I could see he had a wholesome awe of me.

One day Alexander Abraham astonished me by appearing at the dinner-table with his hair brushed and a white collar on. We had a tip-top dinner that day and I had made a pudding that was positively wasted on a womanhater. When Alexander Abraham had disposed of two platefuls of it he sighed and said: "You can certainly cook. It's a pity you are such a detestable crank in other respects."

"It's kind of convenient being a crank," I said. "People are careful how they meddle with you. Haven't you found that out in your own experience?"

"I am not a crank," growled Alexander Abraham resentfully. "All I ask is to be let alone."

"That's the very crankiest kind of a crank," I said. "A person who wants to be let alone flies in the face of Providence, who decreed that folks for their own good were not to be let alone. But cheer up, Mr. Bennett. The quarantine will be up on Tuesday and then you'll certainly be let alone for the rest of your natural life so far as William Adolphus and I are concerned. You may then return to your wallowing in the mire and be as dirty and comfortable as of yore."

Alexander Abraham growled again. The prospect didn't seem to cheer him up as much as I'd expected. Then he did an amazing thing. He poured some cream into a saucer and set it down before William Adolphus.

Neither Alexander Abraham nor I had worried much about the smallpox. We didn't believe he would take it for he hadn't even seen the girl who was sick. But the very next morning I heard him calling me from the up-stairs landing.

"Miss MacNicol," he said in a voice so uncommonly mild and polite that it gave me a jump, "what are the symptoms of smallpox?"

"Chills and flushes, pain in the limbs and back, nausea and vomiting," I answered promptly, for I had been reading them up in a patent-medicine almanac.

"I've got them all," said Alexander Abraham solemnly.

I didn't feel as much scared as I should have expected. After enduring a woman-hater and a brindled dog and the early disorder of that house, smallpox seemed rather insignificant. I went to the window and called to Thomas Wright to send for the doctor.

The doctor came down from Alexander Abraham's room looking grave.

"It is impossible to pronounce on his disease yet," he said. "There is no certainty until the eruption appears. But of course there is every likelihood that it is the smallpox. It is very unfortunate. I am afraid that it will be very difficult to get a nurse. All the nurses in town who will take smallpox cases are overbusy now, for the epidemic is still raging there. However, I'll go into town to-night and do my best. Meanwhile, as Mr. Bennett does not require any attendance at present, you must not go near him, Peter.

I wasn't going to take orders from any man and as soon as the doctor had gone I marched straight up to Alexander Abraham's room with some dinner for him on a tray. There was a lemon cream that I thought he could eat even if he had the smallpox.

"You shouldn't come near me," he growled. "You are risking your life."

"I'm not going to see a fellow creature starve to death, even if he is a man," I retorted.

"The worst of it all," groaned Alexander Abraham between mouthfuls of lemon cream, "is that the doctor says I've got to have a nurse. I've got so kind of used to you being in the house that I don't mind you, but the thought of another woman coming here is too much. Did you give my poor dog anything to eat?"

"He has had a better dinner than many a Christian," I said severely.

Alexander Abraham need not have worried about another woman coming in. The doctor came back that night with care on his brow.

"I don't know what is to be done," he said. "I can't get a soul to come here."

"I will nurse Mr. Bennett," I said with dignity. "It is my duty and, thank Heaven, I never shirk my duty. He is a man and he has smallpox and he keeps a vile dog, but I'm not going to see him die for want of attendance for all that."

"Well, if you're not afraid to take the risk," said the doctor, looking relieved, manlike, as soon as he found a woman to shoulder the responsibility.

I nursed Alexander Abraham through the smallpox and I didn't mind it much. He was much more amiable sick than well and he had the disease in a very mild form. Below stairs I reigned supreme, and Mr. Riley and William Adolphus lay down together like the lion and the lamb. I fed Mr. Riley regularly and once, seeing him looking lonesome, I patted him gingerly. It was nicer than I'd thought it would be.

When Alexander Abraham got able to sit up he began to make up for the time he'd lost being pleasant. Anything more sarcastic than that man during his convalescence you couldn't imagine. I just laughed at him, having found out that that could be depended on to irritate him. To irritate him still further I cleaned the house all over again. But what vexed him most of all was that Mr. Riley took to following me about and wagging what he had of a tail at me.

"It wasn't enough that you should come into my — peaceful home and turn it upside down, but you have to alienate the affection of my dog," complained Alexander Abraham.

"He'll get fond of you again when I go home," I said comfortingly. "Dogs aren't very particular that way. What they want is bones. Cats now, they love disinterestedly. William Adolphus has never swerved in his allegiance to me although you do give him cream on the sly."

Alexander Abraham looked foolish. He hadn't thought I knew that.

I didn't take the smallpox, and in another week the doctor came out and sent the policeman home. I was disinfected and William Adolphus was fumigated and then we were free to go.

"Good-by, Mr. Bennett," I said, offering to shake hands in a forgiving spirit. "I've no doubt that you're glad to be rid of me, but you're no gladder than I am to go. I suppose this house will be dirtier than ever in a month's time and Mr. Riley will have discarded the little polish his manners have taken on. Reformation with men and dogs never goes very deep."

With this Parthian shaft I walked out of that house, supposing that I had seen the last of it and of Alexander Abraham.

I was glad to get back home, of course; but it did seem queer and lonesome. The cats hardly knew me and William Adolphus roamed around forlornly and appeared to feel like an exile. I didn't take as much pleasure in cooking as usual, for it seemed kind of foolish to be hissing over oneself. The neighbors avoided me pointedly, for they couldn't get rid of the fear that I might erupt into smallpox at any moment; my Sunday-school class had been given to another woman, and altogether I felt as if I didn't belong anywhere.

I had existed like this for a week when Alexander Abraham suddenly appeared. He walked in one evening at dusk, but at first sight I didn't know him, he was so spruced and barbered up. But William Adolphus knew him. Will you believe it, William Adolphus, my own William Adolphus, rubbed up against that man's trouser leg with an undisguised purr of satisfaction?

"I had to come, Angelina," said Alexander Abraham. "I couldn't stand it any longer."

"My name is Peter," I said coldly, although I was feeling ridiculously glad about something.

"It isn't," said Alexander Abraham stubbornly. "It is Angelina for me and always will be. I will never call you Peter. Angelina just suits you exactly. And Angelina Bennett would suit you still better. You've got to come back, Angelina. Mr. Riley is moping for you and I can't get along without somebody to appreciate my sarcasms, now that you've accustomed me to the luxury."

"What about the other five cats?" I demanded.

Alexander Abraham sighed.

"I suppose they'll have to come too," he said. "It's awful to think of living with six cats, but it's worse to think of living without you. How soon can you be ready to marry me?"

"I haven't said that I am going to marry you at all, have I?" I said tartly, just to be consistent. For I wasn't feeling tart.

"No, but you will, won't you?" said Alexander Abraham anxiously. "Because if you won't I wish you'd let me die of the smallpox. Do, dear Angelina."

To think that a man should dare to call me his "dear Angelina"! And to think that I shouldn't mind!

Marjorie Pickthall

Marjorie Pickthall, born in England in 1883, came to Canada in 1889 and later became fairly successful as a poet and short story writer. Today, though she is still known as a writer of a few fine lyrics, she is forgotten as a short story writer — even though in the first decade of this century she was touted by American magazines as one of the best of her day. Perhaps her early death in 1922 curtailed an otherwise promising career and doomed her to relative oblivion. The following short story was first published in Pall Mall Magazine *in 1913 and subsequently in* Century Magazine *in 1922.*

Luck

There were four bunks in the shanty, and three of them were filled.

Ohlsen lay in one, a great bulk under the Hudson Bay Company blankets, breathing like a bull; in the next was Forbes, with eyes as quick as a mink's, and now red rimmed from snow blindness, twinkling from time to time over his yellowish furs. Nearest the door was Lajeune, singing in his sleep. In one corner an old Indian cowered, as little regarded as the rags and skins in which he was hidden; and Desmond sat by the stove, drinking to his luck, fingering it and folding it.

It was all there in a bag — raw gold, pure gold, the food of joy. At the weight of it in his rough palm, Desmond chattered and chuckled with delight. He had sat there talking and laughing for hours, while the glow of the stove grew darker and the cold crept in. Little blots of snow from the snowshoes first melting had turned again to dark ice on the floor, the red light clung to them until each little circle seemed to be one of blood. Outside the world trembled under the shafts of the bitter stars; but Desmond, with the very fuel of life in his hand, was warm. Dreams ran in his brain like a tide and dripped off his tongue in words. They were strangely innocent dreams of innocent things: sunlight on an old wall, honey, a girl with sandy eyebrows, and yellow ducklings.

"And maybe there'll be a garden, with fruit you pick off the bushes. 'Twas under a thorn bush she used to stand, with the wind snapping her print gown. Or maybe I'll see more of the world first in an easy fashion, never a drink scarce, and no man my better at it. I know how a gentleman should behave. Are you hearing me, boys?"

Ohlsen breathed as slowly and deeply as a bull, Forbes blinked a moment over the greasy furs and said, "I'm hearing you." Lajeune gave a sudden little call in his sleep, like a bird.

"They're all asleep, like so many hogs," said Desmond, with a maudlin wonder, "they don't care. Two years we've struggled and starved together in this here freezing hell, and now my luck's come, and they don't care. Well, well."

He stared resentfully at the bunks. He could see nothing of Ohlsen but blanket, yet Ohlsen helped him to a new outfit when he lost everything in a snowslide. Forbes was only an unheeding head of grimy fur, yet once he had pulled Desmond out of a log jam. And Lajeune had nursed him laughingly when he hurt his foot with a pick. Yet now Lajeune cared nothing; he was asleep, his head flung back, showing his smooth, lean throat and a scar that ran across it, white on brown. Desmond felt hurt. He took another drink, strode over to the bunk, and shook him petulantly.

"Don't you hear when a friends talks t'ye?"

Lajeune did not move, yet he was instantly awake. His eyes, so black that they showed no pupil, stared suddenly into Desmond's muddled blue ones. His right hand gripped and grew rigid.

Desmond, leaning over him, was sobered by something in the breathless strain of that stare. He laughed uneasily.

"It's only me, Jooney. Was you asleep? I'm sorry."

He backed off bewildered, but young Lajeune smiled and yawned, showing his red tongue curled like a wolf's.

"Still the gold, my friend?" he asked, drowsily.

"I — I can't seem to get used to it, like," explained Desmond, "I have to talk of it. I know I'm a fool, but a man's luck takes him all ways. You go to sleep, young Jooney. I won't talk to you no more."

"Nor before your old savage in the corner, *hein*?"

Desmond glanced at the heap of rags in the corner.

"Him? What's the matter? Think he'll steal it? Why, there's four of us, and even an Injun can have a corner of my shack for an hour or two tonight. I reckon," finished Desmond, with a kind of gravity, "as my luck is making me soft. It takes a man all ways."

Lajeune yawned, grinned, flung up his left arm, and was instantly asleep again. He looked so young in his sleep that Desmond was suddenly moved to draw the blanket over him. In the dim light he saw Forbes worn and grizzled, the wariness gone out of him, a defeated old man with horrible eyes. Ohlsen's hand lay over the edge of the bunk, his huge fingers curved helplessly, like a child's. Desmond felt inarticulately tender to the three who had toiled by his side and missed their luck. He piled wood on the stove, saying, "I must do something for the boys. They're good boys."

At the freshened roar of the stove the old Indian in the corner stirred and lifted his head, groping like an old turtle in the sunlight. He had a curious effect of meaningless blurs and shadows. Eye and memory could hold nothing of his insignificance. Only under smoked and puckered lids the flickering glitter of his eyes pricked in a meaning unreadable. Desmond looked at him with the wide good nature born of his luck.

"I ain't going to turn you out, Old Bones," he said.

The eyes steadied on him an instant, and the old shadow spoke fair English in the ghost of a voice.

"Thanks. You give grub. I eat, I warm, I rest. Now I go."

"Jest as you like. But have a drink first." He pushed over the dregs of the whiskey bottle.

The old man seized it; seemed to hold it to his heart. While he could drink whiskey he might drink and forget; when he could get no more, he must remember and die. He drank, Lethe and Paradise in one, and handed back the bottle.

"How," he said. "You good man. Once I had things to give, now nothing. Nothing but dreams."

"Dreams, is it, Old Bones?"

The eyes were like cunning sparks.

"Dreams, yes," he said, with a stealthy indrawing of breath. "You good man. I give you three dreams. See."

With a movement so swift the eye could hardly follow it, he caught three hot wood coals from the ash under the stove and flung them on the floor at Desmond's feet. He bent forward, and under his breath they woke to a moment's flame. The strangeness of his movements held Desmond, and he also bent forward, watching. He had an instant's impression that the coals were burning him fiercely somewhere between the eyes, that the bars of personality were breaking, that he was falling into some darkness that was the darkness of death. Before his ignorance could find words for his fear, the old

Indian leaned back, the fire fled, and the spent coals were no more than rounds of empty ash, which the old man took in his hands.

"Dreams," he said, with something that might have been a laugh. He blew the ash like little grey feathers toward the men in the bunks. He eyes were alive, fixed on Desmond with a meaning unreadable. He thrust his face close. "You good man. You give me whiskey. I give you three dreams, little dreams — for luck."

Desmond was staring at the little floating feathers of wood ash. As they slowly sank and settled, he heard the door close and felt a sharp stab of cold. The old Indian had gone; Desmond could hear his footsteps dragging over the frozen crust of the snow for a little while. He got up and shook himself. The drink had died out of him; he felt himself suddenly and greatly weary of body and mind. The fire would last till morning. "Dreams — dreams, for luck!" he muttered, as he rolled in to the fourth bunk. He was ready for sleep. And as he lay down and yielded to the oncoming of sleep, as a weed yields to the tide, he knew of a swift, clear certainty that he would dream.

II

He opened his eyes to the pale flood of day; Lajeune was cooking pork and making coffee; Ohlsen was making snow shoes; Forbes bent over his bunk, black against the blind square of the frozen window, feeling blindly with his hands, and snuffling a little as he spoke, "We'd ha' let you sleep on, but we wanted to know what you'd be doing. Will ye stay here with me and the rest — I'm all but blind the day — or will ye go into Fort Recompense with Jooney here and the dogs, and put the dust in safety? Or will ye try to short cut across the pass with Ohlsen?"

Desmond stretched, grunted and hesitated. He felt curiously unwilling to decide. But Forbes was waiting, his yellow fingers twitching on the end of the bunk.

"Oh, I dunno," he said. "What's the hurry? Well — I guess I'll try the pass with Ohlsen."

"Right." Ohlsen nodded his heavy head, for he seldom spoke. He had the physique men always associate with a kind and stupid fidelity. Desmond said of him, "Them that talks most ain't the best at heart." Desmond said it to himself as he rolled out of the bunk for breakfast.

Forbes stayed in his bunk, and made little moaning animal noises while he fed. Lajeune bubbled over with quick laughter. Desmond beamed on everyone and talked of his luck. Ohlsen sat immovable, working his jaws like an ox, watching Desmond with his small, pale eyes.

He did not speak as they drew on their furs and packed the gold; nor as they turned out of the shack, shutting the door swiftly behind them, and faced the stinging splendour of the windy winter day. The cold had lessened with the sunrise, but what cold there was the wind took and drove to the bone. The air was filled with a glittering mist of blown snow, and all the lower slopes of the hills and the climbing spruce forests were hidden. Above the *poudre* the mountains lifted like iron in the unpitying day, and every snowfield and glacier was crowned with a streaming feather of white against a hard turquoise sky.

"You think we'll get through?" asked Desmond, doubtfully.

"Ay t'ank so." Ohlsen was striding heavily, tirelessly, just behind his shoulder. His grey eyes, still fixed on Desmond, were like little bits of glacier ice inset above his high cheek bones.

"We may."

"We may. It ain't far." Desmond was talkative. "This gold weighs heavy. I like the colour o' gold. Ohlsen, you got any children?"

"Ay, got two kids."

"Wisht I had. Maybe I will, though — little boy 'n' gal, with kind o' gold hair. See here, you ever had a garden?"

"No."

"I've me a garden on me back here, hey? With them blue things that smell, and hens. You come and see me, Ohlsen, and you'll have the best there is."

"T'anks. I like fresh eggs."

"So do I. And apples. Say, Ohlsen, I'm sorry this ain't for you."

Ohlsen did not answer or slacken his heavy, stooping stride against the wind. The curved hills opened slowly, swung aside. The spruce stood up, came nearer, and closed in around them like the outposts of a waiting army. The wind roared through the trees like a flood of which the surf was snow.

"Do you think we'll do it?" shouted Desmond again and Ohlsen answered, "Ay t'ank so."

In a little while the trees were a dark mass beneath them, and they were out on the bare heights, fighting with the wind for every foothold. Desmond staggered under it, but Ohlsen seemed untiring, climbing very close at his shoulder. The glare of the sun seared their eyes, but they had no heat of it. In all the vast upheaval of the hills, in all the stark space of the sky, there was no warmth, no life.

Something took Desmond by the throat. "We'll not do it," he cried, to Ohlsen. "Let's turn back."

For answer Ohlsen unstrapped the heavy pack of gold, fastened it on his shoulders, and went on. This time he was ahead, and his huge body sheltered Desmond from the wind.

"I been drinking too much," thought Desmond, "and here's Ohlsen having to do my work for me. It ain't right."

They were on a high ridge, and the wind was at its worst. On the left lay a precipice, and the dark masses of the spruce. On the right the depths were veiled with glittering silver, now and then shot through with the blue-green gleam of a glacier. It was fair going for a steady head, but the wind was dangerous. It took Desmond, as with hands, and thrust him to his knees at the narrowing of the ledge. He slipped a little. The dark grey ice, white veined, gave him no hold. He lost his head, slipped a little farther, and the white driven foam of snow and cloud above the glacier was suddenly visible. He called to Ohlsen.

Ohlsen could not have heard, yet he turned and came slowly back. Desmond could have raged at him for his slowness if his lips had not been so stiff and dry. Inside his fur mitts his hands were suddenly wet. Gently he slid a little farther, and the wind-driven white below was plainer, cut through with turquoise as with a sword. He shut his eyes. And when he opened them Ohlsen had stopped and was standing quietly watching him.

Desmond shrieked hoarsely, for he understood. Between the two drove the torrent of the wind, shutting slayer and all but slain into a separate prison of silence. But even the wind did not stir Ohlsen; he stood like a grey rock, watching Desmond. Presently he leaned forward, hands on knees, his back humped grotesquely under the pack, as the cruel or the curious might watch the struggles of a drowning kitten. Desmond was shaken to his fingers by the terrible thudding of his heart. He could not make a sound. Earth and sky flashed away. There remained only the grey inhuman shape beyond the barrier of the wind.

Presently that also flashed away. Yet, as Desmond fell, he was aware of light, a great swift relief, for he knew that he dreamed.

Then came darkness.

III

It was a darkness glittering with stars. Such stars as the men of the South, the men of the cities, never see. Each was a blazing world hung in nothingness, rayed with sapphire and rose. Now and then the white ice-blink ran over and died beyond them in the spaces where even stars were not. Desmond was lying on his back, staring at them through a cranny in his sleeping bag. He knew where he was, yet in his brain was a sort of cold confusion. He seemed to hear Forbes speaking.

"Will ye stay here with me and rest — I'm all but blind the day — or will ye go into Fort Recompense with Jooney here and the dogs, and put the dust in safety? Or will ye try the short cut across the pass with Ohlsen?"

"And here I am, halfway to the fort, and sleeping out with Jooney and the dogs," Desmond muttered, "but I can't remember coming."

Yet, as he turned in his sleeping bag, his knowledge of his whereabouts was exact. He was in a stony little gully beyond Fachette, where high banks cut off the wind and ground willows gave firing. The huskies were asleep and warm in deep drift under the bank, after a full meal of dried salmon.

"I'll say this for young Jooney," said Desmond, drowsily, "he's got some sense with dogs."

Lajeune was beside him, asleep in another bag. Between them was the pack of gold and the sledge harness. And the great plain, he knew, ran north and south of the very lip of the gully, silver under the stars, ridged and rippled by the wind, like white sand of the sea. The wind was now still. The earth was again a star, bright, silent, and alone, akin to her sisters of the infinite heavens.

"There ain't so much gold in a place like this here," Desmond whispered, resentfully, to the night, "but jest you wait till I get south-east again." He was filled with blind longing for red brick, asphalt, and crowded streets; even the hens and ducklings were not enough. He hungered in this splendour of desolation for the little tumults of mankind. It seemed as if the stars laughed.

"There ain't nothing my gold won't get me," said Desmond more loudly. His breath hung in little icicles on the edges of his spy-hole. It was cruelly cold. He drew his hood closer round his head, and thrust it out of the bag.

Lajeune was gone.

He did not feel afraid; only deadly cold and sick as he struggled to his feet. Under their shelter of canvas and snow he was alone; everything else was gone. He fell on his hands and knees, digging furiously in the trodden snow, like a dog.

The gold was gone also.

"My luck," whispered Desmond, stupidly. "My luck."

He was still on his knees, shaping a little rounded column of snow; suppose it might be Lajeune's throat, and he with his hands on each side of it — so. Lajeune's dark face seemed to lie beneath him, but it was not touched with fear, but with laughter. He was laughing, as the stars had laughed, at Desmond and his luck. Desmond dashed the snow away with a cry.

He scrambled out of the gully. The dog trail was easy to read, running straight across the silvery plain. He began to run along it.

As he ran he admired Lajeune very much. With what deadly quietness and precision he must have worked! The gully and the deserted camp were a grey streak behind him, were gone. He was running in Lajeune's very footprints, and he was sure he ran at an immense speed. The glittering levels reeled away behind him. A star flared and fell, staining the world with gold. Desmond had forgotten his gold. He had forgotten food and shelter, life and death. He could think of nothing but Lajeune's brown throat with the scar across it. That throat, his own hands on each side of it, and an end for ever to the singing and the laughter.

He thought Lajeune was near at hand, laughing at him. He felt the trail, and searched. The dark face was everywhere, and the quick laughter; but silence was waiting.

Again he knelt and groped in the snow; but he could feel nothing firm and living. He tore off his mitts, and groped again, but there was only the snow, drifting in his fingers like dust. Lajeune was near at hand, yet he could not find him. He got up and began to run in circles. His feet and hands were heavy and as cold as ice, and his breath hurt; but Lajeune was alive and warm and lucky and laughing.

He fell, got up, and fell again. The third time he did not get up, for he had caught young Lajeune at last. The brown throat was under his hands, and the stricken face. He Desmond, was doing all the laughing, for Lajeune was dead.

"My luck, Jooney, my luck," chuckled Desmond.

His head fell forward, and the dry snow was like dust in his mouth. Darkness covered the stars.

IV

In the darkness and the shadow something moved. Desmond was in his own bunk at the shack. There seemed to be an echo of words in the air, yet he knew that he had slept for some time. He was not asleep now, yet sleep lay on him like a weight, and he could not move.

Forbes was silent, too. He was quite clear that he was alone with Forbes, and that the other two had gone prospecting beyond Fachette. Forbes had asked him, "Will ye stay here with me and rest, — I'm all but blind the day, — or will ye go into Fort Recompense with Jooney here and the dogs, and put the dust in safety? Or will ye try the short cut across the pass with Ohlsen?" And he knew he had chosen to stay in the shack with Forbes.

It was night. The shack was dark, save for the red glow of the stove, and something moved very softly in the dusk and the shadow.

Desmond, weighted with sleep, could not move; but he listened. Someone was shuffling very softly and slowly round the wall of the shack pausing at the bunks. It was Forbes. He was snuffling to himself, as some little soft nosed animal might snuffle, and feeling in his blind way with one yellowed hand.

Desmond was amused. "If I was to yell out, old Scotty'd have a fit," he thought. He decided to wait until Forbes was quite near, and then yell, and hear the old man curse. Old Forbes' cursing was the admiration of the camps. Desmond lay very still and listened.

Forbes was coming nearer, feeling his way as if over unseen ground, and whimpering to himself very softly. Desmond could hear the scratch, scratch of his long clawed fingers as he slipped his hand over the empty bunk near the door. He was silent and still for a minute, then the shuffling came again.

"I'll wait till he's at the foot o' my bunk," thought Desmond, grinning foolishly, "and then I'll bark like a dog. Used to do it in school when I was a kid and scare the teacher. Lord! how a bit of luck does raise a man's spirits!" He lay very quiet, grinning to himself in the dark.

Forbes' blind, bent head showed, swaying slightly, against the dull, red glow of the farther wall. A tremulous touch, as light as a falling leaf, fell on Desmond's foot, and suddenly he was stricken with the black, dumb terror of dreams; for he knew there was death in the touch of that hand.

The walls reeled about him, shot with streaks of red. He could feel the hand hovering lightly at his knee. The blind man's soft, whimpering breathing sounded close above him. But he could not move. His whole life was centered in the quivering nerves which recorded the touch of the blind man's hand.

It travelled very slowly and lightly up his body, and lingered above his heart. His life gathered there also like a cold flame. And he could not move.

Visions rose before him. The gold was under his head and he heard again the sound of wind in a garden among tall flowers, and thud of ripe apples falling, soft croons, and cluckings of hens, a whirring of the wings of doves. He saw a straight girl in a stiff print dress, with very blue eyes under brows and lashes the colour of sea sand. He saw two children with hair the colour of gold.

The blind man moaned and bent waveringly near, his right hand gathered to his breast.

The flowers of the hollyhocks were gold, and the little ducks were gold, and gold sunlight lay on the gold hair of the children. "Gold," said Desmond, faintly — "gold; my luck." The blind hand crept upward. Like a blown flame, the golden visions flickered and went out.

Desmond awoke, fighting upward out of darkness and the dreams of the night. He felt reality coming back to him as a tide comes back to a beach, and opened his eyes on a glad world. His terrors fell away from him. He came near to thanking God. Dark words he had dreamed, dark deeds, but they were not true. Thank God! They were only dreams. He stirred in the bunk, sat up, and brushed a white feather of wood ash from his sleeve. Only dreams!

Lajeune was cooking pork and making coffee; Ohlsen was mending snow shoes; Forbes bent over his bunk, black against the frozen window, feeling blindly with his hands and snuffling a little as he spoke, "We'd ha' let you sleep on, but we wanted to know what you'd be doing. Will ye stay with me and rest — I'm all but blind the day — or will ye go into Fort Recompense with Jooney here and the dogs, and put the dust in safety? Or will ye try the short cut across the pass with Ohlsen?"

He stopped suddenly. Desmond shrank back slowly against the wall of the bunk, his eyes staring on them as a man stares on death, a fleck of froth on his lips. There was no sound in the shack but the quick breathing of four men.